Policymaking and Prosperity

Studies in Public Policy

Series Editor: Paul J. Rich, Policy Studies Organization

Government in the new millennium demands creative new approaches to managing change. Faced with the impact of globalization, technological revolution, and political reform, what can be done to encourage economic growth, develop more effective public administration at home, and forge strong and lasting relationships abroad?

Lexington Books and the Policy Studies Organization's **Studies in Public Policy** series brings together the very best in new and original scholarship, spanning the range of global policy questions. Its multi-disciplinary texts combine penetrating analysis of policy formulation at the macro level with innovative and practical solutions for policy implementation. It provides the political and social scientist with the latest academic research and the policy maker with effective tools to tackle the most pressing issues faced by government today.

Titles in the Series

Public Policies for Distressed Communities Revisited
Edited by F. Stevens Redburn and Terry F. Buss

Analyzing National and International Policy: Theory, Method, and Case Studies by Laure Paquette

Developmental Policy and the State: The European Union, East Asia, and the Caribbean by Nikolaos Karagiannis

Policymaking and Democracy: A Multinational Anthology
Edited by Stuart Nagel

Policymaking and Prosperity: A Multinational Anthology
Edited by Stuart Nagel

Policymaking and Peace: A Multinational Anthology
Edited by Stuart Nagel

Policymaking and Prosperity

A Multinational Anthology

Edited by
Stuart Nagel

LEXINGTON BOOKS
Lanham • Boulder • New York • Oxford

LEXINGTON BOOKS

Published in the United States of America
by Lexington Books
A Member of the Rowman & Littlefield Publishing Group
4720 Boston Way, Lanham, Maryland 20706

PO Box 317
Oxford
OX2 9RU, UK

British Library Cataloguing in Publication Information Available

Library of Congress Cataloging-in-Publication Data

Policymaking and prosperity : a multinational anthology / [edited by] Stuart Nagel,
p. cm.—(Studies in public policy)
Includes bibliographical references and index.
ISBN 0-7391-0460-8 (hardcover : alk. paper)
1. Commercial policy. 2. International trade. 3. International economic relations. I. Nagel, Stuart S., 1934– II. Studies in public policy (Lanham, Md.)

HF1411 .P588 2002
380.1'3—dc21 2002009878

Printed in the United States of America

∞™ The paper used in this publication meets the minimum requirements of American National Standard for Information Sciences—Permanence of Paper for Printed Library Materials, ANSI/NISO Z39.48-1992.

For Seymour Martin Lipset, extraordinary scholar

Contents

Introduction

Paul J. Rich

The authors in this three-volume series about policy issues in the new millennium were challenged in this volume to write about policy on an international level as it concerned issues of prosperity. The end of the Cold War is generally and properly given credit for sparking an increased discussion about ways of supporting the cultural environment that nurtures democracy and prosperity. Indeed, the claim is made that without democracy, the chances for economic prosperity are sharply reduced.

The surprisingly quick dissolution of the Communist system meant there was a receptive audience for any suggestions about which directions policy studies relating to reform would or should take. The number of "customers" (i.e. embryo democracies), seemingly in need of advice was dramatically increased. Marxist scholarship seemed at a dead end. The former Soviet bloc states as well as other states interpreted the emergence of the United States as the lone superpower as virtually a command to learn the mores of a Western lifestyle, whose signs and tokens were not only McDonalds's but Rotary and Kiwanis.

Civil society in consequence has become popular as a term, defined as "that set of diverse nongovernmental institutions which is strong enough to counterbalance the state, and while not preventing the state from fulfilling its role of keeper of the peace and arbitration between major interests, can nevertheless prevent it from dominating and atomizing the rest of society."[1] This attention to volunteerism, with its obvious implications for economics, is in fact a rediscovery of the part it has played in the political process over centuries.[2]

By no means is the current increased number of countries espousing democracy and an open economic system certain to be permanent. Fears are constantly expressed that there will be regression. Much of the debate expresses concerns about whether revived democratic institutions have staying power. A commonly stated reservation is that the legacies of oligarchy and dictatorship are not going to be quickly overcome.[3] That curious fact that nationalism is so strong at the same time that globalism is growing has been much noted.

Mercantilism is a principal contributor to the ethos of state-building. The decline of mercantilism as a philosophy has been a barometer reading that points to the decline of statism, and indicts that proponents of an exclusive loyalty to the nation state and its organizations have at least temporarily yielded to an internationally minded class. Nevertheless, recently an increasing concern over stubborn social problems has been accompanied by a stirring of mercantilism sentiments. Statism has been around too long to depart without a battle: "The moderate statist ideology of neomercantilism, however, has forebears as old as the medieval parliaments that grew into our institutions of representative government. If age lends interest and dignity, therefore neomercantilism must be approached in a spirit of respectful inquiry."

The temptation to which those who will espouse mercantilism in the future may be to use government as the "hair of the dog," believing that corrective administration of some sort is a means to economic prosperity. This "one more for the road" is as enticing to conservatives as it is to their liberal foes.

The classical position of Mun and other seventeenth-century writers may return as the garnishment for a repackaged mercantilism: the continued imbalance of trade and the persistence of poverty could result in the stone being rolled away from the tomb. The objections to mercantilism—the narrowness of its focus, the way it restricts policy concerns, its failure to contribute to the construction of an adequate general economic theory—are being forgotten.

So mercantilism remains part of the ethos of state-building and thus an ever attractive policy option. A rationale will be found for its continuance regardless of whether the right or the left is politically in ascendancy. Its demise seemingly threatens *la patrie*. When mercantilism is out of favor, the exclusive loyalty to the nation state thought so desirable gives way to an internationally minded class. That is not what is on the mind of the resurgent right in the United States, and should the right win there is a collision course set with such new instrumentalities as GATT and NAFTA.

With the collapse of the Soviet Union, economic models have far outstripped war games as a think tank pursuit. The next war is seen as an economic one and the voters' revenge would be swift for that rash politician who would subordinate growth and employment to grand diplomatic strategy.

But Japan is not today's Venice, Germany is not an enlarged Hanseatic League, and Microsoft is not the East India Company. All economic philosophies face a vastly more complex world than that of pirate adventurers. Much more realism about the pain that is going to accompany a genuine shift to free trade is needed. This is demonstrated by the fact that often *jejeune* arguments for winning the trade wars via government intervention are being made at the same time by the same people who advocate staunch individualism and demand independence from the tentacles of government organization.

Much of the current rhetoric is against interventionism.

Paul Krugman and others have charged that an obsession with trade competitiveness has diverted policy makers from what should be the real focus of the future, domestic productivity. Of course, in the case of the United States where only about 10 percent of the U.S. output goes in exports, that argument has some merit. Administrators in such a situation would appear to get their priorities wrong when they concentrate on trade wars as opposed to domestic issues. In more heavily export-oriented countries, the concern about other countries as rivals would still seem valid.

Adam Smith's accusation that mercantilists were unable to differentiate between wealth and treasure, seeing gold bars as the end when the real end was consumable and usable goods, still may hold true. The chances in the future are that there is going to be a continued "yes but" effort to interfere under the table, colored by misperceptions about what really contributes to trade competitiveness. For politicians to genuinely repudiate mercantilism as a philosophic approach, sincerely abdicating the power to intervene in the market and thus letting the chips fall where they may, would be to witness the greatest collective *hara-kiri* in organizational history. Mercantilism like the proverbial cat has many lives.

However, as a number of the contributors to this volume make clear, economics are not the whole story in the search for prosperity. The forces that nurture democracy and prosperity are a mixed blessing. While in any discussion about democratization and economics the encouragement of volunteerism and the activities of NGOs or Non-Governmental Organizations is seen as being crucial, reservations are expressed about the destabilizing influence of decentralization and pluralism,[4] a pluralism including the proliferation of harmful organizations.[5] At issue is the *quality* of the pluralism. The belief that pluralism per se, as represented in the growth of associationalism, is essential has produced sweeping endorsements of the benefits derived from the private sector, fulsome accolades which need reconciling with the political role of powerful but secretive anti-democratic movements[6] that are widespread.

In other words, praise for NGOs sometimes fails to consider that not all NGOs are unambiguously committed to democracy. Often they believe so firmly in their own viewpoint that they would welcome the chance to impose it if they could on everyone. Treating voluntary groups as if they were unexceptionally a benign influence is simplistic. Seymour Martin Lipset, to whom this volume is dedicated, has argued convincingly that an organization can be internally undemocratic but as a challenge to state power can perform a democratizing function, but that tradeoff has limits. No one would claim that the Ku Klux Klan ends up on the positive side of the ledger.

Certainly the argument has authority that not having durable intermediate associations that stand between the family and state is a threat to both democratization and economic development. Prosperity, many observers believe, needs the open society. The now-gone Soviet Union and Eastern Europe, where civil society was so long nonexistent, provide a prime example of how not to achieve prosperity, but are not the only instance: "Many Latin Catholic countries like France, Spain, Italy and a number of nations in Latin America exhibit a saddle-shaped distribution of organizations, with strong families, a strong state, and relatively little in between. These societies are utterly different from socialist ones in any number of important ways, particularly with regard to their greater respect for the family. But, like socialist societies, there has been in certain Latin Catholic countries a relative deficit of intermediate social groups in the area between the family and large, centralized organizations like the church or the state."[7]

The growth of volunteerism is desirable as large parts of the world attempt to democratize and embrace a free economy.[8] There is concern that the odds are against these changes, and against both prosperity and democracy.[9] Given the previous intellectual pursuit by intellectuals of Marxist answers, recent concern about the relationship between civil society and economics has an element of irony—apparently associations that promote democracy can even do so when they are not themselves particularly democratic.[10]

Another conundrum is whether one can be free and poor, or free and poor for very long. It is not just an operatic question. In any event, the diverse and even antagonistic opinions in the following pages should contribute to the current debate about how, having escaped Marx, we can avoid chaos.

NOTES

1. Ernest Gellner, qtd. Marc F. Plattner, "The Uses of 'Civil Society.'" *Journal of Democracy* 6(4) October 1995, 170.

2. Margaret Jacob, *Living the Enlightenment: Freemasonry and Politics in Eighteenth-Century Europe* (New York and Oxford: Oxford University Press, 1991), 20. For re-analysis of a specific incident focusing on the influence of voluntary societies, see Martin Phillip Johnson, *The Paradise of Association: Political Culture and Popular Organizations in the Paris Commune of 1871* (Ann Arbor: University of Michigan Press, 1996).

3. Howard J. Wiarda, "Mexico: Too Early to Celebrate." *The Washington Post*, 11 August 1997, A17.

4. In Mexico, interest groups have long been controlled by the ruling oligarchy, but this corporatism is now yielding to "free associationalism."

5. Weber comes to mind increasingly: "Perhaps no issue is more prominent in Latin American religion or more evident to visitors than the expansion (some would say invasion) of Protestantism and new religious movements. Five hundred religious groups, most of them new to Latin America, were registered with the ministry of foreign relations in Bolivia, one of the more remote places for their activity. Throughout the Caribbean and Central America, one sees new chapels springing up, seemingly everywhere. In one Maryknoll parish in Guatemala where there had been one non-Catholic chapel, there are now 50." Edward L. Cleary, "The Catholic Church Since Puebla." James M. Malloy and Edurardo A. Gamarra, eds., *Latin America and Caribbean Contemporary Record, 1987–1988*, vol. VII (New York and London: Holmes and Meier, 1990), A93.

> 6. If one looks up the dictionary definition of "secret society," one finds a description of organizations exactly like Masonry—i.e., the normal usage of the term "secret society" is to refer to a group with oath-binding and secret rituals, whether or not its existence, place of meeting, membership, or whatever else is secret or public information. We may object to being called a "secret society," but according to recognized usage, that's what we are.

Probably true, but this same definition puts us in very good company! Scouting has the same sort of "oath-binding and secret rituals." I have participated in it. The Order of the Arrow, a fraternity within Scouting, even has more. When I was in the U.S. Navy, I was bound by several oaths, and participated in many "secret rituals." Several of the employers I have worked for have required me to swear oaths, and participate in "secret rituals." I wonder how many *other* places in our society would fit within this definition?

7. Francis Fukuyama, *Trust: The Social Virtues and the Creation of Prosperity* (New York: The Free Press, 1995), 55.

8. See Mariclaire Acosta, "Democracy, Governability, and Human Rights in Mexico." *Enfoque* Spring/Summer 1997, 1.

9. Kurt Weyland, "Latin America's Four Political Models." *Journal of Democracy* 6(4) October 1995, 138.

10. See Daniel H. Levine, "Popular Groups, Popular Culture, and Popular Religion." Daniel H. Levine ed., *Constructing Culture and Power in Latin America* (Ann Arbor: University of Michigan Press, 1993), 173–74.

1

Liberalizing Capital Controls: Economic Pluralism or Political Institutions?

Quan Li and Dale L. Smith

Financial globalization has been proposed as the single most important characteristic of the contemporary international political economy. Conventionally, this means the financial markets of different nation states are more integrated than ever before. Movement of portfolio and direct investments encounter increasingly fewer barriers and ever lower transaction costs. Although it is widely believed financial globalization has reached such an extent that capital moves frictionlessly across borders, empirical evidence has yielded a somewhat different conclusion. International financial markets have not yet reached the degree of integration found in domestic financial markets, and even the industrialized countries vary greatly in the degree to which they have reduced barriers to financial flows.

In this article, we take on the issue of financial globalization by arguing that financial market integration and the high levels of international capital mobility we observe are but the outcome of domestic policy processes. What we must first understand is why nation states consciously choose to remove various restrictions on capital movement across their borders.[1] As Cohen (1996) notes in a recent review article, capital liberalization has been explained from a number of different approaches.[2] A systemic approach relies on changes in the distribution of financial power or the spread of technology to explain globalization. Since this approach ignores domestic influences, a policy of liberalization is assumed to be the rational choice of a unitary national actor. Alternatively, domestic explanations can be divided into two groups. A societal approach argues that changes in the economic fortunes of powerful societal and economic interest groups lead to competition for control of government policy. Termed by some as economic pluralism, this approach sees government policy as a reflection of the balance of power among these socioeconomic groups. While acknowledging the importance of societal influences, a statist approach contends that a state's governmental and institutional structures play an independent role in determining policy choice. These approaches have often been presented as competitors in explanations of financial liberalization, but they are obviously complementary. Systemic changes alter the economic and political interests of societal groups. However, that new constellation of power and interest is not seamlessly translated into changes in government policy, as economic pluralism would have us believe. Rather, changes in the power and interests of these groups are mediated by existing governmental institutions.[3] Thus, the different models are essentially complementary rather than competing.

Drawing explanations from each of these approaches, but focusing particularly on the pluralist and statist approaches, we seek to explain both cross-sectional and cross-time differences in governmental decisions to remove controls on capital transactions. We expect that capital control liberalization reflects domestic societal interests and their share of power, but that societal support is not sufficient. The policy is also affected by the incumbent government's ideological composition and political institutions. Using a sample of 18 OECD countries over 24 years (1967–1990) we statistically test the hypotheses drawn from each of these approaches and evaluate their complementarity in explaining states' capital decontrol decisions.

The rest of the paper is organized as follows. In the next section, we review different measures of capital control liberalization and market integration and make a case for the measure of this important variable we choose. A discussion of the different theoretical explanations of capital liberalization policies is followed by a presentation of our methodology and specification of hypotheses. We then present the results of our statistical analysis, and conclude the paper with a discussion of the theoretical implications of our findings.

CAPITAL CONTROL LIBERALIZATION

Financial globalization has been empirically assessed using several different measures. Frankel (1993) reviews different measures of capital mobility based upon some economic relationships, including capital flows, onshore-offshore interest differentials, deviations from covered interest rate parity, and the Feldstein-Horioka saving-investment approach. He shows that international financial integration has advanced much less than the integration of domestic financial markets. More recent analyses using time series techniques have shown some evidence of international financial market integration, but again only to a certain extent (Cavaglia 1992; Goodwin and Grennes 1994). However, this type of research focuses on the increased flows of capital, and the liberalization policy is assumed but not directly measured.

Attempts to measure the capital control or liberalization policy usually rely in some form on the IMF's *Annual Report of Exchange Arrangements and Exchange Restrictions*. In summary tables, this publication reports the presence (or absence) of twelve different types of restrictions on exchange rates and capital and current transactions.[4] These data have been used widely by economists and are beginning to appear in the political science literature (Alesina, Grilli, and Milesi-Ferretti 1994; Grilli and Milesi-Ferretti 1995; Rose 1994; Garrett 1995; Haggard and Maxfield 1996). Authors have often summed across these categories to produce a simple aggregate index of restrictions. While such an aggregated index has the advantage of providing an interval level measure, and thus facilitating statistical analysis, it might distort the extent of capital control for at least two reasons. First, it treats very different restrictions with equal weight, and second, some of the restrictions are functionally complementary and are usually lifted (or imposed) concurrently.

A different approach to measurement of policy change is to focus upon the most essential types of capital control restrictions. One of the most important capital flow restrictions deals with restrictions on payments for capital transactions.[5] The imposition of these restrictions are carefully studied in Mathieson and Rojas-Suarez (1994), Alesina, Grilli and Milesi-Ferretti (1994), and Grilli and Milesi-Ferretti (1995).[6] Such a restriction curtails capital flows across borders and thus, produces stabilizing effects upon national economies with respect to the balance of payments situation and the real sector of the economy. The restraining impact is most acutely felt by domestic financial institutions in terms of their foreign asset and liability positions and by nonbank residents such as the multinational corporations in terms of foreign direct investment. Corporations and domestic financial intermediaries are suggested to be the prime political actors who might have strong interests in seeing the removal of such capital restrictions (Goodman and Pauly 1993; Frieden 1991; Sobel 1994). Given that our major theoretical interest is to specify the conditions under which state leaders make decisions to liberalize capital controls, we focus on examining the removal of this essential restriction limiting capital transactions.

THEORETICAL EXPLANATIONS

The Pluralist Model

The pluralist view of democracy argues that policy is a result of competitions among societal interests and that elected politicians have to meet the demands of their own constituencies in the process of pursuing reelection. When capital liberalization is explained in terms of economic pluralism, it is suggested that the liberalization policy simply reflects the wishes of the dominant interest groups (Goodman and Pauly 1993; Sobel 1994). The expected distributional consequences of a liberalization policy will generate an incentive for different domestic interest groups to compete for influence over the policy outcomes.

Frieden (1991) identifies several key societal actors who are affected by financial globalization: owners of capital, owners and workers in specific sectors, producers of traded goods, international investors and producers of nontraded goods. The distributional effects of capital mobility lead to political realignments among these different groups. Thus he suggests that support for greater financial integration can be expected from owners and managers of financial assets and from multinational corporations with internationally diversified investments. In a comparative analysis of the capital decontrol experiences of Japan, Germany, France and Italy, Goodman and Pauly (1993) also conclude that multinational firms and domestic financial intermediaries in these countries have more and more interest in investing abroad and diversifying their portfolios internationally. Consequently, as these societal interests have become increasingly powerful in domestic politics, their interests in liberalizing capital flows usually coincide with the adoption of such policies. In this article, we specifically examine whether domestic deposit money banks and multinational firms are the primary supporters of the liberalization policy and whether policy adoption is correlated with their interests in removing restrictions on capital transactions. We expect that as domestic deposit money banks are more and more interested in owning foreign assets, they are more likely to support policies liberalizing capital controls. We also hypothesize that as multinational firms increase foreign direct investment abroad, they will increasingly support removing restrictions on capital flows across borders.

The Statist Model

According to this model, state leaders are rational political actors who act to realize their policy preferences within various institutional and environmental/contextual constraints. The question at issue is whether state leaders enjoy some degree of policy autonomy with respect to capital decontrol in the face of systemic changes and societal pressures. More specifically, if they do play some autonomous role, state leaders should be able to take advantage of domestic political institutions and pursue their own policy preferences, regardless of systemic and societal pressures.

State leaders make decisions based on their policy preferences, and their policy preferences derive from their value assumptions and how they think the economic world works. Helleiner (1994) argues that shifts in the beliefs of state leaders provide an important explanation to why capital decontrol is adopted. Two kinds of beliefs may be important to the adoption of liberal financial policies. The first is a state leader's belief about how the economy works. The belief that Keynesian type economic interventionism and demand side management do not work is the driving force behind the policy of financial de-regulation (Cerny 1994). Only when state leaders believe that capital control liberalization is desirable will they act in favor of removing capital movement restrictions. Thus, policy preferences are related to the decision makers' cognitive belief. Second, state leaders may be ideologically pro-labor or pro-capital. Pro-labor state leaders are more likely to impose a higher tax rate on capital and, therefore, are less likely to liberalize capital controls in order to avoid capital flight (Alesina, Grilli and Milesi-Ferretti 1994; Grilli and Milesi-Ferretti 1995). On the other hand, pro-capital leaders tend to adopt policies in line with the interests of their own constituencies such as multinational corporations and domestic financial institutions. They are more likely to liberalize capital controls. Thus, ideology is related to the decision-makers' policy preferences.

Both the cognitive beliefs of state leaders and their attitude toward capital and labor are reflected in the ideological composition of the government and correlated with the partisanship of the government. Extensive evidence has been garnered about the effects of political partisanship in the choice of macroeconomic policies of the industrialized countries (Quinn and Shapiro 1991, Hicks and Swank 1992; Alesina 1995; Garrett 1995). The leftist or liberal party is more prone to adopt a Keynesian type of economic interventionism whereas the rightist or conservative party is more inclined toward laissez faire, neoclassical economic policy packages.

State leaders may be successful in seeking their most preferred policies, but only within existing institutional constraints. In the making of foreign economic policies, state leaders are bound by state political institutional features (Ikenberry 1988; Gourevitch 1986). Two institutional features are relevant to the adoption of capital decontrol policies: the degree of government cohesion, and the degree of central bank independence. One feature of modern democracy is the dispersion of power among disparate political institutions. In a parliamentary system, governments can be formed based upon coalitions of different parties or a single party. Coalitional government is undoubtedly characterized by more compromises than single party government. Government cohesion in policy adoption and implementation can be reasonably expected to be lower in the former than in the latter. Similar situations also exist in presidential systems. Laver and Shepsle (1996) and Fiorina (1996) draw an analogy between coalitional government under a parliamentary system and divided government under a presidential system. In terms of policy adoption and implementation, both lead to the expectation of more compromises and lower government cohesion, compared to single party government and unified government respectively.

The level of government cohesion is especially relevant to capital liberalization. Frieden (1991), Goodman and Pauly (1993) and Sobel (1994) argue that capital liberalization has important distributive effects upon different groups in the domestic economy. Accepting their argument, we may reasonably expect that the adoption of a liberalization policy will be quite controversial. The issue itself can have a very divisive impact upon a coalitional or divided government. Ceteris paribus, it is less likely for a coalition or divided government to remove capital restrictions, but more likely for a single party or unified government to do so.

One other institutional feature state leaders have to take into account in liberalizing capital controls is the degree of central bank independence. Greater central bank independence implies greater monetary discipline. Thus, not surprisingly, it is found to be significantly correlated with lower inflation and smaller variability of inflation and real interest rates (Cukierman, Webb, and Neyapti 1992; Alesina and Summers 1993). Lower inflation does not produce the need for contractionary monetary policy, and less variability in inflation and real interest rates eliminates another reason for drastic capital flows across borders in search of higher returns. Thus, greater central bank independence serves as a facilitating factor when state leaders consider the removal of capital and exchange restrictions. In a sense, financial liberalization is expected to be easier to achieve when the central bank is independent enough to instill monetary discipline.

In the next section, we discuss the methodology used to evaluate these hypotheses and the operationalization of the relevant theoretical concepts so that they are amenable to empirical assessment.

METHODOLOGY

We are interested in explaining the conditions under which states liberalize controls over capital flows across national borders. As we discussed earlier, there are different approaches to the measurement of global financial liberalization, and each approach has its strengths and weaknesses. Given that our theoretical focus is state policy choice, we follow Mathieson and Rojas-Suarez (1994) and Alesina, Grilli and Milesi-Ferretti (1994) and focus on "restrictions on payments for capital transactions." The IMF's *Annual Report on Exchange Arrangements and Exchange Restrictions* has reported (since 1967) whether member states imposed or lifted this restriction for a given year. We use this measure to represent state capital liberalization policy. It is coded zero if an IMF member state restricts payments for capital transactions for a given year, and one if it does not impose restrictions for that year. While this measure does not reflect the intensity or degree of capital liberalization for a given state, it does capture whether a state allows domestic financial institutions and multinational firms to invest freely abroad. Therefore, it aptly fits our theoretical interest in assessing the explanatory power of pluralist and statist explanations.

Since our dependent variable, the adoption of capital liberalization policy, is dichotomous, regular regression analysis is not appropriate. Thus, assuming that our sample is drawn from a normal distribution, we use a probit model. Our sample includes 18 OECD countries from 1967 to 1990.[7] This gives us a pooled time series cross-sectional design. One assumption we make in using the pooled time series cross-sectional design is that the parameters for the independent variables are stable across time and over space. Since we believe that our theoretical model is generalizable to the liberalization processes in all industrial countries, the pooled time-series cross-sectional design is most appropriate here.[8]

Economic pluralism argues that state capital liberalization policy is simply an outcome of domestic interest group competition. According to Frieden (1991), Goodman and Pauly (1993), and Sobel (1994), multinational firms and domestic financial institutions are the most important domestic groups that may have interests in liberalizing capital controls. To test whether the pluralist model explains capital decontrol, we use two different measures to gauge the relative interest of these two important domestic actors in capital decontrol. The first measure is a state's foreign direct investment as a percentage of its gross domestic investment. It reflects the extent to which home country based multinational firms are interested in liberalizing state restrictions over capital flows across borders. The greater the ratio, the more interested multinational firms based in a state will be in having the state's capital controls liberalized, and the more active they will be in pushing for such a policy change.

The second measure is the domestic money deposit banks' foreign assets as a percentage of their assets in the (domestic) private sector. This measure is meant to capture the relative interest of domestic financial intermediaries in diversifying their portfolios at home and abroad. The higher the ratio, the more we anticipate domestic financial institutions want to see capital controls liberalized.

Since loosened capital controls may lead to the purchase of more foreign assets by domestic financial institutions and more foreign direct investment flows by multinational firms, the direction of causality between these two independent variables and our dependent variable may run in both directions. Using contemporaneous observations of the independent and dependent variables could result in spurious findings. To correct for the possibility that capital decontrol policy may lead to greater capital outflows, we use one-period lagged values for these two variables. Data on these variables are taken from the IMF's *International Financial Statistics Yearbook*.

We argue that even in the face of systemic and societal pressures, state leaders enjoy some policy autonomy to make politically rational policy choices. They may act on their beliefs and policy preferences, or they may be constrained by political institutions in pursuing their policy choices. To test this statist model, we use one measure to capture the state leaders' cognitive and ideological beliefs that inform their policy preferences, and two measures to examine the influence of domestic political institutions. As discussed earlier, state leaders' beliefs and policy preferences are correlated with their partisanship. Alesina, Grilli and Milesi-Ferretti (1994), and Grilli and Milesi-Ferretti (1995) use a dummy variable for government partisanship. We believe that in modern democracies where power is dispersed among different political actors and institutions, a dummy variable is too crude a measure to truly reflect government partisanship. Instead, we use an interval level measure of government ideological complexion developed by Woldendorp, Keman, and Budge (1993).[9] The measure is a five point scale with 1 representing most conservative and 5 representing most liberal. The higher the scale, the more liberal the government, and the less likely it is to liberalize capital controls.

Government cohesion can affect the adoption of a capital decontrol policy that can have important distributional consequences. Government cohesion is to a large extent determined by the structure of domestic political institutions. We measure government cohesion using the "type of government" measure created by Woldendorp, Keman and Budge (1993).[10] The measure is again a five point (1–5) scale. The higher this measure, the less cohesive the government is, and the less likely it is to liberalize capital controls.

The degree of central bank independence also affects the adoption of a capital decontrol policy. We obtained the aggregate legal index of central bank independence from Cukierman, Webb and Neyapti (1992). It is expected that greater central bank independence facilitates the adoption of capital liberalization policies.[11]

In considering the liberalization of capital controls, state leaders may also be influenced by several other important factors: systemic level pressures, the exchange rate regime, a country's trade openness, and its current account status. Valid evaluations of the pluralist and statist models require that we control for these other relevant variables. Systemic level pressures constitute the impact of the market and global financial developments. We measure them by the lagged number of countries in our 18 nation sample which have liberalized capital controls for any given year. As more countries lift restrictions on capital flows, pressures for liberalization are exerted on other countries in the international system.

The type of exchange rate regime also affects a country's likelihood of capital liberalization. Since 1967, different states have experienced different types of exchange rate regimes: fixed rates under Bretton Woods, managed floating, target zones, and freely floating exchange rate regimes. The general trend is a movement in exchange rate regimes from more fixed to more flexible. The more flexible the exchange rate, the more difficulty states will have in maintaining stringent capital control policies. We use two dummy variables to control for the effects of different exchange rate regimes. One dummy variable is coded one if a country is under the Bretton Woods fixed rate system, and zero otherwise. The other dummy variable is coded one if a country is under some pegged system and zero otherwise. Both variables are expected to be negatively related to capital liberalization.

There is no definitive expectation on how a country's trade openness might affect a state leader's decision on capital liberalization. On the one hand, trade openness is often used as a measure of economic interdependence among countries. When a state is more open to trade, it is more dependent upon other countries, and it has a greater interest in capital decontrol. On the other hand, greater exposure to the world economy implies more exposure to international market risks. As a result, state leaders might be reluctant to liberalize capital controls, since free capital flows could lead to greater volatility and loss of policy autonomy. The lagged value of exports plus imports divided by GDP allows us to estimate the effect of trade openness on capital liberalization. These data are from the Penn World Tables (Mark 5.6a).

As suggested in Goodman and Pauly (1993) and Grilli and Milesi-Ferretti (1995), current account surpluses provide favorable conditions for capital liberalization whereas countries in deficit are less likely to liberalize capital controls. We use the lagged current account balance as a percentage of GDP to account for the effect of macroeconomic conditions upon capital liberalization.

To summarize, our dependent variable, restrictions on payments for capital transactions, is dichotomous with one representing no restrictions on payments (i.e., liberalization) and zero representing the existence of restrictions. The independent variables (along with their expected signs) are as follows:

Control/contextual variables:

- Number of states in the sample with liberalized capital controls, lagged (expected sign: +)
- Fixed exchange rate regime (−)
- Managed floating/pegged exchange rate regime (−)
- Trade openness, lagged (+,−)
- Current account balance as a percentage of GDP, lagged (+)

Pluralist Variables:

- Domestic banks' foreign assets as a percentage of their assets in the private sector, lagged (+)
- Foreign direct investment abroad as a percentage of gross domestic investment, lagged (+)

Statist variables:

- Ideological complexion of the government (−)
- Type of government (−)
- Index of central bank independence (+)

FINDINGS AND IMPLICATIONS

The first step in our analysis was to estimate the pluralist model with all the control variables. However, we began this paper by arguing that these two models are really complementary, and so the next step was to add the statist model to our pluralist estimation. We attempt to show that the pluralist model provides an important explanation for state adoption of capital decontrol policies, but that the inclusion of the statist model can significantly improve our understanding of state policymaking. We use probit to analyze the pooled time series cross-sectional data on 18 OECD countries from 1967 to 1990. The statistical estimation results are presented in table 1.1.

The overall model fit measures show that both the pluralist and the statist models provide significant variables for explaining a state's capital liberalization policy. The likelihood ratio (LR) test, essentially a chi-square test, allows us to reject the null hypothesis that all coefficients are jointly zero at the .01 level for both the pluralist and the full model. The percentage reduction of error for the pluralist model and the full model, as compared against the null model of a constant only, is 44 percent and 59 percent, respectively. The percentage of correctly predicted observations is 74.6 percent and 81.4 percent respectively, which can be computed from the data in Appendix 2. The pseudo R-square, computed as the likelihood ratio index according to Greene (1993: 651), is reasonably high for both models. Thus, both the pluralist model and the full model have significantly improved our predictions of state capital liberalization policy.

The findings also reveal the complementary nature of the pluralist and the statist models. The LR test comparing the pluralist model and the full model rejects the null hypothesis that all three independent variables from the statist model are jointly equal to zero. Compared to the pluralist model, the full model improves the reduction of error by 27 percent. These statistical results imply that a model without the statist variables is underspecified in explaining capital liberalization.

Table 1.1 also shows that all the major theoretical hypotheses have received statistical support for both the pluralist and the full model. Drawn from the pluralist model, the percentage of domestic banks' foreign assets and the percentage of a state's foreign direct investment abroad turn out to be statistically significant and in the expected direction. The more domestic financial institutions increase their portfolios in foreign assets and the more multinational firms invest abroad, the more likely a state is to liberalize its

Table 1.1. Pooled Time-Series Cross-Sectional Probit Estimation of State Capital Liberalization Policy in Industrialized Countries from 1967 to 1990

		Pluralist Model	*Full Model*
Constant	Parameter	−0.2705	−0.9045*
(expected sign: +,−)	Z-score	−0.855	−1.78
Banks' foreign assets as a percentage of assets in		0.0072***	0.0087***
the private sector, lagged (+)		1.989	2.46
Government cohesion (type of government)			−0.1374*
(−)			−1.882
Government ideological complexion			−0.1088*
(−)			−1.787
Aggregate legal index of central bank			2.8393***
independence (+)			4.246
Number of states in the sample with liberalized		0.1754***	0.1908***
capital controls, lagged (1)		4.154	4.311
Fixed exchanged rate under Bretton Woods		−0.9135***	−1.155***
(2)		−2.649	−3.143
Pegged or managed floating exchange rate regime		−0.8423***	−0.9196***
(2)		−3.74	−3.393
Current account balance as a percentage of GDP,		0.1417***	0.125***
lagged (1)		3.914	3.225
Trade openness, lagged (1, 2)		−0.0136***	−0.0143***
		−3.018	−2.895
Sample size		295	295
Log-likelihood		−146.59	−133.18
LR-test (Chi-Square)		113.31***	140.11***
% reduction of error		44%	59%
Pseudo R-square		0.28	0.35
LR-test comparing the two models			26.8036***
% reduction of error comparing the two models			27%

Notes:
1. *** (**, *) statistically significant at 0.01 (0.05, 01) level (two tail).
2. Reduction of error is computed using the following formula:
   % reduction of error = (% correctly classified − modal category)/(100 − modal category).
3. Pseudo R-square is computed as the likelihood ratio index (LRI) as in Greene (1993, 651).

capital controls. The policy coincides with the interests of powerful societal actors and supports the tenets of economic pluralism.

Under the full model, both of the pluralist variables continue to be significant and exhibit their robustness to different model specifications. Their effects are not washed out by the inclusion of the statist variables. All three statist variables, government cohesion (type of government), the ideological complexion of the government, and central bank independence, are statistically significant and in the expected directions. The lower government cohesion (represented by higher values on our "type of government" scale), and the further left the state leaders are (represented by higher values on the "government ideological complexion" scale), the less likely a state is to liberalize capital transactions. And the more independent a state's central bank is, the more likely the state is to adopt a policy of liberalization. These results appear to support the notion that capital decontrol policies are the result of rational and conscious decision making on the part of state leaders and that they have some policy autonomy in making such decisions. They are able to follow their beliefs within the constraints of political institutions. It seems a reasonable inference that although state leaders are constrained by the political institutions in their policy-making capacity, they can also design political institutions in ways that may increase their own policy autonomy, even in the face of strong societal interests. Therefore, political institutions may be a double-edged sword for state leaders.

There are also interesting findings for our control/contextual variables in these two models. The lagged number of states with liberalized capital controls is statistically significant and has the expected sign. As more states within the system liberalize over time, pressures for the remaining states to liberalize increase. In addition, relative to a flexible exchange rate regime, the fixed exchange rate regime under Bretton Woods and pegged systems such as the EMS exert less pressure upon nation states to liberalize capital transactions. These results suggest that systemic factors may indeed set broad parameters, within which more complex political interactions between societal and statist forces take place. Consistent with previous research (e.g. Goodman and Pauly, 1993), the current account balance is found to serve as either a facilitating factor or a hindrance to capital liberalization, depending on whether the current account is in surplus or deficit. Lagged trade openness is statistically significant and takes on a negative sign. If our theoretical conjectures about its effects are correct, then the inference here is that fear of exposures to international financial market risks supersedes the positive influence of economic interdependence upon capital liberalization.

Our major theoretical expectation is that the statist model complements the pluralist model in the sense that state leaders are able to exercise some degree of policy autonomy even under the influence of systemic and societal forces. If the empirical results shown in table 1.1 support this notion, then it is reasonable to expect that a capital liberalization policy is most likely to be adopted when state political factors, societal interests, and the systemic level influences all point in a favorable direction. A single (majority) party, right-wing government, accompanied by a highly independent central bank, is most likely to liberalize capital controls when domestic financial institutions and multinational firms have large percentages of foreign assets and transactions, and when a relatively large number of countries have already liberalized capital controls. Unfortunately, the extent to which such an expectation is substantiated is not explicit in table 1.1, because in probit analysis we cannot directly interpret the coefficient estimates as the marginal effect of the respective independent variable upon the dependent variable as we do in regular regression analysis. Thus, in order to translate the statistical results into evidence supporting our major theoretical argument, we need to calculate the marginal effects of the major statist variables upon the probability a state will adopt a capital liberalization policy. We compute some probability estimates using the parameter estimates from the full model and present these results in tables 1.1 and 1.2.

The tables illustrate the effects of the major statist variables on the probability of the adoption of a capital liberalization policy under a pegged exchange rate system and a freely floating exchange rate system. In both cases, we are interested in the extent to which government cohesion and government ideological complexion affect the probability of the policy choice, even in the presence of high societal and systemic pressures. Thus, we set both the pluralist model variables (banks' foreign assets and foreign direct investment abroad) and the number of states having liberalized capital controls at values equivalent to the eightieth percentile of their respective distributions. We hold all other variables at their mean levels.

Table 1.2 shows that under a pegged exchange rate system, ceteris paribus, a single-party, right-wing government will liberalize capital controls with a probability of 0.72. Alternatively, a multiparty, minority government with a centrist/balanced ideological orientation has a probability of only 0.42 of adopting capital decontrols. Holding everything else constant, but now shifting to a flexible exchange rate system, table 1.3 shows the probability for a single-party, right-wing government to liberalize capital controls is 0.93. This is very similar to the ideal scenario we identified above. A single-party, right-wing government, facing high societal demands from banks and multinational corporations, a highly liberalized international environment, and a

Table 1.2. Effects of the Major Statist Variables on the Probability of Capital Liberalization Policy Adoption under a Pegged Exchange Rate System as in the Full Model

	Single Party Majority Government	*Surplus Coalition Government*	*Multiparty Minority Government*
Right-wing dominance	0.72	0.62	0.51
Balanced situation	0.64	0.53	0.42
Left-wing dominance	0.55	0.45	0.34

Notes:

1. The row variable is government cohesion (type of government); the column variable is government ideological complexion. Each variable is a 5-point scale, we show the effects of these two variables only at their minimum (1), median (3) and the maximum (5) values.
2. The two pluralist model variables and the number of states liberalized in the system are set at their 80th percentile values; all other variables are set at their mean values.

Table 1.3. Effects of the Major Statist Variables on the Probability of Capital Liberalization Policy Adoption under a Flexible Exchange Rate System as in the Full Model

	Single Party Majority Government	*Surplus Coalition Government*	*Multiparty Minority Government*
Right-wing dominance	0.93	0.89	0.83
Balanced situation	0.90	0.84	0.77
Left-wing dominance	0.85	0.78	0.69

Notes:
1. The row variable is government cohesion (type of government); the column variable is government ideological complexion. Each variable is a 5-point scale, we show the effects of these two variables only at their minimum (1), median (3) and the maximum (5) values.
2. The two pluralist model variables and the number of states liberalized in the system are set at their 80th percentile values; all other variables are set at their mean values.

freely floating exchange rate is almost certain to liberalize. However, the probability of liberalization for a multiparty minority government with a left-wing orientation is only 0.69. High societal demands, a highly liberalized international environment, and freely floating exchange rates all remain unchanged in our example. We have only altered the structure and ideological orientation of the government, and yet the probability of liberalization has dropped significantly.

Clearly, the probability estimates, computed using estimated parameters from our statistical model, help drive home the point that the ideological orientations of state leaders and the characteristics of political institutions make a real difference in terms of policy choice, with respect to capital liberalization. It is reasonable to infer that state leaders can manipulate the chances of policy adoption by altering the design of relevant political institutions. Providing the central bank with greater legal independence would increase the probability of adopting more liberal capital controls. State leaders may also use the characteristics of their political institutions to deflect societal pressures. For example, a leftist government, ideologically reluctant to liberalize capital controls, can always blame the sluggishness of policy adoption on the lack of government cohesion, even in the face of paramount societal and systemic pressures. Our results illustrate the central role that politics play in the choice of capital liberalization policies and have rendered statist explanations more relevant.

CONCLUSION

Whether referred to as globalization or internationalization, it is widely accepted that barriers to a whole range of international transactions have been falling throughout the post-war period. These systemic changes alter the power and interests of powerful socioeconomic groups within states. In turn, these groups press their governments for changes in policy. However, changes in government policy do not directly and truly reflect the changes in the power and interests of those societal groups. There is another set of actors involved. Government structures and institutions have an independent role to play in translating societal demands into government policy.

Within a sample of industrialized states, we have examined governmental decisions to liberalize on an essential dimension of capital controls—restrictions on capital transactions. We explained policy choice in terms of a relatively parsimonious statistical model that draws from systemic, pluralist and statist explanations. Our results provide powerful evidence for the links described in the previous paragraph. Explanations drawn from the pluralist model are strongly supported, but the addition of statist explanations significantly improves the explanatory power of our model. Economic pluralism is important, but only tells part of the story. Politics matter.

NOTES

1. Any complete understanding of the financial globalization must include the complex and dynamic relationship between government liberalization, the resulting increase in capital mobility and the pressures for greater liberalization that follow. Both Goodman and Pauly (1993) and Cohen (1996) have recognized the importance of this dynamic interaction between national choices and systemic processes. However, as a first cut, we believe it is important to focus on the determinants of governmental decisions to reduce barriers to capital flows, without ignoring the effect of earlier liberalization on the government's current decision.

2. After reviewing a number of recent books on capital liberalization and the approaches both employed and rejected by the various authors, Cohen admits that, "the organization of inquiry seems to be treated very much as a matter of personal taste" (1996: 274). The taxonomy we employ—systemic, societal and statist—is quite standard and, within this field, can be traced back at least to the work of Ikenberry, Lake and Mastanduno (1988).

3. This is essentially the argument found in Garrett and Lange (1996).

4. See Appendix 1.1 for a listing of the types of restrictions.

5. Restrictions are defined as "official actions directly affecting the availability or cost of exchange, or involving undue delay other than restrictions imposed for security reasons" (IMF, AREAER).

6. We follow Alesina, Grilli and Milesi-Ferretti (1994) in using this measure as our focus of study, but our design is different from theirs in terms of the fundamental research question, operationalization of some of the political variables, and the inclusion of other independent variables.

7. Although we began this project expecting to test our model with 24 OECD countries, six (Greece, Luxembourg, Portugal, Spain, Switzerland, and Turkey) had

to be dropped due to missing data on some of the variables. Due to the creation of the lagged variables, the year 1967 had to be dropped from the estimation. The final sample includes 414 observations with 18 countries for 23 years.

8. In order to test the robustness of our results, we also carry out analysis on the measure of capital restrictions/mobility in Garrett (1995). Since the variable has multiple rank-ordered categories, we use a pooled ordered probit. All the major statistical findings in terms of hypothesis testing are the same as those presented in the text. Results are available from the authors upon request.

9. See Appendix 1.1 for an explanation of this measure.

10. See Appendix 1.1 for details on the coding used to create this variable.

11. Cukierman et al. compose two measures for central bank independence: central bank turnover rate and the legal independence measure. They find that the aggregate legal independence index is a better measure for the industrialized countries, whereas the central banker turnover rate is a better measure for the developing countries. In this paper, since our sample includes only the industrialized countries, we use the legal independence index. One drawback of the measure is that it lacks variation over time for many countries. Thus, it does not inform us much about over time changes, but it does show cross-national differences.

REFERENCES

Alesina, Alberto. 1995. "Elections, Party Structure and the Economy," in *Modern Political Economy,* Jeffrey S. Banks and Eric A. Hanushek, eds. Cambridge: Cambridge University Press.

Alesina, Alberto and Lawrence H. Summers. 1993. "Central Bank Independence and Macroeconomic Performance: Some Comparative Evidence." *Journal of Money, Credit and Banking* 25: 151–63.

Alesina, Alberto, Vittorio Grilli and Gian Maria Milesi-Ferretti. 1994. "The Political Economy of Capital Controls," in *Capital Mobility: The Impact on Consumption, Investment and Growth,* Leonardo Leiderman and Assaf Razin, eds. Cambridge: Cambridge Press, 1994.

Cavaglia, Stefano. 1992. "The Persistence of Real Interest Differentials: A Kalman Filtering Approach." *Journal of Monetary Economics* 29: 429–43.

Cerny, Philip G. 1994. "The Dynamics of Financial Globalization: Technology, Market Structure, and Policy Response." *Policy Science* 27: 319–43.

Cohen, Benjamin J. 1996. "Phoenix Risen: The Resurrection of Global Finance." *World Politics* 48: 268–96.

Cukierman, Alex, Steven B. Webb and Bilin Neyapti. 1992. "Measuring the Independence of Central Banks and Its Effect on Policy Outcomes." *The World Bank Economic Review* 6: 353–98.

Fiorina, Morris P. 1996. *Divided Government.* Boston: Allyn and Bacon.

Frankel, Jeffrey A. 1993. *On Exchange Rates.* Cambridge: MIT Press.

Frieden, Jeffrey. 1991. "Invested Interests: The Politics of National Economic Policies in a World of Global Finance." *International Organization* 45: 425–51.

Garrett, Geoffrey. 1995. "Capital Mobility, Trade and the Domestic Politics of Economic Policy." *International Organization* 49: 657–87.

Garrett, Geoffrey and Peter Lange. 1996. "Internationalization, Institutions, and Political Change," in *Internationalization and Domestic Politics,* Helen V. Milner and Robert O. Keohane, eds. Cambridge, UK: Cambridge University Press.

Goodman, John B. and Louis W. Pauly. 1993. "The Obsolescence of Capital Controls? Economic Management in an Age of Global Markets." *World Politics* 46: 50–82.

Goodwin, B.K. and T.J. Grennes. 1994. "Real Interest Rate Equalization and the Integration of International Financial Markets." *Journal of International Money and Finance* 13: 107–24.

Gourevitch, Peter A. 1986. *Politics in Hard Times: Comparative Responses to International Economic Crises.* Ithaca: Cornell University Press.

Greene, William H. 1993. *Econometric Analysis.* New York: Macmillan.

Grilli, Vittorio and Gian Maria Milesi-Ferretti. 1995. "Economic Effects and Structural Determinants of Capital Controls." *IMF Staff Papers* 42(3): 517–51.

Haggard, Stephan and Sylvia Maxfield. 1996. "The Political Economy of Financial Internationalization in the Developing World." *International Organization* 50: 35–68.

Helleiner, Eric. 1994. *States and the Reemergence of Global Finance: From Bretton Woods to the 1990s.* Ithaca, N.Y.: Cornell University Press.

Hicks, Alexander and Duane Swank. 1992. "Politics, Institutions and Welfare Spending in Industrial Democracies, 1960–1982." *American Political Science Review* 86: 658–75.

Ikenberry, G. John. 1988. "Conclusion: An Institutional Approach to American Foreign Economic Policy," in *The State and American Foreign Economic Policy,* G. John Ikenberry, David A. Lake, and Michael Mastanduno, eds. Ithaca, N.Y.: Cornell University Press.

Ikenberry, G. John, David A. Lake and Michael Mastanduno. 1988. "Introduction: Approaches to Explaining American Foreign Economic Policy." *International Organization* 42: 1–14.

IMF. Various years. *International Financial Statistics.* Washington D.C.: IMF.

———. Various years. *Annual Report on Exchange Arrangements and Exchange Restrictions* (AREAER). Washington D.C.: IMF.

Laver, M. and K.A. Shepsle. 1996. *Making and Breaking Government.* Cambridge: Cambridge University Press.

Mathieson, Donald J. and Liliana Rojas-Suarez. 1994. "Capital Controls and Capital Account Liberalization in Industrial Countries," in *Capital Mobility: The Impact on Consumption, Investment and Growth,* Leonardo Leiderman and Assaf Razin, eds. Cambridge: Cambridge Press.

Quinn, Dennis P. and Robert Y. Shapiro. 1991. "Business Political Power: The Case of Taxation." *American Political Science Review* 85: 851–74.

Rose, Andrew K. 1994. "Exchange Rate Volatility, Monetary Policy, and Capital Mobility: Empirical Evidence on the Holy Trinity." *NBER Working Paper,* 4630.

Sobel, Andrew C. 1994. *Domestic Choices, International Markets: Dismantling National Barriers and Liberalizing Securities Markets.* Ann Arbor: University of Michigan Press.

Woldendorp, Haap, Hans Keman and Ian Budge. 1993. "Political Data 1945–1990: Party Government in 20 Democracies." *European Journal of Political Research* 24(1): 1–119.

Appendix 1.1 Types of Exchange and Capital Restrictions

Source: IMF, AREAER.	
Exchange Arrangements:	separate exchange rates for some or all capital transactions import rate(s) differ from export rate(s) more than one rate for imports more than one rate for exports
Prescription of Currency	
Bilateral Payments Arrangements:	with members with non-members
Payments Restrictions:	restrictions on payments for current transactions **restrictions on payments for capital transactions**
Cost-Related Import Restrictions:	import surcharges advance import deposits
Surrender Requirement for Export Proceeds	

Government Cohesion:

Source: Woldendorp, Keman and Budge (1993)

Data for states under parliamentary systems came from Woldendorp, et al. Data for the United States were coded by the authors. For parliamentary systems, the variable is based on the number and status of parliamentary parties. We created analogous scenarios for our coding of the U.S. presidential system. The government cohesion variable uses the following five point scale:

1 = single party majority government. Parliamentary: the party in government possesses a majority in parliament. Presidential: one party controls the executive branch and both Houses of Congress.

2 = minimal winning coalition. Parliamentary: all participating parties are necessary to obtain a majority in parliament. Presidential: no such correspondence for the U.S.

3 = surplus coalition. Parliamentary: coalition government exceeds the minimal winning criterion. Presidential: one party controls the executive branch, but only one House of Congress.

4 = single party minority government. Parliamentary: the party in government does not possess a majority in parliament. Presidential: no such correspondence for the U.S.

5 = multiparty minority government. Parliamentary: the parties in government do not possess a majority in parliament. Presidential: one party controls the executive branch, but the other party controls both Houses of Congress.

Ideological Complexion of the Government:

Source: Woldendorp, Keman and Budge (1993)

Data for states under parliamentary systems came from Woldendorp, et al. Data for the United States were coded by the authors based on the rules below. The variable reflects the relative strength of parties in government with reference to the ideological or partisan Left-Right dimension. It uses the following five point scale exhibiting the degree of party control of the government:

1 = right-wing government: share of seats of the right-wing party in government and their supporting parties in the parliament is larger than 66.6%; or the Republicans control both the presidency and the Congress.

2 = right-center complexion: share of seats of the right and center parties in government and their supporting parties is between 33.3% and 66.6% each; or the Republicans control the presidency and one House of Congress.

3 = balanced situation: share of the center party is larger than 50% in government and in the parliament, or the left and right parties form a government together not dominated by either side; or one party controls the presidency and the other party controls both Houses of Congress.

4 = left-center complexion: share of seats of the left and center parties in government and their supporting parties is between 33.3% and 66.6% each, or the Democrats control the presidency and one House of Congress.

5 5 left-wing government: share of seats of the left party in government and their supporting parties is larger than 66.6%; or the Democrats control both the presidency and the Congress.

Appendix 1.2 Frequencies of Actual and Predicted Outcomes for the Pluralist Model and the Full Model

The Pluralist Model

	Predicted (y = 0)	*Predicted (y = 1)*	*Total for Actual*
Actual (y = 0)	128	33	161
Actual (y = 1)	42	92	134
Total for Predicted	170	125	295

The Full Model

	Predicted (y = 0)	*Predicted (y = 1)*	*Total for Actual*
Actual (y = 0)	137	24	161
Actual (y = 1)	31	103	134
Total for Predicted	168	127	295

2

International Firms, Strategic Trade, and Reciprocity

Jonathan Crystal

INTRODUCTION: THE GLOBALIZATION OF PRODUCTION AND DOMESTIC POLITICAL RESPONSES

Every day the business press reports on another planned foreign direct investment, another cross-border merger, another international strategic alliance, another cooperative RandD, licensing, or subcontracting agreement; these individual stories, in turn, comprise a wider trend (often termed the "globalization" or "internationalization" of production) in which firms increasingly organize and control the production of goods and services on a scale that traverses national borders.[1] This is especially evident in many high-technology industries where firms face added incentives to become more globally oriented.[2] In these sectors, economies of scale require firms to produce a larger volume of output than their own national market can absorb. Also, as production costs and RandD requirements skyrocket, firms are forced to look abroad for partners in order to spread out these immense costs as well as the associated risks. Other motives for investing abroad or forming global alliances include the need to gain access to complementary technologies, to gain knowledge of local markets and better serve foreign customers, to evade discriminatory government policies, and so forth (Contractor and Lorange 1988; Cowhey and Aronson 1993).

How do these economic trends affect nation-states? What are the implications for national governments? These questions have attracted an enormous amount of attention from scholars as well as journalists. Much of the resulting literature, however, has had an evaluative and/or prescriptive flavor. For example, among the journalistic commentary, management "gurus" paint a generally positive picture of globalization while other observers present a much more critical view.[3] Among the academics, while some economists and business scholars have explicated the factors behind these trends and their implications for managers[4], others have looked at the effects on national (and global) welfare and, from this, have drawn conclusions about the appropriate policies states should pursue.[5] Finally, many political scientists have weighed into the discussion about how globalization affects the power and interests of national governments, noting, for example, that economic efficiency is not and can not be the sole criteria by which national governments judge the effects of different policies.[6]

Thus, there has been a wide-ranging interdisciplinary debate about how states *can* and *should* react to these important changes in the world economy. However, as social scientists, we might also want to ask how states *have* reacted and *why*? What kinds of trade, investment, or technology policies have they adopted? Answering this question will tell us something about the ways in which states are likely to respond to increasing globalization in the future, and thus help us predict how the international economy is likely to evolve.[7] If national reactions have varied, what accounts for these differences?[8] In fact, students of international political economy are just beginning to develop models and theories that focus on explaining the national-level responses to changes in the global economy. But much of this new literature, while insightful, is, I believe, deficient in two major respects.

First, much of the most recent work by IPE scholars on the domestic political effects of globalization has analyzed the consequences of international *financial* integration.[9] Given the magnitude and importance of these capital flows, this emphasis is understandable. Yet the globalization of finance differs in some fundamental respects from the globalization of production. In fact, the latter kind of integration often does not entail the actual movement of capital across international borders; even in the case of equity investments, MNCs often raise the funds from capital markets in the host state. Rather than affecting broad macroeconomic variables like the interest or exchange rate (Frieden 1991), corporate mobility has micro-level, sector-specific effects. To the extent political economists have looked at the politics around the production structure, they have tended to confine their focus to explaining *trade* policy outcomes.[10] Unfortunately, looking only at trade politics without taking into account FDI produces a distorted picture about how firms and governments respond to international competition. Domestic producers understand that import protection can not block (and indeed, often induces) competition by foreign-owned firms who jump over trade barriers (Encarnation 1992; Goodman, Spar, and Yoffie 1996). How do these societal groups react to this new form of competition? What kinds of government policies do they seek, if any, to regulate the activities of foreign-owned firms operating within their home market? At least in the developed countries (where most FDI takes place), the *political* consequences and responses to these trends has not been the subject of much analysis by political economists.[11]

The second major problem with the literature on the political effects of globalization—the issue I will discuss in this paper—is a broader one and relates to the assumptions that most analysts make regarding the reactions of societal groups to the pressures of the world economy. One of the main debates among political scientists who try to explain the domestic political responses to globalization has centered on the relative role of the state and political structures as opposed to societal interests in determining these policies.[12] For example, a recent volume on the domestic political effects of globalization (Keohane and Milner 1996) is centered on two theoretical essays: one, by Frieden and Rogowski (1996) provides a framework that uses economic theories to derive the interests and incentives of the relevant social actors. The second article, by Garrett and Lange (1996: 49), criticizes the implicit political model embodied in the Frieden/Rogowski piece (which they label "economic pluralism") according to which "policy outcomes are a function of political conflict shaped by the preferences of different actors, weighted by their market power and their propensity for collective action." Instead, Garrett and Lange argue, one must understand how institutions "mediate in the relationship between internationally induced changes in the policy preference of domestic actors . . . and political outcomes. . . . " Only then can one understand the national responses to the international economy because differences in domestic institutions will produce different policy outcomes.[13]

It is notable that this "debate" has not been a very acrimonious one: Frieden and Rogowski (1996: 47) admit that the preferences they explain, "of course, go on to be mediated by existing political coalitions and institutions . . ." Nor do Garrett and Lange argue with the models from which the preferences are derived; they simply claim one can not infer policy outcomes directly from these preferences. Thus, the consensus that has developed reflects something of a division of academic labor. Economic theories are used to explain the domestic distribution effects of international economic transactions.[14] From this, political scientists then derive the societal demands (that is, which groups want which policies) and plug these into their models of the policy-making process. In a societal or pluralist model, the preferences of the most powerful groups (measured by money, votes, ability to organize, etc.) are translated into policy. In a statist model, these preferences are overruled or ignored (while in an international/systemic model, they are also irrelevant). Finally, in an institutional model (like Garrett and Lange's) these preferences are sifted and filtered through domestic structures. The debates revolve around which approach best explains the actions that states take (or do not take) in response to these changes in the international economy.

However, I want to argue that this whole approach to understanding the domestic political consequences of globalization is inadequate. To understand how states are affected by, and react to, the world economy, analysts need to step back from the debate over *policy outcomes* and "problematize" the derivation of *societal demands*. This is for two reasons. First, as I will discuss below, alternative economic theories exist that predict alternative (and often incompatible) preferences. We need some criteria to distinguish among them if we want to make any judgment about the importance of societal demands; otherwise, one could always argue that social actors did in fact get what they wanted—when one has "properly" understood just what it was that they wanted. The second reason has to do with an empirical puzzle: firms in internationalized industries have reacted to changes in the structure of the international economy in contradictory ways. At times, even in the face of severe international competition, producers have "resisted the protectionist temptation"[15] and even pressed for further opening of their own markets; at other times, however, they have lobbied for a more nationalistic or aggressive approach, for example supporting protectionist trade contingent on other countries' agreeing to further liberalize their markets (or even to guarantee foreign market share). As discussed below, both types of responses are economically rational and entirely explicable with existing theories. The problem, however, is that we end up with one theory to explain one type of behavior and another theory to explain another type of behavior. But we can not explain the *variation* itself.

This chapter represents a very preliminary attempt to think about this question of how producers respond to the threats and opportunities presented by the increasingly rapid globalization of production. So far, I have explained why, theoretically and empirically, it is important to understand these domestic political reactions and I have indicated why I think the existing literature is incomplete. Next, I will look more closely at different theories that account for why producers, faced with the growing integration of the world economy (which, by the way, I take as exogenous), demand the policies they do. I will focus specifically on firms (as opposed to labor) and their demands for commercial policy. One argument, in particular, that I examine derives corporate demands for commercial policies from the insights of strategic trade theory. Ultimately, however, I will argue that this literature leaves us with indeterminate predictions and incomplete explanations about what kinds of policies producers will demand. Again, this matters because we can not understand the policy responses that states put forth—or how nations define their national interest—without a firm understanding of these societal level responses. Only after we explain societal demands can we assess their relative importance in determining state behavior. I will then suggest potential ways to address the problem by "bringing politics in" but, in contrast to the Garrett/Lange approach described above, bringing politics in from the beginning. That is, societal responses to globalization, while often juxtaposed or combined with domestic political structures as potential determinants of policy outcomes, are *themselves the result of political variables.*[16]

"WHO WANTS WHAT?" CORPORATE DEMANDS FOR TRADE PROTECTION

As I mentioned above, IPE scholars who study the effects of globalization have paid disproportionate attention to trade politics; precisely for that reason, then, I will focus on trade demands.[17] This is to show that even here where the literature has been most fully developed, analysts still have a problem in explaining producer demands. For the most part, discussions of societal trade preferences have consisted of a debate over the issue of how actors affected by import competition mobilize and organize. Three main "camps" have evolved. One approach derives political consequences from the Stolper-Samuelson theory taking *factors* of production (land, labor, capital) as the relevant unit of analysis. Most notably, Rogowski contends that relatively scarce factors within a country will favor protection while relatively abundant factors lobby for free trade.[18]

By contrast, others emphasize that many factors are specific to a particular economic activity. In this Ricardo-Viner model, *sectors* are the relevant actors: import competitors battle against export-oriented or nontradable industrial sectors.[19] If, as seems reasonable, one assumes that factors are fixed in the short-run but mobile over time (the Mayer-Mussa approach), then the two perspectives can be thought of as complements rather than alternatives.[20] Magee's (1980) investigation of political activity around U.S. trade legislation in 1973 concluded that the sector-specific model better accounts for the pattern of trade lobbying, but he added that the Stolper-Samuelson theorem explains the long-run political interests of U.S. capital owners.

More recently, a third approach has emerged which, in discussing how increasing exposure to the world economy affects societal groups, differentiates producers by *firm*. After all, firms that are in the same sector may have very different structures and strategies and thus may be differently affected by international competition. As a result, trade associations are often driven by conflict. What variables affect the preferences of firms with regard to trade policy? The most obvious is the extent of its *international ties*. G. K. Helleiner (1977) was the first to highlight the role of U.S.-based multinational corporations in supporting a global regime of openness, citing the costs of disrupting intrafirm trade and the danger of provoking retaliation against their own exporting or investing activities as the main motivation for this position.[21] Helen Milner (1988) tested this argument by comparing the trade policy preferences of various industries over different time periods and across nations. Export dependence as well as multinationality push firms toward opposing protectionism.

In addition to reiterating Helleiner's argument about obstacles to intrafirm trade and fear of retaliation, Milner adds that protection will disproportionately benefit a multinational's domestically based rivals and that it can spur foreign MNCs to evade trade protection by creating new and potentially more threatening competition in the domestic market (1988: 23).[22]

Finally, Destler and Odell, in their study of "anti-protection" forces in U.S. trade politics, found that industries dependent on exports and/or dependent on imports as intermediate goods (along with retailers, foreign companies and foreign governments) were most likely to take an active role in fighting against "product-specific" trade protection. Interestingly, Destler and Odell play down the role of MNCs who, they argue, tend to avoid involvement in trade battles over particular products. Why is this? Large MNCs may simply decide it is not worthwhile to expend effort on restrictions that affect a small part of their business. Similarly, an enterprise that participates in many different markets may find itself simultaneously benefiting and suffering from trade restrictions; these conflicting interests create a paralysis that prevents the firm from taking a definite position on specific trade measures.[23] Finally, multinationality itself may make trade politics less significant for these firms insofar as their global networks allow them to evade trade barriers, for instance by relocating production to the protected market (1987: 34).[24]

Nevertheless, the theory that increased globalization will lead to increasing demands for a liberal commercial policy has attained the status of conventional wisdom, both among academics and in the business and mainstream press.[25] Cowhey and Aronson (1993: 56–7) write:

> Even firms that make strong pleas for limited protection would be negatively affected if the world economy suddenly limited flows of products, technologies, and investments. . . . Thus, globalized firms are more sensitive to all forms of barriers that prevent them from operating in specific national markets. . . As globalization proceeds, they are likely to push strongly for openness.

The hypothesis also leads to the expectation that, as more firms develop more extensive international ties, the balance of political power among groups will continue to shift away from pro-protectionist coalitions and we should see a secular movement toward greater openness.[26] This is one important reason that many students of IPE are sanguine about the prospects for world trading system, despite the relative decline of U.S. hegemony or the movement toward increased regionalization.

Other firm-level variables that are said to have an effect on trade policy demands relate to aspects of the *production process*, especially to high-tech sectors which tend to be characterized by large economies of scale. Frieden and Rogowski (1996: 39) note:

> Inasmuch as the already largest firms are most likely to be able to implement the redeployment of assets and physical relocation necessary to reap fully the larger scale economies, political support for integration is expected from these firms; conversely, smaller firms will be less enthusiastic.

They also present an analogous argument about firms involved in activities with steep learning curves. Those companies that have experience in the international marketplace will have an advantage in terms of the accumulated benefits from networks and information that will therefore lead them to favor maintaining, and intensifying, international openness. Often, these characteristics overlap with international orientation; precisely because firms faces large-scale economies, they are forced to look to a global market from the very beginning. Thus, they would be expected to favor liberal commercial policies, both because these policies would give them a relative advantage over smaller firms, and because they fear retaliation for protectionist policies at home. The bottom line is that multinational companies, especially those in high-tech industries, should favor policies that support and advance the cause of "technoglobalism;" they should not, by contrast, look favorably on "technonationalist" policies, even if they might provide short-term benefits.

Has this happened? Have we entered a new era in which internationalized producers no longer seek the rents that result from their home governments adopting nationalist or discriminatory policies? To some degree, the answer is yes (as seen, for instance, in the active role of American electronics companies in pushing for the market-opening information technology trade agreement (*Financial Times* 12/4/96)). But, at the same time, the liberal consensus is not as prevalent as we might expect given the implications of the above discussion. For instance, in the United States, there is abundant evidence of corporate political activity seeking restrictive and/or discriminatory policies to favor domestically based producers at the expense of foreign-based competitors. The semiconductor industry's campaign for "managed trade" is perhaps the most prominent example, but this kind of behavior also occurred in other sectors such as machine tools, aerospace, and telecommunications.[27] The disjuncture in these sectors between the international orientation of producers and their nationalist policy demands has puzzled many observers. Stevens (1990: 46) writes that "today's multinationals tend to pursue their technoglobalist corporate strategies while at the same time supporting technonationalist government policies." Why is this? She provides a number of potential explanations; many of which seem implausible on their face (e.g. MNCs have little influence on trade policy, MNCs are outnumbered by smaller domestically oriented firms, industry trade associations take nationalist positions to justify their own existence). Other, seemingly more tenable, explanations look within the firm to explain this contradiction. For instance, Stevens posits that there may be little "spillover" between corporate divisions that engage in different industrial pursuits so that firms may cooperate in some areas with foreign rivals while competing in others. Also, firms may emphasize short-term gains from technonationalist policies while discounting the long-run gains of an open world economy.

Ultimately, however, Stevens argues that this "conflicted" corporate identity is the result of incomplete globalization; for most firms, overseas activities are still subordinate to national corporate headquarters, RandD is largely conducted in the home state, and business practices and organization reflect national cultural variables. Instead of global or even multinational corporations, one writer suggests we call these entities "National Firms with International Operations" or NFIOs (Hu 1992; for other versions of this argument, see Wade 1996 and Pauly and Reich 1997). The "incomplete globalization" explanation does not necessarily challenge the hypothesis that firms *will* support liberal commercial policies as they become (or if they become) more truly global. The argument, however, is that this global orientation has not yet emerged. These authors often underline the point that the nation's well-being is still tied to that of the MNCs headquartered in them; in other words, "we are still us" (Tyson 1991; Kapstein 91/92). But we can easily deduce the implications for producer demands: even firms involved in extensive overseas activities are still dependent enough on conditions in their home market to provide them with the incentive to seek nationalist policies from their home governments. If and when these firms do become more truly globalized, presumably they will correspondingly modify their policy demands.

STRATEGIC TRADE THEORY AND CORPORATE DEMANDS FOR RECIPROCITY

There is, however, an alternative theory that does not predict this eventual movement toward liberal attitudes. This approach suggests that economies of scale and steep learning curves are not necessarily associated with demands for free trade, but may in fact lead firms to favor more protectionist policies. Milner, whose original argument (1988) was based on evidence drawn from the 1970s, recognized that by the 1980s support for protectionism was emerging among firms whose reliance on exports and multinationality should have made them unconditional anti-protectionists. She thus revised her earlier argument in an article cowritten with David Yoffie (1989). Extending some of the findings from the new strategic trade literature in international economics to the study of foreign economic policy, the authors constructed a theory of what they called "strategic trade demands"; that is, advocacy of trade barriers for the home market, but only for the explicit purpose of eliminating foreign trade barriers.

The underlying economic insight is that in certain oligopolistic industries characterized by large economies of scale, steep learning curves, and substantial RandD requirements, protectionist or promotional policies on the part of foreign governments gives overseas companies significant "first-mover advantages" in world markets. A protected markets allows these firms to reap the scale-benefits and reduce their marginal costs, subsequently damaging the competitive position of the shut-out firms—even in other nonprotected markets (1989: 244; also see Tyson 1992). If the industry is characterized by the economic conditions listed above, if it is relatively homogenous in terms of the competitive strategies pursued by firms, and if its foreign rivals are receiving government support, then domestically based MNCs that would otherwise favor free trade instead support various protectionist policies designed to pressure the foreign government to liberalize. The authors try to distinguish these demands for reciprocity from old-fashioned protectionist appeals by looking, first, at whether the industry communicates to the government that its demands are conditional on foreign market access, and second, at whether evidence exists that firms have made concrete efforts to gain access to foreign markets (1989: 251).[28]

Many economists have expressed skepticism concerning the practical applicability of strategic trade policy. For example, Krugman (1987: 219) wonders whether the benefits from this type of policy would accrue to the citizens of the state implementing it given the extent of global interdependence. For the firm in question, however, this does not pose a problem. He (1987: 218–19) says (in arguing against adopting such a policy), ". . . nations are not firms writ large. . . . " In other words, the firms may benefit even if the nation does not. But while the theory's critics (appropriately) use the criteria of national welfare, Milner and Yoffie's concern is on the interests of firms and their subsequent policy demands. Thus, the critique is not really relevant. The same principle holds for other arguments against strategic trade theory—for example that supporting one industry will harm others or that overall benefits are probably not that large.[29] These contentions imply that strategic trade theory makes for bad policy; they say nothing about the benefits for the affected domestic firms.

Milner and Yoffie's theory is an important corrective to work that sees a secular movement toward free trade as more and more industries become globalized. Instead, they see an increasing number of industries experiencing the economic changes and intensifying competition that tend to lead to strategic trade demands. One could even extend their arguments in a number of ways that the authors chose not to. For example, elsewhere I have argued (Crystal 1998) that if trade barriers are meant to pressure foreign governments to liberalize, one has to account for the possibility that foreign firms could jump over these import barriers via FDI, thus diluting the sanctioning effect these actions were designed to have. Milner and Yoffie discount FDI because, they argue, the increasing returns to scale mean that shifting production abroad might reduce cost advantages (1989: 246–47). But a firm could shift all of its production abroad, preserve the scale economies, and serve its own home market by exporting from the foreign subsidiary. More likely, firms can unbundle the various parts of the production process, shifting enough production abroad to escape the effects of trade barriers, but maintaining the most technologically advanced production (where the greatest scale and learning economies occur) at home.[30] Thus, industries find that unless they extend their strategic trade demand to incoming FDI, putting forth "strategic investment demands," their gains may be illusory.[31]

Another possible extension involves expanding the number of sectors in which we would expect to find producers putting forth these kinds of demands. Milner and Yoffie emphasize the importance of scale economies and steep learning curves. In sectors without these characteristics, they argue, MNCs facing discriminatory policies abroad could either move offshore to reduce their costs or invest directly in the protectionist country. But is this always true? Savings from offshore production may not counterbalance the costs of being shut out of an important foreign market; besides, if there were gains to be had from relocating production, we might expect firms to have already taken advantage of this option. As for the second option of neutralizing foreign protectionism by jumping over trade barriers and producing in the offending country, this may not be possible if the foreign country also has (formal or informal) barriers to FDI or discriminates on the basis of corporate ownership. Therefore, it is worth considering expanding the domain of the Milner-Yoffie argument to other sectors.

In fact the international business literature on FDI provides some theoretical support for the hypothesis that reciprocity considerations will influence a wider range of industry actors than those indicated in the Milner-Yoffie model. The so-called "oligopolistic" or "rivalistic" theory of foreign direct investment asserts that FDI often occurs in clusters because the oligopolistic structure of the home country forces firms to "follow-the-leader" and invest abroad in order to prevent their rivals from obtaining a potential relative advantage (Knickerbocker 1974). Edward Graham (1978) extended the theory to international oligopolies showing that firms invest abroad in order to defend their relative position against global competitors based in other countries. Thus he found that much of the European FDI in the U.S. market that occurred during the 1970s was undertaken precisely to challenge U.S. MNCs on their home turf; in this way, the Europeans hoped to even the global playing field and improve their competitive position at home. More recently, Yoffie (1993: 434) summarizing the industry case studies in his edited volume, concludes that MNCs in global oligopolies invested in each other's markets irrespective of profits. "Firms aggressively pursued cross investments because they wanted to prevent their competitors from having safe havens, they wished to pre-empt new entrants, or they wanted to maintain industry discipline and stability." However, if there is an asymmetry of access, domestically based MNCs will be put at a competitive disadvantage since they will not be able to engage in rivalistic FDI or, for that matter, in export activity. Foreign-based competitors will have a sanctuary market, earning excess profits that they can use to subsidize their exporting or subsidiary activities. Although the strategic and rivalistic theories differ in their logic, both predict injuries to firms unable to gain access to their competitors home market (albeit for different reasons) and both would therefore predict demands from globally oriented producers for reciprocal treatment, or in the absence of this, contingent closure. The rivalistic approach, however, would expect to see these kinds of demands in global oligopolies, regardless of the extent of economies of scale, RandD requirements, or learning curves.

Although Milner and Yoffie, in discussing foreign governmental actions, characterize state involvement as a dichotomous variable, it seems more accurate to think of a continuum ranging from complete laissez-faire and openness to imports and FDI on one end to active industrial targeting and strict regulation of or barriers to imports and FDI on the other.[32] Finally, the authors also unnecessarily restrict their theory by limiting objectionable foreign practices to governmental actions (industrial and trade policies). But the line between public and private sector actions, or between actual policies and the residual consequences of past policies is contested, especially in Japan where the issue of reciprocity most often arises. Thus, much of the U.S.-Japanese bilateral trade conflict revolves around issues such as the allegedly discriminatory keiretsu networks, though many dispute whether this is a legitimate basis for complaint.[33] However, in order to account for the policy demands of firms, we need only determine that the producers themselves considered foreign nongovernmental practices a legitimate issues of concern for their government's foreign economic policy. Admittedly, if the practices at issue involve domestic institutions, deeply ingrained private sector practices, or even the industrial structure of the offending foreign country, the domestic firms will have to decide whether a "results-oriented" approach would be likely to succeed in inducing the foreign government to make such comprehensive reforms. If the companies do not believe that this goal is realistic, the reciprocity motive may be weakened. However, firms could demand that, regardless of whether these practices are continued, they receive some quantitative market share guarantee. Indeed, it is this very practice which the critics of reciprocity attack most vigorously.

THE INDETERMINACY OF POLITICAL DEMANDS

In sum, I have claimed that we can broaden the types of industries in which firms will seek strategic trade demands; not only economies of scale and learning curves, but any oligopolistic sector in which foreign competitors enjoy the benefits of protective or promotional industrial policies. Moreover, one can broaden the type of foreign practices that might provoke these demands from formal policies to nongovernmental practices or even industrial structure. Why then do we not see more of these kinds of demands for reciprocity? Milner, in a separate article (1990), suggests a couple of reasons. First, aggressive sectoral reciprocity, if it leads to a larger market share for domestic producers, may lead the target country (and third suppliers) to ship their excess production abroad, thus intensifying competition elsewhere and providing no net benefits to the initial petitioning firm (169). Second, she emphasizes (170–71), "the high probability that aggressive reciprocity will lead to mutual retaliation and the high costs of this outcome for internationally oriented firms, especially relative to the low potential gains from reciprocity, as in Super 301."

But it is not clear why this uncertainty and indeterminacy do not apply to other firms as well, including those in high-tech sectors to which Milner still insists the strategic trade demand model applies.[34] Firms in industries characterized by large economies of scale will also wonder whether these policies might backfire on them, either by leading to intensified competition elsewhere or retaliation.[35] Risk-averse executives may decide to maintain their support for liberal policies, despite the injuries they sustain, because they fear that taking a tough line could lead to a tit-for-tat spiral of retaliation. Nevertheless, Milner (171) argues that for high-tech sectors "the risks imposed by threats to pry open foreign markets are probably less than the costs of living with such unequal access." How do we know? Theoretically, this is an extremely complicated analysis of competing risks; why should we assume firms will err on the side of activist trade policies? Empirically, this theory *overpredicts* strategic trade demands. That is, we often do *not* observe these kinds of demands even though firms, according to the Milner-Yoffie criteria, may have an interest in seeking them. Strangely, the same industry that in one instance expresses these demands will, at other times, favor liberal policies.

The changing positions of firms in the U.S. semiconductor industry exemplifies this ambivalence: Milner and Yoffie emphasize economic changes in the industry to explain the shift from unilateral free trade in the 1970s to strategic trade demands in the 1980s, despite this sector's international orientation. But then by the early 1990s, with Japanese and American firms jumping into various kinds of strategic alliances, domestic producers seemed to swing back toward liberal demands. Despite uneven Japanese compliance with the Semiconductor Trade Agreement, trade tensions dissipated and many observers agreed with *The Economist* (7/18/92) that increased "collaboration between American and Japanese firms should end the long-running quarrel . . ." at least as far as the firms themselves were concerned. As one *Business Week* headline (3/29/93) put it: "Suppose They Gave a

Trade War and Nobody Came." However, by the summer of 1996, the majority of semiconductor firms were again pressing the Clinton Administration to negotiate for an extension of the controversial trade agreement guaranteeing market share in Japan. In other words, joint ventures and strategic alliances did not prevent U.S. firms from demanding commercial policies that emphasized reciprocity.

The strategic trade demand theory has difficulty explaining why strategic sectors are inconsistent in their demands for reciprocal policies. At the same time, however, it also *underpredicts* demands in that, as mentioned above, producers in industries that are often not thought of as cutting-edge high technology sectors have adopted positions in favor of reciprocity. Examples, again drawn from the U.S. would include the automobile, photographic film (i.e. Kodak), and insurance industries which all advocated a tougher trade policy against their Japanese competitors unless comparable market access was given (which sometimes meant a pre-determined share of the market). Japan was not the only country targeted in these disputes; the financial service sector and the airline industry also demanded commercial policies incorporating various degrees of reciprocity. All of these sectors are internationally oriented though not necessarily "strategic"; yet they adopted political demands for contingent protection. Of course, it is no mystery why they were interested in gaining better access to foreign markets, just as it is no mystery why high-tech firms had the same interest. The difficulty lies in explaining why this manifests itself as strategic trade demands at some times but not at others.

My argument is that political demands are indeterminate. International firms have an interest in liberalism *and* an interest in reciprocity. Theoretically, we can explain demands for either type of trade policy in terms of profit-maximizing behavior. Empirically, we observe both types of behavior but the correlation between these demands and the independent variables that the original theory of strategic trade demands highlights is a weak one. It might be noted that this same problem of indeterminacy exists with reference to trade policy more broadly. Firms, after all, can increase their profits by obtaining increased protection for their outputs, decreased protection for their inputs, or even subsidies for their exports. In the abstract, it is not obvious which policy the firm should pursue.[36] Douglas Nelson's survey of the endogenous tariff theory literature also makes this point (1988: 813–16). As he puts it, "Somehow the range of choice must be systematically limited." Elsewhere, Nelson (1989a) has suggested one potential way to solve this puzzle: specifically, analysts need to look firm characteristics beyond just export dependence and multinationality. To deduce what policies producers will seek, one has to focus on the firm-specific assets (such as its technologies, managerial strategies and so forth) and link these characteristics to economic interests.[37]

The indeterminacy is even greater when we realize that producers can also choose to pursue a private (nonpolitical) strategy as well, such as exit from the industry, economic adjustment, or the formation of a strategic alliance. Analysts have used Hirschman's insight that social actors have a choice between voice (in this case, political demands for government assistance) and exit (in this case, private adjustment up to and including divestment).[38] Another way of phrasing this point is that asset specificity should be correlated with the preferences for policies that provide rents for the owners of those assets (Alt et al. 1994: 17). Given the lack of alternative uses for their assets, firms have no choice but to use voice in order to seek public aid. A recent example of this kind of argument can be found in Robert Uriu's discussion of Japanese industry preferences (1996: 15) in which he criticizes political scientists for assuming firms will respond to economic distress by turning to the government; instead, he argues, ". . . industries with viable economic alternatives available to them will have fewer incentives to seek political solutions." Large oligopolistic firms, because they have the capabilities and incentives to pursue economic strategies of divestment and adjustment, will not lobby for government help. But why assume firms turn to political action only *after* calculating the costs of economic adjustment and without calculating the costs of political action? In other words, what is the theoretical justification with privileging private over public action? It is more useful to think of actors comparing this private cost with the political cost of lobbying for policies. Any political or nonpolitical behavior only makes sense when compared to the alternatives. Uriu's argument is thus weakened by his not including political variables into the model *before* he explains how preferences are shaped into governmental policy choices.

EXPLAINING THE AMBIGUITY: THE TRANSLATION OF PREFERENCES INTO DEMANDS

In part, the problem stems from terminological confusion between *preferences* and *demands*. Most political scientists, like most economists, make assumptions about (but do not try to explain) an actor's ranking of various goals (Riker 1990: 173). For example, we take as given that firms want to maximize their profits and, although that assumption may be problematic,[39] we accept it as useful in helping us to explain behavior. But actors must then decide, given their preferences, what specific policies to demand, what governmental tools to focus on, and what specific actions to take in order to persuade the state to supply the desired policy outputs. These are their "political demands" as opposed to their (assumed) "preferences."[40] For most IPE scholars, this has not been an important distinction. For instance, in the debate over the effects of globalization, as I mentioned above, political scientists rely on economic theories to explain how exogenous shocks will affect relative prices; plugging in these results, they then can easily deduce how different groups will be affected and thus what policies they will seek. Most of the discussion then concentrates on how important those groups are. But the missing step is an explanation of *how preferences are translated into demands.*

We can think of the actor's decision of what policy to demand as a cost-benefit calculation in which he or she compares alternative courses of action. The costs might consist of the direct expenses of political action: salaries of lawyers, lobbyists, advertisements, contributions, and so forth. These costs, while not trivial, are usually not prohibitive, especially when compared to the value of the rents that firms are lobbying for. The value of these rents comprise the benefits that private actors will receive (or preserve) by engaging in political action; these are what can be derived from economic theories (Alt et. al. 1994). But because producers are deciding between alternative courses of action (including "doing nothing"), these cost-benefit calculations have to be compared with those of other possible actions. Of course, it can often be very difficult to measure the benefits of various policies precisely enough to compare them; the information requirements can be staggering. Presumably, however, economic analysis, if it were detailed enough, would provide a basis for comparison of these rents from alternative policies.

But what matters for the producer is the *expected* benefit; all actors weight the utility they receive from a policy by the probability of successfully obtaining it. As Daniel Verdier (1994: 6) has pointed out:

> Producers try to maximize the product of the two variables (return discounted by political risk [that is, the chance of winning the return through lobbying]). High risk might make an expected high return look less attractive, whereas low risk might make an expected low return appear more attractive. . . . To a great extent, producers choose sides on the basis of political feasibility.

Political feasibility, in turn, is a function of the domestic political system. Thus, political variables that reduce the chances of obtaining one's demands will subsequently increase the relative costs of pursuing that option and will lead the actor to consider pursuing an alternative course (that, hopefully, will still allow him or her to realize the same underlying goal).

TOWARD A POLITICAL EXPLANATION OF PRODUCER DEMANDS

Returning to our initial puzzle, then, one way to try to explain the inconsistent political responses by international firms to increased globalization is to look more carefully at the domestic political context in which these firms are situated. After all, while their economic activities may become more and more international, lobbying for favorable policies is still a very domestic endeavor. When the domestic political context is favorable for strategic demands, we should expect to see them; when it is less favorable, we should not expect to see them. This naturally brings up the next question: what constitutes the "domestic political context"? What variables do societal actors believe are important in determining policy outcomes?[41] One way to try to get at this question is to turn to the voluminous political science literature that explains policy outcomes and see whether these same explanations can account for political demands as well. That is, the "supply-side" explanations tell us what factors make some demands more likely to be acted upon or privilege the demands of some groups while disadvantaging those of others. Because these variables determine which demands will be listened to, we might expect them also to have an effect on which (or whether) demands are made in the first place. Producers, facing the prospect of costly political action with little chance of success, will simply opt for a different strategy that is more likely to allow them to achieve their underlying preference.

Verdier himself argues that *electoral pressures* shape the rules by which elected officials make policies and this, in turn, affects producer demands (1993; 1994). For example, firms find it much less costly to pursue rent-seeking policies when the trade issue is neither salient nor divisive. Conversely, when a large number of voters are mobilized and represented in the policy-making process, producers have to present trade demands consisting of more general policies reflecting broader socioeconomic interests in order to have any chance of success. Verdier's approach is attractive both because he is one of the few political scientists to depart from the common practice of simply deriving demands from a producer's economic position in the world economy, and because, in his book (1994: chapters 1–5), he integrates the demand and supply side analyses by showing how different combinations of issue salience and divisiveness result in distinctive trade policy processes: party politics, executive politics, competitive pressure politics, and logrolling pressure politics. The nature of the policy process, in turn, explains not only policy demands and the identity of principle units of organization (factor, sector, or nation), but also the orientation of the policy itself and the specific tools employed. Nevertheless, the drawback of his theory is that, as he explicitly notes (1994: 63), the argument applies only over an extended period of time in which periodic elections affect the policy process which then affects demands. It would therefore be difficult to explain variation over shorter periods of time.

Another possible explanation would look at the difficulties of overcoming the *collective action* problem—one of the costs of political activity to which IPE scholars have indeed devoted considerable attention. Most analyses claim that there will be more pressure for protection when there are fewer firms in an industry (or at least a few large firms), when the industry is more concentrated, or when a crisis exists that leads firms to discount the free-rider problem (e.g. Anderson and Baldwin 1987: 263–64). But this does not explain why the firms have chosen to seek protection in the first place, only why they may have trouble organizing to pressure government officials to get it. Still, because in more concentrated sectors, each firm will be able to enjoy a larger share of the rents for a longer period of time before they are eroded by competition, these variables do affect the relative cost-benefit ratio and thus the initial decision to demand the policy (Milner 1988: 237–38). It is also likely that producers in sectors with high organization costs will anticipate the difficulties of forming a coalition and thus will choose an alternative course of action (e.g.. economic adjustment). On the other hand, the variables that explain collective action can not, for instance, account for different or contradictory demands from the same industry (or firm). Nor is the empirical evidence for the importance of these variables in explaining corporate activity very solid.[42]

A comparable issue also arises with regard to the nature of the rents themselves—specifically, the extent to which they are public goods. Thus, for example, in the mid-1980s, U.S. manufacturers lobbied for trade protection (a divisible and hence, potentially private good) rather than a downward adjustment of the exchange rate (a public good), despite the fact that the overvalued dollar was largely to blame for their difficulties. The reason was that the exchange rate adjustments were less excludable and so the costs of overcoming the free rider problem were prohibitive for the affected industries (Gowa 1988). Similarly, within the category of trade policies, for the same reason, producers tend to seek product-specific protection rather than generic trade protection and tend to favor firm-specific policy instruments over general tariffs or quotas (Destler and Odell 1987: 117; Weck-Hanneman 1992: 737)

Collective action costs depend on more than characteristics of the groups involved. Different domestic *political institutions* have different implications for the severity of the collective action problem. Many analysts have pointed out that the RTAA of 1934, by shifting responsibility for U.S. trade policy to the executive, increased the organizational costs for rent-seekers (e.g. Destler 1992; Haggard 1987). Similarly, the increasing popularity of "administered" or "low-track" protection is not due just to its excludability but also to the fact that, because of the way the rules are structured and implemented, it is less politically costly to obtain (Finger, Hall, and Nelson 1982: 414; Nelson 1989b: 94). Alt and Gilligan (1994) have argued that domestic institutional structures can affect, not only what policies are supplied (as Garrett and Lange show), but also what type of lobbying behavior we will observe among social groups. Majoritarian institutions in which numbers matter will reward large mass movements. The collective action costs here will be higher and exit will be an attractive alternative; thus we will most likely see factoral coalitions along the lines of the Stolper-Samuelson model. By contrast, institutional arrangements that are insulated from popular pressures will reward small groups and lead to sectoral demands, the Ricardo-Viner model. Following Verdier's logic (above), this will also affect whether demands are put forth broadly or narrowly.

More generally, the argument that producer demands are a function of domestic political institutions has been made recently by those who call themselves "historical institutionalists." As Thelen and Steinmo (1992:8) argue, "While rational choice deals with preferences at the level of assumptions [that is, by deducing preferences from the structure of the situation], historical institutionalists take the question of how individuals and groups define their self-interest as problematical." In some ways, however, the dichotomy they depict may be too stark. While a rational choice approach may assume profit-maximization as the underlying preference, there is nothing in a rationalist approach that rules out institutions affecting an actor's conception of what policies are in his or her self-interest, that is, what strategy to adopt in order to achieve one's ends or what demands to make in order to further one's preferences.[43]

Pauly and Reich (1997) have argued that durable and distinctive state structures in the U.S., Japan, and Germany lead to distinctive strategic behavior on the part of multinational firms. The argument here builds on this analysis in two respects. First, it focuses on a component of "strategic behavior" which the authors do not address: namely, demands for government policy. Secondly, although institutional variation is starkest among different countries, even within a single political system, there exists significant institutional variation (e.g. see Goldstein 1993; Finger, Hall, and Nelson 1982), and thus, different demand outcomes. Hansen's study of industry petitions to the International Trade Commission (1990: 37–38) concludes that ". . . industries do self-select themselves in deciding to file applications for protection . . . The industries that believe their requests will probably be rejected will not bother to apply, since their expected utility from applying will be lower than the utility they derive from not applying." And, as Wendy Takacs (1981: 692) notes, this belief itself will depend on "the degree of severity of the criteria for obtaining protection, as set forth in current legislation, and the experience of previous petitioners." She finds that the Trade Enhancement Act of 1962 (which tightened the escape clause injury test) reduced the number of industry petitions whereas the Trade and Tariff Act of 1974 (which eased the test) had the opposite result.

We can expect that industries will seek reciprocal policies when some institution already exists to channel their policy and supply the desired output. Thus, supporters of the multilateral trading system are right to worry about the consequences of new legislation such as Super 301; once the instrument exists, it becomes less costly for producers to put forth demands for reciprocity (Irwin 1994: 70). By contrast, groups will not mobilize to champion a policy when they anticipate confronting an absence of any institutional channels to address their complaints. For instance, firms in sectors that are covered by existing regulations that govern foreign ownership will find these tools useful to demand policies for reciprocity. Globalized firms in industries like the airline industry, the telecommunications industry, or the financial services industry will seize upon these sectoral regulations in order to oppose foreign encroachment into the domestic market unless the home markets of these foreign-based MNCs are themselves significantly liberalized. But had these instruments not existed, the demands from producers would have been different.

CONCLUSION

This paper has argued that, in order to explain how industry actors (and thus, eventually, national governments) react to the pressures of the international economy, analysts need to move beyond deducing how price changes affect different groups and thereby determine their interests. Instead, I emphasize that producers translate these interests into political demands and that this translation process is a function of the domestic political context. There are at least two potential objections to this approach. First, there is the potential for an endogeneity bias. That is, if, say, domestic political institutions reflect, rather than shape, the political demands of producers, then I will have overestimated the effect these variables have on political demands; economic interests dictate demands for policies *and* for changing political structures. Frieden and Rogowski (1996: 6–7) write that, "Given that socioeconomic and political agents have preferences about policies, and political institutions affect the adoption and implementation of policies, it follows that private agents must have preferences about institutions themselves." But, on the other hand, the collective action costs are much higher for the general policies that would create or modify domestic institutions. Producers will not want to bear the costs of demanding policies for which the benefits can not be appropriated.[44] In the short- and medium-term, institutions tend to be rather sticky.

A second objection asserts that an advantage of the academic division of labor (in which political scientists rely on economists to explain what groups want) is that we end up with more parsimonious models of domestic responses to the global economy. By contrast, with a political theory of producer demands, it becomes much more difficult to generate clear ex ante predictions of how groups will respond to international economic integration. However, I believe this tradeoff is justified. Because producers have multiple and conflicting interests, deducing their policy positions from their economic situation will lead to ambiguous predictions and will not allow us to be able to explain much of what we observe in the domestic politics of globalization. Furthermore, although we must sacrifice some parsimony for greater explanatory accuracy, we can work on improving the "terms of trade"; that is, it is not inevitable that bringing in domestic politics means that one must eschew rigorous theorizing. Verdier's argument represents an attempt to present a coherent model that accounts for policy supply and policy demand in a systematic way recognizing that both processes are affected by economics *and* politics. Thus, in looking at the effects of globalization, a more explicitly political analysis of how business reacts might help to explain some of the anomalies mentioned above. I have criticized the division of academic labor in which economists explain the interests of private groups and political scientists explain policy outcomes, not because economists are wrong, but because the way groups formulate their demands is a supremely political activity. Firms from different countries, because they exist in different domestic political contexts, will behave differently. Within a single country, firms will present varying demands depending on whether the political situation makes it more or less likely their demands will be listened to and acted upon.

Finally, how much difference will this make for the final policy outcome? If a nation's domestic political context is such that it blocks nationalist policies, then demands for these kinds of policies will be less common. In this case, the effect on demands only reinforces the supply-side effect; the policy outcome was likely to be liberal before, and incorporating the effect on demand means the policy result is even more likely to be liberal. In fact, although we are unlikely to observe political conflict over the issue (since groups will not raise demands), we should not infer from this that societal groups favor a liberal approach; overt conflict is avoided only because the law of anticipated consequences means the issue is not raised in the first place. But if the domestic political context is not uniform—if it varies across issue areas for instance, that will affect the mix of demands we will observe, and thus the policy outcome as well.

The globalization of production is real. Even if it has not yet progressed as far as many in the "who-is-us" school would have us believe, these observers have gotten the trend right. At the same time, political conflict over the effects of international economic integration is likely to persist, even as more firms develop ties to the international economy. Largely, I argue, this is because domestic political variables such as state institutions are durable (if, perhaps, not unchangeable). And as long as the political opportunities exist, there will be an incentive for producers to seek favorable treatment. But to understand why, when, and how groups react the way they do, it is essential to incorporate these political variables into our models rather than just relying upon economic theories to explain how actors will behave.

NOTES

1. The ratio of FDI stock to world GDP doubled from 1980 to 1994, as did the ratio of FDI flows to gross domestic investment. Within that period, the years between

1986 and 1990 saw the most rapid surge; during this period, World GDP grew at around 6 percent annually, exports at around 9 percent, and FDI at around 23 percent (UNCTAD 1996: 16; Graham 1996: 10). These figures do not include nonequity arrangements such as strategic alliances. Incidentally, myriad definitions exist for the term "globalization" and many have criticized the concept as vague and/or misleading. Without entering into this argument, I simply use the term as shorthand to refer to the growing international activities of multinational corporations.

2. Between 1975 and 1990, the share of capital- and technology-intensive industries of the total manufacturing inward stock of FDI increased from 27 percent to 40 percent (Ostry and Nelson, 1995: 24). The authors refer to these trends as examples of "technoglobalism" which they define as the process by which "multinational firms are *exploiting* their technology globally and, to a lesser though increasing degree, are gaining *access* to new technology globally through the worldwide diffusion of RandD and through collaboration." (1995: 24 emphasis in original). Similarly, Stevens (1990: 42) defines the term as referring to the "internationalization of industrial activities due to technological needs."

3. For the positive assessments, see e.g. Ohmae 1990, Kanter 1995. For the negative assessments, see Greider 1996; Barnet and Cavanaugh 1994; or, from a more mercantilist perspective, Tolchin and Tolchin 1992.

4. See, for example, Contractor and Lorange 1988; James and Weidenbaum 1993; Mytelka 1987; Ostry and Gestrin 1993; Ostry and Nelson 1995.

5. See Graham 1996; Graham and Krugman 1995; Tanzi and Coelho 1993; Thompson 1992.

6. Moran (1996: 188) for example, in looking at economic analyses of an Airbus project, wonders "Would less than a half billion dollars a year...seem like a large or small price to pay in comparison to the freedom to conduct foreign and defense policy without being constantly under the scrutiny, and approval, of an external monopolistic supplier of airframes and avionics?" See also Kapstein 1991/92; Borrus and Zysman 1992. On the other hand, for arguments that concur with the economists' prescriptive conclusions, see, for example, Kline 1989 and Milner 1993. Finally, a few scholars have emphasized the variation in economic behavior among firms headquartered in different countries and have argued that this complicates the effect that globalization has on the host state's calculation of its national interests, even from a purely economic standpoint (Reich 1996; Pauly and Reich 1997).

7. Richard Cooper (1973: 168–72) for example, argued that governments can respond to international economic interdependence in five different ways: (1) passively (accepting the constraints on state power); (2) defensively (e.g. adopting protectionist policies); (3) exploitatively (e.g. defecting from an agreement); (4) aggressively (attempting to extend national control to other countries); or, (5) constructively (pursuing cooperative agreements). Obviously, the options states choose will shape (if not determine) the character of the international system.

8. These questions would seem to be the domain of political scientists who supposedly have something of a "comparative advantage" in explaining government policies and state behavior. This is not to imply that only state actions are "political." Susan Strange (1996: 35) has criticized political scientists for using overly narrow definitions of politics. Instead, she argues, "...it follows that forming any kind of association of individuals for a commonly agreed purpose is political." Nonetheless, for analytic purposes, it is useful to distinguish between activity that is more directly related

to the state and state power (e.g. lobbying for policies in response to economic competition) and that which is not (e.g.. adjusting economically in response to competition). Of course, such a distinction makes no prejudgments about which kind of action is more significant or worthy of study..

9. See for example: Andrews 1994; Cerny 1993; Cohen 1996; Frieden 1991; Goodman and Pauly 1993; Kapstein 1994.

10. Garrett (1996: 100–102) points out that financial integration and trade integration, while often combined together in discussions of globalization, actually have very different consequences in terms of the constraints they impose on national governments.

11. I have dealt with this issue in some depth elsewhere (Crystal 1998).

12. The debate is often framed as being about the "relative importance of the constraints and incentives imposed by the world economy, on the one hand, and the constraints and incentives inherent in preexisting national institutions, on the other" (Keohane and Milner 1996: 6). The debate between the "convergence" and "nonconvergence" schools is not equivalent to the societal vs. statist debate. (For one thing, the two debates are arguing about different dependent variables). Nonetheless, a common issue in both literatures is the extent to which state institutions are able to resist the forces of globalization, whether experienced directly (e.g. balance of payments crises) or through the demands of social actors (e.g. multinational corporations). See the essays in Berger and Dore 1996; Boyer and Drache 1996.

13. For example, more veto points in the policy-making process, or more bureaucratic insulation, or a more indirect method of voter preference aggregation, means that there will be a greater gap or lag between international economic changes and the domestic political response. Of course, the argument over the importance of the state and of institutions is neither new nor unique to IPE; for an earlier example of this theme applied to the question of how the globalization of the world economy affects nation-states and conditions their responses, see the essays in Katzenstein 1978; and Ikenberry, Lake, and Mastanduno 1988.

14. Indeed, Keohane and Milner (1996: 7) criticize the earlier interdependence literature for not being "firmly grounded in economic theory" and thus unable to provide a systematic way to understand the linkages between changes in the international economy and domestic political reactions.

15. The phrase comes from Milner 1987 (whose arguments I discuss in greater detail below).

16. What follows is in the nature of a review essay and theoretical discussion. Until I have systematically tested these hypotheses against the empirical record , any conclusions, of course, remain preliminary.

17. Elsewhere I have explored the extent to which one could extend the conclusions from the trade policy literature to an analysis of foreign direct investment (Crystal 1998). Frieden (1991) discusses these issues in the context of international finance.

18. Rogowski 1989; Midford (1993), while essentially endorsing Rogowski's approach (563), argues for further differentiating the factors (e.g. professional and semiskilled labor, tropical, temperate, and forested land, etc.) and altering the measurement of factor abundance to control for relative size of the country's economy.

19. Frieden (1991) argues for this approach. This approach is also commonly adopted in the endogenous tariff literature, which then goes on to make a variety of arguments about what other variables (e.g. labor-intensity, falling profit rates,

declining market shares, low RandD spending, etc.) will determine protectionist demands as well as what variables affect the "supply side" of trade policy. For a couple of surveys of this enormous literature, see Nelson 1988 and Marks and McArthur 1990.

20. Frieden (1991), however, insists that the short and medium run are "more relevant to political analysis." Alt and Gilligan (1994) point out that if factor owners are able to obtain policies that supplant market forces, then even in the long run, factors may stay fixed and Ricardo-Viner type behavior may persist.

21. "In their efforts to rationalize their worldwide activities and to maximize long-run profits, national boundaries are decided nuisances to them" (1977: 108). See also Pugel and Walter (1985: 469), who, by surveying CEOs, found a correlation between a liberal trade policy orientation and the "benefits of access to foreign markets" measured by company sales in foreign markets, its RandD/sales ratio, and its advertising/sales ratio. (The last two variables are proxies for, respectively, international competitiveness and the extent of multinationality.) On the other hand, Anderson and Baldwin (1987: 21) argue against this hypothesis "since the likelihood of any particular exporter or investor being hurt by retaliatory actions is very small."

22. Firms that are both multinational and big exporters are the biggest free-trade advocates and those that neither export nor invest abroad are the most protectionist. The intermediate cases are more ambiguous; multinational firms that export little and lack substantial intrafirm trade will, she argues, seek selective protection against their stronger competitors, and are, therefore, more protectionist than domestic firms that do depend heavily on exports. However, domestically based MNCs will oppose protection if they re-import the goods produced abroad back to the home country (whether this trade consists of arm-length or intrafirm transactions.) Firms that only export care more about opening foreign markets and see home market opening only as a means to that end; if there were another more effective means, presumably they would support it (1988: 24–25).

23. Milner (1988: 248–57) makes an analogous point on the industry level, showing how divisions among firms can inhibit trade associations from playing an active role in trade politics.

24. One reason why Destler and Odell see MNCs as much less vigorous in support of free trade than do Helleiner and Milner might be that, although Destler and Odell consider exporters, import-users, and multinationals as separate categories, they underemphasize the extent to which these groupings coincide. This is especially true given the importance of intra-firm trade, which the authors tend to downplay—perhaps because their case selection leans more heavily toward traditional products rather than high-tech (1987: 9). See also Yoffie 1993.

25. Not all scholars agree that these shifting preferences can account for the persistence of a liberal trading regime after the decline of U.S. hegemony. For instance, Lenway (1985) emphasizes the importance of international regimes while Goldstein (1993) emphasizes the role of ideas and state institutions. The dependent variable in these studies, however, are either state policy or international openness, not firm demands. My point is the widespread acceptance of the view that demands will become more liberal as globalization intensifies.

26. As Busch and Milner (1994: 269) write, "...states are more likely to act on the demands of exporters and multinationals as these firms gain political clout and

achieve privileged access to policy makers. We posit that these firms will wield more political clout as they account for a greater share of national income."

27. See Milner and Yoffie (1989) which I discuss below. On U.S.-Japanese sectoral conflicts, see Bergsten and Noland 1993. On the semiconductor industry in particular, many good accounts exist of the trade friction that emerged as Japanese import competition increased. See, for example, Borrus 1988; Irwin 1992; Tyson and Yoffie 1993.

28. Nollen and Quinn (1994: 495–97) further distinguish "strategic trade policy" which they define as measures designed to promote the relative competitiveness of domestic firms in key industries (in other words, an industrial policy) from, on the other hand, "fair trade policy" which is designed to pressure foreign governments into adopting reciprocal policies. I find this distinction not to be useful. When a government wants to protect its own industry from injury caused by the industrial or trade policies of a foreign government, it can respond with either a fair trade or strategic trade policy; both have the same intent. The main difference seems to be that the ultimate aim of fair trade policy is to achieve reciprocity and the ultimate aim of strategic trade policy is to improve the competitiveness of the domestic industry regardless of what foreign competitors do. But since competitiveness in this sense is a relative term, the distinction disappears (relevant only, perhaps, in arguments over which country was the first to violate free-market precepts).

29. For these arguments and others, see Grossman 1986.

30. Froot and Yoffie (1994: 142–44) argue that "Activities such as RandD, product development and design, and the actual production of new generation products may have the greatest increasing returns associated with them. Yet these activities may be the least likely candidates to be moved abroad—at least in the short to medium run." In the long run, however, they argue that firms will eventually move if it becomes necessary and so therefore the incentives for protection will decline.

31. See Encarnation 1992 for another extension of the argument to FDI, although he only argues that there would be "strong incentives" for governments and oligopolists to adopt such a policy (34).

32. Note that these really comprise two different spectrums: an open or closed market access regime does not necessarily have to correlate with industrial policies that aid domestic firms (Reich 1988). But if the industrial policies privilege national firms over foreign firms, than both sets of policies will harm the competitive advantage of the non-national firm. See footnote 29 above.

33. On this question, see Bhagwati 1988; Irwin 1994.

34. She (1990: 169) writes (somewhat tautologically), "The type of reciprocity in Super 301 is theoretically less likely to appeal to groups interested in open markets." The question, of course, is when will firms be interested in open markets and when will they be attracted by reciprocity strategies.

35. For example, theorists of the original strategic trade framework (Krugman 1987: 212) have emphasized that the case for export subsidies depends on the assumption that firms compete on quantities; if, instead, they compete on price, then the same policy will lead the foreign target firms not to reduce its output, but rather to engage in a price war.

36. Alt, et. al. (1994: 23–25) write, "An enduring question to which the literature has paid insufficient attention is why do we observe trade restrictions in the first place? . . . . [I]f the beneficiaries of trade restrictions are indeed powerful enough to

redistribute income to themselves, why do they not do so more directly?" This "difficult puzzle," they conclude, has yet to be satisfactorily addressed.

37. However, he has also argued (1988), as I do below, that there is an external political dimension to producer demands as well. For example, in looking at petitions to the ITC for trade relief, he says (309), "If access to the administered protection mechanism is sufficiently less costly than access to alternative (more economically appropriate) mechanisms for responding to general (nontrade-related) competitive problems, firms will seek administered protection even if it is less productive for them."

38. Aggarwal, Keohane, and Yoffie (1987: 350), for instance, emphasize the importance of exit barriers in their discussion of pressure for VERs.

39. For instance, in a satisfying model, firms want to attain a given profit level. Or perhaps firms (or rather managers) are pursuing other ends such as maximizing sales volume, growth rates, managerial perquisites or discretionary resources, etc. (Moe: 1984: 747). Aaron Wildavsky (1987) has criticized this practice of taking preferences as given, maintaining that "why people want what they want" has been unjustifiably neglected. Political preference formation, he says, "ought to be one of the major subjects of political science." (His own explanation emphasizes cultural variables.)

40. The distinction is somewhat analogous to that between, on the one hand, interests, goals, or preferences over outcomes, versus, on the other hand, means, strategies, or preferences over policies. (Frieden and Rogowski 1996: 28fn). I use the term "demand" rather than policy preference or strategy because I want to emphasize the external dimension; that is, whatever managers may secretly desire, the dependent variable of this study confines itself to the public positions and actions of industry actors that can be observed by outside agents (including, most importantly, government officials).

41. One obvious factor is previous success; already protected industries not only have more to lose, but have some indication, based on experience, that their efforts will succeed. However, this seems to beg the question; what then explains the earlier successful demands? Furthermore, successful protection that provides benefits to producers may weaken their subsequent need for protection and thus lead to demands for openness (Milner 1988: 238; Aggawal Keohane and Yoffie 1987: 350; Hansen 1990: 37).

42. Milner cites evidence to this effect from Lavergne 1983 and Baldwin 1986.

43. Peter A. Hall and Rosemary C. R. Taylor (1994: 22) write that "even if behavior is seen as goal-oriented and strategic, we might posit that the range of options that strategic actors canvass can be limited by the templates for action that existing institutions or norms make available to them."

44. In their work on trade politics, Destler and Odell (1987: 109–19) find that antiprotection political activity was confined to product-specific trade protection and that there was no comparable increase (if anything, a decline) in opposition to generic trade restriction proposals. These issues, they contend, do not generate political participation by narrow industry-specific interest groups because of collective action costs; instead, these questions interest the larger business coalitions who do not face the collective action problems but who find themselves immobilized on product-specific issues because of the heterogeneity of their members' interests.

REFERENCES

Aggarwal, Vinod K., Robert O. Keohane and David B. Yoffie. 1987. "The Dynamics of Negotiated Protection." *American Political Science Review* 81: 345–66.

Alt, James E. and Michael J. Gilligan. 1994. "The Political Economy of Trading States." *Journal of Political Philosophy* 2: 165–92.

Alt, James E., Jeffrey Frieden, Michael J. Gilligan, Dani Rodrik and Ronald Rogowski. 1994. "The Political Economy of International Trade: Enduring Puzzles and an Agenda for Inquiry." Unpublished paper. New York: New York University.

Anderson, Kym and Robert E. Baldwin. 1987. "The Political Market for Protection in Industrial Countries," in *Protection, Cooperation, Integration and Development: Essays in Honour of Hiroshi Kitamura*, edited by Ali M. El-Agraa. New York: Macmillan Publishing, 20–36.

Andrews, David M. 1994. "Capital Mobility and State Autonomy: Toward a Structural Theory of International Monetary Relations." *International Studies Quarterly* 38: 193–218.

Baldwin, Robert. 1986. *The Political Economy of U.S. Import Policy*. Cambridge: MIT Press.

Barnet, Richard J. and John Cavanaugh. 1994. *Global Dreams: Imperial Corporations and the New World Order*. New York: Simon and Schuster.

Bhagwati, Jagdish. 1988. *Protectionism*. Cambridge: MIT Press.

Borrus, Michael. 1988. *Competing for Control: America's Stake in Microelectronics*. New York: Ballinger.

Borrus, Michael and John Zysman. 1992. "Industrial Competitiveness and American National Security," in *The Highest Stakes: The Economic Foundations of the Next Security System*, edited by Wayne Sandholtz, et. al. New York: Oxford University Press, 7-52.

Boyer, Robert and Daniel Drache, eds. 1996. *States Against Markets: The Limits of Globalization*. New York: Routledge.

Busch, Marc L. and Helen V. Milner. 1992. "The Future of the International Trading System: International Firms, Regionalism, and Domestic Politics," in *Political Economy and the Changing Global Order*, Richard Stubbs and Geoffrey R. D. Underhill, eds. New York: St. Martin's Press, 259–76.

Cerny, Phillip G., ed. 1993. *Finance and World Politics*. Aldershot, England: Edward Elgar.

Cohen, Benjamin J. 1996. "Phoenix Risen: The Resurrection of Global Finance." *World Politics* 48: 268–96.

Contractor, Faro J. and Peter Lorange. 1988. *Cooperative Strategies in International Business*. Lexington, Mass.: Lexington Books.

Cooper, Richard N. 1972. "Economic Interdependence and Foreign Policy in the Seventies." *World Politics* 24: 59–181.

Cowhey, Peter F. and Jonathan D. Aronson. 1993. *Managing the World Economy: The Consequences of Corporate Alliances*. New York: Council on Foreign Relations.

Crystal, Jonathan. 1998. "New Kind of Competition: How American Producers Respond to Incoming Foreign Direct Investment." *International Studies Quarterly*.

Destler, I. M. 1992. *American Trade Politics*. Washington, D.C.: Institute for International Economics.

Destler, I. M. and John Odell. 1987. *Anti-Protection: Changing Forces in United States Trade Politics*. Washington, D.C.: Institute for International Economics.

Encarnation, Dennis J. 1992. *Rivals Beyond Trade: America Versus Japan in Global Competition*. Ithaca, N.Y.: Cornell University Press.

Finger, J. M., H. Keith Hall and Douglas R. Nelson. 1982. "The Political Economy of Administered Protection." *American Economic Review* 72: 452–66.

Frieden, Jeffery A. 1991. "Invested Interests: The Politics of National Economic Policies in a World of Global Finance." *International Organization* 45: 425–51.

Frieden, Jeffrey A. and Ronald Rogowski. 1996. "The Impact of the International Economy on National Policies: An Analytical Overview," in *Internationalization and Domestic Politics*, edited by Robert O. Keohane and Helen V. Milner. New York: Cambridge University Press, 25–47.

Froot, Kenneth A. and David B. Yoffie. 1994. "Trading Blocs and the Incentives to Protect: Implications for Japan and East Asia," in *Regionalism and Rivalry: Japan and the U.S. in Pacific Asia*, Jeffrey Frankel and Miles Kahler, eds. Chicago: University of Chicago Press, 125–33.

Garrett, Geoffrey. 1996. "Capital Mobility, Trade, and the Domestic Politics of Economic Policy," in *Internationalization and Domestic Politics*, Robert O. Keohane and Helen V. Milner, eds. New York: Cambridge University Press, pp. 79–107 i.

Garrett, Geoffrey and Peter Lange. 1996. "Internationalization, Institutions and Political Change," in *Internationalization and Domestic Politics*, edited by Robert O. Keohane and Helen V. Milner. New York: Cambridge University Press, 48–75.

Goldstein, Judith. 1993. *Ideas, Interests, and American Trade Policy*. Ithaca: Cornell University Press.

Goodman, John B. and Louis W. Pauly. 1993. "The Obsolescence of Capital Controls? Economic Management in an Age of Global Markets." *World Politics* 46: 50–82.

Goodman, John B, Debra Spar and David B. Yoffie. 1996. "Foreign Direct Investment and the Demand for Protection in the United States." *International Organization* 50: 565–91.

Graham, Edward M. 1996. *Global Corporations and National Governments*. Washington, DC: Institute for International Economics.

———. 1978. "Transatlantic Investment by Multinational Firms: A Rivalistic Phenomenon?" *Journal of Post Keynesian Economics* 1: 82–99.

Greider, William. 1996. *One World, Ready or Not: The Manic Logic of Global Capitalism*. New York: Simon and Schuster.

Grossman, Gene M. 1986. "Strategic Export Promotion: A Critique," in Paul R. Krugman, ed. *Strategic Trade Policies in a Changing World Economy*, 47–68. Cambridge: MIT Press.

Haggard, Stephan. 1987. "The Institutional Foundations of Hegemony: Explaining the Reciprocal Trade Agreements Act of 1934," in *The State and American Foreign Economic Policy*, G. John Ikenberry, David A. Lake, and Michael Mastanduno, eds.. Ithaca: Cornell University Press, 91–119.

Hall, Peter A. and Rosemary C. R. Taylor. 1994. "Political Science and the Four New Institutionalisms." Paper presented to the Annual Meeting of the American Political Science Association, New York.

Hansen, Wendy L. 1990. "The International Trade Commission and the Politics of Protectionism." *American Political Science Review* 84: 21–46.

Helleiner, Eric. ed. 1994. "The World of Money: The Political Economy of International Capital Mobility." *Policy Sciences* (special issue) 27: 4.

Helleiner, Gerald K. 1977. "Transnational Enterprises and the New Political Economy of U.S. Trade Policy." *Oxford Economic Papers* 29: 102–16.

Hu, Yao-su. 1992. "Global Corporations Are National Firms with International Operations." *California Management Review* 34: 107–26.

Ikenberry, G. John, David A. Lake and Michael Mastanduno, eds. 1988. *The State and American Foreign Economic Policy*. Ithaca: Cornell University Press.

Irwin, Douglas. 1994. *Managed Trade: The Case against Import Targets*. Washington, DC: American Enterprise Press.

———. 1992. *Trade Politics and the Semiconductor Industry*. (NBER Working Paper no. 4745.) Cambridge: National Bureau of Economic Research.

James, Jr., Harvey S. and Murray Weidenbaum. 1993. *When Businesses Cross International Borders: Strategic Alliances and Their Alternatives*. Westport, Conn.: Praeger.

Kanter, Rosabeth Moss. 1995. *World Class: Thriving Locally in the Global Economy*. New York: Simon and Schuster.

Kapstein, Ethan B. 1994. *Governing the Global Economy: International Finance and the State*. Cambridge: Harvard University Press.

———. 1991. "We Are U.S.: The Myth of the Multinational." *The National Interest*. Winter: 55–62.

Katzenstein, Peter, ed. 1978. *Between Power and Plenty: Foreign Economic Policies of Advanced Industrial States*. Madison, Wis.: University of Wisconsin Press.

Keohane, Robert O. and Helen V. Milner, eds. 1996. *Internationalization and Domestic Politics,* New York: Cambridge University Press.

Kline, John M. 1989. "Trade Competitiveness and Corporate Nationality." *Columbia Journal of World Business* Fall: 25–32.

Knickerbocker, F. T. 1974. *Oligopolistic Reaction and Multinational Enterprise*. Cambridge: Harvard University Press.

Krugman, Paul R. 1987. "Strategic Sectors and International Competition," in R. M. Stern. ed. *U.S. Trade Policies in a Changing World Economy*. Cambridge: MIT Press, 207–31.

Lavergne, Real. 1983. *The Political Economy of U.S. Tariffs: An Empirical Analysis*. Toronto: Academic Press.

Lenway, Stephanie. 1985. *The Politics of U.S. International Trade*. Boston: Pitman.

Magee, Stephen. 1980. "Three Simple Tests of the Stolper-Samuelson Theorem," in Peter Oppenheimer, ed., *Issues in International Economics*. London: Oriel Press, 138–53.

Marks, Stephen V. and John McArthur. 1990. "Empirical Analyses of the Determinants of Protection: A Survey and Some New Results," in John S. Odell and Thomas D. Willett, eds. *International Trade Policies—The Gains From Exchange Between Economists and Political Scientists*. Ann Arbor: University of Michigan Press, 105–39.

Midford, Paul. 1993. "International Trade and Domestic Politics: Improving on Rogowski's Model of Political Alignments." *International Organization* 47: 535–64.

Milner, Helen V. 1993. "American Debt and World Power." *International Journal*: 527–60.

———. 1990. "The Political Economy of U.S. Trade Policy: A Study of the Super 301 Provision," in *Aggressive Unilateralism: America's 301 Trade Policy and the World Trading System,* Jadgish Bhagwati and Hugh T. Patrick, eds. Ann Arbor: University of Michigan Press, 163–90.

———. 1988. *Resisting Protectionism: Global Industries and the Politics of International Trade.* Princeton: Princeton University Press.

———. "Resisting the Protectionist Temptation: Industry and the Making of Trade Policy in France and the United States during the 1970s." *International Organization* 41: 639–65.

Milner, Helen V. and David B. Yoffie. 1989. "Between Free Trade and Protectionism: Strategic Trade Policy and a Theory of Corporate Trade Demands." *International Organization* 43: 239–72.

Moe, Terry. 1984. "The New Economics of Organization." *American Journal of Political Science* 28: 739–77.

Moran, Theodore H. 1996. "Grand Strategy: The Pursuit of Power and the Pursuit of Plenty." *International Organization* 50: 175–205.

Mytelka, Lynn Krieger. 1987. "Knowledge-Intensive Production and the Changing Internationalization Strategies of Multinational Firms," in *A Changing International Division of Labor,* James Caporaso, ed. Boulder: Lynne Reiner, 43–70.

Nelson, Douglas. 1989a. "The Political Economy of Trade Policy." *Economics and Politics* 1: 301–14.

———. 1989b. "Domestic Political Preconditions of U.S. Trade Policy: Liberal Structure and Protectionist Dynamics." *Journal of Public Policy* 9: 83–108.

Nelson, Douglas. 1988. "Endogeous Trade Theory: A Critical Survey." *American Journal of Political Science* 32: 796–837.

Ohmae, Kenichi. 1991. *The Borderless World.* New York: HarperCollins.

Ostry, Sylvia and Michael Gestrin. 1993. "Foreign Direct Investment, Technology Transfer and the Innovation-Network Model." *Transnational Corporations* 2: 7–30

Ostry, Sylvia and Richard R. Nelson. 1995. *Technonationalism and Techno-Globalism: Conflict and Cooperation.* Washington, D.C.: The Brookings Institution.

Pauly, Louis W. and Simon Reich. 1997. "National Structures and Multinational Corporate Behavior: Enduring Differences in the Age of Globalization." *International Organization* 51: 1–26.

Pugel, Thomas A. and Ingo Walter. 1985. "AUS Corporate Interests and the Political Economy of Trade Policy." *Review of Economics and Statistics* 67: 465–73

Reich, Simon. 1989. "Roads to Follow: Regulating Direct Foreign Investment," *International Organization* 43: 543–84.

Riker, William H. 1990. "Political Science and Rational Choice," in *Perspectives on Positive Political Economy,* James E. Alt and Kenneth A. Shepsle, eds. New York: Cambridge University Press, 163–81.

Rogowski, Ronald. 1989. *Commerce and Coalitions: How Trade Affects Domestic Political Realignments.* Princeton, N.J.: Princeton University Press.

Stevens, Candace. 1990. "Technoglobalism vs. Technonationalism: The Corporate Dilemma." *Columbia Journal of World Business* Fall: 42–49.

Strange, Susan. 1996. *The Retreat of the State: The Diffusion of Power in the World Economy.* New York: Cambridge University Press.

Takacs, Wendy E. 1981. "Pressures for Protectionism: An Empirical Analysis." *Economic Inquiry* 19: 687–93.

Tanzi, Vito and Isaisas Coelho. 1993. "Restrictions on Foreign Investment: A New Form of Protectionism?" in *Protectionism and World Welfare,* Dominick Salvatore, ed. New York: Cambridge University Press, 200–208.

Thelen, Kathleen, Sven Steinmo and Frank Longstreth, eds. 1992. *Structuring Politics: Historical Institutionalism in Comparative Analysis.* New York: Cambridge University Press.

Thompson, Stephen. 1992. "We Are All Us.'" *Columbia Journal of World Business* Winter: 7–13.

Tolchin, Martin and Susan J. Tolchin 1992. *Selling Our Security: The Erosion of America's Assets.* New York: Alfred A. Knopf.

Tyson, Laura D'Andrea. 1992. *Who's Bashing Whom? Trade Conflict in High-Technology Industries.* Washington DC: Institute for International Economics.

———. 1991. "They Are Not Us: Why American Ownership Still Matters." *The American Prospect*: 37–49.

Tyson, Laura D'Andrea and David B. Yoffie. 1993. "Semiconductors: From Manipulated to Managed Trade," in *Beyond Free Trade: Firms, Governments, and Global Competition,* David B. Yoffie, ed. Boston: Harvard Business School Press, 29–78.

United Nations Conference on Trade and Development. 1996. *World Investment Report 1996: Investment, Trade and International Policy Arrangements.* New York: United Nations.

Uriu, Robert. 1996. *Troubled Industries: Confronting Economic Change in Japan.* Ithaca: Cornell University Press.

Verdier, Daniel. 1994. *Democracy and International Trade: Britain, France, and the United States, 1860–1990.* Princeton: Princeton University Press.

Wade, Robert. 1996. "Globalization and Its Limits: Reports of the Death of the National Economy are Greatly Exaggerated," in *National Diversity and Global Capitalism,* Suzanne Berger and Ronald Dore, eds. Ithaca, N.Y.: Cornell University Press, 60–88.

Weck-Hanneman, Hannelore. 1992. "Institutional Analysis of Protectionism," in *European Integration in the World Economy,* Hans-Jurgen Vosegerau, ed. New York: Springer-Verlag.

Wildavsky, Aaron. 1987. "Choosing Preferences by Constructing Institutions: A Cultural Theory of Preference Formation." *American Political Science Review* 81: 3–21.

Yoffie, David. 1993. Conclusions and Implications," in *Beyond Free Trade: Firms, Governments and Global Competition,* David Yoffie, ed. Boston: Harvard Business School Press, 429–50.

3

Multilateralism and Bilateralism in Transatlantic Trade Policy Relations: The Road to a Nebulous and Platonic Relationship?

Bart Kerremans

THE QUESTION OF BILATERALISM AND MULTILATERALISM IN EU-U.S. RELATIONS

The context of EU-U.S. economic relations abounds in declarations on improving transatlantic relations. The adoption of the Transatlantic Agenda in Madrid in December 1995 is generally seen as an important step, if not a qualitative leap in the economic relations between the United States and the European Union. After a period of increasing trade conflicts and acrimonious discussions on agriculture in the GATT Uruguay Round, a new era in EU-U.S. relations seemed to start. The goal of these improved relations would not be the establishment of a Transatlantic Free Trade Area or Agreement but rather the gradual creation of a Transatlantic Marketplace. Such an approach is reminiscent of the approach for the European Economic Area between the EC and the EFTA-member states before 1989.[1]

A number of questions could be raised however, on these ambitious plans. The first question concerns the real significance of the New Transatlantic Marketplace (NTM) compared with the current situation of transatlantic economic Marketplace for the WTO. To what extent will the NTM create an added value for the WTO and to what extent could it jeopardize the multilateral principles of the WTO? Last, but not least, questions can be raised about the limits of the Transatlantic Marketplace. Is it going to contribute to a qualitative improvement in transatlantic trade relations or is it just an overstated political project to disguise the modest performance in ongoing transatlantic trade negotiations?

Behind these three questions, one question lingers. It concerns the question on the role of multilateralism and bilateralism in EU-U.S. trade relations.

Because the United States and the EU are the two major trade partners in the WTO, this question is relevant, not only for the relations between them, but also for the operation of the WTO as a whole. This question will be answered by looking at the state of current relations between the United States and the European Union as seen from the perspective of trade relations. Then, the problems with the Transatlantic Agenda will be analyzed. Different possible roads of cooperation will be assessed. Does this agenda lead to exclusive bilateralism between both sides of the Atlantic, or to a limited bilateralism in which there is room for both bilateralism and multilateralism?

In the answers to these questions, it will become clear that the Transatlantic Marketplace, a concept developed through the Transatlantic Agenda, is a nebulous concept, a concept with more political meaning than with a real material content; a concept that has to accommodate relations between two partners that are at the same time eager to cooperate in the trade field, but that nevertheless entertain relations in which consensus-building is accompanied by mutual distrust and acrimonious disputes. Rather than forming the basis for a qualitative leap in transatlantic relations, this paper will conclude, the Transatlantic Agenda has to be seen and assessed as a mechanism whose major objective is to enable the maintenance of transatlantic trade relations at its current, decent level.

THE CURRENT STATE OF THE EU-U.S. TRADE RELATIONS

Trade and Investment between the EU and the United States

Much has been written and said about the trade relations between the United States and the European Union. In almost every publication on this issue one can read about the impressive amount of trade between the two sides of the Atlantic and about the huge amount of mutual foreign investment. Especially the last one is emphasized to indicate that there exists a large constituency in both the United States and the EU that has an interest in smooth transatlantic relations, in the removal of barriers to trade and investment, in the absence of trade conflicts, in the maintenance or building of a mutual consensus on multilateral trade policies and in the creation or development of a marketplace that spans the Atlantic Ocean.

Such a consensus-directed constituency is said to be strengthened by the large amount of intra-industry trade between the EU and the United States. Intra-industry trade leads to lower adjustment costs as a consequence of trade liberalization because "jobs lost due to customers shifting to more efficient foreign suppliers may to a large extent be offset by the job-enhancing expansion in foreign demand for similar goods produced domestically" (Hoekman and Kostecki 1996: 215). As the United States and the EU have a large amount of such trade, the basis for trade liberalization between them is strong.

The trade figures speak for themselves. As indicated by the last United States Trade Representation (USTR) report on the National Trade Estimate (1997 NTE), the EU and the United States share the largest two-way relationship in trade and investment in the world. In 1996, EU merchandise exports to the United States were valued at $142.7 billion whereas the value for U.S. merchandise exports was $127.5 billion. This accounts for almost one fifth of total EU exports and total U.S. exports.

In terms of foreign direct investment (FDI), U.S. FDI in the EU accounted for 74 percent of all inward FDI in the European Union in 1996.[2] In 1995 EU inward FDI in the United States accounted for 54 percent of total FDI in the States (European-American Business Council 1997a) which represented about 52 percent of all outward investment of the EU in 1995, 30 percent in 1994, 57 percent in 1994, 57 percent in 1993, and 39 percent in 1992 (European Commission 1996a and 1997).[3]

From the figures on trade and investment between the EU and the United States one can derive at least two conclusions. Firstly, that there is a high level of interdependence between the EU and the United States and secondly, that the quality of their mutual relations potentially affects the quality of their trade relations in the context of the World Trade Organization in general. Paralyzing trade disputes or conflicts between the two sides of the Atlantic clearly affect a large share of world trade and for that reason the quality of trade relations in general (Vogel 1997: 3; Green Cowles 1997: 1).[4]

Trade figures are just trade figures however. They may indicate the possible influence of trade relations, but not the quality of them. The assessment has to be done on a multilateral and a bilateral level.

The State of the Transatlantic Relations

In the past, the quality of EU-U.S. trade relations has played an important role in the quality of the relations inside and the effectiveness of the GATT. This has been true for the Uruguay Round, for the rounds before this one and for the issues that are on the table for the implementation of the agreements of the Uruguay Round. Indeed, the extent to which the United States and the EU have been cooperating in the WTO has to a large extent determined and influenced the extent to which the post–Uruguay Round Agenda has been implemented. And even if one of the two transatlantic partners blocked negotiations in the WTO because of a conflict with a third country, the transatlantic partner concerned has often been criticized for endangering progress in the multilateral negotiations. This makes clear that in many cases, the policies and behavior of both partners in their relations with third countries affects the quality of their mutual relations. This is to a certain level logical, since the size of the two partners (in terms of market power) makes their actions, even if unilateral, relevant for the other and for the world trading system as a whole. So if the United States concludes a semi-conductor agreement with Japan (the Vancouver Agreement), the European Union cannot look the other way if this agreement is an example of managed trade that violates the principles of nondiscrimination in the GATT/WTO. Even so, it is not surprising that the United States has showed and still shows interest for decisions taken by the European Union in its relations with third countries. The Customs Union with Turkey or the banana regime with the ACP countries are not just trade issues with a European relevance. They are issues with a relevance for large parts of world trade, and for that reason for the United States as well.

For that reason, it is not surprising that during the Uruguay Round, the relationship between the United States and the European Union played a substantial role. Cooperation and conflict between the United States and the EU influenced to a large extent, but not completely as other actors are becoming more important (see for instance Pigman 1996), the degree of progress or stalemate in the Uruguay Round (see Kerremans 1996). For the implementation of the Uruguay Round, the same is true.

For the same reason, one is not surprised to see that both the European Union and the United States stress at regular intervals the importance of the relations between them.

THE TRANSATLANTIC AGENDA

Motives for Strengthened Relations

In the context of the high interdependence between the two sides of the Atlantic, one would not be surprised to see emerging something like the Transatlantic Declaration and Agenda. The reasons for their emergence, however seem to be more political than economic.

When James Baker launched the idea of strengthened transatlantic relations, in his speech of December 12, 1989 in Berlin, the Berlin Wall had just fallen and the process of German reunification had just started (Coffey 1993: appendix 5). In this context the United States was looking for the reaffirmation of its special relationship with Europe. This search was intensified because of the reaction of the European Community itself to the process of German reunification. By way of direct linkages between German reunification, the Economic and Monetary Union and the intergovernmental conference on European Political Union, the European Community seemed to react to German reunification with a new step in its own integration (Dinan 1994: 161 and 165). The effect of this on EU-U.S. relations has been indicated clearly by Peterson (1996: 58; see also Zelikow and Rice, 1995):

> Germany unified in less than a year. The pace of European integration was accelerated in the process, as American and wider European positions converged on its desirability as a response to German unification. The United States moved to ensure that its relations with both Germany and (especially) the EU were intensified. The New Transatlanticism may be viewed largely as a byproduct of German unification.

The conclusion is, therefore, that the Transatlantic Declaration served political objectives in the first place and that references to economic or trade issues were not the first goal. After all, in the field of trade, EC-U.S. relations were nearing their point of escalation as the agricultural dispute between them became the issue that dominated the negotiations for the Uruguay Round and that led to the failure of the Heysel Conference in Brussels (December 1990) (Kerremans 1996). This conference was supposed to conclude the Uruguay Round negotiations.

Seen from the European perspective, the "New Transatlan-ticism" was also an instrument that had to serve political purposes in the first place. It was a way to reaffirm the American commitment in Europe, in the first place in the field of security. The end of the Cold War could not, as far as the Europeans were concerned, mean the end of the United States security commitment in Europe. The Transatlantic Declaration was a way to convince the United States of this. As Kohl, quoted by Peterson (1996: 59) has put it: "A transatlantic security union is of existential significance for Germans and Europe. Only it can create a true balance in Europe. A look at the map underlines this."

In the attempts to reaffirm the good relations between the European Union and the United States by way of the Transatlantic Agenda, trade did play a much more important role than in the case of the Transatlantic Declaration. Whereas in the case of the latter, political motives seem to have played a central role, like German reunification and European integration, in the case of the former, the main motive was related to trade and economics. In the period between 1988 and 1994 the United States started to conclude preferential agreements with other countries. The first was the CUSFTA, the Canadian-U.S. Free Trade Agreement in 1988. It was preceded by the preferential agreement between the United States and Israel (1985), a country with which the EC also concluded a preferential agreement (Association Agreement). In this vein, 1993 was a "key year." The United States started to conclude regional arrangements, the first of which was the North American Free Trade Agreement. That agreement was approved by Congress in November 1993. In the same period, on the initiative of President Clinton, the first APEC[5] summit was held in Seattle.

The conclusion of all these agreements by the United States, was the result of mixed motives, in which market access, migration (from Mexico) and the Uruguay Round played a role (Cuyvers and Kerremans 1997: 308–09).

United States frustrations about its paralyzing conflict with the EU on agriculture and audiovisual services in the Uruguay Round triggered an increased interest in NAFTA and APEC (Jütte-Rauhut 1995). The timing of the three (Uruguay Round, NAFTA, and APEC) was remarkable. On November 17, 1993, the House of Representatives approved the NAFTA-agreement by 234 votes against 200. On November 18–19, 1993 the first APEC-Summit took place in Seattle. On November 20, 1993 the U.S. Senate approved NAFTA by 61 votes against 38. On December 15, 1993 the final agreement on the Uruguay Round was reached. Also important was the initiation of the process towards a Free Trade for the Americas Agreement in December 1994 (Economic and Social Committee 1995: 2; see also Cuyvers and Van den Bulcke: 6; Buelens, 1997: 45).

This timing seems to indicate that the formation of the NAFTA and the start of the APEC process was part of a U.S. strategy to press the Europeans and other negotiating partners in the Uruguay Round (see Abbott 1995: 119; Rolle 1995: 472; Peterson, 1996: 122).[6] The idea was simple. If no agreement would be reached in the multilateral Uruguay Round, the United States would use bilateral and regional strategies to achieve market access, or, as Vernon (1996: 625) has put it:

> The emergence of a NAFTA possibility offered the Americans a splendid opportunity to send a signal to the negotiators in Geneva that, if those negotiations [the Uruguay Round negotiations, BK] failed, the United States had an attractive option, namely, to build its own trading block from a North American base.

From the European side this was perceived as threatening because of two reasons. First because the bilateral and regional alternative for the United States could reduce its preparedness to support a multilateral framework such as the new WTO or to concede in negotiations on its formation. It is in this context important to remember that one of the big objectives of the EC in the Uruguay Round consisted of the "disciplining" of section 301 by a reinforced dispute settlement procedure in the GATT.[7]

Another, perhaps even more important reason was the fear of the EC and its member states that APEC and NAFTA would divert attention away from Europe. Moreover, the United States was working on better relations with a region that enjoyed remarkable rates of economic growth and has an impressive potential outlet for Western products. The involvement of China (the People's Republic) in APEC was especially important in this context.[8]

The fear of a "turning away" of the United States' attention in favor of the Asia-Pacific area was to a large extent due to the fact that the end of the Cold War meant that the United States was not tied anymore to Europe in the field of security as it was before 1989–1990. This gave the impression that the United States was freer now to choose its preferential partners in the world trading system. In some circles, this fear was probably overstated, as was the U.S. fear for a "Fortress Europe" in 1989. But it nonetheless exerted an influence on EU decision makers, especially in DG I. The following quote from a report of the European Commission on transatlantic relations indicates this (European Commission 1995a: 2):

> Of course, the end of the Cold War has changed the nature of [transatlantic] relationship. There is no longer a single, common adversary and the need to guarantee military security has ceased to be the overriding feature of the relationship. . . . There can be no return to the time when political and economic issues were subordinate to the central question of security. Today it is necessary to demonstrate anew why this unique partnership is more valid than ever, for reasons which have more to do with the future than a past common heritage.[9]

The lingering fear in the European Union of the U.S. attention to Asia was not so much due to the attention itself but to the possibility of the development of preferential relations with that region. By definition, such preferential relations would exclude the European Union. This fear still exists,[10] although it has been reduced somewhat since the reinforcement of relations between the APEC countries in the field of trade seems to be more difficult than originally expected. This is partly a consequence of the attitude of the Asian countries which see APEC as a tool to tie the hands of the NAFTA countries to the multilateral trading system (Kohler-Koch 1996).[11] Nevertheless, the European concern about possible preferential relations in APEC to the detriment of Europe, still exists, as was indicated by a speech given by Sir Leon Brittan on March 19, 1996 at the Capitol Hill Club in Washington D.C. in which he compared the American and the European approach to the Asia-Pacific region:[12]

> We must not fall back into the Cold War trap of thinking we have to choose between partners. Ours will not be an exclusive relationship. We are not setting out to create a rival regional group, nor do we propose to set up a regional trade liberalization system along the lines of APEC. We wish APEC well, as long as it remains a force for further multilateral liberalization. So far we are satisfied that APEC liberalization will be open on a most favored nation basis and thus compatible with the WTO agreements. However, there are voices in America which argue that market opening in Asia should be on a preferential basis, in other words only available to members.[13]

The European answer to this diversion of U.S. attention consisted of two parts. Firstly, the improvement of its own relations with the Asian-Pacific Region. Secondly, the re-emphasis on the importance of transatlantic relations, which basically resulted in the Transatlantic Agenda.

The renewed European stress on transatlantic relations clearly struck a sensitive cord in some parts of the federal administration in Washington D.C.

It clearly reinforced those, in the administration and in the business communities, that were eager not to let the United States turn itself exclusively or too much to the Pacific; it reinforced the "Atlantic lobby" in Washington.[14] Among them were certainly the Secretary of Commerce, the late Ron Brown and Mickey Kantor, at that time still U.S. Trade Representative. Also involved was Stuart Eizenstat, then Head of the U.S. mission (ambassador) to the EU in Brussels and now under-secretary of commerce and largely involved in the EU-U.S. dispute on the Helms-Burton and the D'Amato Acts (see later).

An additional factor in American receptiveness towards the idea of a reinforced transatlantic relationship were—as Peterson (1996: 184) has called it—the "teething problems of NAFTA and APEC [which] (. .) acted to weaken the assumption in Washington that the country's economic future lay in North America and Asia, not Europe" (see also Orme 1996; and Rich 1997: 96). This certainly reinforced the "Atlantic lobby" in Washington D.C. and reinforced the conviction, even in Congress, that improving transatlantic relations is in the interest of the United States.

It was Ron Brown who launched the idea of a Transatlantic Business Dialogue (TABD), which was warmly welcomed by European Commission vice-president Sir Leon Brittan and by his German colleague, Martin Bangemann.

In the course of 1995, both the TABD and the Transatlantic Agenda were developed, which resulted in the TABD meeting in the presence of Brown, Brittan and Bangemann in Sevilla in November 1995 and the EU-U.S. Summit in Madrid in November 1996. These meetings resulted in reports in which the formation of a Transatlantic Marketplace was ushered. At the summit, both the United States and the EU adopted the Transatlantic Agenda including an Action Plan. The role of the TABD in shaping the Action Plan had been essential, according to Brittan and Bangemann. This confirmed their conviction that as far as transatlantic relations are concerned, "the best way to identify and to discuss all (. .) [the] problems is to let the businessmen speak (. .)" (AE[1], no.6599: 5).

In the Agenda the concept of a Transatlantic Marketplace was used for the first time. It pointed at a number of initiatives that would be developed between the United States and the EU. These are (AE,[15] no.6619: 6):

- An agreement on standards and verification.
- An agreement on veterinary issues.
- Greater openness on public procurement.
- An effort to resolve outstanding difficulties on intellectual property.
- Dialogue on financial services.
- The development of dialogue on the information society (with several specific initiatives).
- The continuation of bilateral cooperation on competition.
- Discussion of data protection.
- Specific initiatives on air and maritime transport.
- Intensification of cooperation in energy matters.

One can wonder what is the real meaning of this Transatlantic Marketplace. Is it a kind of Transatlantic APEC? Is it meant to develop a preferential trade agreement between the United States and the EU, or is it meant to be an instrument that can promote a policy of proactive multilateralism by both the United States and the EU jointly and separately? The answer to this question is far from agreed as the discussions during the preparation of the Transatlantic Agenda and the declaration after its launching have indicated. Nonetheless, these questions are of a fundamental importance as transatlantic trade, and as a consequence also transatlantic trade relations, in one way or another affect the WTO and its multilateral rules. The question is therefore, whether the Transatlantic Agenda aims at an exclusive bilateralism or at a limited bilateralism at the service of multilateralism?

Exclusive Bilateralism?

Exclusive bilateralism refers to a relationship between two countries that is based on mutually granted preferences that are not granted to third countries. In the case of the EU-U.S. relationship, the once proposed TAFTA (Transatlantic Free Trade Agreement) would have been an example of such bilateralism.

The arguments in favor of and against TAFTA have been outlined extensively elsewhere. It is important to look at them, however, in order to clarify the concept of the Transatlantic Marketplace, a concept that has been developed as soon as it became clear that a TAFTA was neither feasible nor desirable.

The idea of a TAFTA became popular in the first half of 1995 when both European and North American leaders defended the idea. In Europe, politicians such as Klaus Kinkel and Malcolm Rifkind raised the issue (Devuyst 1995: 17). On the North American side, the Canadian Prime Minister, Jean Chrétien raised the issue by pleading a general trade liberalization agreement between NAFTA and the EU (Economic and Social Committee 1995: 26). American politicians such as Jeffrey Garten, Under Secretary of Commerce for International Trade and Clayton Yeutter, former U.S. trade representative and agricultural secretary, found the idea attractive. Former U.S. Secretary of State, Warren Christopher even stated that the United States would make a serious analysis of the issue.

A number of problems have barred the road to a TAFTA however. In the first place, there is article XXIV of the GATT and the Understanding on the Interpretation of Article XXIV of the GATT 1994. Article XXIV: 8(b) clearly states:

> A free-trade area shall be understood to mean a group of two or more customs territories in which the duties and other restrictive regulations of commerce (except, where necessary, those permitted under articles XI, XII, XIII, XIV, XV and

> XX) are eliminated on substantially all the trade between the constituent territories in products originating in such territories.

One of the questions about this definition has concentrated on the exact meaning of "substantially all the trade." A clear figure (80 percent of total trade), as originally suggested by the EEC member states when the consistency of the EEC-Treaty with article XXIV was examined, has never been accepted.[16] Instead, a negative criterion (i.e. a criterion that defines when the condition of "substantially all the trade" has not been met) have been adopted. This criterion, as adopted by several GATT Working Parties on Agreements Presented Under Article XXIV, stated that (WTO 1995: 825): "Article XXIV: 8(b) had to be interpreted to mean free trade in all products and not carved out by sectors; the exclusion of a whole sector, no matter what percentage of current trade it constituted was contrary to the spirit of both Article XXIV and the General Agreement."

This reasoning has been included in the Understanding on Article XXIV, following the Uruguay Round. In the preamble of this Understanding, after having recognized the contribution to the expansion of world trade that customs unions and free-trade areas *may* make, the Members of the WTO recognize: "(. .) that such contribution is increased if the elimination between the constituent territories of duties and other restrictive regulations of commerce extends to all trade, and diminished if any major sector of trade is excluded."

One could easily say that this interpretation probably represents the major stumbling block to the formation of the TAFTA. By definition, a TAFTA would have to include agricultural trade between the United States and the EU.[17] If one looks, however, at the extent to which discussions about trade in this sector paralyzed the Uruguay Round (Ingersent et al. 1996: 707; Paarlberg 1997)[18] and to the way in which this issue continues to affect transatlantic relations—e.g. the issue of the EU reference price system for grain imports;[19] the role that grain and rice played in the EU-U.S. negotiations based on Article XXIV: 6 after the EU-enlargement with Austria, Sweden and Finland; the question of the EU-banana regime for which a WTO Panel has been established in 1996 (USTR 1996; 1997; European Commission 1995b; 1996a), it would be realistic to predict that the inclusion of this sector in TAFTA negotiations would paralyze such negotiations from the beginning. Such a paralysis would not only be the consequence of disputes between the EU and the United States, but also because of the conflicts it would engender (again) among the EU-member states (Kerremans 1996). Revealing here is a quote from Franz Fischler, the current EU Agricultural Commissioner on the TAFTA. Saying that he "cannot imagine a free-trade agreement on agriculture between the United States and the EU," he added: "I can only recommend caution in free trade" (quoted in AE no.6618: 2).

A TAFTA without agriculture would be unimaginable, however. This is for two reasons. Firstly, because of the pressure in the United States itself (especially in Congress) to use the opportunity of TAFTA negotiations to force more access to the European agricultural market, in a period where the enlargement negotiations with the Central European countries would put serious strain on this market anyway. The recalcitrance of France towards TAFTA was, besides its traditionally complex relations with the United States, partly due to this "fear" of weakening or losing Community preference in agriculture.

The second reason, of course would be the WTO itself. If the two biggest trading blocs in the WTO, the two customs territories on whose loyalty the legitimacy and the very existence of the WTO depends, violates one of the basic provisions of the GATT 1994, they would probably give the *coup de grâce* to the current multilateral trading system. A preferential trade agreement between the United States and the EU that violates the "substantially all the trade" provision would certainly open a Pandora's box and would reinforce trends in regional bloc formation everywhere in the world.

Besides the problem of the sectoral coverage of a TAFTA, an additional problem that basically jeopardized the whole idea consisted of the effect that a TAFTA would have on the WTO, even if it respected the WTO-rules. As Devuyst (1995: 17) has indicated, a TAFTA would probably be perceived by most developing countries as a "rich men's club, leaving the rest of the world behind." A similar impression would certainly arise in Japan and in the newly industrialized countries such as South Korea and Taiwan (Forward Studies Unit 1995: 38). This would probably reduce the credibility of the multilateral trading system and reduce the preparedness of the developing world and the Asian countries to make reciprocal concessions in the WTO (see Kahler 1995: 60). In other words, TAFTA risks to block the permanent process of trade liberalization that was launched by the Uruguay Round timetable for further negotiations and by the establishment of the WTO as a permanent forum for multilateral trade negotiations. Abbott (1995: 137), not referring to TAFTA but to the relations between NAFTA and the EU, comes to a similar conclusion: "It is perhaps ironic that the relative compatibility of the NAFTA and the EU social welfare systems may provide an impetus more for biregional Fortress Atlantic than for either Fortress North America or a Fortress Europe."

TAFTA would not only, however, have a negative impact on the ongoing negotiating process in the WTO but also on the meaning of what can be considered to be the nucleus of the WTO, the MFN-principle. A TAFTA would put a large amount of trade, currently ruled by the MFN-principle, on a discriminatory basis, thereby eroding the basis on which the whole GATT/WTO has been built. Consequently, neither the United States, nor the EU wanted to take such a risk. This shows how trade relations between such two big trading blocs as the EU and the United States cannot be conducted without affecting the whole trading system. This, to a certain extent, ties the hands of those that are responsible for these relations.

The overall conclusion about TAFTA cannot be different than—as Kahler has put it (1995: 60)—that TAFTA is the "least attractive" formula to reinforce transatlantic relations. It would jeopardize the WTO-system and it would risk blocking any progress in transatlantic relations because negotiations on a TAFTA would inevitably involve acrimonious discussions on sensitive issues. Besides that, opposition to a TAFTA in both the EU and the United States, because it ties the United States and the EU too much together (which is especially a concern in Congress), makes the conclusion, let alone the ratification of such an agreement highly improbable. Rather than being the basis for a qualitative leap in transatlantic relations, a TAFTA would risk becoming a factor of deterioration in these relations.

What conclusions can be drawn from this? The first one is clear: in shaping their mutual relations the EU and the United States have to take into account the effects of their agreements and disagreements on the multilateral system. Secondly, to tie the EU and the United States too much together is both unfeasible (because of domestic opposition) and too risky for the quality of their relations. The latter may sound paradoxical. It is in the interest of the EU and the United States to reinforce their trade policy relations, but to limit such reinforcement to a certain level. After all, and whatever the political rhetoric of transatlantic relations, the United States and the European Union do not only share a large number of common values, but are also each other's competitors in the international trade arena. This is not only true for American and European companies. If one sees how anxious the EU has become to improve its relations with the Asian-Pacific countries since the APEC process started (cf. the Asia-Europe Meetings, called ASEM, see Dent 1997: 8) or how much effort is put into concluding a preferential agreement with Chile now that the perspective of Chilean accession to the NAFTA has faded away (Rich 1997: 96), one can clearly conclude that both the public authorities of the EU and of the United States are collaborating and competing at the same time. That clearly sets limits to the depth and the quality of transatlantic cooperation.

In terms of the Transatlantic Agenda, what was required instead of the TAFTA, was the search for another formula to define and to structure transatlantic trade relations.

LIMITED BILATERALISM AND INTERNATIONAL SUBSIDIARITY

Limited Bilateralism?

The fact that TAFTA was dropped resulted in a search for another way to restructure the transatlantic relationship. In the discussions on this subject, the idea of TAFTA loomed in the background. Some EU-member states were afraid that, in spite of a different name, the acceptance of a new framework for these relations could mean that they would engage themselves in a process that would result in something similar to a transatlantic free-trade area. Especially the Southern member states did not want to go so far.

As a result, new concepts to define the renewed transatlantic relation were looked for. Concepts such as the Transatlantic Economic Space and the Transatlantic Marketplace emerged. The nebulous character of these concepts (what is a marketplace?) made them more suitable to be accepted by all the EU member states.

Whatever the name, the great distinction between the TAFTA and the new concepts was that in the new framework enhanced cooperation between the EU and the United States would be compatible with the multilateral way of liberalizing trade. This puts two constraints on transatlantic cooperation. Firstly, whenever the United States and the EU cooperate on issues that are already dealt with in the WTO or that are part of the ongoing post–Uruguay Round negotiating process, cooperation must aim at promoting multilateralism. This is the idea of "co-leadership" in which the EU and the United States jointly provide leadership in favor of multilateralism in the WTO.

The second constraint is a consequence of the first. On issues that are not dealt with in the WTO, EU-U.S. cooperation must aim at improved mutual market access by dealing with market barriers that are difficult if not impossible to deal with on a multilateral basis. In principle, such cooperation would have to lead to "open regionalism." This means that, at least in theory, issues that are dealt with on a bilateral basis should be brought into the multilateral realm as soon as multilateral solutions on these issues come within reach. The second constraint refers to the idea of "subsidiarity." It points at the fact that EU-U.S. cooperation aims at elevating mutual market access at a "higher qualitative level" than is possible or feasible in the multilateral framework of the WTO. By definition, this means that transatlantic bilateral cooperation will mostly deal with "behind the border issues," i.e. with regulatory cooperation. By looking at the Transatlantic Marketplace, as defined in the 1995 Transatlantic Agenda, one clearly sees that most issues that have been enumerated concern regulation. Issues such as Mutual Recognition Agreements on Standards and Certification, sanitary and phytosanitary measures, and competition policy agreements are predominant. It concerns issues that can only be dealt with by countries or trading blocks with similar or comparable levels of economic development, regulation and economic structures. Countries with intra-industry trade, for instance, will encounter less difficulties in reaching agreements on such issues than countries that maintain inter-industry trade (cf. infra and Hoekman and Kostecki 1996: 215). Let us look deeper into the concept of subsidiarity and the role it plays in the transatlantic trade relationship.

International Subsidiarity and the Transatlantic Trade Relationship

The concept of international subsidiarity is an attractive one in the context of the EC-U.S. trade relations. International subsidiarity relates to the concept of "subsidiarity" which is central in federalism and federal thinking. It points at the rationale behind the division of power among different government levels which is effectiveness. Applied to the international realm (as has been done on a smaller and very controversial scale inside the European Union), this means that the extent to which problems will be dealt with domestically, bilaterally, plurilaterally or multilaterally, will be determined by the most effective government level or level of cooperation to deal with them. In this case the nature of the problem determines the required government level or level of cooperation. Two perspectives can be used here: the bottom-up approach and the top-bottom approach. In the case of international subsidiarity, the first approach mainly points at an economic rationale, whereas the second one is more political.

The Bottoms-Up Perspective (the Demand Side)

There are problems that an individual state or customs territory cannot deal with effectively because of their scale. The globalization of the economy makes a number of national decisions meaningless and requires an international approach. This is not only true for the global commons but also for problems directly related to trade and investment. For such problems, it is precisely the increased amount of FDI and international trade that has made purely national trade strategies obsolete. In order to reach a decent level of policy efficacy states have to cooperate with others. What was once dealt with at a purely national level (i.e. the "lower level") has now become the subject of international negotiations (i.e. the "higher level"). Failure to do so is generally perceived as being a serious political problem since economic integration results in cross-border spillovers between countries which means that one country is exposed to problems created by or in another country or that the benefits of one country's policies "leak away" (i.e. externalities) to other countries (e.g. the benefits of French economic policies between 1981 and 1983 for Germany). As there is "a growing mismatch between the economic and the political structures of the world" (Lawrence 1996: xvii), the problem of cross-border spillovers and externalities becomes more urgent.

The problem of the "mismatch" is not a static one, however, nor is it similar for the world as a whole. The extent of market integration between countries or customs territories will determine the need for international cooperation or the extent of the mismatch in case there is a failure to cooperate. As the extent of market integration evolves, cooperation will have to evolve as well. The failure to do so will become increasingly problematic as market integration proceeds. In the case of transatlantic relations this is important since the level of transatlantic trade and market integration is quite important, this largely due to the high amount of transatlantic investment (see above). In addition, almost all tariff barriers between the United States and the EU have been removed. This exposes traders and investors to other, domestic, barriers, mostly of a regulatory kind.[20] This requires, not only transatlantic cooperation in the traditional meaning of at-the-border issues, but also cooperation on behind-the-border-issues. What Lawrence (1996: xvii–xviii) has written about trade and investment in general, therefore, applies in the first place to the transatlantic relations:

> As separation fences have been lowered and technological innovations have shrunk economic distances, a multitude of formerly neglected differences among nation's domestic policies have become exposed to international scrutiny. National governments and international negotiations must thus increasingly deal with deeper—behind-the-border-integration

One could call this the demand side of international subsidiarity. In the case of international trade this demand side has, literally, been reflected by the activities of interest groups and companies in favor of an international rules-based trading system. As international economic integration has been intensified by increasing trade and investment (globalization) and by technological developments (especially in telecommunications), the demand has evolved as well (cf. Krugman 1997). Issues like nontariff barriers (NTBs), investment, services and intellectual property rights have all been put on the multilateral trading agenda during the last twenty years.

In the transatlantic realm, the increasing demand for a transatlantic level playing field, with its increasing stress on behind-the-border issues, has been reflected in the activities of the Transatlantic Business Dialogue (TABD, 1995; 1996a; 1996b; 1997), the Transatlantic Policy Network and more informal and less open attempts by interest groups to open the borders and to allow for more transatlantic coordination on issues that have traditionally been domestic issues (such as competition policy). Some of them really infringe deep into the domestic realm. In EuroChambres' report on Non-Tariff Barriers (1996: 6), for instance, the "complicated American legal system" is said to be a trade barrier.

The "demand side" is not only reflected in nongovernmental activities, however. Both the United States and the European Union have started to look deeper into each other's domestic policies in order to assess the effects of domestic policy decisions on trade in general[21] and on transatlantic trade in particular. On the EU-side, one can see this in the annual reports on the United States trade and investment barriers in which a good deal refers to barriers engendered by decisions that traditionally belonged to the domestic realm. On the U.S. side there are the annual National Trade Estimates. Besides that, the United States followed very precisely the steps that have been taken in the European Community in the completion of the internal market and its effects on the United States. For that purpose, the United States International Trade Commission issued six Follow-Up Reports on the 1992 Internal Market between 1988 and 1994.[22]

The Top-Bottom Perspective (the Supply Side)

The Technical Rationale and Subsidiarity It is not sufficient, however, to have a demand for cooperation in order to have cooperation itself. Equally, the demand for multilateral cooperation will not always be met by cooperation on that level. In other words, there can be a large difference between the demand and the supply of international cooperation. As on the demand side, subsidiarity also plays a role on the supply side.

An often-heard reply to the question why the United States and the EU use the bilateral approach on the Mutual Recognition Agreements on Standards and Certification[23] is that the equivalence between the United States and the EU standards and certification procedures makes bilateral agreements on these more feasible. Negotiations with countries with radically different standards or certification procedures would just not result in an agreement. That is why the EU succeeded concluding MRAs with Australia, New Zealand, and Canada as well. That is also why it is unrealistic to expect MRA-negotiations on a multilateral level. There is just too much diversity on that level to allow for agreements.

Another aspect is enforcement (for the theoretical arguments, see Martin (1993: 97) and the reaction from Caporasso (1993: 64). In MRAs, the question of trust plays a central role. One recognizes the certification and the standards of the other. That requires that one can be sure that the other will apply the required levels of safety and quality for one's own export products. That seems to be possible only in the case of economic systems with equivalent levels of economic development and consumer demands. This, by definition (at least in the current world) restricts the number of potential counterparts in MRA-negotiations. The same could be said for other trade issues such as financial services (where regulations play a very important role, cf. Herring and Litan, 1995), intellectual property and competition policy. It seems logical, therefore, to conclude that the effectiveness of policy making on these issues requires that agreements should be concluded, not on a multilateral, but on a bilateral or minilateral level. As the world economic system becomes less divergent, the geographical extension of such agreements would become feasible.

This subsidiarity logic gives the impression that technical arguments (effectiveness) can account completely for the choice of the geographical level of cooperation in general and between the United States and the EU in particular. Because the last two have similar systems in terms of economic development, consumer preferences, the role of the state in the economy, and the current level of standardization, they can provide bilateral agreements on issues where multilateral agreements still are unfeasible.

The Political Rationale: Reverse Subsidiarity This technical rationale behind the supply side of international subsidiarity is one part of the picture, though. The other part is more political and could be termed "reverse subsidiarity." It points at the paradox of EU-U.S. trade relations. As these relations have led to a reduction in trade barriers between the two sides of the Atlantic and to an increased investment in both directions, the future transatlantic relations can almost exclusively concentrate on issues that impinge upon questions that have been traditionally dealt with in the domestic realm only. This is true for the EU as it is true for the United States. This has two consequences: firstly it confronts the process of market opening and market integration with issues that reflect domestic values and interests much more than the traditional issues of trade policies. Such issues relate to questions about the organization of society, social welfare, tax policies and environmental protection (cf. Vogel 1997; Ives 1997: 27). Secondly—and this is to a large extent related to the first consequence—these issues mobilize more domestic political actors more intensively. Domestic interest groups that had nothing to do with international trade policies will now be directly affected by them. This puts a serious strain and a lot of pressure on those domestic institutions and actors that take part in the decision making on international market integration and results in much more domestic controversy on such issues. More controversy leads to more domestic visibility of international trade issues and to more political salience for the subjects concerned. The "reverse" aspect of subsidiarity is then, that the more international cooperation on trade and investment is "domesticized," the more difficult such cooperation will become. The conclusion is then, that subsidiarity and reversed subsidiarity are the two sides of the same coin. On one side there is the internationalization of previously domestic issues. On the other hand there is the "domesticizing" of international trade policy. Whereas the first points at the need for international cooperation, the second refers to the problems to satisfy this need. The combination of the two leads to a difficulty in overcoming the mismatch between economic integration and the political structures in both international trade in general and transatlantic market integration in particular.

In recent EU-U.S. trade relations this has become very visible as these relations affect actors and issues "behind the border" more than most other trade relations do. The MRA negotiations, for instance raised the question of the role of private normalization bodies on both sides of the Atlantic. They raise the question of certification procedures and of the competence and autonomy of national certification bodies, the most famous (or infamous) of which is the Food and Drugs Administration. Equally, in the case of public procurement and financial services, the autonomy of the states-level (in the United States) and the substate-level (in the EU) is at stake. To what extent are the 50 U.S. states committed by obligations accepted by the federal government (cf. Paarlberg 1995: 47)?[24] In the case of the EU a similar problem occurred on TRIPs[25] and services which entailed first a Court Ruling (Opinion 1/94, see Kerremans 1996a) and then political discussion on the competencies of the EU and its member states in this field.[26]

The question goes deeper, however. It not only concerns the autonomy of actors but also the opinions of a society towards fundamental issues such as environment and health safety. The hormones is a relevant example here (cf. Vogel 1997: 23–24 and 58–59). Does it matter that scientific research proves that particular kinds of hormones have to be allowed in beef, if this risks jeopardizing beef consumption in a whole market? Whatever the answer, it is clear that it will attract a lot of public attention, even turmoil. Also in the case of financial services, legal frameworks build on socially well embedded premises about the ways to protect the banks and the public from too much financial risks (cf. the Glass-Steagal Act), are confronted with completely different opinions about banks and finances. As this will mobilize domestic actors, negotiations between the EU and the United States become more difficult. In the case of the United States, this leads to two problems: firstly, whether Congress, by tradition more receptive to local and parochial pressures (see Peterson 1996: 80–82), will accept the concessions made by the United States Trade Representative. As Silverstein (1997: 163–64) has put it:

> Foreign trade intimately and immediately effects most industries in the United States as well as having a direct impact on the prices paid by all consumers. Many lobbyists and all constituents, then, have a direct interest in foreign trade legislation, and increasingly constituents are coming to realize the impact these policies actually do have on their lives.[27]

Secondly, whether other actors, such as the 50 states and other federal administrations like the FDA, either are committed by or will accept the commitments conceded by the USTR (cf. Ives 1997: 29; Shapiro 1997), and the extent to which they will be able to define trade policy outcomes themselves.[28] These two questions, which will become more urgent as transatlantic cooperation impinges more upon the domestic U.S. system, create problems for the U.S.'s partner, the EU. As Peterson (1996: 81, see also Silverstein 1997: 199 and Paarlberg 1995: 25 and 35) has put it: "For EU policymakers, it became more difficult to identify a single 'American view' on most issues of foreign policy, particularly those concerning trade."[29]

Exactly the same holds for the European Union however. As more "behind the border issues" come to be dealt with between the United States and the EU, proportionately fewer issues will be issues directly related to trade in goods where the European Union enjoys exclusive competencies. That means that more and more transatlantic agreements will take the form of "mixed agreements" which equally confuses the picture who negotiates for who and who commits who (Kerremans 1996b).[30] The only difference between the EU and the United States is perhaps then, that the EU has already built a certain tradition in negotiating, concluding, ratifying and implementing mixed agreements. But the question of the TRIPs and services in the Uruguay Round and the recent debate on the EU competences in the "Open Skies" negotiations indicate that the question still bears a lot of political controversy.

The Fallacy of Commonality

The question of "reverse subsidiarity" refers to a fundamental problem in EU-U.S. trade relations which, and this is the paradox, points at the relative depth and success of these relations in the past. Whereas it is generally accepted that the future for EU-U.S. trade relations augurs quite well because of the large extent of commonality in the economic structures and development levels of both customs territories,[31] the reality will be the presence and the absence of this commonality at the same time. One could call this the fallacy of commonality in transatlantic relations. Because of the existent commonality and the removal of trade barriers, the United States and the EU have deepened their trade relations so much that they have to deal with issues where the pretended commonality does not exist anymore or is at least qualitatively less than in the case of general concepts such as economic welfare and economic structures. This is one of the lessons to be drawn from the rejection of the concept of a Transatlantic Free-Trade Area (TAFTA).[32] Because of the risk it would pose for multilateralism, it would engender more conflicts than agreements since it would impinge too much upon the domestic economic and trade systems of both the EU and the United States. It is also a reason to remain skeptical when Europeans talk about the Transatlantic Marketplace as a "transatlantic extension of the Internal Market." As the European Economic Area (EEA) negotiations with the former EFTA-countries have shown, such a extension is difficult because it has fundamental consequences for both the countries concerned and the decision-making autonomy of the EU (Kerremans 1996a: chapter VI). In the case of transatlantic relations, different from the case of the EEA, the EU will not have a predominance in the negotiations, which will make it all but easy to arrive at something close to a Transatlantic Economic Space.

The conclusion is clear therefore, because of its inherent constraints, EU-U.S. bilateralism has its limits. It is limited because deeper than shallow transatlantic integration (to use the words of Lawrence) means impinging upon the sovereignty and the domestic politics of the two sides. This does not mean that transatlantic bilateralism is unfeasible or impossible. It already exists. But going deeper on "behind the border" issues will be a slow, incremental and difficult process which will be impeded by all those that try to jealously preserve their nationally (or European-wide) protected prerogatives. It will equally be hindered by those that believe that the values on which one's own environmental, health and social policies are built are better than those of the other side of the Atlantic are. Transatlantic bilateralism will be limited bilateralism therefore, a bilateralism that will hardly damage the already existing multilateral rules in the international trading and investment system. A bilateralism with a limited scope.

CONCLUSION: THE TRANSATLANTIC MARKETPLACE AS A NEBULOUS CONCEPT

What are the conclusions from the above for the future of transatlantic trade relations and the concept of the New Transatlantic Marketplace (NTM)? The answer to this question can be provided by looking at the scope of the NTM and the depth of cooperation inside the NTM (see table 3.1).

As far as the scope of the Transatlantic Marketplace is concerned, there are clear limitations. Whereas there are still a number of issues for which the Transatlantic Marketplace could provide a framework of cooperation, it is clear that the NTM can never come close to a TAFTA nor to a Transatlantic Economic Space if the definition of this "space" would be analogous to the European Economic Space or Area between the EU and the EFTA (except Switzerland). It is clear that sensitive issues such as agriculture, textiles, subsidies (in some sectors), maritime services and audiovisual services will be difficult to deal with on a bilateral basis. The factors that inhibit this are on the EU-side the division among the member states, on the U.S. side the role

Table 3.1. Scope and Depth of Transatlantic Trade Policy Cooperation

Dimension of Cooperation	*Extent of Cooperation*	*Inhibiting Factors*
Scope of cooperation	• Note in sensitive areas • No TAFTA or Economic Space	• Division among the EU member states • Resistance from Congress • Article XXIV GATT and Article V GATS
Depth of cooperation	• Reverse subsidiarity	• Resistance of Congress, the member states and the public at large • the fallacy of commonality • economic rationale versus societal rationales

that Congress plays and the fact that the United States has no strategic interest in linking itself too much to Europe, and on the WTO-side article XXIV GATT.[33] For these reasons, there is no risk that the Transatlantic Marketplace would result in an exclusive bilateralism between both sides of the Atlantic to the detriment of the multilateral principles of the WTO.

As far as the depth of the transatlantic trade policy relationship is concerned, there are also certain constraints despite the fact—and it is important to emphasize this—that the depth of this relationship is already far-reaching. It is precisely the current depth of the relationship that accounts for the limitations on its possible future deepening. In the first place there is the "reverse subsidiarity" which points at the fact that deeper cooperation makes better cooperation more difficult as such cooperation has to deal with traditionally domestic issues and impinges therefore, into the domestic realm of both customs territories. This "fallacy of commonality" puts serious constraints on transatlantic trade policy cooperation, as recent disputes between the United States and the EU have shown. Congress, the EU member states and the public at large show a certain recalcitrance in allowing international trade arrangements (like the transatlantic ones) to intervene in issues that affect basic principles of society, health, consumer protection or environment. The deeper trade cooperation goes—i.e. the more successful trade cooperation is—the more the traditional *rationale* of competition will be confronted with other less economic and more societal *rationales*. In the case of EU-U.S. relations, this not only affects the bilateral relationship but also the capacity for the transatlantic partners to provide co-leadership in the WTO. In the latter, there is an additional factor that impedes the deepening of cooperation: the strategic interest of both the United States and the EU to keep their hands free in choosing their partners whenever these are needed to defend their own interests in WTO negotiations (cf. the support of the Cairns countries for the U.S. approach on agriculture in the Uruguay Round).

The confrontation between the political and economic interests of both the United States and the EU to emphasize the importance of the transatlantic relationship on the one hand, and the constraints inherent in this relationship on the other hand, has entailed an interest in creating and preserving a concept that emphasizes the special character of the relationship while keeping the concrete content of this relationship as vague as possible. This concept is the Transatlantic Marketplace.

What has been put in the NTM, were almost all issues that would have been dealt with anyway. In addition, the NTM did not seem to make any concrete difference in the negotiations on these issues in the one and a half-year that the NTM-idea exists. On the contrary, according to some, the problem with the NTM, compared with the Transatlantic Declaration, is that it is precisely too concrete. This makes it possible to measure its real meaning on concrete issues and results, at least until now, in a "low grade." It equally gives the impression, as one European Commission official has put it,[34] that the Transatlantic Agenda is just window-dressing.

The conclusion is then, that it is in the interest of both the EU and the United States to take into account the constraints on the deepening of their mutual relationship and to try to improve this relationship by using a nebulous framework such as the NTM. In its vagueness, the NTM is most instrumental for both the transatlantic trade relationship and for the role of this relationship (in positive and negative terms) in the WTO. As one DG I official has put it:[35] "The NTM contains a long open list of issues that can be dealt with between the United States and the EU. This has the benefit of always providing issues on which we agree. That can be very useful whenever serious conflicts between the two of us erupt."

Otherwise stated, the Transatlantic Marketplace is most instrumental for EU-U.S. relations and for the WTO (i.e. no risk for transatlantic trade bloc formation) if it continues to be the nebulous framework in which a platonic trade relationship—not too close and not too distant from the concrete issues at stake—between the United States and the EU can develop further. In this way, the limited bilateralism that it engenders can remain easily compatible with multilateralism and with the mixed-trade-strategies[36] of the two sides of the Atlantic.

NOTES

The author is assistant professor in International Relations, deptartment Politieke Wetenschappen, Katholieke Universiteit Leuven (Belgium), and visiting scholar of the National Scientific Fund Flanders at the Elliott School of International Affairs, George Washington University, Washington D.C.

1. The European Economic Area was basically an extension of the EU's internal market to the EFTA member states (except Switzerland).

2. Total outward FDI of the United States accounted for $85.1 million in 1995 and $85.6 million in 1996, more than half of which went to Europe (Deloitte Research, 1997: 5–7).

3. Taking into account that the total outward investment from the European Union represents 44 percent of all world outward FDI whereas all EU inward investment represents 37 percent of all world inward FDI (Echinard 1997: 195).

4. Maria Green Cowles has phrased it this way: ". . . virtually all trade disputes between the U.S. and EU affect other countries as well. Every bilateral dispute has the potential to become a multilateral dispute."

5. APEC: Asia-Pacific Economic Cooperation.

6. Abbott claims that one of the major factors behind the U.S. attitude towards NAFTA consisted of ". . . the developments involving the European Union." It was not however, the fear for a Fortress Europe that was decisive, but the fact that the EU would assemble so much bargaining power that it could create a "sufficient risk of imbalance in future trade negotiations with the United States" (1995: 119).

7. For the text of section 301, see Coffey (1993: appendix 6).

8. Recently published figures from a RAND study (published in *The Wall Street Journal Europe*, April 8, 1997) are revealing. In this study it is estimated that the five largest Asian states (China, Japan, India, South Korea, and Indonesia) would account for 45 percent of the world product in 2015. The United States would account for 25 percent (its current share) and the EU for 15 percent. These figures date however from before the Asian crisis that started in the summer of 1997.

9. For a similar American perspective, see Paarlberg (1995: 26 and 29–30).

10. As has been put by the European Commission's Forward Studies Unit (Forward Studies Unit 1995: 15) "Regional projects are now important variables on both sides of the Atlantic, and their development, at varying speeds, will be one of the primary contextual factors shaping Transatlantic relations."

11. It must be mentioned here that especially Mexico saw NAFTA as a way to attract Japanese investment. In practice however, NAFTA attracted Japanese FDI more to the United States than to Mexico (Orme 1996: 265–66).

12. "Brittan Describes EU-U.S. Disparities on Asia Policies," in *Europe in Washington* 6(2) 1996: 1 and 3.

13. One could say that Brittan's assessment of APEC largely points at the big plans to realize a free trade area on a preferential basis between the APEC countries, plans that were largely supported by the United States. In practice however, APEC has become a framework that presses in favor of multilateralism. As Kahler (1995:23) has put is: "A key role of APEC since its inception has been to lobby within the global trading system for multilateral negotiations and multilateral resolution of outstanding trade conflicts."

14. Interview with a member state representative of the Working Party Responsible for Transatlantic Relations, April 1997. This Working Party has been erected by the COREPER in January 1996.

15. AE refers to Agence Europe (English version).

16. Nonetheless, the idea of such an agreement continues to erupt once and a while as has recently been the case with rumors on a EU-U.S. Free Trade Pact (*Financial Times*, February 2, 1998). This last rumor was denied however by the U.S. Trade Representative, Barchefsky, although her words seem to indicate that something may be on the table: "What is clear is that we do not evision a free trade agreement. Our dialogue on this is at the very preliminary level. The breadth and scope and timing of any mutual set of recommendations on this has not been decided. There are no announcements of any sort that are in any sense imminent" (*Bridges Weekly Trade News Digest* 2(4) February 9, 1998). The EEC countries proposed that "substantially all" would mean: "a free-trade area should be considered as having been achieved for substantially all the trade when the volume of liberalized trade reached 80 percent of total trade" (WTO 1995: 824). According to Grossman and Helpman (1995: 681–82) however, "substantially all trade" can be interpreted ". . . to place a limit on the number of industries that can be excluded from an agreement, on the fraction of bilateral trade excluded, on the fraction of total trade excluded, or perhaps on something else" (see also Senti 1994: 145).

17. One can imagine similar problems in other sectors, such as maritime services, audiovisual services, and the subsidization of airplane production.

18. Paarlberg emphasizes the importance of the conflict on the corn-gluten case that affected the Uruguay Round negotiations but that was basically a bilateral

EC-U.S. question (see also Kerremans 1996a) interpreted ". . . to place a limit on the number of industries that can be excluded from an agreement, on the fraction of bilateral trade excluded, on the fraction of total trade excluded, or perhaps on something else" (see also Senti 1994: 145).

19. Where the EU blocked the composition of a WTO-Panel in February 1997 (see *Financial Times*, February 27, 1997).

20. As Lawrence (1996: 7) has put it: "Once tariffs are removed, complex problems remain because of differing regulatory policies among nations."

21. As an example, EuroCommerce claims in its Manifesto of European Commerce that ". . . the rules and disciplines of the WTO should be extended to new areas such as international competition policy and foreign investment." It defends the opinion that "multilateral negotiations on these issues should be started as soon as possible, with the EU taking a clear lead" (EuroCommerce 1996: 23).

22. The reports were the consequence of a joint request by the House Committee on Ways and Means and the Senate Committee on Finance based on section 332(g) of the Tariff Act of 1930 (see USITC 1994: i).

23. As an example, EuroCommerce claims in its Manifesto of European Commerce that ". . . the rules and disciplines of the WTO should be extended to new areas such as international competition policy and foreign investment." It defends the opinion that "multilateral negotiations on these issues should be started as soon as possible, with the EU taking a clear lead" (EuroCommerce 1996: 23).

24. Better known as the MRAs. These negotiations, which at times proved to be very difficult, have been concluded at the end of May 1997.

25. Cf. the reaction of the U.S. states on the Uruguay Round Agreement on Public Procurement and the decision of the Massachussetts Legislature on companies investing in Burma.

26. TRIPs: Trade-Related Intellectual Property Rights.

27. This resulted in, *inter alia*, the adding of a fifth paragraph to article 113 of the Treaty on European Union in June 1997 (see Kerremans 1998: forthcoming).

28. TRIPs: Trade-Related Intellectual Property Rights.

29. Cf. the way in which the FDA develops its own ways of international regulatory cooperation, as indicated by Horton (1997: 34), and the EU-U.S. antitrust cooperation, as indicated by Stark 1997. For a closer look at the role of the USTR in trade policy making, see Noland (1997: 366–67).

30. The analysis of Silverstein on those policies that Congress tries to keep within its own control seems to confirm the point that is made here, namely that "behind the border issues" will increase the interest of Congress in international trade and investment policies. The course of the 1997 attempt by Clinton to get fast-track authority points in that direction. As Silverstein has put it: "Legislators have been most successful in gaining power and influence in those areas of foreign policy that lie clearly within the constitutional authority of Congress, where the problems at hand are reasonably responsive to the tools Congress has its disposal, and where the issues at stake have real and direct connections to the legislator's electoral interests" (Silverstein 1997: 199).

31. Cf. the way in which the FDA develops its own ways of international regulatory cooperation, as indicated by Horton (1997: 34), and the EU-U.S. antitrust cooperation, as indicated by Stark 1997. For a closer look at the role of the USTR in trade policy making, see Noland (1997: 366–67)

32. See for instance the more general argument (e.g. not limited to EU-U.S. relations) of Ruggie (1993: 33) where he explains the continued existence of the multilateral system as created by the United States after the decline of U.S. hegemony by referring to the lack of a strong "domestic divergence" between the major powers of today, especially after the fall of the Berlin Wall and the implosion of the Soviet Union.

33. The same conclusion could be drawn from the recent MRA-negotiations between the United States and the EU. As Ives (1997: 27) has indicated: ". . . the United States and the EU are politically and culturally similar. . . . But, the differences when diving into something like the MRAs tend to emerge much more readily than the similarities. . . . the differences seem to stand out more than our wish to cooperate and find common ground."

34. And article V GATS.

35. Interviews with DG I officials (March–May, 1997).

36. Multilateral, regional, bilateral, and unilateral.

REFERENCES

Bhagwati, J. and D. Irwin. 1987. "The Return of the Reciprocitarians—U.S. Trade Policy Today." *The World Economy* 10(2): 109–30.

Buelens, F. 1997. "After the Presidential Elections: Will the United States 'Open Door' Trade Strategy Continue?" *Intereconomics* 32(1): 41–50.

Caporasso, J. A. 1993. "International Relations Theory and Multilateralism: The Search for Foundations," in *Multilateralism Matters: The Theory and Practice of an Institutional Form*, J.G. Ruggie, ed. New York: Columbia University Press, 51–90.

Coffey, P. 1993. *The EC and the United States*. London: Pinter.

Cuyvers, L. and D. Van den Bulcke. 1996. "Regionalisering van de wereldeconomie: een goede zaak?" *Noord-Zuid Cahier* 21(3): 5–21.

Cuyvers, L. and B. Kerremans. 1997. *Internationale economische organisaties*. Leuven: Garant.

Deloitte and Touche Consulting Group. 1997. *1996 Foreign Direct Investment Trends of U.S. Manufacturers*. New York.

Dent, C.M. 1997. "Economic Relations between the EU and East Asia: Past, Present and Future." *Intereconomics* 32(1): 7–12.

DeVuyst, Y. 1995. *Transatlantic Trade Policy: U.S. Market Opening Strategies*. Pittsburgh, Penn.: University of Pittsburgh, Center for West European Studies Papers, no. 1: 1–20.

Echinard, Y. 1997. "L'Union européenne: régionalisation ou mondialisation?" *Révue du Marché commun*, 406: 192–202.

Economic and Social Committee. 1995. *Information report on Relations between the European Union and the United States (Rapporteur: Mrs. Davison)*, Brussels: CES-Report 978/95.

EuroChambres. 1996. *Non Tariff Barriers in Third Countries, NTBs Encountered by EU Companies Trading with Third Countries: A Survey*. Brussels: EuroChambres: Association of European Chambres of Commerce and Industry.

EuroCommerce. 1996. *The Manifesto of European Commerce*. Brussels: EuroCommerce: The Retail, Wholesale and International Trade Representation to the European Union.

European-American Business Council. 1997. *The United States and Europe, Jobs, Trade, and Investment: A Picture of the Economic Benefits to Each of the 50 States from European Trade and Investment.* Washington, D.C.: European-American Business Council.

———. 1997. *Is the Price Too High? The Cost of U.S. Sanctions Policies.* Washington, D.C.: European-American Business Council, October.

European Commission. 1995. *Communication from the Commission to the Council: Europe and the U.S.: the Way Forward.* Luxembourg: Office for Official Publications, COM (95) 411 final.

———. 1995. *Eleventh Report on United States Barriers to Trade and Investment.* Brussels: Services of the European Commission, May.

———. 1996. *Twelfth Report on U.S. Barriers to Trade and Investment.* Brussels: Services of the European Commission, May.

———. 1997. *1997 Report on the United States Barriers to Trade and Investment.* Brussels: Services of the European Commission, July.

Forward Studies Unit. 1995. *Perspectives on Transatlantic Relations.* Brussels: Forward Studies Unit of the European Commission, November 5.

Goldstein, J. 1993. "Creating the GATT Rules: Politics, Institutions, and American Policy," in *Multilateralism Matters: The Theory and Practice of an Institutional Form,* edited by J.G. Ruggie. New York: Columbia University Press, 201–32.

Green Cowles, M. 1997. "The Limits of Liberalization: Regulatory Cooperation and the New Transatlantic Agenda: A Conference Report" in *The Limits of Liberalization: Regulatory Cooperation and the New Transatlantic Agenda.* Washington, D.C.: American Institute for Contemporary German Studies, The Johns Hopkins University, 1–25.

Grossman G.M. and E. Helpman. 1995. "The Politics of Free-Trade Agreements." *The American Economic Review* 85(4): 667–90.

Herring, R.J. and R.E. Litan. 1995. *Financial Regulation in the Global Economy.* Part of the "Integrating National Economies" Series. Washington, D.C.: The Brookings Institution.

Hoekman, B. and M. Kostecki. 1996. *The Political Economy of the World Trading System: Form GATT to WTO,* Oxford: Oxford U.P.

Horton, L. 1997. "Regulatory Cooperation with the EU on Food, Drugs, and Medical Devices," in *The Limits of Liberalization: Regulatory Cooperation and the New Transatlantic Agenda,* Washington, D.C.: American Institute for Contemporary German Studies, The Johns Hopkins University, 34–39.

Ingersent, K.A., A. J. Rayner and R.C. Hine. 1996. "Ex-Post Evaluation of the Uruguay Round Agriculture Agreement," in *The World Economy* 18(5): 707–28.

Irwin, D.A. 1995. "The GATT in Historical Perspective," in *The American Economic Review* 85(3): 323–28

Ives, R. 1997. "The ABC of MRAs," in *The Limits of Liberalization: Regulatory Cooperation and the New Transatlantic Agenda.* Washington, D.C.: American Institute for Contemporary German Studies, The Johns Hopkins University, 27–33.

Jutte-Rauhut, J. 1995. "NAFTA: Results after One Year," in *Intereconomics* 30(2): 70–76

Kahler, M. 1993. "Multilateralism with Small and Large Numbers," in *Multilateralism Matters: The Theory and Practice of an Institutional Form,* J.G. Ruggie, ed. New York: Columbia University Press, 295–326.

———. 1995. *Regional Futures and Transatlantic Economic Relations.* New York: Council on Foreign Relations Press and ECSA.

Kerremans, B. 1996a. *Besluitvorming en integratie in de externe economische betrekkingen van de Europese Unie*, Brussels: Royal Academy.

———. 1996b. "De bevoegdheden van de Europese Unie op het terrein van de externe economische betrekkingen: een juridische en politieke analyse" in *Tijdschrift voor Bestuurswetenschappen en Publiek Recht* 51(5): 257–70.

———. 1998. "Le systéme économique international et l'Union européenne après Amsterdam: vers une politique commerciale extérieure plus cohérente," in *L'Union Européenne: les grands défis de l'an 2000*, J. Vandamme, ed. Bruxelles, TEPSA, forthcoming.

Kohler-Koch, B. 1996. *The European Union Facing Enlargement: Still a System sui Generis?* Paper prepared for the 1996 ISA-JAIR Joint Convention, Panel on Comparative Regionalism—Asia, Europe, and North America.

Krugman, P. 1997. "What Should Trade Negotiators Negotiate About?" in *Journal of Economic Literature* XXXV(1): 113–20.

Lawrence, R.Z. 1996. *Regionalism, Multilateralism, and Deeper Integration*. Washington, D.C.: The Brookings Institution, "Integrating National Economies" Series.

Martin, L.A. 1993. "The Rational Choice of Multilateralism," in *Multilateralism Matters: The Theory and Practice of an Institutional Form*, J.G. Ruggie, ed. New York: Columbia University Press, 91–121.

Morici, P. 1997. "The United States, World Trade, and the Helms-Burton Act," in *Current History*, February 1997, 87–88.

Noland, N. 1997. "Chasing Phantoms: The Political Economy of USTR," in *International Organization* 51(3): 365–87.

Nunnenkamp, P. 1993. "The World Trading System at the Crossroads." *Aussenwirtschaft* 48(2): 177–201.

Orme, W.A. 1996. *Understanding NAFTA, Mexico, Free Trade and the New America*. Austin: University of Texas Press.

Paarlberg, R.L. 1995. *Leadership Abroad Begins at Home: U.S. Foreign Economic Policy after the Cold War*. Washington, D.C.: The Brookings Institution.

———. 1997. "Agricultural Policy Reform and the Uruguay Round: Synergistic Linkage in a Two-Level Game?" *International Organization* 51(3): 413–44.

Petersmann, E.-U 1994. "Why do Governments need the Uruguay Round Agreements, NAFTA, and the EEA?" *Aussenwirtschaft* 49(1): 31–55.

Peterson, J. 1996. *Europe and America: The Prospects for Partnership*. 2nd edition. London, Routledge, 1996,.

Rich, P.G. 1997. "Latin America and Present U.S. Trade Policy." *The World Economy* 20(1): 87–101.

Rolle, J. 1995. "EU Enlargement and the World Trade System." *European Economic Review* 39(3–4): 467–73.

Ruggie, J.G. 1993. "Multilateralism: The Anatomy of an Institution," in *Multilateralism Matters: The Theory and Practice of an Institutional Form*, J.G. Ruggie, ed. New York: Columbia University Press, 3–47.

Senti, R. 1994. "Die Integration als Gefahr für das GATT." *Aussenwirtschaft* 49(1): 131–50.

Shapiro, M. 1997. "The Problems of Independent Agencies in the United States and the European Union." *Journal of European Public Policy* 4(2): 276–91.

Silverstein, G. 1997. *Imbalance of Powers: Constitutional Interpretation and the Making of American Foreign Policy*. Oxford: Oxford University Press.

Stark, C. 1997. "U.S.-EU Antitrust Cooperation," in *The Limits of Liberalization: Regulatory Cooperation and the New Transatlantic Agenda*. Washington, D.C.: American Institute for Contemporary German Studies, The Johns Hopkins University, 52–56.

U.S. International Trade Commission. 1988–1993. *1992: The Effects of Greater Economic Integration Within the European Community on the United States*, five follow-up reports. Washington, D.C.: USITC.

———. 1994. *1992: Implementing the European Community Single Market: Sixth Follow-up Report*. Washington, D.C.: USITC.

U.S. Trade Representative. 1997. *1997 National Trade Estimate*. Washington, D.C.: USTR, April 1997; available on the Internet.

Vernon, R. 1996. "Passing Through Regionalism: The Transition to Global Markets." *The World Economy* 19(6): 621–33.

VOGEL, D. 1997. *Barriers or Benefits? Regulation in Transatlantic Trade*. Washington, D.C.: The Brookings Institution.

Zelikow P. and Rice, R. 1995. *Germany Unified and Europe Transformed: A Study in Statecraft*. Cambridge, Mass.: Harvard University Press.

4

Trade Conflicts during the Multilateral Negotiations on the International Trade Liberalization

Zdzislaw W. Puslecki

INTRODUCTION

In the contemporary conditions of the economic development, apart from the phenomenon of growing interdependence between various countries which participate in the international economy, in the course of increasing competition in the area of new markets and of capital investments, there arise conflicts which can be mainly observed in trade contacts. They become more intensive during the multilateral negotiations concerning the foreign trade liberalization issues, negotiations conducted on the General Agreement on Tariffs and Trade (GATT), which after the Uruguay Round, has been transformed into the World Trade Organization (WTO).

The decisions taken by the representatives of the governments participating in the negotiations are, to a significant degree, influenced by various lobbies, such as organizations and unions of food producers or other extra-governmental organizations, including trade unions. The problems of mutual relations between the representatives of governments and those extra-governmental organizations which influence the course of multilateral trade negotiations are the subject of the analysis in the undertaken research program, while special attention has been paid to the trade conflicts between the European Union and the United States of America.

The biggest confrontations within GATT involved agricultural problems. They could also be observed in other areas, such as the steel industry, textile industry or in an environmental protection. There are serious conflicts existing between the idea of international trade liberalization and environmental protection since one has to consider what is more profitable—environmental protection or international trade liberalization.

Different positions of the U.S. and the European Community representatives could be observed during the next round of trade negotiations. In recent years (Uruguay Round) the governments of those two economic powers found themselves under significant pressure from food producers who had serious difficulties with the sale of agricultural products surplus in the situation of the limited world market and lower prices. The problems of agriculture protection in the European Union, the protection resulting from the Common Agriculture Policy (CAP) of member countries, were becoming a serious obstacle on the way to the final compromise. However, at the same time, like in previous negotiations, global solutions prevailed, the solutions that had to take into consideration the propositions coming from different regions and different interest groups. The World Trade Organization (WTO) which was established in order to strengthen the global trade system, received broader competence than GATT for implementing the decisions of the Uruguay Round, through the mechanism which allows the insight into the foreign trade policies of individual countries and through participating in the process of decision making in the ministries.[1]

THE ROLE OF GATT/WTO IN SOLVING TRADE CONFLICTS

In the second half of the nineties, the governments of the countries participating in an international economy were still facing the problem of how to define the general principles of world competition. GATT was established in order to solve that problem, and WTO continues this task, although the economic situation nowadays is completely different from that which existed fifty years ago. GATT was formed by 23 countries in Geneva, on October 30, 1947.[2] The organization was established within the Preparatory Committee for Havana Conference which was to deal with the forming of the International Trade Organization (ITO). Meanwhile, that is, until ITO has been established, GATT came into existence on the basis of the protocol that was operative since January 1, 1948. However, ITO has never been formed and therefore GATT, as an international agreement, became a permanent organization.[3] The main task of GATT was aiding and regulating open trade using clear, stable rules based on the free competition principles, and on the mutual balance of rights and duties.

GATT/WTO besides its strong points also has some weaker ones. It deals mainly with the problems connected with lowering customs duties and with eliminating the extra-tariff limits in international trade. Article I of GATT/WTO states that in case of customs duties and customs duty formalities the participating countries will apply the most-nation-nation clause (MFNC). Article V speaks about free transit across the territory of the countries participating in the organizations and exempts the goods in transit from customs duties and from transit fees. Article VII deals with the evaluation of goods for customs duty purposes. It presents common, for all participant countries, principles of evaluating those goods. Article XXIV establishes the principles that should be observed by the countries participating in GATT/WTO in case of forming customs duty unions and free trade zones. This article defines the customs union as forming one customs area out of a few different customs areas and eliminating customs duties within this union, while forming, at the same time, one external customs duty tariff, which actually took place during the process of building the European Union. The free trade zone has been defined as a group of countries, which mutually eliminate customs duties for all the goods or part of them.

The strength of GATT/WTO lies in a great number of international negotiations, negotiations organized under their auspices. Already in the very beginning, that is, in the years 1947–1956, there were four conferences held on tariffs (in Geneva—1947, in Annecy—1949, in Torquay—1951, and once more in Geneva—1956), during which the problems of international trade liberalization were discussed. The initiator was the United States, the country which while applying high customs barriers by lowering them, wanted to open the way for their own exports. These initial talks did not bring any significant changes into the tariff order operative at the time. Neither did they lead to a significant decrease in customs duty rates. At the same time, many countries, trying to strengthen their own position in tariff negotiations, began to modernize and change both tariffs and customs laws. In the years 1950–1959 a number of western European countries, the United States and Japan adapted them to their own needs.

During the next few decades there were four further rounds of trade negotiations (Dillon Round, Kennedy Round, Tokyo Round and Uruguay Round). So far, there were eight of those rounds held. Due to numerous mutual adjustments during the four consecutive and most important rounds, significant areas of world trade have been liberalized and the means for further liberalization expansion have been established. The decisions of the last one—the Uruguay Round—have not been implemented in full yet. However, three years after its completion, we can state that this round prevented us from a few potentially destructive conflicts in the trade area and helped to achieve further liberalization in trading agricultural products and services.

GATT/WTO have also worked out a legal system of solving conflicts and the rules for trade with the principle of bigger openness. The organization, by prohibiting the discrimination of partners during the negotiations, was trying to protect the weaker against the stronger imposing their will on them. All the co-signatories of GATT had, theoretically, equal status (unlike in Bretton Woods institutions), although in the past it was the stronger that defined the rules and set conditions during the negotiations.[4]

So far, the limited mandate of GATT/WTO was its main weakness. The organizations did not deal with all the goods, such as, for instance, energy raw materials. Also trading in services, although their share in the trade turnover reached 20 percent of is overall value, could be found, for the first time, in the program of the Uruguay Round. Another limitation for GATT/WTO could be observed in the character of negotiation processes. One of the basic problems resulted from the fact that negotiations were based on the principle of mutuality, and this, in turn, on the assumption that granting broader access to imports is a concession that is also expected from the other parties. This led to a certain atmosphere, in which the protectionistic tendencies were being overcome more slowly and there were problems with solving the trade conflicts. In spite of all those problems and interminable negotiations (the Uruguay Round, for example, lasted for almost ten years), the participants usually managed to reach a compromise and solutions favorable for the development of international trade.

PROTECTIONIST PRESSURES EXERTED BY THE PRODUCERS AND URBANIZED LABOR FORCE (TRADE UNIONS)

Causes of Protectionistic Pressure

The branches demanding protection in the western industrialized countries justify their demands saying that they cannot compete with the suppliers from developing countries because of lower wages paid in those other countries. Higher competitiveness of those threatened goods could be obtained in industrialized countries by lower prices, which, in consequence, could lead to lower incomes of production employees and lower profits for owners. Whole branches and individual firms suffering from the foreign competition demand the introduction of import restrictions, which would allow to keep the price of home products on the same level, and, at the same time, to keep jobs and incomes intact. If the magnitude of protection is big enough, the home industry not only is able to survive but it can even develop.

The comparison of income units in the industries threatened by competition and demanding protection, and in the corresponding branches in developing countries, shows a significant gap between their levels, which obviously influences the competitiveness of the relevant goods. Such a comparison, however, does not take into account the fact that unit individual incomes do not constitute the only element defining the competitiveness of goods, and their prices. The wages in western industrialized countries, to a significant degree, are higher because the efficiency of work there is higher, when compared with less developed countries. The difference in the levels of efficiency neutralize, to a certain extent, that influence which those differences in wages exert on the system of comparative benefits between countries. If that were not so, it would be rather difficult to explain why the United States is a major exporter of textiles, in spite of the fact that the wages in the American textile industry are higher than those in the analogical industry of such important textile goods producers as South Korea, Taiwan or Hong Kong.

The relative benefits of the given branch or product are defined mainly by the relation between the increase of wages and the increase of work efficiency in that branch or product. As long as the work efficiency growth rate is higher than wage increase rate, a given branch can, assuming it was competitive at the starting point, remain competitive in relation to foreign suppliers.[5] In that situation, however, the gap between wages in different branches of the national economy will become broader. This does not necessarily have to lead to the absolute drop of wages in the branches competing with imports. As long as work efficiency in a given branch grows, the wages can also grow.

Since there are different possibilities of obtaining work efficiency increase in different areas of economic activity, there are also different reasons for increasing the level of wages. The branches that compete with imports are usually characterized by a well developed technology, relatively slow work efficiency growth, they do not tend to accept the deepening gap between wages, because this would make their position weaker in relation to those branches that are most efficient and most dynamic. The condition necessary to keep a stable relation of wages in relation to the most efficient branches could then be found in lower employment. However, trade unions, a pressure group, strongly oppose such a solution. In order to achieve both goals, that is, keeping a stable gap between wages and an absolute level of employment, it is necessary to apply trade protection.

We can see from the above that in our present situation protectionism results not only from the endeavors to stop the decrease of incomes but is also the result of protecting employment and higher wages for the most efficient producers. So, this protection is supposed to save jobs and assure higher incomes than those that are defined by the general trends in work efficiency growth.[6]

Protection, however, cannot be applied indefinitely because it would cause a permanent gap between wages. It would also mean a further existence of all those unprofitable results that accompany permanent aiding of inefficient branches, that is, lowering the efficiency in co-operating branches, higher costs for consumers, etc. A permanent protection of those production branches which are threatened by the outside competition could also lead to a weakening supply of labor force for more dynamic branches.[7] Potential employees would stay in inefficient branches and they would not be motivated to move to more efficient branches, because the wages would not properly reflect the difference in inefficiency between those branches.[8]

It is therefore necessary, in order to shorten the protection period, to introduce, as quickly as possible, technological innovations into the production processes and thus to cause the fastest efficiency growth in the branches threatened by foreign competition. At the same time it would be advisable to conduct schooling and training for the employees so they could hold jobs requiring higher qualifications. All this should be accompanied by the actions that would result in more innovative products, in other words, new products that had not existed in the market before. If big enterprises were not able to show proper flexibility in introducing the said changes, it would be advisable to form smaller enterprises, more energetic and dynamic, basing their production on the newest achievements in the research and developments (RandD) sphere, that could consequently employ more labor force and assure higher wages than the previously existing, bigger firms. That bigger firm, on the other hand, could, by applying automation and robotics, increase its efficiency and therefore the wages for those who stayed employed. Then, any further protection would not be necessary.

The second reason for demanding trade protection, in order to protect employment and incomes, is the imports growth.[9] It is being pointed out that in recent years the rate of imports was so high that it made very difficult, or impossible, to adapt the economy to new conditions. According to this conception a fast imports growth brought a number of bad results for western industrialized countries, it especially caused higher unemployment. To aid this argument most often the growth of so-called imports penetration coefficient, that is, the share of imports in home consumption of a given product, is being quoted.[10]

One should notice, however, that changes in imports are not the only factor causing the change of conditions in which producers act, and causing the adaptation problems associated with those conditions. There are also other factors, such as changes in work efficiency, changes in production technology, in the structures and dynamics of demand, etc. Quite often the changes caused by imports are even smaller than those which are caused by the work efficiency growth.[11] The level of imports penetration index depends also on a number of factors of natural character, that is, on a demographic factor, the structure of demand, and so on. Its growth may mean, for instance, that the specialization of a given country is growing. Thus, the argument that any imports growth influences unfavorably the situation on a labor market, given the above, is not so strong. Nevertheless, in the situation of structural changes and adaptation problems, it was treated very seriously and was taken into account when the decisions about the introduction of temporary trade protection were being taken.

Considering the argument about import growth as the basis for the application of temporary trade protection, one has to add that sometimes some production branches profit from foreign trade exchange while others lose because of it. This asymmetry between profits and losses connected with the foreign trade exchange may be the basis for the introduction of temporary protectionistic means in order to weaken or spread in time the costs connected with the adaptation to the situation of bigger imports. From the point of view of protected producers they are undoubtedly more comfortable than costly and not quite so certain technological and organizational adaptations, requalifying the employees, etc., but when they assume a permanent character their cost for the whole national economy becomes significant.

One should also stress here that protectionism, resulting from the pressures exerted by trade unions, is often applied in order to assure employment and the required level of income in inefficient branches. The tendency to keep both jobs and the existing levels of wages in economy, that is, blocking the drop of incomes in comparison with more efficient production branches, is, in the opinion of many economists, the leading motivation of contemporary trade protectionism in western industrialized countries. W. M. Corden—one of the major theoreticians of contemporary trade policy—defined that motivation as "the function of the conservative social welfare."[12] In W. M. Corden's opinion a permanent trade protectionism in inefficient areas has no economic basis. Long lasting protectionism practices, in declining production branches, lead to lower economic effectiveness, fuel inflation and may cause other negative phenomena in economy. However, as Corden states, there are very few countries that are resistant to the application of protectionism.

The efficiency of protectionism, as the means of increasing employment, is doubtful also because it stimulates the employment growth, especially through the expansion of those branches that compete with import production and not those branches which produce goods for export. The instruments applied in the area of prices and in the area of currency exchange rates may bring better results.[13] Devaluation, for example, causes the increase of home prices for foreign goods (similarly to customs duties), but it also lowers the price of exported goods, which allows it to increase employment in pro-export production. The negative side of protectionism can also be seen in that by lowering the turnover of international trade exchange, it causes unemployment on the partners' side.

In order to keep a given income structure, it is much better, in Corden's opinion, to apply a direct compensation of incomes instead of protectionism. Instead of customs duties and extra-tariff means, which influence the trade exchange, one can use, for instance production subsidies.[14] Although they also are a form of aid for less efficient production branches, they are considered to be the means of adaptation aid, because foreign trade is not directly influenced by them.

The Role of Trade Unions in Different Political Systems

The role of trade unions in different political systems may be, to a high degree, different. In authoritarian systems it is, as a rule, smaller than in democratic systems. It would seem that if protectionistic pressure on the part of trade unions is weaker, the situation for economic growth is much better. Following that line of reasoning we could come to the conclusion that the authoritarian system is better for the effectiveness of the labor market. The examples of Chile, South Korea, Singapore and Turkey from the seventies and early eighties could confirm that point of view. In many cases during those two decades the authoritarian regimes persecuted trade unions and put restrictions on basic labor rights. During that period of oppression, South Korea, Singapore and Turkey experienced a spectacular growth in the sector of processing industry and in the growth of demand for labor. Growing profits and the demand for labor in a processing industry, caused a general growth of prosperity of the employed. Although similar results were not noted immediately during the authoritarian phase of development in Chile, a number of observers express the opinion that the reforms introduced at that time helped to reorganize Chilean economy in the nineties.[15]

The application of democratic rules, on the other hand, may lead to lower productivity of the labor force. In a number of years, different democracies had to use significant financial resources for the employment of those who belonged to trade unions.

A different point of view says that government legislation concerning the labor market may be applied more effectively in an authoritarian system than in a democratic one. The authoritarian regimes often make use of individual interests of given circles. In most democratic countries there is no broad enough basis that would allow labor market policy for gaining the support from pressure groups, the urbanized labor marked elite included. The major difference between authoritarian and democratic regimes lies in the level of the outside influence. In a well functioning democracy, the outside opinions are also taken into account and there occur some limitations that come from the outside, which restricts the achievements of given groups of interest. In a dictatorship, a government cares only that those groups are not too strong.[16]

There are, however, a number of democracies among the industrialized countries where an effective labor market exists. There are also a number of democracies with effective labor market policy among the developing countries. Similarly, in the countries in which the transformation from the authoritarian regime towards a democracy is taking place, avoiding unfavorable phenomena on a labor market is often a priority. For example, the Chilean government moved towards democracy and to free trade unions without home income growth. The end of oppression in South Korea, in 1987, started the partnership relations in full of conflicts industry.[17]

Analytical Construct

It is worth considering which of the two points of view presented above should be given support, that is, which of them is the proper one. The analysis of that problem may be based on the Grossman and Helpman model.[18] This model describes economic development on the basis of two sectors—urbanized, regulated processing sector, and rural, unregulated agricultural sector. The protection of the labor market, especially of minimum wages, is usually applied in order to bring the benefits for the employees of the regulated sector, since the sector of unregulated employees does not come under the legislation concerning the labor market.

The sector of regulated employees, and also the owners, demand from the government that it leads an economic policy that is favorable to them. The employed demand high minimum wages, while capitalists demand high profits. Both groups demand the restrictions on the degree of economy openness. In a closed economy, higher market minimum wages and higher profits are usually connected with higher prices for home consumers, and this is not easy when those consumers are free to buy the substitutes in the form of imported goods. Thus, incomes in an economy may be created by protection and later divided among the employees of the regulated sector and the capitalists, although sometimes the government itself takes a part of those incomes.[19]

A government conducting an economic policy takes into account a number of factors. Firstly, it has to decide the degree of obtaining the resources, that is, how much from those resources it wants to obtain. Hence the importance of investments and of future economic growth, and also of defining the possibilities for keeping the power it is currently holding. Secondly, the government should define the scale of support from each of the pressure groups that can influence the situation. The position and importance of each group for the development of political processes should be considered. For example, in the country where the regulated labor market is divided, and politically weak, only the capitalists may have a deciding voice in political processes. And the contrary also happens—in the societies where the labor market is organized, it may play the important role in mobilizing voters.

How can we recognize the type of power, the type of rule? First of all, we should investigate what level of resources a given government is going to achieve. If an authoritarian government is more or less corrupted than a democratic one, it will be creating the income, to a bigger or lesser degree, through protectionism. It will also appropriate some part of that income. Secondly, a given type of government may remain under the influence of different pressure groups. If an authoritarian government is trying, to some extent, to subordinate special pressure groups including the regulated labor sector, it will be, to some extent, generating incomes through protection and it will be turning over some part of them to those special pressure groups.

The above arguments show that the policy is defined by political factors (including the type of the government and the burdens resulting from obligations towards employees and capitalists), and by economical factors (wages, prices, the structure of production and consumption). On the basis of the present discussion, we can present two equations, one pertaining to the level of protection, and the second pertaining to the national economy and deformation of wages.

1) $\pi = f(e, l, k, R)$
2) $\varphi = f_1(\pi, e, l, k, R)$,

The level of protection (π) depends on the economic parameters (e), a relative political importance of urbanized employees and capitalists (l and k, respectively), and on the type of the government (R). Deformation of wages is, on the other hand, the function of π and of e, l, k and R. In case of a small economy, economic parameters that can influence π and φ include flexible consumer and producer prices, demand flexibility, wages and the demand for labor force, and also the price of goods on an international market.

One can expect, a priori, that the growth of π is dependent on l and k. If interest groups become stronger, the pressure to form incomes based on protectionism may become stronger. The influence of R, that is, the influence of a political authoritarianism on the level of protectionism, that is, π, depends on the fact whether the opinion, that the level of protectionism depends on the effects of democratization, is correct. It is also thought that the increase of the deformation of wages depends on π and l, while its decrease depends on k. As long as the incomes are obtained from trade protections, those incomes can be handed over to urbanized employees. An important problem in the case of an urbanized labor force as an interest group with growing strength is the fact that urbanized employees may gain a big share in the division of incomes but the growth of political importance of the capitalists may cause that the shared incomes, handed over to the labor force in regulated sectors of economy will become smaller.[20]

There is no doubt that it is easier for wealthy rather than poor societies to choose democracy.[21] Since those wealthier societies at the same time have a tendency to a bigger openness, the direction of cause-result events may run from the openness of society to the political system, and not, as was suggested earlier, in the opposite direction. The research showed also that the level of education plays an important role in this respect. The countries with a higher level of education of labor force are more open.

On the basis of earlier considerations, one can come to the conclusion that authoritarian systems have a tendency towards a broader application of protectionism than democratic systems, and that, in turn, the trade restrictions accompany significant deformations of wages on the labor market. This opinion may be justified on the basis of the observations of the situation in a number of countries in the seventies, eighties and nineties.

Freedom of association is one of the elements of good management and the necessary condition for development. The authoritarian governments do not respect, however, the freedom of association, which is connected with the policy of trade restrictions and with the deformations on the labor markets. One cannot state, however, that improper or ineffective policy on the labor market belonged exclusively to authoritarian regimes or that authoritarianism automatically generates this kind of policy. There are a number of examples of authoritarian countries that do not conduct policies of that kind. The works of such authors as Fields[22] or Freeman[23] show that the repression against the labor force is not necessary, if one wants to achieve a required economic growth.

Finally, it should be pointed out that there exists a close relation between democracy and economic growth. There are well known examples of open societies that stimulate economic growth. This is true mainly in the case of highly developed and strongly urbanized countries. In the countries with a developed democracy, the pressure groups have a bigger opportunity for acting. The research shows that the presence of trade unions helps to accelerate economic reforms.[24] The benefits resulting from the liberalization of international trade are bigger when the trade unions exist in the sector of the economy under protection. The growth of import abilities leads to the decrease of wage pressures, and when the trade unions agree to that, such a situation allows for a better allocation of labor force in the economy. This is true both in the case of active and passive trade unions, although the effects are better in the case of active trade unions.

The Influence of Trade Unions on the Course of Trade Negotiations within GATT

The trade unions active on an urbanized labor market had a significant influence on the decisions of governments, in the course of multilateral trade negotiations within GATT. It was especially evident in the negotiations on lowering customs duties and extra-tariff means in steel, shipbuilding, textile and clothing industries, and in coal mining. In the so-called "sensitive" industries, which, for example, in the European Union were under special trade protection, the position of trade unions was very strong.[25]

From the proposal of a textile agreement, which is an element of negotiations within the Uruguay Round, it was evident that a number, or probably most, restrictions in an international textile and clothing trading (existing on the basis of MFA decisions) will not be abolished before the year 2003.[26] Taking into account a possibility of conflicts in that area, the European Union and the United States proposed, for the reduction of restrictions, a transitional period of 10 to 15 years. Major textile and clothing experts from developing and from new industrialized countries express the opinion that 6,5 years would be enough for that purpose. This caused some intensification of the conflict between the United States and the European Union.[27]

The negotiating group involved in textile and clothing trade negotiations made the completion of all the negotiations within the round a condition of implementing the textile agreement. The discrepancies in opinions between the participants of the round show, however, that this cannot be expected soon. Meanwhile, according to the planned schedule of a 10-year liberalization program of the textile trade, the first partial elimination of import quotas was supposed to take place in the importing countries on January 1, 1993. In that situation this date did not seem at all certain.

The proposal of the textile agreement included also many decisions that favored the importers, which was criticized strongly by the developing exporting countries. This referred, among others, to the clause protecting the importing countries against the sudden growth of imports from the countries of the Third World. This clause allowed introducing new import quotas on the goods that earlier had not been regulated. According to the proposition, the importing countries could also decide which goods were to be subjected to the rules of the free trade (in accordance with GATT rules), regardless of whether they are regulated or not. In the opinion of 22 developing countries, major textile exporters and members of the International Textile and Clothing Bureau (ITCB), this meant that the current restrictions would not be eliminated before the year 2000. The importing countries would "liberalize" first of all the goods not regulated by the MFA decisions, the goods that constitute about one third of the imports.

During the Uruguay Round the conflict between the United States and the European Union involved also the steel industry, the industry which suffered serious development troubles. For a number of years the demand for steel was going down, old steel mills were being liquidated and the unprofitable divisions of steel mills were being closed down. In the first half of 1992, the six largest American steel companies lost a total of about $500 million, while the European steel giant—French Usinor-Sacilor—lost almost $600 million. Japan reduced the employment in steel industry by 10 percent, while the production of steel dropped from 110 million tons in 1991, to less than 100 million tons in 1992. Although the demand for steel products in the United States, Western Europe and Japan dropped, and the production was accordingly reduced, still the production of steel was by 15 percent bigger than required by the market.

The worsening condition of the American steel industry impelled the representatives of that industry to start, in the first half of 1992, the anti-dumping procedures and the actions against the subsidies applied by the European exporters of steel bars and rolled steel, among others against Usinor-Sacilor, and against another French company Ascométal, which was considered by the European Union to be "the steel war." The European Commission expressed regret over that new interventionist offensive on the steel market, especially when the United States broke the well going negotiations within the Uruguay Round, the negotiations on the multilateral agreement on steel products trade.

In the course of the last Uruguay Round, there arose also conflicts involving the area of services, especially banking. Multilateral negotiations on trading services are very complicated considering the complexity of exchange in that field. So far, there is no one explicit theory of service exchange, which is the result of the great variety of forms of services. The thesis saying that the liberalization of service exchange would bring similar benefits as a free good exchange has not been convincingly proved yet. Therefore, it is not clear whether those classic GATT norms, such as lack of discrimination, or mutual benefits, could be applied in exchanging services. The situation would become even more complicated in the case of the detailed rules, especially if we consider the fact that even the identification of the barriers is a very complex task. Thus, the negotiations can be conducted in a selective way, only in those service sectors in which the potential benefits from the liberalization of exchange are most obvious.[28] Similarly, in the case of negotiations on trading in latest technologies, most interested are the highly developed countries, the European Union included. This is the result of a similar level of their development, of their great experience in negotiating, and of the reluctance of the less developed countries to participate in these types of negotiations.

During the Uruguay Round the United States accused the European Union that 75 percent of financial and telecommunication services in their mutual exchange was inadmissible, and that the European Union drew significant profits out of this exchange.[29] The United States justified their position in this respect with the incapacity to satisfy the offers of other parties, especially those from the developing countries. At the same time, they hinted that they could change their position in this matter. The European Union, however, always insisted on a global character of negotiations, and had no guarantees that they would be conducted in this way. Trade unions, to a significant extent, were influencing the position of the European Union. That position in some cases could accelerate and in others retard the course of negotiations on the liberalization of international trade.

PRESSURE EXERTED BY FOOD PRODUCERS ON THE POSITION OF GOVERNMENTS IN MAJOR TRADE CONFLICTS

The biggest conflicts between the United States and the European Union within GATT/WTO were caused by agricultural problems. The first major confrontation is remembered under the name of a "chicken war." It was a serious encounter between foreign economic interests of the United States and the European Union. It broke immediately after the fifth multilateral trade negotiations within GATT on lowering customs duties, known under the name of the Dillon Round. The initiator of those talks, which started in 1960, that is, two years after the EEC had been established, was the government of the United States.

The trade negotiations during the Dillon Round were a direct attack of the United States against the customs barriers of the European Economic Community. A common European Community customs tariff was just being introduced, and the U.S. government, which was under the pressure of food producers, hoped to weaken its effects. The negotiations were long and difficult. They were finished in March 1962 with a temporary agreement between the United States and the EEC, the agreement which lowered the customs duties of the EU by 20 percent on an average, and those of the United States by 8 percent.

The conflict between the United States and the European Community intensified just before the beginning of the Uruguay Round of GATT.[30] The reason for that was the announcement of the U.S. government of the introduction of 200 percent customs duty on agricultural products imported from the EEC. The admission at that time of Spain and Portugal to the EEC, which caused the problems for American grain exports to those countries, was a direct reason of the conflict. In the spring of 1986, the Americans threatened retaliation, if the Community did not compensate for the losses in the Iberian Peninsula, which they counted as $400 million a year. Although the Community did not treat those demands as justified, no mutual restrictions followed, because the Community complied to the requests and guaranteed, temporarily, the same level of American cereal sales on its territory.

The conflict appeared again in the end of 1986, when that temporary agreement expired, and the efforts for a permanent compromise did not bring positive results.[31] Both the United States the EEC found themselves, at that time, on the brink of the new trade war. The governments of the two economic powers were under very strong pressure from food producers, who had problems with the sale of agricultural product surpluses in the situation of the shrinking world market and lower prices. One should note, however, that previous conflicts between the EEC and the United States were always ended with a compromise, although the European side had to agree to bigger concessions. That conflict between the United States and the EEC showed also the necessity of convening the Uruguay Round.

So far, a significant liberalization in agricultural products trading has not been achieved. Presently, the most intensive protectionism in this area exists in the countries of the EU, where the internal market is protected by variable compensatory fees and intervention purchases, financed from the Union budget. Common agricultural policy, although frequently criticized, is often treated as the biggest achievement in the integration of the EU, and it brings benefits for the net exporters of agricultural products (especially France). High prices of agricultural products within the Union create incentives and stimulate production, which results in the production surpluses that have to be sold on the world market. This, in turn, reduces the world prices, which is against the economic interests of major food exporters, such as: the United States, Canada, New Zealand, Australia, Argentina. The major net importers of food, on the other hand, benefit from that situation.

The classic methods of trade liberalization, that is, through the reduction of customs duties, in the case of agricultural products, have little influence, since the internal markets are protected with extra-tariff means, and exports are subsidized. The only solution, in this situation, may lie in a coordinated reduction of subsidies for agriculture in developed countries. This is linked with the relative reduction of prices for intervention purchases in the EU, and with limiting the production using the direct budget subsidies (mainly in the United States). For social and political reasons, this solution, proposed already during the Kennedy Round, is not popular among western, industrialized countries. It would lead to the bankruptcy of many small farms, causing, temporarily, higher unemployment, and perhaps also a lack of food independence in the EU. The countries that benefit from the common agricultural policy are also against such a solution. However, the application of harder and harder budget restrictions show that this could be the right solution. Those restrictions are being felt painfully in the EU countries, where 3/4 of the budget is spent for financing the common agricultural policy, and in the United States which has a serious budget deficit. This solution is also attractive when we consider a relatively low level of world prices for major agricultural products, which makes the intervention policy more costly. [32]

The problem of liberalization of agricultural products trading is linked to the problem of subsidy application. According to the GATT decisions (Art. XVI), exports of the agricultural products, as so-called basic goods, can be subsidized, if this fact does not interfere with the economic interests of other participants of the agreement. Actually, subsidizing exports of agricultural products may have many different forms, starting with a direct subsidy, through variable compensatory fees, and finally through various forms of government guarantees and preferential credits. In the ministers' declaration we read only about a better discipline among the members of GATT. The total prohibition of subsidies would be the simplest course, but it does not seem to be realistic.

The problem of protection of agriculture by the European Union, resulting from the common agricultural policy that had been conducted for years, was considered, during the Uruguay Round to be the main reason of the fact that the talks were so difficult. Major food exporters that participated in negotiations decided to force the Union to change its attitude towards agricultural problems. The United States and the group of fourteen biggest exporters of agricultural products, under the name of Cairns,[33] for a certain time were trying to lower the level of interventionism in the agricultural sector of the EU.[34] At the same time, the final general outcome of the round was to depend on satisfying that demand. The European Union was also lagging with its proposals, concerning trading in agricultural products, behind the United States and the Cairns Group. The difference of opinions was difficult to overcome, since the agricultural sector remained the only negotiated sphere in which the proposals of GATT partners on liberalization could be precisely quantified. That was also a reason why this problem could be so openly discussed.[35]

The disputes, within GATT, between the United States and the European Union on agricultural problems, especially on oleiferous seeds, could be, this time, called "the fat war." This conflict was much more serious then previous "trade wars" between the United States and the EU. Its solution could, in the future, be very important for the countries of Central and Eastern Europe.

In an effort to limit the EU budget expense for subsidizing agricultural products, it was decided, among other things, that in the case of fats, the money will be transferred from the processing sector to the production sector. Instead of compensating the industry for higher costs of purchasing more expensive, local raw materials (the prices paid to the growers of rape or sunflower in the EU are much higher than the world prices), it was decided that subsidies would go directly to farmers, and the size of farms was to be the basis for calculations. At the same time, the Union authorities disclosed that they would be trying to reduce gradually those expenses by reducing guaranteed prices.[36]

The conflicts between the United States and the European Union, arising as a result of the introduction by the EU of new rules in agricultural policy concerning oleiferous plants, caused that the United States wanted to finish the negotiations on subsidizing the agricultural exports, within the Uruguay Round, as quickly as possible. The United States was afraid that they would have to spend more money for subsidizing the exports, if they wanted to compete successfully with the EU on the world market. They pointed out the fact that the EU spends at least $12 billion on export subsidies, while the United States not more than $1 billion.

In the middle of 1992, the member countries of the EU agreed to a packet of basic changes in the common agricultural policy, the policy that for the last decades had been the most influential factor in the agricultural development of the European Union. The most important decision was the consent to reduce by one third, during three years, the guaranteed prices for cereal producers. In 1992 they reached 155 ECU for one ton, and in 1993, 1994 and 1995, 130, 120 and 110 ECU for one ton, respectively.[37] The cereals, throughout the food channel were influencing the profitability, and the volume, of meat and milk production. Farmers received compensation for their losses, on the condition that they exclude the growth of cereals from the 15 percent of their land.[38]

This reform was the first in which the attempt was made to eliminate the structural surpluses, the surpluses that had been disorganizing the EU agricultural market and international trade for many years. It is worth pointing out here that the direct result of announced changes in the agricultural policy of the EU might not be favorable for Poland and other countries of Central and Eastern Europe. The simplest form of compensation for farmers is usually the restrictions for the suppliers from abroad. The agricultural lobby in France is especially active in this area. As a result of its activity and the pressure exerted on the government the agricultural goods from abroad have been successfully blocked from the EU market. The position taken by that agricultural lobby influenced also the position of the EU representatives in the debates on the agricultural questions during the multilateral trade negotiations within GATT.

In spite of the trade conflicts, most clearly visible in the United States—the EU relations, all the countries participating in the international trade were interested in the successful completion of the Uruguay Round. The reduction or the elimination of trade restrictions stimulates significantly the growth of the world trade exchange, while the foreign trade, in turn, is an important factor of the economic growth of individual countries.

Mutual consultations between the representatives of the European Union and the United States resulted, on November 20, 1992, in an agreement (known as Blair House agreement) on the reduction of production of oleiferous plants by the European farmers. Concessions made by both sides prevented a transatlantic trade war. According to the agreement the Union would reduce the subsidies for farmers by 21 percent, and, during the following years, it will reduce by 36 percent the subsidies for the exports of agricultural goods. Also the size of the area where oleiferous plants were grown would be reduced, which would reduce their production from 13 million tons annually to the maximum of 9.7 million tons.[39]

This compromise was considered to be of historical significance.[40] And not only because it helped to avoid a trade war. The success was seen in the resumption of the talks on the international trade liberation during the GATT Uruguay Round. The Uruguay Round itself was finished on December 15, 1993, after seven years of negotiations, with the agreement on lowering the customs duties for industrial goods by 1/3 on an average, to 3 percent, and with establishing the World Trade Organization (WTO) which was to replace GATT. The agreement on ending the Uruguay Round was ratified by 117 countries on April 15th in Marrakech, Morocco, and became operative on January 1st of 1995.

There followed a reduction of trade protection in the area of industrial products, further significant reduction of customs tariffs, decisions to consider important extra-tariff barriers—such as voluntary exports reduction (VER) or multilateral textile agreements—as illegal. In spite of this success, it is worth noticing that individual countries can still use, for protection purposes, antidumping procedures and the mechanism of protection clauses, the rules of which were not significantly changed during the Uruguay Round. Notable successes were reached, however, in the area of agricultural goods and services trading. In case of agricultural goods it was agreed that the reduction of trade protection will result from the reduction of extra-tariff means and from substituting them with customs duties.[41] Thus, there was a renaissance of customs duties and once more they became most important for trade protection.

The successful results of negotiations will certainly lead to the growth of the international trade and will help to overcome the development difficulties of the world market participants. The Uruguay Round will bring the growth of the global income by $200 billion annually, starting with 1995.

It is estimated that in 2005 the value of world trade will grow by $230 billion. So, the agreement will result in more investments, more jobs and higher incomes as the function of economic growth. The economic powers will benefit most, however the countries of Central and Eastern Europe, and the developing countries, will get easier access to new markets for their commodities.

CONFLICTS BETWEEN INTERNATIONAL TRADE LIBERALIZATION AND ENVIRONMENTAL PROTECTION

The tendencies to liberalize international trade often stand in clear conflict with the protection of the natural environment which, during the intensification of production, found itself in the center of attention. The process of pollution was one of the negative results of scientific-technological revolution. Water and air pollution in many industrialized countries has reached such dimensions that it threatens the health of the population, and, in the near future, may become an obstacle for reproduction. Many countries introduced special legal regulations in order to protect the environment against pollution. Ecological organizations of different types were established, and also pressure groups, especially in industrialized countries, interested in the use of trade restrictions by governments for protection of the environment.

The pressure groups acting for natural environment protection see the trade policy in two aspects: as the way of improvement the standards of environmental protection in individual countries and over their borders, and as the instrument for persuading those countries to sign the international agreements on environmental protection. The imports restrictions against the producers coming from the countries with low standards of environmental protection may lead to the improvement of production standards by the local companies resulting from fighting with low competitiveness, and from the attempts to compete with foreign firms.[42]

The application, in trade policy, of discriminating means in relation to the environment, which happened in the countries of western Europe, is in accordance with Article XX of GATT, and it testifies to the fact that trade barriers are used for the protection of the environment. Thus, the activities related to environmental protection are in conflict with the tendencies leading to international trade liberation, and with higher investments. From the theoretical point of view, we cannot say that trade liberalization may help environmental protection, especially when serious steps have to be taken in order to protect this environment against further degradation.[43] On the other hand, when some government finds itself in a difficult situation, the trade reforms will be much more advantageous for that government than the actions in the environmental protection area.[44] That is why the pressure groups connected with environmental protection are against international trade liberalization.

The actions of those groups on GATT/WTO forum, and their regional activity against the reduction of trade barriers, have three reasons: (1) free trade means the growth of production and income, which, in turn, leads to the degradation of the environment, (2) free trade and growing investments cause the growth of transport activity and encourage companies to transfer the production to the countries with low ecological standards, which from the environmental point of view is wrong, 3) freedom for foreign investments discourage local companies to develop the technologies favorable for environmental protection.[45] The problems of environmental protection, considering their antagonistic nature in relation to the liberalization of international trade, were noticed by GATT at the beginning of the seventies. A Working Group on Environmental Measures and International Trade was formed. However, its first meeting took place as late as 1991. Since then, the meetings of the group members have been more frequent, and it should be pointed out here that a number of Uruguay Round agreements included the clauses on environmental protection.

The question of reaching some form of an agreement between the problems of international trade liberalization and the protection of the natural environment became an important task for the World Trade Organization (WTO), which continues the activities of GATT. Managing the work on trade and environmental protection can be found in a preamble to an agreement on establishing a new trade organization. The program of WTO activities, worked out in the final stage of the Uruguay Round included:

- The relations between the means used in trade and in environmental protection.
- The relations between multilateral trade systems and the environmental protection means, applied for protection of the environment.
- The influence of the effects of environmental protection on the liberalization of international trade.

- The relations between the mechanisms leading to compromises within WTO and within the multilateral agreements on environmental protection.[46]

Reaching the effective agreements on international trade liberalization and on environmental protection is considered to be both a very difficult and a very delicate question. The problems of environmental protection have become most important issues. Therefore, it is evident that the international market has to take them into account. The key problem is to make a proper choice: is the introduction of restrictions on international trade the best solution, or will the benefits from environmental protection (as applied by a multilateral trade system) be higher than the costs?

NOTES

1. W. Martin and L. A. Winters, "The Uruguay Round: Widening and Deepening the World Trading Systems." *World Bank Policy Research Bulletin* 6(5) November–December 1995: 1.

2. See Z. W. Puślecki, *Ochrona Handlowa Wspólnoty Europejskiej* (Poznań: The European Community Trade Protection, 1994), 161.

3. See A. Dunkel, "Das GATT—Hüter des globalen Wettbewerbs, Die Herausforderung an die Uruguay—Runde," *Neue Z¸rcher Zeitung*, no. 352, October 31, 1987, GATT–Information, 1393, Geneva 1986.

4. *Nasze swiatowe podwórko* (Our world backyard). Raport komisji do Spraw Światowego Kierowania (Warszawa: Report of the Commission on World Management, 1996), 198.

5. Cf. R. Blackhurst, N. Marian, and J. Tumlir, *Trade Liberalization, Protectionism and Interdependence*, "GATT Studies in International Trade, Geneva 1977, no. 5, 47.

6. Cf. E. Kawecka-Wyrzykowska, *Protekcjonizm w polityce handlowej Stanów Zjednoczonych* (Protectionism in the U.S. trade policy), Warszawa, 1983, 12.

7. See *Structures and Changes in European Industry* (New York Economic Commission for Europe, 1977), 99.

8. Cf. H. Giersch, "Eurosclerosis, the Malaise that Threatens Prosperity." *Financial Times* from January 8, 1984.

9. Cf. S. Burenstam-Linder, "How to Avoid a New International Economic Disorder." *World Economy* 3(3) November 1980.

10. See E. Kawecka-Wyrzykowska, op. cit., 14.

11. See c. Hsieh, "Measuring the Effects of Trade Expansion on Employment. A Review of some Research." *International Labour Review* January 1973.

12. See W. M. Corden, *Trade Policy and Economic Welfare* (Oxford: Clarendon Press, Oxford, 1974), 36.

13. See P. F. Drucker, "The Changed World Economy." *Foreign Affairs*, Spring 1986.

14. Cf. W. M. Corden, op. cit., 108.

15. Cf. A. Banerji and H. Ghanem, "Does the Type of Political Regime Matter for Trade and Labour Market Policies?" *The World Bank Economic Review* 11(1) January 1997: 173.

16. Banerji and Ghanem, "Does the Type of Political Regime Matter?" 173.

17. Banerji and Ghanem, "Does the Type of Political Regime Matter?" 174

18. G. Grossman and E. Helpman, "Protection for Sale." *American Economic Review* 84(4) 1994: 833–50.

19. See Banerji and Ghanem, "Does the Type of Political Regime Matter?" 175.

20. Banerji and Ghanem, "Does the Type of Political Regime Matter?" 176.

21. See J. F. Helliwel, "Empirical Linkages between Democracy and Economic Growth." *Working Paper 4066*. National Bureau of Economic Research, Cambridge, Mass. Processed. 1992.

22. G. Fields, *Changing Labor Market Conditions and Economic Development in Hong Kong, Singapore and Taiwan* (Ithaca, N.Y.: Cornell University, 1994).

23. R. Freeman, *Does Suppression of Labor Contribute to Economic Success? Labor Relations and Markets in East Asia* (Cambridge, Mass., and London: Harvard University and London School of Economics, 1993).

24. See S. Devarajan, H. Ghanem and K. Thierfelder, "Economic Reform and Labor Unions: A General Equilibrium Analysis Applied to Bangladesh and Indonesia." *The World Bank Economic Review* 11(1) January 1997: 145–70.

25. More in Z. W. Puzlecki, *Ochrona Handlowa Wspólnoty Europejskiej* (Poznań: The European Community Trade Protection, 1994).

26. "Rynki Zagraniczne" (Foreign Markets) March 28, 1992, no. 38.

27. See R. J. Langhammer, *Nachsetzen der Uruguay—Runde: zu viele Streitpunkte zu wenig Ergebnisse* (Kiel: Institut für Weltwirtschaft, 1991), 7.

28. Cf. H. P. Gray, "A Negotiating Strategy for Trade in Services." *Journal of World Trade Law* 5, 1983: 383.

29. *Le Monde*, April 22, 1992.

30. As a result of economic stagnation, of the crisis in the international trading and the escalation of trade protectionism in the first half of the eighties the members of GATT decided to start multilateral negotiations on the reduction of fast growing trade restrictions. During the ministerial session in Punta del Este in Uruguay on September 20, 1986, they accepted the declaration about a new round of negotiations within GATT, known as the Uruguay Round, or Growth Round, which was to be completed at the end of 1990. It should be pointed out that the GATT principles were, at that tome, accepted by 92 countries, the countries that conducted 95 percent of the world trade. The share of trade exchange in the world gross national product (GNP) rose significantly. While in 1950 it was about 8 percent, in 1987 it was more than 15 percent. It is evident that international trade contributes significantly to the growth of the world gross social product. Therefore the problems connected with its further development were the reason for multilateral trade negotiations.

31. On December 30, 1986, the American government announced the introduction, before January 1987 at the latest, higher customs duties for imported from the European Union alcohol beverages, cheese and vegetables (from 20 to 200 percent). The European Union threatened the retaliating actions. It should be pointed out that many months earlier the EU was preparing a list of countermeasures against many America agricultural products, such as cereals, fruit juices or beer. The United States

expecting such response prepared further countermeasures against the European Union.

32. Cf. J. J. Micha?ek, "A New Round of Multilateral GATT Negotiations." *Sprawy Mi?dzynarodowe* (International Affairs) 2, 1987: 52.

33. Cairns Group includes 14 countries exporting agricultural products: Argentina, Australian, Brazil, Chile, Fiji, Philippines, Indonesia, Canada, Columbia, Malaysia, New Zealand, Thailand, Uruguay, and Hungary.

34. See R. J. Langhammer, op. cit., 3.

35. R. J. Langhammer, op. cit., 3.

36. Some opinions that appeared in the context of the conflict, concerning agricultural products, between the United States and the European Union seem to be very interesting. Contrary to the opinions expressed by the United States, the representatives of the fat industry in the EU were anxious that the new agricultural policy might lead to the drop in production of oleiferous plants on the EU territory. Linking the subsidies for farms with their area could encourage farmers to the growth of cereals. Meanwhile, in the eighties the industry made big investments, adapting its processing capabilities to local soft rape and sunflower seeds. For technical reasons, not all the oil producing plants could process imported soybeans. In case of lower local supplies they would have to turn to imported soft seeds. The suppliers could be then found in such countries as Hungary, Poland and Russia.

37. *Rynki Zagraniczne* (Foreign Markets), May 5, 1992.

38. See A. Kalicki, "Reform or Correction?" *Rynki Zagraniczne*, June 6, 1992.

39. *Życie Gospodarcze* (Economy Life) 48, November 29, 1992: 23.

40. In such a strain spoke the then-president of the United States, George Bush. Also, before a French-German summit meeting, a former German Minister of Economy, Jürgen Moellemann expressed his support for the GATT agreements on agricultural products trading between the EU and the United States. France was at the time under strong pressure from its farmers and that is why the agricultural policy was more important for that country than for Germany. The German minister expressed the opinion that the benefits resulting from signing the treaty on world trade liberalization would prevail over the objections of the French agricultural lobby.

41. See W. Martin and L. A. Winters, op. cit., 1.

42. See K. Anderson, *Environmental Standards and International Trade,* in Annual World Bank Conference an Development Economics 1996, M. Bruno and B. Pleskovic, eds. (Washington, D.C.: The World Bank, January 1997), 319.

43. Cf. G. Chichilnisky, "North South Trade and the Global Environment." *American Economic Review* 84(4) 1994: 851–74; B. R. Copland and M. S. Taylor, "Trade and Transboundary Pollution." *American Economic Review* 85(4), 1995: 716–37; W. M. Corden, "The Environment and Trade Policy," in *Trade Policy and Economic Welfare*, W. M. Corden, ed. (Oxford: Clarendon Press. 1996).

44. See J. N. Bhagwati and T. N. Srinivisan, "Trade and the Environment: Does Environmental Diversity Detract from the Case for Free Trade?" in *Fair Trade and Harmonization: Prerequisites for Free Trade?* J. N. Bhagwati and R. E. Hudec, eds. (Cambridge, Mass.: MIT Press, 1996).

5

The Global-Continental-National Dynamic: Hypotheses for Comparative Continentalism

Stephen Clarkson

INTRODUCTION: CONTINENTALISM AND POLITICAL SCIENCE

If comparative continentalism is opening up as a new niche at the interstices of comparative politics, international relations, and international political economy, it is not because the existence of continental systems is novel. From the beginning of time, vast land masses have witnessed cultural, commercial, and migratory intercourse among the various peoples spread over their territory. Although the consolidation of states over the past few centuries divided up these geographical spaces with political boundaries, these national frontiers did not stop transnational interaction at the societal level. For social scientists this sub-political, extra-economic reality has been of marginal interest compared with the formalized, more easily documented intergovernmental relationships that states sustain with other states and the statistically manipulable trade, investment, and information flows that economies sustain with other economies. What has brought continental regimes into focus for academic consideration is the institutionalization of inter-state arrangements among contiguous groupings of countries, which, following often protracted negotiations, have agreed to establish intergovernmental and even supranational institutions with varying degrees of legislative, administrative, and judicial authority.

A rapid review of the past fifty years shows that what we can now call a comparative continentalism has evolved through two stages coinciding with the evolution of the global trade order itself.

THE FIRST FORTY YEARS: ASYMMETRICAL COMPARISON

In sharp contrast with North America, which was little recognized as a system by political science in the first decades following World War II (Clarkson 1988), the vicissitudes of the European Community have been the subject of a burgeoning literature since 1952 when its first formal association was created by treaty as the European Coal and Steel Community. Because the bulk of these studies naturally centered on the *sui generis* process of continental integration, their main comparative component was intra-systemic: the characteristics of one country were contrasted with those of another member state, producing works comparing the party politics, industrial policies, or welfare systems of the European Community's various components.

The precursor of inter-systemic comparison was inspired by the contrast between the United States of America and the evolving European Community. These explorations, whether on the nature of federalism or a specific issue such as agricultural policy (Skogstad) had much in common with the problem of comparing an apple (albeit a big apple) with a bunch of grapes (albeit a small bunch). While much could be learned from contrasting different entities, there were definite limits to setting a highly integrated, if federal super power against a quite imperfectly integrated grouping of heterogeneous states which operated supranationally (civil servants in the European Commission or judges of the European Court of Justice owing their allegiance only to the continental regime), intergovernmentally (national politicians defending their country's interests in the Council of Ministers), intranationally (state civil servants developing a common culture in Coreper), and transnationally (interest groups operating at the pan-European level) and which had separate currencies, distinct cultures, different policy processes, and varying legal systems. In some fields such as competition policy, where there was a good deal in common between the systems, comparative analysis had significant heuristic value. In others such as federalism, the United States offered a vision towards which some Europhiles aspired rather than a regime with which fruitful empirical comparisons could be undertaken (Paolini).

THE LAST TEN YEARS: A NEW, TWO DIMENSIONAL DYNAMIC

The recent consolidation of other continental groupings in Australasia, South-East Asia, Latin America, West Africa, and North America has made it possible to compare different bunches of grapes with each other, presenting the potential for authentic comparative analysis of these new formations along many different dimensions. As political economies they can be compared in terms of

- The historical process of their formation (gradual and consensual vs. rapid and forced).
- The institutional sophistication of their organizations (from highly articulated to loosely structured).
- Their internal distribution of power revolving around a hegemon (whether symmetrical or asymmetrical).
- Their economic structure (from laissez-faire to state interventionist).
- Their societal type (from neo-liberal to solidaristic).

Such inter-continental comparison presents a severe intellectual challenge because of the interdisciplinary capacity, knowledge base, cultural sensitivity, and linguistic competence required of the analyst who ventures along this path. The order of difficulty was raised further still because, during the years when many states were experimenting with these new continental systems, they were engaged in the painstaking commercial negotiations of GATT's Uruguay Round. As a result the same decade, which created the opportunity for serious horizontal comparisons among a number of new continental systems, introduced in the World Trade Organization a new form of global trade authority (Winham 1996) which has made possible the analysis of the vertical linkages connecting these new levels of global and continental governance with national, sub-national, and even municipal governments.

The superimposition of this two-dimensional dynamic on the already tangled skein of intergovernmental and transnational relationships suggests the need for new hypotheses for consideration—whether we are interested in the recent past, the prospects for the future or the immediate present.

THE PAST: COMING TO THE WTO

As we reflect on the years leading up to the creation of the World Trade Organization—a surprisingly robust international body with the power to discipline its signatory nation states in the cause of "deep integration" (Ostry 1977)—we can consider a number of causal interconnections between the continental and the global levels of action.

Hypothesis 1. The Consolidation of Continentalism Varied Inversely with that of Globalism[1]

Did continental regimes emerge because of the failure of globalism? This question cannot be posed in the same sense for the more senior European Community, which formed up under the cloud of a third, ideological World War, as for NAFTA, which emerged in the more benign post–Cold War era. A strong case can be made that the consolidation of western Europe was stimulated by the failed globalism symbolized by the Berlin Wall and the threatened westward push of the Stalinist menace through the central European people's democracies. An analogous case can be made that the consolidation of the new North America as NAFTA was the product of a double set of fears about the inadequacy of global governance: apprehension by the dominant of losing ground in the competitive race and anxiety by the weaker about failing completely. The continental hegemon feared it was losing its global dominance. Its protectionist responses to Asian and European competition caused its two dependent neighbors to fear for their own prospects.

The Hegemon's Fear of Failing

In the late 1970s the United States was suffering a collective depression. The gloomy cold warrior was obsessing bitterly that, having expended colossal resources to build up its military might to win the Cold War against its ideological enemy, it was facing hegemonic decline by losing the economic peace to its ideological allies who were exploiting their free ride under the U.S. security blanket in order to play a different, economic game. Their use of industrial policies, public monopolies, and other versions of business-government collaboration in Europe and Asia resulted in American firms losing market share not just abroad but, more ignominiously, at home where they were out-competed by lower cost, higher quality products sometimes even of their own invention.

One way for the United States to deal with such state-led competitive behavior was to respond by using its superior muscle. Congress toughened its trade measures so as to deprive a successful foreign exporter of the government-provided benefits that had helped produce its competitive advantage. Such unilateral actions became increasingly popular in Washington in the early 1980s but they contradicted the United States's long-standing advocacy of multilateral solutions for international trade problems through the General Agreement on Tariffs and Trade (GATT).

The multilateral way to deal with unacceptable foreign-government practices was to expand the scope of GATT's authority to address the most egregious subsidy programs such as the European Community's common agricultural policy and to establish new rules to deal with emerging issues that were needing regulation. This objective was accepted by GATT's member states in the early 1980s when agreement was reached in Punta del Este to launch a new, "Uruguay" round of negotiations. But reservations in Europe about subjecting state subsidies to international control and fears in leading Third World countries about accepting rules on, *e.g.* services, concocted to serve the interests of the industrialized world made the prospects for a successful global trade-rule deal highly dubious.

There was a third way. A significant component of Ronald Reagan's appeal to have America stand tall in the saddle once again was the "North American accord" he had called for in his 1980 presidential campaign. An economic integration pact with Mexico and Canada offered an intermediate strategy between using Congress's unilateral trade weapons and waiting for the uncertain results of the multilateral Uruguay Round. Given its competitive advantage in the information, telecommunications, and entertainment industries, the United States wanted to have services and intellectual property rights brought within the discipline of international trade rules. The continental option offered a step towards achieving that objective. What better way to force a new proposal onto the international negotiating table than to create a fait accompli by writing these rules into bilateral deals with neighboring countries whose economies were so dependent on trade with the United States that they could hardly refuse Uncle Sam's commercial offer?

The Reagan administration's North American project was in effect a strategic retreat, a classic *reculer pour mieux sauter*. The United States wanted to broaden and deepen its hemispheric hegemony in order to strengthen its capacity to take up the economic challenge coming from across both the Atlantic and the Pacific Oceans. Seen in this light, the emergence of North America as a continental system appears as the United States's clear-headed response to a stalled process of globalism which it could no longer control. Had the United States been able to get its way at the GATT, it is unlikely Washington would have wanted to divert its energies into bilateral negotiations with secondary powers. The American *recul* of the late 1980s created the set of trade rules, investment norms, and embryonic institutions known to the world as the North American Free Trade Agreement. When the GATT negotiating logjam broke and it came time to *sauter* into the new era of the WTO, a continental regime was left in place in North America. Whether or not it was losing global hegemony, NAFTA showed the United States had enhanced its dominance on its own continent and was poised to extend it through the hemisphere.

Fear of Failing among the Hegemon's Partners

If a defining characteristic of hegemony is acceptance by the led of the leader's leadership, the bilateral agenda of the United States's neighbors also has to be understood. While a complex of factors is needed to explain how Canada came suddenly to abandon its decades-long, if often half-hearted and contradictory, effort to develop a national mode of regulation superimposed on a national regime of accumulation, the conversion of its governing elite to a neo-conservative mindset was central. (Clarkson 1991) Here too, fear of failing provided the prime motivation for action. A century-old development model of industrialization by import substitution and staple export seemed to be on the ropes by the early 1980s—particularly after world oil prices started to fall. Competitive forces from across the seas were threatening Canadian markets at home and abroad. More ominous still, the largest, nearest, and still most sophisticated market to which it looked for its continuing export hopes seemed to be closing its doors to Canada because Congress was turning ever more protectionist.

The best way to deal with a bully is to exert the collective discipline of the whole community, so Canada's preferred option was to support a strengthening of the GATT's rules in the hope that they could temper American high-handedness. In this it was following a traditional strategy of trying to offset the overwhelming asymmetry of its relationship with the United States by participating in the multilateral fora created by the post–World War II set of specialized international political, military, cultural, and economic institutions.

But if the Uruguay Round was so blocked that there was little, if any hope that GATT would provide relief from the Americans' highly politicized trade politics within a foreseeable future, then a second best solution might be a direct deal: "If you can't beat them, join them." When in October 1985 Ottawa requested the opening of trade negotiations with the U.S. government, its objective was to obtain a bilateral free trade pact that gave Canadian exporters enhanced and secure access to the American market. "Enhanced access" meant reduced border barriers, a fairly easy objective for Ottawa to achieve if it were itself willing to give up tariff levels which, though low, were twice the American average. "Secure access" in Canadian trade discourse meant exemption from exposure to U.S. trade remedy sanctions, a naïvely ambitious objective given how jealously Congress guarded its economic sovereignty. When it became evident that Congress would not consider such an exception, the Canadian negotiators nevertheless settled for a palliative dispute mechanism while still agreeing to abandon substantial fields of policy autonomy.

Making a leap of faith endorsed more by its government than by its electorate,[2] Canada signed the Canada-United States Free Trade Agreement on January 1, 1989 and so heralded its move towards adopting the American mode of regulation. Joining with Mexico to sign the North American Free Trade Agreement on January 1, 1994[3] signaled formally that there was to be but one continent-wide regime of accumulation, not three national economies. This system, which was the aggregation of the more than ten thousand firms operating as corporate citizens of the greater North America across the two national boundaries, had in NAFTA the mode of regulation business required for mobility, efficiency, and—in some sectors such as automobiles and textiles—rules-of-origin protection against Asian, Third-World, and European competition.

While this inverse relationship between faltering globalism and resurgent continentalism can be documented convincingly for the North American case, testing the hypothesis with other continental systems poses a number of questions for researchers.

1. Was continental coalescence in Southeast Asia and the cone of South America driven less by a defensive, tactical fear of loss of position within the globalization process or more by an aggressive, strategic expectation of greater trade muscle?
2. NAFTA entrenched a paradigm shift, pushing Canada to abandon its social-democratic system of mixed economy and social programs in favor of the hegemon's neo-liberal stance. Did developing a continental accord require less value change in Mercosur because the Brazilian hegemon does not represent a different development model that of its associated neighbors and in ASEAN because the member states were more willing to accept a consensual and voluntary, rather than a rules-driven process?
3. The prime motivation for member-state concertation in Mercosur may have been responding to the inter-continental challenge of the United States rather than to the intra-continental leadership of Brazil. If this is the case, was the apparent stasis of the Uruguay Round a more insignificant factor in the development of continentalism?
4. Asymmetry between hegemon and partners was aggravated by NAFTA and mitigated by the structures established for the European Community. If in ASEAN the largest countries are poor and the smallest members are rich, concern about hegemony within the system may be negligible.
5. Do the conditions of entry for new members to a continental system necessarily oblige the radical transformation of a candidate country before admission or do they depend on the power of the candidate vis-à-vis that of the system? The inclusion of Greece, Spain, and Portugal in the EC necessitated major adjustments both in terms of democratic politics and welfare state practice. Extensive tariff reductions, privatization, and deregulation by Mexico were prerequisites for its negotiations with the United States and Canada of NAFTA which required further acts of institutional conformity to neo-liberal norms. Admission of Central and East European states to the EU will demand even greater internal transformation in the form of the adoption of the European Union's whole aquis communautaire. The conditions imposed on China for entry to ASEAN or APEC, however, may be far less onerous, given its economic and military power.

Hypothesis 2. Continental Emergence in Turn Furthered the Process of Globalism

Even if continental regimes emerged in response to the dysfunctionality of globalism in the late 1980s, it is still possible that continentalism can be functional to globalism. The argument would not be that NAFTA, ASEAN, or APEC became new global players similar to the European Commission and acted as supranational participants to break the multilateral logjam. Rather the hypothesis suggests that the rules worked out and accepted in CUFTA and then NAFTA acted as precedents that facilitated their acceptance by the participating members in GATT negotiations. Services first found a place in a trade agreement in CUFTA and were expanded in NAFTA before being accepted in the Uruguay Round for inclusion in the WTO. Similarly, once trade-related intellectual property rights (TRIPS) were included in NAFTA they were acceptable by GATT's negotiating partners as part of the WTO package. This proposition argues that both innovations were incorporated within the WTO in part because the world community had already been given a chance to observe them in practice at the continental level.

This rule building was not just a product of the hegemon pressing for new services rules and TRIPS. Canada also used the experience gained in its continental accords to argue for the changes it wanted. For example, lessons learned from CUFTA's bilateral dispute settlement mechanism, as weakened by NAFTA's trilateral processes, suggested to Canadian negotiators improvements which they proposed to turn GATT's system into the more effective and authoritative structure ultimately ratified for the WTO.

Beyond the evolution of new norms, NAFTA's continentalism may have contributed to the globalism of the WTO through both demonstration and intimidation.

Demonstration effect. When Mexico as a developing country entered a formal trade and investment regime with the highly developed countries to its north, other Third World countries saw a concrete example of a Third World–First World liberalization relationship that made it easier for them to contemplate accepting the disciplines of the new global agreement.[4]

Intimidation effect. There was negative as well as positive learning in the difficult years of the Uruguay Round. The emerging continental trade blocs of NAFTA, ASEAN, and Mercosur presented an implicit threat that, if a global settlement was not reached by the GATT, then states such as India would be left on the outside facing a world of continental fortresses.

For our hypothesis to be established we would need to know whether participation in the development of ASEAN and Mercosur helped prepare their members to accept the disciplines of the new World Trade Organization. It would be equally pertinent to know to what extent the countries outside these continental systems were prodded by their fear of isolation to prefer membership in the WTO regime to no membership at all.

THE FUTURE: POSSIBLE CONNECTIONS BETWEEN THE GLOBAL AND THE CONTINENTAL

Even if the continental trade blocs contributed to the creation of the global trading system, it does not follow that continentalism and globalism will be mutually reinforcing in the future. Indeed, of the various variants of our third hypothesis—(a) the global order will strengthen at the expense of the continental blocs; (b) the global and continental orders will covary, waxing and waning together; (c) continental trade blocs will strengthen at the expense of the global order—the most persuasive appears to be the first, suggesting an inverse relationship between continentalism and globalism in the years ahead.

Hypothesis 3a. The Global Trade Order Will Prosper at the Expense of the Continental

To the extent that the development of trade rules by the WTO preempts their formulation at the continental level, growth of global governance will constrain continental development. The upwards extension of the subsidiarity principle in which continental regimes lose function to the universal level of governance could affect the prospects for both broadening their membership and deepening their political integration. A more authoritative WTO with wider jurisdiction could reduce the value of continental membership. This would facilitate the broadening of continental regimes since present members would have less to lose by conceding privileges to new entrants. As more candidates join these continental systems they could become shallower rather than deeper in their institutional substance.

Much will depend on each continental system's internal dynamic and maturity as well as on its position in the global balance of forces. Unless endogenous centrifugal forces cause them to self-destruct, the WTO is unlikely completely to supersede any but the weakest continental regime. As for the strongest, the European Union's prospects as a coherent political-economic system will depend more on its internal dynamics than on the success or failure of the WTO. Still, if the WTO effectively expands its global competence from trade matters to include investment rules, competition law, cultural policy, human rights issues and even environmental or labor policy, the EU would *ipso facto* lose equivalent amounts of policy-making authority with a consequent erosion of the European fortress.

With its deliberately weak institutions and minimally supranational mechanisms, NAFTA's prospects in the light of WTO's aggrandizement are murkier both for deepening and for broadening.

Deepening. The hostility of the United States Congress to any diminution of its sovereignty is so profound that little is to be hoped for in the direction of building stronger NAFTA institutions unless it be through the gradual, behind-closed-doors consensus building that can take place in functionally specific, stakeholder-staffed working groups or collectively inspired epistemic communities tackling particular continent-wide problems. The problem is that NAFTA's geo-strategic value to the U.S. has already declined in the space of a decade during which time Washington has experienced a substantial attitude shift. From a defensive, Monroe-Doctrine stance in the mid-1980s, it became buoyant and aggressive in the 1990s. Its neo-liberal economic model appears to be proving superior in job creation and even technological progress to the state-centered models, whether social-democratic or communitarian, still in vogue in Europe and Asia.

The resurgence of the U.S. economy vis-à-vis its Asian and European rivals accounts for some turning away from continentalism. The mood change is also related to the troubles in Mexico—corruption, drugs, emigration, and general political instability—which have made NAFTA anathema as a path to pursue for many members of Congress. In addition, the realization that the WTO is a forum where the United States can negotiate trade rules that apply to the whole world takes further luster away from NAFTA whose scope is relatively parochial.

Paradoxically, it is Uncle Sam's partners—those who made the greatest concessions by giving up broad fields of policy-making sovereignty—who cling to NAFTA. Canadian and Mexican diplomats and trade officers use the document every day as they fight in the corridors of the American capital against protectionist moves by U.S. lobbies. Some fifty working groups mandated by NAFTA are beavering away on specialized intergovernmental issues giving both officials and private sector representatives from Mexico and Canada highly valued leverage in the American political system. (Jacek 1995)

Business supports NAFTA as a depoliticized constitution that, positively, guarantees it rights of investment and establishment from the Yucatan to the Tuktoyaktuk. Negatively, NAFTA also provides capitalism with insurance against more activist politicians in the future who would be prevented by it from rolling back its provisions with ambitious, government-led initiatives that get in the way of free market decision making.

But beyond the confines of ongoing intergovernmental relations and corporate strategizing, NAFTA does not seem to have a positive dynamic. Bilateral relations between sub-national governments are not spontaneously transforming themselves into trilateral state-province-state relations. (Munton and Kirton 1996) There are some indications that elements of civil society are developing a continental praxis in what has been called "continentalism from below" as trade union leaders, and environmental activists, for example, learn about their comrades' struggles in the other countries of North America. (Gutiérrez-Haces 1996)

Since these cautious moves towards increased transnationalism do not endow NAFTA with either a political center or a popular base, the agreement seems doomed not to develop into a sophisticated, institutionally complex, politically participatory supranational system analogous to the EU and able eventually to overshadow the WTO in importance. On the contrary, if the WTO manages to maintain its early momentum and becomes the effective locus for regulating trade conflicts and developing a global economic regime, NAFTA could continue to lose its geo-strategic centrality in the minds of its member governments. If "use it or lose it" is a valid way to summarize this argument, then the global order will affirm itself at the expense of continental regimes if it is found to satisfy member states' trade needs and used by them more actively. But if the continental framework continues to fill a valid need, the two levels of inter-governmentalism will coexist, if uneasily, for years, leaving us with the third variant of this hypothesis.

Broadening. In principle NAFTA is explicitly open to the adhesion of new members. Chile, the Caribbean Basin, post-Castro Cuba, an independent Québec would head the waiting list, but the short shrift that President Clinton received when seeking fast-track negotiation authorization in 1997 suggests that the United States does not see its interests as crucially linked either to an expanded continental regime or even to the grand hemispheric scheme envisaged in 1994 by the Miami Declaration that a Free Trade Agreement for the Americas (FTAA) should be in place by the year 2005. (Palacios 1996)

The more it expands, the less value an organization is likely to have for its members. But, on the assumption that exports create jobs,[5] Canada wants to keep the process aimed at hemispheric free trade in motion, having already negotiated a separate agreement with Chile in 1996. Mexico is adopting Canada's outward-looking stance in seeking to establish bilateral accords with partners in Asia as well as Latin America. Some kind of free trade agreement is envisaged for APEC's advanced economies by 2010 and for its developing members by 2020, though the severe crisis that has Asia in its grip is likely to decelerate the process of liberalization. The APEC process could be rendered unnecessary if the WTO maintains its policy-making momentum.

Weak candidates for entry on the margins of the continental systems are being pressed by global institutions such as the World Bank, the OECD, and the International Monetary Fund radically to transform their state-centered political economies and adapt neo-liberal standards of greater laissez-faire. The Central and East European countries who are anxious to belong to the European Union are striving to transform their legal systems, to privatize their public monopolies, to deregulate their investment and trade regimes in order to qualify for entry. Actual accession to these trade blocs may give the new member state some help in dealing with the resulting economic and social dislocations: structural adjustment funds from Brussels for Portugal, Spain, and Greece in the 1980s; financial support from Washington and Ottawa for Mexico's peso crisis of 1994. But those countries languishing on a waiting list may have to rely on the new disciplines imposed by the WTO's rules to obtain better access to the markets of continental fortresses.

In short, the future of continental regimes seems uncertain. Some may well consolidate over the next few decades, sheltered by the WTO umbrella. If global institutions are stymied by persistent obstruction of their leading members, continental associations could be expected to consolidate further.

PRESENT CONSIDERATIONS: BRINGING THE STATE INTO THE GLOBAL-CONTINENTAL DYNAMIC

Contemplating the phenomenon of continentalism and globalism from the viewpoint of the federal state,[6] one can see two reasons why national capitals may prefer to support the consolidation and expansion of the WTO's jurisdiction rather than that of their continental system.

1. Many states have already lost some of their raison d'être thanks to the decline of security concerns following the end of the Cold War. Given their loss of internal function as their sub-national levels of government become more active in micro-economic and industrial policy-making, the task of representing the national interest at the global level of negotiations remains a role in which the federal state has a continuing monopoly of legitimacy. For countries such as Canada, which is suffering a drastic loss of internal legitimacy, this trade representation function abroad is a precious bulwark for its challenged credibility at home.
2. Whereas continental regimes tend to develop supranational practices that reduce the autonomy of their member states, this sovereignty is less jeopardized by the World Trade Organization. True, the WTO's members agree to have their trade behavior scrutinized by an international dispute settlement jury. But they retain the sovereign ability to refuse to implement a WTO judgment even though such a refusal gives the grieving trade partner the right to retaliate against it. This may be preferable to being subject to a supranational, continental-level process over which the federal state has lost effective control, and suggests further hypotheses need to be explored.

Hypothesis 4. Incoherence between Levels Threatens the Trade Order

As anyone with experience of federalism well knows, every extra level of autonomous government creates the possibility for further conflicts of jurisdiction and contradictions of policy. When continental and global trade regimes coexist, the notion of "two-level games" takes on a new meaning. Member states engage in calculations as to whether it is to their advantage to Ago to Geneva" or deal with their partners according to the norms of their continental system. A recent example will make the point. Bridling at the vaunted cultural exemption that CUFTA and NAFTA offered Canada, the U.S. took its complaint about Ottawa's discrimination against *Sports Illustrated* as a dumped split-run edition to the World Trade Organization. Washington's success there largely nullified the value to Canada of CUFTA's problematic cultural exemption, Article 2005. Nullifying CUFTA's Article 2005 by invoking the WTO undid a deal Canada had "paid for" by specific concessions (Magder). There will be no point for countries in the future in negotiating an agreement at the continental level if it can be nullified at the global level.

This conundrum suggests a number of questions:

1. Will the subsidy code embodied in the WTO's rules prevail over U.S. trade law as applied to a NAFTA partner?
2. Will precedents created at the global level prevail for disputes adjudicated in a continental dispute panel?
3. Will anti-dumping procedures, if they are better articulated in NAFTA's rules, complement or complicate the settlement of anti-dumping cases at the WTO?

The issue of incoherence between the continental and the global systems could have a serious impact on either level of governance.

Hypothesis 5. Differing Continental Value Systems Presage Conflict at the WTO

Coherence is not just an issue between the global and the continental levels. To the extent that continental regimes overlap—NAFTA and APEC have common members; so too would Mercosur and FTAA—variations in the deals struck will cause uncertainty, a condition abhorred by the transnational corporation. Eliminating such discrepancies will likely reinforce one of the most striking characteristics of the present global trade order, the constant renegotiation of the rules and the continual addition of new items to the agenda.

While this phenomenon of continuous bargaining is seen by some as a linear progress towards a more rational, universal order, such an interpretation conceals the extent to which global negotiations provide the forum for a significant clash of values among competing continental power systems. As the U.S. trade representative Charlene Barshefsky proudly claimed in the wake of the WTO telecommunications agreement, "the United States has effectively exported American values of free competition, fair rules and effective enforcement."[7] But the effort to export U.S. values can encounter resistance. Smaller powers can also play the game of negotiating rules in order to influence American norms: Canada and Chile in their bilateral accord of 1996 agreed that anti-dumping suits would no longer be permissible between the signatory parties in sectors where tariffs had already fallen to zero. Collective resistance to American pressure has been most obviously manifest in APEC, which refused to establish a rules-based regime in favor of a consensual approach to working out its trade and investment norms. Indeed the Asian system of capitalism may be so different in its normative base that conflicts in future rounds of global negotiation may become intractable.[8]

CONCLUSION

If globalization were not a big enough challenge for students of international relations and international political economy, the phenomenon of continentalism has emerged to complicate their intellectual life still further. While continental regimes will not likely render the nation-state defunct, they do not appear about to disappear within the new global order. Developing and testing hypotheses about this new multi-level reality in the lives of nations and in the future of the world appears to have a valid claim for scholarly resources.

NOTES

1. In this chapter I distinguish continentalism and globalism as political and institutional developments from globalization as economic, technological, or cultural phenomena.
2. In the 1988 federal election 43 percent of the voters supported the pro-free trade Progressive Conservatives who, thanks to the first-past-the-post electoral system, walked off with 57 percent of the seats giving them a clear majority in the House of Commons. Public opinion polling continued to show the majority of the population opposed to free trade.
3. A parallel analysis of Mexican motivations for a trade deal with the United States would put less emphasis on the blockage of GATT than on Mexico's economic crisis and its governing elite's ideological transformation. If import substitution was to be abandoned by this capital-poor country as its development strategy, then Mexico needed foreign direct investment if it was hoping to become globally competitive. To attract nervous capital required a radical restructuring of economic policies from high levels of state interventionism to high levels of laissez faire. NAFTA, which gave Mexico more assured access to the U.S. market, represented both Washington's reward to President Salinas for good economic behavior and its hope that the Mexican political system could be stabilized enough and the Mexican economy boosted enough for the pressure of illegal immigration to the United States to be contained.
4. Interview with Luis de la Calle, February 21, 1997, Embassy of Mexico in the United States.
5. Ottawa's Foreign Affairs and International Trade department reckons that every additional $1 billion of exports creates some 7,000 new jobs—a figure that has been revised downwards from its previous assumption of 11,000.
6. Given the difficulty of applying the concept of nation-state to countries such as Canada where Québécois and native peoples identify themselves as nations or peoples, "federal state" will be used throughout to designate the phenomenon generally

referred to as nation-state. Even France, the prototype for the nation-state, contains vestigial non-French nationalities and, however unitary its political system may be thought to be, has introduced significant measures of decentralization.

7. *New York Times*, February 17, 1997, 1.

8. Richard Stubbs, "Asian's Distinctive Capitalism: Implications for International Trade Rules." Paper presented to the International Studies Association, March 1997.

REFERENCES

Blank, Stephen and Stephen Krajewski. 1995. "U.S. Firms in North America: Redefining Structure and Strategy." *North American Outlook* 5(2) February.

Clarkson, Stephen. 1988. "Continentalism: the Conceptual Challenge for Canadian Social Science." *The John Porter Memorial Lectures: 1984–1987.* Canadian Sociology and Anthropology Association, 23–43.

———. 1991. "Disjunctions: Free Trade and the Paradox of Canadian Development," in *The New Era of Global Competition: State Policy and Market Power,* Daniel Drache and Meric S. Gertler, eds. Montreal: McGill-Queen's University Press, 103–26.

Gutiérrez Haces, Teresa. 1996. "Globalization from Below: The Awakening and Networking of Civil Societies in North America." Paper presented to Association of Canadian Studies in the United States conference, Toronto, November 8, 1996.

Jacek, Henry J. 1994. "Public Policy and NAFTA: The Role of Organized Business Interests and the Labor Movement." *Canadian American Public Policy* 19, October.

Magder, Ted. 1998. "Franchising the Candy Store: Split-Run Magazines and a New International Regime for Trade in Culture." *Canadian-American Public Policy* 34, April.

Munton, Don and John Kirton. 1996. "Beyond and Beneath the Nation-State: Province-State Interactions and NAFTA." Paper for the International Studies Association, San Diego, April 1996.

Ostry, Sylvia. 1997. *The Post–Cold War Trading System: Who's on First?* Chicago: Chicago University Press.

Palacios, Juan J. 1994. "The Dual Logic of Trading Bloc Building in the Pacific Rim: Mexico vs. South East Asia under NAFTA?" Mimeo.

Paolini, Edmondo. 1989. *Altiero Spinelli e l'unificazione dell'Europa.* Movimento Federalista Europeo: Roma.

Skogstad, Grace. 1997. "Ideas, Paradigmatic Stability and Change: Agricultural Exceptionalism in the European Union and the United States." Paper presented to the Canadian Political Science Association, June 1997, 35 pages.

Winham, Gilbert R. 1996. "International Trade Policy in a Globalizing Economy." *International Journal* LI:4, Autumn: 638–50.

6

Diffusion of Power in Agro-Food Policy Networks

Henri J. M. Goverde

All the world's people need a secure, sufficient and sustainable food supply. This paper draws attention to the political aspects of the agro-food system, particularly from a power perspective. The central hypothesis of the study is that power relations in the agro-food system today, although much more complex than the ancient agrarian societies, are related to the same basic human activities particularly producing, saving, allocating, orientating, disciplining and polity constructing. The research design is mainly based on "the analysis of the power balance," an approach deducted from the sociology of human figurations. Theoretically, the agro-food system is perceived as a network. Therefore, all human activities concerning food and nutrition are supposed to be interrelated in a loosely coupled way. Six case studies illustrate the dimension of power in the agro-food system today. These studies draw attention to shifts in power in the (mutual related) fields of biogenetic engineering, fundamental rights of plant breeders, liberalization of the world trade for agro-food products, the EU-CAP policy during and after the EU-expansion with Central and East European countries, the public management of animal diseases (BSE) and the renewal of regional and local polity. In all cases state- and non-state actors are involved. These interrelated actors cause a fundamental diffusion of power.

The results of the case studies allow some reflections concerning general shifts of power in the agro-food system, particularly about chances and constraints for policy making by (mainly EU) nation-states in the field of agro-food production and the future of the rural areas.

INTRODUCTION

The agro-food system is involved in and responsible for the fulfillment of the demand of the world's people for a secure, sufficient and sustainable food supply. This paper will not draw attention to the whole food system. It focuses on the political aspects of this system, particularly from a power perspective. Agrarian societies, religious as well as military ones, have shown that human beings were involved in very characteristic activities. These human activities were necessary to survive as a community not only in the short but also in the long term. From a historical point of view, section 2 focuses on the question of how the production, saving, and allocation of food is related to increasing social stratification (based on power, property, and prestige), so to the development of power relations in these societies. The central premise is that the food system today, although far more complex than in the ancient agrarian societies, operates on the same basic human activities which are particularly producing, saving, allocating, orientating, disciplining and polity constructing. Of course, in every issue in the agro-food system all analytically distinct human activities are relatively present. However, each of these activities was used to select a specific case in order to illustrate the dimension of power in the agro-food system today (section 4). Section 5 introduces these case studies. Attention is drawn to shifts in power in the fields of biogenetic engineering, fundamental rights of plant breeders, liberalization of world trade also for the agro-food products, the expansion of the EU with Central and East European countries, the public management of an animal disease (BSE), and the renewal of rural areas caused by the trends mentioned before. In all cases, state- and non-state actors are involved. Theoretically, the agro-food system is perceived as a network. Therefore, all human activities concerning food and nutrition are supposed to be interrelated in a loosely coupled way. The concept of (policy-) network is used as a theoretical basis for descriptive-analysis as well as for explanation (section 3). In section 6, an attempt is made to summarize the ever-shifting balances of power as well as the complexity of the diffusion of power in the agro-food (sub-)network(s).

PRELUDE: POWER AND AGRICULTURE IN HISTORICAL PERSPECTIVE

In the agrarian societies of the ancient world increasing productivity and growing vulnerability had not produced equity in the standards of living. On the contrary, this combination of conditions caused a process of ongoing social stratification. People became different in power, property and prestige. Besides regional and local variations, a general pattern of stratification could be observed during the ages in different parts of the world. Goudsblom (1997: 84) refers to the old Mesopotamia, to pre-Columbian Mexico and Peru, to pre-industrial Britain as well as pre-industrial Nippon, to Celtic agrarian societies, and the like. The majority of the population was professional farmers. Most of the people worked on the land and they formed the base of the social pyramid. Sometimes an individual farmer could reach a high social position. Still his social prestige was relatively low. The real top positions in the hierarchy of power, property and prestige were monopolized by priests and warriors, who created for themselves (and in advanced agrarian societies also for their heirs) the position of a ruling elite. Farmers became dependent on priests, because they intermediated between human beings and the "higher powers." In fact, the priests were responsible for timing the right moment to start sowing. They owned the fanners calendar. In this way they had the power to *orientate* people to a certain sequence of activities and by doing this they produced a severe *discipline*. In general, the discipline was based on values that were important in order to survive as a community. For example, values like working hard, being careful with the stocks of seeds and products, distribution of available goods, diligence, economy, communal sense, and obedience (to God) orientated these agrarian societies to think in a long term perspective. In fact the priests worked out *an agrarian regime*: a polity which regulated the behavior of the farmers. Marvin Harris (1978) has explained that in agrarian societies the production of food is less stressful than the problems of saving (conservation) and allocating (distribution and consumption) the stocks. The rituals performed by priests served to ensure that internalized codes of people's behavior remained intact (see "Fremdzwang" to "Selbstzwang," Elias, 1939/1969).

Although orientation and discipline helped the fanners to survive in the long term, the tools and rituals of the priests could not protect the crops in the fields as well as the stocks in the temples. Gangs and passing warriors often destroyed the fields and plundered the stocks. For this reason the farmers were *productive* as well as *vulnerable*. The farmers could not protect their harvests by themselves. It would take too much of their scarce labortime. They needed their working-hours, because the physical protection against natural catastrophes was very modest, the seasons were short, and the technical tools almost nonexistent. So, the farmers in the rural areas were ready to accept legitimate (legal) and also illegal forms of threat and tributary power. For the same reason (scarcity of time) agrarian societies were not able to produce enough surplus to exempt many people from routine farming duties. This explains the relatively small size of the cities and the small number of "lords." The warriors were *destructive* and *defensible*. Therefore, these nonfarmers competed for the power positions in the society. In fact, the majority of the people had almost no influence in this competition. Wichers (1965: 53) has argued that almost till the beginning of the twentieth century the majority of the people had no real power in influencing the borders of kingdoms or empires, neither could they influence changes in the public administration. In many colonial, later-developing countries, this type of influence is still rather weak. However, the fanners and the warriors became mutually interdependent. The farmers produced food and they demanded protection in exchange. The warriors offered protection to the farmers who were ready to exchange it for food. Being destructive, however, the warriors could only dominate the farmers, not rule them. The farmers were still ruled by the priests, who disciplined them to obey God in order to receive the benefit of metaphysic protection. As soon as the warriors and the farmers became double-bound to each other (protection was exchanged for production; lifting destruction and vulnerability), warriors got the position to take over the ruling power of the priests. Three components were the basis for the change in the power relations: a) training (how to use the sword and how to collect courage and authority); b) organization (military discipline and leadership); c) equipment. In this process of increasing mutual interdependence between the farmers and the warriors the *religious-agrarian regime* has been elite, they often needed alliances with the former persons in power. The priests continued to be specialists in socializing and disciplining ordinary people and therefore they controlled it with lower costs (i.e., without means of violence). In fact, the transition from the religious-agrarian regime to the military-agrarian regime gives insight in the sociogenesis of a social order with three estates.[1]

For the purpose of this paper it is not necessary to work out the history of agrarian regimes throughout the world. In fact the sociogenesis of ancient agrarian regimes helps to conceptualize some characteristics which seem to be very basic in understanding the mechanisms of power in the agro-food system today. This conceptualization helps to put the right research questions concerning power in current agro-food policy networks. Table 6.1 summarizes the construction of the dependencies in the agro-food system from the perspective of the farmers. Table 6.2 demonstrates the same but from the perspective of the priests and the warriors.

From the distinct perspectives of the main actors in the ancient agrarian regimes (tables 6.1 and 6.2) the following human activities, which dominated the agro-food system, can be deduced:

- Economizing (producing, saving, allocating).
- Orientating (timing, planning, dividing, managing).
- Disciplining (controlling agro-circle: controlling consumption; intermediating between actors; promoting collective values and norms).
- Polity constructing (training, organizing, regulating, equipping, taxing, treasuring, guarding).

In our view, the same activities are still fundamental in the agro-food system today. These activities show a historical continuity. Nevertheless, many gradations are relevant as well. The chains of interdependencies between actors had become much longer in modern times in comparison with the an-

Table 6.1. Dependencies from the Farmers Perspective

	Reading from farmers perspective →	*Priests*		*Warriors*	
		Orientators	*Disciplinists*	*Destroyists*	*Protectionists*
Farmers	Production	sacrifices to higher powers	"higher" knowledge on farming	one year crops	agro-food as taxes in natura
	Saving	keeping stocks and seed	short overcon-sumption; later regulation stock-use	treasury of seeds	stock keeping & seeds production
	Allocation	supply to markets; trade	gifts to com-munity; sacrifices	selling surplus; protection daily food	Offering tax and goods to markets
	Vulnerability	security to natural catastroph es, social conflicts and intra human dangers	demands for help of higher powers coalition against warriors	small defense army; coalition with priests	tax and political support

cient world. This implies that all distinct basic human activities in these chains have developed an enormous complexity, too. It is the object of this investigation to deal with this complexity and to indicate its meaning for policy making in a political arena of intergovernmental institutions and nation-states.

FARMERS, PRIESTS AND WARRIORS: METAPHORS FOR POWER RELATIONS IN THE MODERN AGRO-FOOD NETWORK

In this section the terms "farmers," "priests" and "warriors" are metaphors for a variety of different types of actors. The actors often play different roles, because the policy situations make their actions diverse. To approach these facts it is fruitful to use the concept of "social networks." The premise is that altogether the actors participate in a pluriform, relatively closed and complex worldwide agro-food network. Like all networks this agro-food network consists of loosely-coupled individuals, groups, organizations and institutions originating in the public as well as in the pri-

Table 6.2. Dependencies from the Perspectives of Priests and Warriors

	Reading perspectives of priests & warriors→	*Farmers*			
		Production	*Saving*	*Allocation*	*Vulnerability*
Priests	Orientation	timing	planning; long term thinking	equal access to food stocks	managing uncertainties; promoting community values
	Disciplining	calendar control	controlled consumption; (harvest festival)	promoting anti-greediness; diligence	rituals; polity; intermediating to warriors
Warriors	Destructionists	destroying one year harvest and seeds for next years	damaging stocks and seeds banks	steeling and firing stocks; sharing out the plunder	training and organizing killing & wars
	Protectionists	defense actions and police control	guards of stocks in temples and granaries	supporting equal access and justifiable distribution	polity; training; organization; equipment

vate sector. It can be argued also that "networks" (just like "markets" and "systems") are instrumental in diminishing the complexity and uncertainty of the real world. People are focused on reducing this complexity and uncertainty. Therefore interacting people create markets, bureaucracies, institutions and networks for coordination and control.[2] In general, they follow their own *logic of action*. However, almost none of them can realize its goals alone, so that most of the actors are interdependent on other individual actors, sub-networks or institutions. "*Institutions*," distinct from networks, consist of (1) a set of rules and values, (2) the decision-making mechanisms, and (3) groups and organizations. Actors cooperate or clash with specific parts of the network only. The reason is that some participants have access to specific (power) resources. Therefore, they are attractive as (*symbiotic* interdependent) partners or they are repulsive as (*competitive* interdependent) rivals for other actors. Often the interactions between the actors follow a pattern (e.g., cooperation, conflict, exchange, negotiation, and aid).

Power and Networks

An essential remark is that on the one hand, actors are interdependent, so their behavior is embedded in formal and informal institutions, rules and contingencies. On the other hand, they operate autonomously to a certain degree also: they can choose the behavior they prefer and they are responsible for their own choice. From this perspective, Crozier and Friedberg (1977–1980) concluded that *power relations* can be deduced from attitudes, feelings and behavior of individuals. Therefore, it makes no sense to express power in quantitative terms. It is preferable to couch it in qualitative terms expressing a relative balance like "more/less" or "stronger/weaker." In the words of Crozier and Frieberg (p. 32):

> The more B can bargain over his willingness to do what A wants, and the more his available resources allow to keep his future behavior from becoming perfectly predictable for A, then the more power he will have over A in this particular relation. Power, therefore, lies in the margin of liberty available to each partner in a relation of power.

Of course, all actors attempt to turn the network into a position that is profitable according to their action-logic. In order to influence the *power balance*, i.e. to manage the network, the actors ought to have relative control over available power resources. As mentioned above the main activities in the agro-food network are economizing, orientating, disciplining and polity constructing. Following Tansey and Worsley (1995: 167–197) the *main power resources* which can sustain these activities are science, technology, information and management. In addition to Tansey and Worsley, a rather comprehensive typology of power resources (Goverde 1987: 12) learns that, besides the control over resources of production, orientation and organization, the control over the means of violence (police, courts, army, tax systems, prisons) should be underlined. On the one hand, control over these resources of violence is an important prerogative of the nation-state. On the other hand, many lobby actions by public and private actors are trying to influence the competencies and the legitimization of the means of violence. The implementation and maintaining of forbidden synthetic hormones, pesticides, and herbicides, for example, is a very complex public affair in the Netherlands. The Dutch state tried already different steering models (regulation, levying, networking) to control this polluting and unhealthy business. However, a successful approach has not yet been found.

The main research design is the "power-balance analysis" (Goverde and Hinssen 1994). Although the methodological and the methodical aspects of this research design are not an issue to be pursued here, some dimensions of this research design are relevant in order to understand the argument in section 6. From a methodical point of view, the construction of the power-balance is based on three elements (Goverde and Hinssen, 104):

1. Which actor is controlling which power resources at which moment in the analyzed process?
2. Changes observed in:
   - The types of power resources used in the process.
   - The social mobility of the actors caused by the movements in social cohesion between the actors.
   - The access actors create for themselves to the functionaries, who can make the final decision.
3. A coherent description and intersubjective interpretation of the facts.

The power resources, which are relevant in the agro-food system, imply that state- and non-state actors are the subject of this study. This focuses the research also on the agro-food "policy"—networks as well as on "polity constructing." Benson (1982: 148) defines a policy network as "a cluster or complex of organizations connected to each other by resource dependencies and distinguished from other clusters or complexes by breaks in the structure of resource dependencies." The differentiation in social cohesion between the actors implies a continuum along which Rhodes and Marsh (1992: 186–187) have categorized policy networks. One extreme is a "policy community." This is a tightly, closed, highly integrated and highly institutionalized network in which membership is very restricted and all members have resources to exchange. The other extreme at the continuum is an "issue network" in which access is relatively open and in which many actors with unequal resources participate. The degrees of integration and institutionalization are low, which makes this network relatively unstable. Policy networks have a major impact on power relations. These power relations influence in turn, the choice of the policy. In policy networks the control over power resources is distributed unequally among the actors. Moreover, those who are members of the network are more privileged than those who are excluded. In policy communities, some groups have no access to the policy process and the policymaking process is mainly characterized by the exercise of structural power. According to Smith (1990: 39) ". . . the basis of structural power is that rules, procedures and beliefs support the interests of the powerful without the powerful having to decide on every occasion what should be allowed on the agenda." In issue networks, on the contrary, the exercise of power is mainly nonstructural. This type of power is based on the application of resources and skills by the actors, dependent from the specific policy situation.

Social cohesion between the core participants is the *key to explain* coalition building in policy networks. According to Lehmbruch (1991: 126) cohesion refers to "...the sharing of meaning attached to the interactions within the network." Policy communities produce high degrees of cohesion, whereas issue networks and looser networks create only low degrees. Daugbjerg (1997: 127–30) has formulated some hypotheses which permit to use the concept of "policy networks" to explain policy processes. "Consensus on policy principles enables members of cohesive networks to form a strong coalition against outsiders, meaning that the existing policy can be successfully defended." And: "a noncohesive policy network has not developed a consensus on policy principles. Therefore, the pattern of resource dependency remains the most important factor which influences policy making. This does not imply that the network is characterized by permanent conflicts. However, since all members suffer from the lack of consensus *casu quo* the lack of certainty, they may make a temporary compromise on some principles, but the network is unstable because it is not based on a shared understanding (Smith 1993: 126–27).

Research Questions

Theoretically, the relevant research questions are the following. Starting from the metaphors: who are the "priests," "warriors" and "farmers" in the agro-food network today? Who, if anyone, manages the main activities (economizing, orientating, disciplining and polity constructing) at different territorial and functional scales? What distinguishes the state from the nonstate actors or do they operate in diffusion? How do they control who has access to what type of power resources? Is the power balance sheet between dominant actors, (sub)networks and institutions of actors shifting nowadays? Which issues will influence the balance of power in the worldwide agro-food system in the near future? Of course, these questions can not be answered comprehensively here. In fact, the theoretical considerations briefly outlined in this section only provide a background for a plausible selection of topical key issues, which will be described in main lines only (section 4).

Finally, in this paper an attempt is made to find a partial answer to the question of how the diffusion of power produces and sustains patterns of interdependence in some key topics in the agro-food system. The diffusion of power is considered as the interwoven, double-bound relationships of state and nonstate actors in a (policy) network of interactions (state-state; state-firm; state-international governmental organization/IGO; firm-firm; firm-state; firm-IGO; state-IN(on)GO; firm-INGO; IGO-INGO). Further, how does the balance of power (resulting from the interdependence, interactions, strategies and games of the state and nonstate actors involved) reflect in the negotiations between international organizations (for example, GATT/WTO, EU, World Bank) and nation-states (United States; member states of the European Union [EU], 15; Central and East European Countries [CEE], 10; Claims group, etc.)? Of course, this paper can not cover all the institutional impacts. Special attention will be drawn to the administrative mechanisms in the diffusion of power and the relative power of a nation-state.

AGRO-FOOD POLICY NETWORKS: SELECTION OF KEY - ISSUES

Starting from the list of fundamental human activities in the agro-food system table 6.3 shows *six cases* selected. For "economizing" a case is selected for each subactivity (producing, saving, and allocating): Biogenetic engineering; Plant Breeders" Rights; Uruguay Round and the regime created by the World Trade Organization (WTO). The other three activities (orientating, disciplining, and polity constructing) are illustrated by one case each, respectively EU expansion, Quality Control and Animal Diseases, Renewal Rural Areas.

Concerning the selection of the cases two preliminary notes should be made. First, although the cases include affairs that have mobilized actors all over the world, a Dutch bias cannot be excluded entirely. All selected issues in the cases are important for the agro-food system in the Netherlands, which is one of the most advanced countries in agribusiness in the world. Therefore, the selected issues have received much attention already from the agricultural research institutes. Second, the selected cases have overlapping dimensions. They cannot be separated from each other completely. For example, biogenetic engineering is interesting when you can sell your unique product all over the world and make your clients almost fully dependent on your business. Granting patents for these "organic" products as well as liberalization of the world trade system can support this strategy, of course (see 5.2 and 5.3).

Why then were the specific cases selected to illustrate the different human agro-activities? The following arguments are relevant. Via biogenetic engineering new types of plants and animals are produced (case 5.1). Because of the in-built characteristics the new products can compete effectively with well-known natural products. However, the seeds of the new plants (i.e., its reconstructed genetic structure) are a technological output which belongs to the producers, or so it is claimed. That is why the saving of the seeds seems to be no longer a fundamental right of the farmer (case 5.2). The allocation of agro-products was always a private affair in combination with serious governmental interventions and ordering of markets. The WTO will stop this public protection after some period of time (case 5.3). The EU has decided

Table 6.3 Six Cases; Agro-Food Human Activities, Main Actors

Activities	*Cases*	*Actors*		
		"Priests"	*"Warriors"*	*"Farmers"*
Economizing Producing	Biogenetica: genetic engineering	EU/USA state officials; WTO; "philosophers"	R+D-experts; geneticists; multinationals; BINGO's; PINGO's; environmentalists; consumer organizations	regional production differences for farmers; consumers' uncertainties
Economizing Saving	GATT-TRIPs and Plant Breeders' Rights	patent-bureaus	R+D-experts; geneticists; multinationals; BINGO's; PINGO's; environmentalists; consumer organizations	
Economizing Allocating	Uruguay-Round for agri-products; Implementation by the World Trade Organisation	WTO; Free trade promoters (The Economist, etc)	EU-institutions; BINGO's; US-officials Critical political-economists	(French) Farmers, Consumers Interest- and Pressure Groups
Orientating	EXPANSION EU; EU-CEE	European Council; National Central Banks; Eur. Central Institute	Debate on the CAP; Strategic managers and Scenario-writers; Diplomats EU- and applying countries	East-Europe Bank; private Banks; Farmers Organisations TNCs
Disciplining	Quality Control and Animal Diseases: Pork pest and (BSE)	EU-Veterinary Committee; EU Council of Ministers	Nat. Ministeries; Farmers Org's; BINGOs; Envronmentalists	Entrepreneurs (farmers; retailers; transporters; caterers) Consumers
Polity Constructing	Renewal Rural Areas; regional and local scale	Constraints by WTO-& EU-CAP-regimes	Institutes of Education, Information and R + D; Planners, Managers; Strategies + Steering Models	Cultural differences between countries; Professional Specialization; Freedom and Privacy of entrepreneurs

to open the union for new members. Now it is orientating which countries should be allowed to enter the union, when (sequence?) and under which conditions (case 5.4). Plants and animals are attacked by all types of illnesses throughout the history of agriculture. No wonder that there were always attempts to get rid of these uncertainties in the agricultural production system. To tackle these diseases the whole agro-food community ought to cooperate. Disciplining the actors involved is an urgent measure in the case of BSE and pork pest in Europe (case 5.5). Worldwide and continental agro-economic developments have influenced since centuries the rural development on the regional and local scale. Nowadays the pluriformity of agro-food innovations and political-economic developments need reflection in regional and local polity as well. Because of the cultural differentiation in farming and the perception of natural values in different countries, there will be no general recipe for regional and local polity renewal. Only national and particularly more decentralized policies can tackle these problems (case 5.6).

Table 6.3 shows a compilation of the selected cases. The actors involved are labeled under the metaphors "priests," "warriors" and "farmers." An actor is categorized according to the criterion "how he/she stands in the policy network." Actors who just feel involved and participate as an individual or as a member of an organized group, were put in the category "farmers." Actors, who are leaders/representatives of interest and pressure groups or operate as consultants of decision makers, were categorized as "warriors." "Nota bene": representatives of state institutions (ministers and civil servants, for example), being a party or fraction between other parties in the arena, can also be "warriors." The final category "priests" is filled up with decision makers, the formal as well as the informal ones, who can produce institutions which discipline the other actors.

PRESENTATION OF SELECTED CASES: DIFFUSION OF POWER IN AN EMPIRICAL SETTING

This section is dedicated to (the shifts in) the balances of power in the policy arenas of biogenetic engineering, fundamental rights of plant breeders, liberalization of the world trade also for agro-food products, the expansion of the EU with Central and East European countries and the public management of animal diseases (BSE/ pork pest), and the renewal of the rural areas. Of course, the descriptive-analyses present the headlines only.

Biogenetic Engineering

Environmentalists, consumer organizations and individual citizens as well as their "public interest nongovernmental organizations" (PINGOs) have started opposition to crops whose genes have been rearranged by scientists. Politicians in Europe, not in the United States surprisingly, have responded. Governments in Italy, Austria and Luxembourg have banned their farmers from growing genetically modified maize. The European Parliament recently demanded a halt to the sale of this maize throughout the EU. In the beginning of April 1997, one million Austrians signed a petition calling for a total ban on all genetically modified foods. That is why "priests" and "warriors" as well as "farmers" are active in the political arena concerning the products of biogenetic engineering.

However, transferring genes between species of plants is nothing new. Many crops are hybrids of various species. Wheat, for example, is derived from a hybrid of at least three different wild grasses. What is new, is the precision with which genes can be transferred. Unlike traditional hybridization, genetic engineering can take individual genes from one plant and pop them into another. In fact, it can take genes from nonplants, such as bacteria and even animals, and do exactly the same trick. Although many new techniques and products in genetic engineering are for the good, environmental groups argue that a number of things may go wrong once the genetically modified plants are in everyday use. The "warriors" act and counteract of course. Some say that genetic engineering will make people ill, for example, because pests become resistant to different types of antibiotics, which are used to test marker genes in order to speed up the work of the genetic engineers.[3]

A real giant in "the green gene" is Monsanto, a company based in St. Louis (Missouri, United States). Mr. Shapiro, who has led the firm since 1995, announces that Monsanto should be the main provider of the "agricultural biotechnology" the world will need if it is to feed itself in the future without despoiling the environment. On one estimate, the world market for crentically altered seeds will reach one million dollars in 2005, to $450 million in 1995. Some people think biotechnology might revolutionize farm productivity, the same as farm chemicals and irrigation led to huge leaps in world food production in previous decades. Many Wall Street analysts talk enthusiastically about Monsanto becoming the Microsoft of genetic engineering. Last year the company began selling genetically altered soybeans, potatoes and cotton to farmers. Dozes of more genetically altered products still are yet to come, including maize, sugar beet and strawberries. Virtually every other big chemical and drug firm is now in hot pursuit of Monsanto, trying to bring its own genetically modified seeds onto the market. Monsanto has responded by buying several seed producers (to improve its distribution network) and increasing investments in a chain of American biotech firms specializing in gene research. These acquisitions are based on little more than an intelligent guess about where the money is to be made in such a new industry. As Shapiro has said: there are no books on how to sell genetically modified seeds in places like China and India: "We don't know what we're doing most of the time . . . we are making it up."

The "warriors" enact a strategy of conflict not only in the degree of safety of biotechnological products. It is a matter of image as well. On the one hand, environmentalists and consumers show their fear for biological power, just as they have done for nuclear power.[4] Furthermore, the access to biotechnological knowledge is a political issue. Is it a new power resource in the hands of developed countries and its governments to continue their world control? The public dimension of biogenetic engineering needs to be researched much deeper. Is it a plausible hypothesis that biotechnological knowledge in multinational companies (MNCs) can cause almost complete dependency of rather monocultural economies in some nation-states? Then, if the development of this knowledge is supported by nation-states or by economic regions (NAFTA, EU, ASEAN), within which the headquarters of the MNC concerned is located, is it plausible as well that biogenetic engineering can have geo-political impacts? On the other hand, the biotech firms talk passionately not only about how to make money but also how "to feed the world" (the world's population will double inevitably in 2030), how to stop the environmental degradation and how to create real "sustainability." Although the economic impact of biogenetic engineering is relatively limited nowadays, the production of genetic manipulated products is only the first phase in economizing these agrofood goods and services. The next two cases, concerning "saving" and "allocating," demonstrate a direct link to these new production techniques.

Following the summary of *The Economist* (26(4) 1997: 94)

> . . . many of the fears about genetically modified plants are exaggerated. . . . However, these plants are not risk-free. But, provided regulators are vigilant, there is no reason to believe they will make farming inherently more dangerous. Perhaps, though, that will never be enough. For many people, worries about the consequences of genetic modification reflect an underlying spiritual concern about science meddling with the very basis of life. Such concern—the province of priests and philosophers, not scientists and politicians—cannot merely be regulated away.

A first critical note to this summary is that in our view scientists and politicians have also ethical responsibilities concerning the introductions of these new agro-food products. This is not only the field of "softees." Secondly, what is striking in the approach of *The Economist* is its totally abstract from relevant power relations, i.e. from the future balance of power in the world *casu quo* between powerful economic regions.

This case shows a diffusion of power between the United States and MNCs (probably supported by U.S. governmental officials) and the European Committee of the EU-15. The manipulated maize, for example, was already laying in ships alone, the quays of the Rotterdam Harbor before the opposition of the "farmers" and the "consumers" in the EU-15 started seriously protesting. The EU-"priests" seemed to have blessed the U.S. producers and officials in advance, not waiting for the acceptance in the European "civic society" and the formal EP-approval.

GATT-TRIPs and Plant Breeders' Rights

As mentioned above, the selected cases are linked politically as well as economically. On behalf of the advanced biotechnological firms, the United States and the EU have dealt with the developing countries hardly concerning the Trade Related Intellectual Property Rights (TRIPs) during the negotiations in the Uruguay Round. This issue is a key problem in the North-South-relations. Particularly the access to the new technological and scientific research outputs is a controversial issue. The developing countries deduced from the propositions presented at the opening conference at Punta del Este that they would be cut off from these scientific results and consequently from the perspectives of economic growth in these fields. The South feared a new international labor division, which gives access to intellectually interesting and well-paid work to the North and labor intensive, low-paid work to the South. The developed countries argued in turn that a great part of the intellectual and scientific progress was produced in private firms, which need the financial and competitive advantages of these inventions. Almost free access for "outsiders" to their RD products would destroy any reason to invest in these branches. Therefore, most industrial sectors in the rich countries (pharmaceutical, chemical, informatica, and textile industry) demand for severe rules to protect their inventions against imitation and plagiary of firms and institutes in countries which do not control and maintain rules of intellectual property so much. For the North, the TRIP is so important that these countries were ready to give in concerning the elimination of the multi-fibre arrangement, which has allowed them to bar gain (even under the GATT-regime) about export-limits in textiles from the South to the North on a free and bilateral basis (Kerremans 1994: 377–78).

The TRIP seem to have the structural power to change dependencies in the global agro-food network. It creates new rules, procedures and institutions that will have impact on economic and cultural dimensions of the production, the saving and the allocation of food throughout the world. Of course, the main condition is the implementation and the maintenance of this new regime. What is the argument for this revolutionary change? The TRIP intervenes in the worldwide dominant Plant Breeders' Rights. The TRIP obligates the countries to give patent and breeders' rights to plant genes and plant breeds, which meet the criteria for protection of intellectual property rights. Then, the upgraders of breeds can prohibit their competitors in the developing countries to use a protected plant breed for commercial reasons without permission and payments. The local fanners are controlled by this

TRIP regime as well. The impact can be a dramatic decline of the distribution of new, more productive seeds, which are necessary in order to increase the production of food in the developing countries. In these countries, the farmers collect about 80 percent of the seeds from outside the commercial circuit. They buy some fresh seeds in order to multiply them as much and as long as possible. They often buy the seeds on credit: they pay with a part of the harvest. So, because of this exchange in nature, the farmers are less dependent on the currency rates. Because this exchange is not registered, the farmers do not pay royalties and taxes. Therefore, they are less vulnerable. This character of the exchange economy developed in a local network will change under the global TRIP-regime. Exchange trade in seeds of protected plant breeds is illegal. Particularly in Argentina and Chile the foreign plant upgraders try to implement their rights massively nowadays. Reporters are invited to write about the new plant breeders' regime. Lawyers and judges are instructed in the functioning of the seed market. Undercover agents try to find the illegal multiplication of protected seeds. Under these circumstances, the foreign "warriors" try to force the domestic "priests" to accept a new disciplinary regime and to implement it in their praxis. Of course, the farmers in the developing countries are often innocent of the type of private property right that a global regime has given to a foreign firm that is unknown to them. Therefore, the farmers do not feel comfortable in accepting the structural power of this regime.

Of course, the TRIP-regime has a link with the first case. The more the techniques of biogenetic engineering are developed, the more different and protected plant breeds can be introduced in accordance with specific climatological, geo-morphological and ecological conditions. The TRIP regime, if implemented and maintained, is a precondition which allows the MNCs, especially those involved in biogenetics, to control the agro-food production and the saving activities related to it in large areas of the world. The more these MNCs form a policy community with IGOs and nation-states, the more this diffusion of power can imply geo-political externalities.

Implementation Uruguay Round Agreement (GATT/WTO)

The "General Agreement on Tariffs and Trade" (GATT) system is based on four principles: nondiscrimination, market compatibility, predictability and special and differential treatment of products from developing countries. The GATT requires that trade instruments be compatible with the functioning of the price system. According to Nicolaides (1994: 23 1): "The founding fathers of the GATT were less interested in theoretical arguments of the superiority of free markets over other economic systems and more concerned about the dislocation of trade caused by government interventionism." Although the Uruguay Round has decided to found the World Trade Organization, the institutional structure of the GATT[5] is not an international organization (see, for example, the World Bank) which cannot act on its own. It needs continuous approval by its members. In the GATT, a multilateral treaty, decisions should be made by contracting parties jointly. This multilateral character of the GATT guarantees benefits to all participants, although these benefits are not shared equally by all participating countries.

The GATT *operates as a network*, which is in the middle of the continuum mentioned above. The eight rounds of negotiations since 1948 have resulted in many rules and procedures concerning the main principles of the GATT without becoming a real policy community. The GATT is mainly a loosely coupled system of nation-states. Not one single country, not even a large one with great market power, can maintain a worldwide system of rules to guide international transactions and to resolve the disputes that arise from time to time. It is a network based on several outstanding issues. Main disputes in the Uruguay Round concerned issues such as market access in service sectors (e.g., telecommunications, finance, etc.), infringements of intellectual property rights (see 5.2), obstacles to direct investments, and market-dominating cartels in strategic industries. The GATT agenda is complex, because there is a firm belief that now because the scope of the GATT is wide, it would make it easier for participating countries to strike a bargain on the contentious issues. "The conventional wisdom was that agreement on those issues had not been achieved in earlier rounds because they were too narrow in scope" (Nicolaides 1994: 237). The GATT agenda illustrates also the proposition (Hocking and Smith 1995: 92) that "there is no longer a settled hierarchy of issues in world politics. Instead, there is a fluctuating international "agenda" reflecting concerns and influences of a wide range of actors."

The *agricultural trading relations* (concerning 10 to 13 percent of world trade) held a strategic position during the Uruguay Round (1986–1993). The overall aim was to devise "modalities" for incorporating agriculture into the GATT. The "Punta del Este Declaration" was very broad, but the main points of dispute were clear: the degree of liberalization, the extent to which quotas had to be converted into tariffs, the products that would be covered, and the definition of objectionable subsidies. In fact, it is surprising that it was not until 1986 that a serious attempt was made to bring agricultural affairs under the GATT. "The exclusion of agriculture from international trade agreements resulted in a situation in which agricultural trade decisions had to be made in a unilateral fashion. In spite of this, large countries cannot change agricultural policies without triggering repercussions in international commodity markets. As a consequence, the interdependence of agricultural policy decisions has forced countries to take into account the effects of their actions on other countries, and ultimately on themselves" (Lynn Kennedy et al. 1996: 382). After the move from fixed to floating exchange rates in 1973 and the sharp rise of costs of farm programs in the early 1980s, a political demand provoked a reform in agricultural trade policy in many countries. Because the growing international interdependence made unilateral reform politically unattractive, policy makers had to consider the option of starting negotiations in an international arena. However, this suggests that a common political rationality would account for the agro-agenda in the Uruguay Round. According to Skogstad (1994: 246), however, it was the U.S. government, who sought to halt the slide in American international competitiveness by "bolstering" the GATT trading regime and bringing under its rubric those matters (agriculture, services, intellectual property, investment) in which it perceived itself enjoying a competitive advantage in a liberal market economy. At the same time, breaking down other nations' barriers to American exports was seen to be a lever by which a liberal-minded U.S. administration could stem the tide of domestic protectionism. In fact, the U.S. government had already attempted to incorporate agriculture under the GATT during the Kennedy Administration (1963–1967) and the Tokyo Round (1973–1979). In both cases, it had to accept "a largely symbolic outcome in agriculture" when the EC resisted U.S. pressures.

Thus, Skogstad brings in a new variable: *the ever-existing relationship between domestic and foreign politics*. In my opinion, this variable implies generally a serious diffusion of power between state and nonstate actors. The preferential treatment of agriculture in the GATT (1948–1986) reflected the primacy of domestic political forces in the United States, Canada, Australia and, undoubtedly, in the Common Agricultural Policy of the EU. Public support for this protectionism persisted for a long time because: a) policy makers recognized the imperfections of agricultural markets and b) these policies received strong institutional supports from well-organized farm lobbies, autonomous agricultural ministries, and politicians whose electoral survival depended on securing rural votes (Skogstad 1994: 248). From 1982 to 1986, U.S. agricultural exports declined. Therefore, these exports could no longer compensate for the nonagricultural deficit. The EC, who became a significant exporter of grains, dairy products and beef, was offended by the United States. First, U.S. measures caused lower world grain prices that meant higher costs for grain export subsidies for the EC. Then, a devaluation of the dollar was allowed together with the introduction of the 1985 Food Security Act, which lowered loan rates and mandated the reintroduction of export subsidies. Under these circumstances, the EC, who was under severe budgetary pressures as well, accepted the Declaration of Punta del Este (1986) which brought agriculture on the agenda in the Uruguay Round. As a result, the United States and the EC, as the two largest agricultural trading blocks, were competitively interdependent.[6] During the Uruguay Round, this competitiveness caused a long-term deadlock. The balance of power was in an unstable equilibrium. In fact, this situation prolonged the Uruguay Round by two years (1991–1993). According to Skogstad (1994: 253–54), French farmers played a catalytic role in breaking the deadlock between the United States and the EU. Although it was not intended to influence the GATT-negotiations, the EU agricultural ministers' endorsement, in May 1992, of reforms to the CAP, radically altered the degree and nature of agricultural support. The announced reduction of volumes of grains met with the United States *conditio sine qua non* for a GATT agreement. The opposition of the French farmers against this part of the CAP reform, however, worked out negatively for a GATT-agreement, because the French government would not agree with any further compromises that such an agreement might require. A few months later, in November 1992, the EU did not accept the panel results concerning subsidies on oilseed processors. Once again, this was reinforced by French farmers' opposition. After the United States had threatened to impose duties of 200 percent on EC food exports, including French white wine, the EU accepted a reduction of oilseed production and to cut its exports of subsidized goods. Then, the negotiations continued and resulted in the Blair House Agreement, which opened the way so as to conclude the Uruguay Round. Both the U.S.'s flexibility on the implementation of the Blair House Agreement and the EU's assurance that the GATT trade concessions were largely consistent with internal CAP reforms, made it possible for the first time to include a set of international rules for agriculture.

In sum, the Uruguay Round has realized better conditions for a worldwide allocation of agro-products in the future. In comparison with the EU, the U.S. interests—both public and private—have been persistently global in their reach. Still, both blocks approach the regulation of international agricultural trade mainly from their own viewpoints. They are the main "warriors," not the "priests" in this arena. The introduction of agro-products in the GATT/WTO treaty, however, is an important step in sustaining the food supply to the people in the world[7] in the future. On the one hand, the GATT/WTO-arena is urging the EU to change its protecting CAP. New regions (NAFTA, CAIRNS, ASEAN, Pacific) to become manifest concerning CAP reform as well (Vernon 1996). On the other hand, the pressure to reform the CAP is also strong within the EU itself. Without such a change, the German reunification and the opening of the EU for Central and East European candidates seem to be almost unmanageable. It was wise of the United States to understand, after the Blair House Agreement (December 1992), the complexity of the position of its main competitor and ally. In the GATT/WTO arena the nation-states still operate as the main actors. A question which should be further researched is: if and how multinational enterprises and alliances among firms can/will promote regions of nation-states (NAFTA + Latin America; Asia under the leadership of Japan; an integrated Europe?: Vernon 1996). For example, the top ten seed corporations in 1988 controlled 20.65 percent of the seed sales in the world market. The top ten pesticide suppliers in 1988 controlled as much as 75.02 percent of the global market.[8]

MNCs, generally, have an enormous interest in the results of the WTO agreement (see TRIPs and Breeders' Rights, for example) as well as in the opening of the markets to the CEE-countries.

EU-CAP and EU Expansion to Central and East Europe

This section is dedicated to the shifts in the balances of power in the agro-food policy network concerning the expansion of the EU within Central and Eastern European countries (CEE-candidates). The structure and processes of policy making in the EU are complex (Andersen and Eliassen, 1993; Williams 1996) and the juridical order should be clearly distinguished from the political order (Sbragia 1992; van Schendelen 1984). The lobby arenas are extremely complex as well (van Schendelen 1993). Diffusion of power is probably at stake. Van der Zee (1997; app. 10.2) has listed 173 "Euro-groups" involved in the EC agricultural policy formation (based on EU and own observations).

The Common Agricultural Policy (CAP) is often debated (Kol and Kuijpers 1997) not only in relation to the expansion of the EU. The CAP agenda contains more issues[9] than its accommodation to 10 new partners in Central and East Europe[10] as well as to Malta, Cyprus, and Turkey (van der Meer 1997: 23–24). In short, the EU-CAP and the expansion of the EU is a subject related to many other key issues in the field of European agriculture. All actors orientate themselves (by "timing," "planning," "dividing," and "managing") to strategies that can produce a profitable commitment package for all issues at the same time (i.e., 1999–2000). Therefore, it is prime time for scenario writers, business forecasters, and international civil servants as well as diplomats. They are the "warriors," who try to get a favorable position for the forthcoming negotiations.

The European Council decided (Copenhagen summit, June 1993) that new member states from Central and East Europe were welcome to enter the Union. Therefore, the main political decision was passed four years ago. The EU's expansion concerns in essence a matter of implementation. Technically, the job can be delegated to civil servants, technocrats and experts. However, such a mandate to the bureaucracies will probably not be delivered because of the political status of the CAP in the European Community. In fact, the CAP:

> . . . lies at the heart of the practical application of the European vision. . . Enshrined in Article 39 of the Treaty of Rome in 1957, the commitment to common organization of the market for food survived intact and was incorporated unamended into the Maastricht Treaty in 1992. The other common policies do not exercise such symbolic power within the Union . . . More positively, the CAP provides evidence that agriculture carries a cultural and social significance far in excess of its economic importance. . . The totemic role is enhanced at a time when the new elements of European unity outlined at Maastricht, the common currency

> and the common foreign and security policy, are struggling to find a realistic formulation . . . The CAP is the culmination of over one hundred years of state support for agriculture in western Europe. (Ockenden and Franklin 1995: 1–2)

These political roots of the CAP will provide a permanent interest for the "priests" (the politicians who have to take the final decisions) as well as the (organized) "farmers" (agrarian entrepreneurs). Of course, most of the work will be done by the "warriors" (the civil servants, diplomats). However, the image of the political leaders of the EU-member states will require them to be prepared permanently to debate about EU-WTO and EU-CEE membership arrangements. Of course, the "farmers" interest- and pressure ("Euro"-)groups will lobby also to prevent any loss in competitive positions.

The complexity of the political EU-CEE-agenda prohibits a forecast about which countries will enter the Union, at what time and under which conditions. It is expected that none of the CEE countries can enter the Union before the year 2003. Partly, the argument is the economic gap between the EU and the CEE-10 (table 6.4).

The agricultural integration of the CEE-10 is often used as a second argument against a fast expansion of the EU. Agriculture is an important sector in the CEE-10 economies, although there are serious differences as well (table 6.5). The CEE-10 are almost as different as the member states of the EU-15 itself. In general, however, the agricultural productivity is much lower in the CEE than in the EU-15. A third argument against speeding up the EU-expansion is the different levels of prices of interventions in the EU-15 in comparison with the CEE-10. Although this is true (table 6.6), the argument is not very valid. The CEE-10 cannot pay the EU-intervention level. The public budgets in these countries cannot afford it and the governments do not like to take money from other sectors. So that is why the CEE-10 want to start with rural renewal. Therefore, the CEE-10 prefers financial support from the EU for restructuring, modernizing and diversification of the capacity of agricultural production, saving and allocation. The infrastructure in the rural areas has to be especially updated as soon as possible. From this point of view, the Phare program, for example, should offer stronger inputs for the land use reconstruction in the rural areas.

Table 6.4. GNP/Capita in Some EU-Countries and CEE-10 (average together and separate)

	GR	*PT*	*IRL*	*ESP*	*C 10*	*PL*	*CZ*	*H*	*SK*	*SL*	*RO*	*BG*	*BALT*
93	63	70	80	77	28	26	47	33	35	51	21	23	20
94	62	69	83	77	30	28	50	36	38	56	22	25	20
95	61	69	86	77	32	31	53	37	41	58	24	24	21

Source: Eurostat.

Table 6.5 Review of Agriculture in Central and East Europe (CEE-10)

	Agricultural Surface		*Agricultural Production*		*Agricultural Employment*	
	(mil.ha)	*(% total surface)*	*(bil.ECU)*	*(%BNP)*	*(x1000)*	*(% total) employment)*
Poland	18.6	59	4.648	6.3	3661	25.6
Hungary	6.1	66	2.068	6.4	392	10.1
Czech Rep.	4.3	54	0.871	3.3	271	5.6
Slovakia Rep.	2.4	49	0.512	5.8	178	8.4
Slovania	0.9	43	0.250	4.9	90	10.7
Romenia	14.7	62	4.500	20.2	3537	35.2
Bulgaria	6.2	55	1.131	10.0	694	21.2
Lithuania	3.5	54	0.259	11.0	399	22.4
Latvia	2.5	39	0.232	10.6	229	18.4
Estonia	1.4	31	0.266	10.4	89	8.2
CEE-10	60.6	56	214.707	7.8	9540	26.7
EU-15	138.1	43	208.8	2.5	8190	5.7

Source: European Committee 1995.

Table 6.6. Intervention-Prices in Visegrad-Countries and the EU (1994)

	WHEAT		*BEEF*		*MILK*	
	ecu/ton	*%EU*	*ecu/ton*	*%EU*	*ecu/ton*	*%EU*
Poland	89	69%	1110	30%	87	28%
Hungary	66	51%	1609	44%	201	65%
Cz Rep	87	67%	1566	43%	171	55%
Slovakia	92	71%	1546	42%	179	58%
EU	129(=100%)		3680(=100%)		310(=100%)	

Source: European Committee 1995.

The main reason, however, why the integration of the CEE-10 is rather slow seems to be the *absence of an EU vision on the future of the CAP* (Boonstra 1996: 44). On the one hand, economic "purists" want to give the CAP a knockout: no longer financial support to agriculture and a free market as ordering principle. On the other hand, "moderates" foresee a permanent need of governmental intervention in agro-food economic activities. One can imagine that the reality will be somewhere between the purist and the moderate opinion. The EC will probably propose to continue in the MacSharry-line (since 1992). This policy implies (Berichout 1996: 11)

- Deepening the system (read: lower prices) in combination with some compensations.
- Liberalization in more agro-sectors in order to keep competitive power.
- Connecting transfer payments to social and environmental targets (cross compliance).
- Programming the rural renewal comprehensively and orientating the farmers to multifunctional "fanning" (*entrepeneur rurale*): according to the principle of subsidiary the role of national and regional governance will increase.

A few arguments make this policy relatively realistic. First, it implies a compromise between different opinions in the EU-15. Secondly, it helps to discover a negotiable position in the next WTO-round. Thirdly, more liberalization and lower prices are profitable for the consumers. Still, the incomes of the EU farmers keep purchasing power. Next, it promotes some convergence to the prices in CEE-candidate-10 agricultural markets. It also prevents the need for a continuous increase of the EU agro-budget of which the political legitimization is no longer possible. Finally, it helps the CEE-10 to spread their budgets over more economic sectors than agriculture only and by doing so the political stability is supported. Conclusion: this policy helps the CEE-10 to get closer to the EU-CAP in the near future.

However, the *balance of power* between the EU-15 and the CEE-candidate-10 is asymmetric. The economic statistics support the following conclusion: from a competitive perspective the EU-15 has nothing to fear from CEE-EU-membership. In fact, the CEE-market offers an overkill in economic opportunities. However, from an EU perspective this is not wholly a good thing. For example, a booming export (e.g., in some Russian cities EU-exporters are absolute market-leaders in the food-supply, sometimes by 80 percent!) can hinder investments for growing productivity in the near future. Osmosis to non-competitive markets can cause entrepreneurial dysfunction in economic strong markets. The disequity in power between the EU-15 and the CEE-10 seems to have inspired the EU to formulate three severe conditions for entering the union:

- Institutional stability concerning democracy, juridical order, human rights and minorities.
- A functioning market economy as well as competitive power to resist the economic pressure from the union.
- Candidates should be able to accept the EU membership obligations dynamic of the process of integration.

On the one hand, these conditions attempt to guarantee the continuity of the process of EU integration, which is a process of keeping peace and international security. On the other hand, these conditions favor the power position of the EU in the European agro-food network. However, the EU accepts the responsibility to accelerate and to support the reformation in the CEE-countries as well (Phare 1990–1995; circa 4.4 billion ECU). The East European Development Bank works in the same way. Recently, at the 50th Anniversary of the Marshall Plan (May 1997), President Clinton (United States) and the President of the European Council (Prime Minister Kok of the Netherlands) announced the preparation of a US $100 billion plan for the CEE countries. This proposal has been designed by a consortium of international bankers, a strategic "warrior" in this arena. It demonstrates the common interests of western state and nonstate actors in the CEE integration. Yet, it is the asymmetric power of the EU that prescribes the tempo. Of course, an important question is what will happen if political stability in Russia weakens dramatically. In my opinion, a plausible hypothesis is the acceptance of (a serious part of) the CEE-10, almost unconditional and immediate. Indeed, a scenario to give entrance to new members which were not yet ready was used earlier (Greece, 1981). Under political pressure, many macro-economic estimations and political-economic modeling can lose their value rather quickly.

In sum, the EU and the CEE-10 countries are interdependent. The EU is an economic world power. It offers an interesting economic climate for advanced entrepreneurs in the CEE-region. For the EU the CEE-countries offer a market of circa 100 million inhabitants with a potential purchasing power. Agribusiness, agro-food scientific knowledge centers and organizations as well as lobby groups of farmers are also ready to improve and strengthen their power positions in the CEE-10. Several major groups of new players in agriculture ("warriors") have been developed over the past few decades. Most of the new players are businesses that offer input supplies to "farmers." Some are rather powerful. For example, the top ten seed corporations in 1988 controlled 20.65 percent of the seed sales in the world market. The top ten pesticide suppliers in 1988 controlled even 75.02 percent of the global market.[11] MNCs, generally, have an enormous interest in the results of the WTO-agreement (see TRIPs and Breeders' Rights, for instance) as well as in the opening of the markets to the CEE-countries. On the other hand, some advanced entrepreneurs in the CEE are ready to make joint ventures in order to get access to relevant power resources (science, information, and management). Others in the CEE will accept western leadership in their agrarian firm in order to continue employment.

However, the process of economic integration will not continue under a regime of equal division of power resources in Europe. For example, the conditions for agriculture in Talinn and Lisbon will always vary extraordinarily. How could one imagine that a general CAP is capable of tackling all the relevant problems? The cultural differences in agriculture in the member states (Hoggart et al. 1995) as well as in the candidate states are political obstacles to implement the WTO agreement as well as a general EU-CAP. Further re-nationalization of some aspects of the CAP sounds reasonable, but will include the danger of erosion of the process of integration as well. Although the neo-liberal ideology of free trade dominates the political elite of the EU (the "priests"), the agricultural "warriors" and "farmers" often put their feet on the brakes. They demonstrate that they are "moderates" for the most part. Nevertheless, its seems that the process of liberalization will continue. Therefore, it will be a sign of wisdom if the moderates ("interventionists") can produce a vision of the future of agriculture in an EU-25, which contains an alternative scenario. The main subject should be not how to survive in a liberalized perfectly free market, but under the enormous variety in imperfect markets (van Kuyvenhoven 1997: 76; Boonstra 1996: 44).

It is always important to remember that, besides economic interests, there are also political interests on both sides. Germany, the uncrowned king of Europe, especially favors the EU as a legitimization for its own power. The main purpose of the integration of the CEE-10 into the EU (and some of them into NATO) is to help Germany (and by this Western Europe as a whole) to realize its logic in action. Therefore, the CEE integration can also be considered as an instrument that may serve to promote political and military security and economic prosperity throughout Europe.

International Animal Disease Management (BSE)

Bovine Spongiform Encephalopathy (BSE or "mad cow disease") quite possibly causes a variation of Creuzfelt Jacob Disease (CJD), which can probably kill human beings.[12] The BSE-disease has caused many doubts about the quality control of meat first in Great Britain, and later throughout the EU. BSE was found in Britain, France, Switzerland, Germany, Portugal and the Netherlands. The management of the BSE-crisis in the EU can illustrate that a particular sovereign nation state has not enough orientation and organizational power nowadays to resist the common administrative power of a regional authority like the EU in the long term. Great Britain could not continue its domestic politics, after the EU had decided that export of British meat, not only to the EU but also to third countries, was not allowed anymore. Of course, the extra EU demand that Britain would have to destroy properly four million cows aged above 30 months, was not easy to fulfill by the British agro sector. Britain developed some hinder power. In the period May to June 1996, two months before the EU Summit in Florence, Great Britain vetoed about 50 EC proposals in the EU Council of Ministers. At the end of the Florence summit, however, it worked out that Britain realized that the political costs of being a noncooperative member of the EU were too high. By and large the EU, as an intergovernmental authority, claimed political power successfully against the British hinder power. However, the financial-economic price of the EU anti-BSE measures is high as well. The EU will pay 70 percent compensation to the British fanners. Although this percentage is regular under the EU-CAP policy, it is still a high price particularly because both the British government and the agro-sector were clearly neglecting advice to take measures against BSE for almost 10 years. Especially, the registration of cattle families should be better organized. Further on, the use of organs meat in burgers and sausages for human consumption should be avoided. Remember also that the United States and Canada closed imports of British meat since 1991 already.

Why did Britain not take enough measures? A plausible hypothesis concerns a successful lobby of meat manufacturing industries and destruction houses to deregulate and liberalize this food sector in the late 1970s, and early 1980s (Kralt 1997). These suggestions were in accordance with the dominant political ideology at the start of the Thatcher regime. Especially, the food industry was allowed to work with lower temperatures, which diminished production costs but, alas, gave also scrapie procreators a chance to survive. Therefore, it seems that domestic political variables—lobby by nonstate actors, being part of a powerful electorate, as well as the ideology of a new political regime—coincided, creating different circumstances for the production of cattle fodder which in its turn promoted, unfortunately, optimal conditions for the procreation of BSE in cows. Doubts expressed from abroad e.g. by the EU Veterinary Committee of Experts (1990) and from the German Minister of Health Care ("BSE is the AIDS problem of the nineties," 1995; quoted by Hoogstraten 1997: 12), were not accepted. Scientists could not prove to be right when stating that BSE could pass the species barrier of human beings at that time. Just this picture has been changed in March 1996, when the British Minister of Health said in the Parliament that BSE most probably caused the CJD in some (young) people.

The BSE case, which could be completed by the way how the EU and some nation states manage the pig pest crisis during 1997, demonstrates that the EU Agencies—the "priests"—could not implement and maintain their regime in a specific nation state for a long time. As stated above, the United Kingdom could produce hinder power effectively for a rather long period of time. Only when the "farmers" (farmers and consumers) continued to worry about the possible impacts of the BSE disease, the "warriors" came under political and economic pressure to solve this problem, at least to control the effects by disciplining one member state.

Rural Renewal: From "Farmers" to "Rural Entrepreneurs"

The data analyzed in the cases above are relevant for "farmers" throughout the world. Particularly biogenetic engineering, the GATT-TRIP, and the implementation of the agricultural part in the Uruguay Round agreement will change the style of farming almost everywhere in the near future. The fanners in the EU and the CEE countries have to accommodate to the new market conditions after the expansion of the EU. As a part of the EU "Agenda 2000," the EU-CAP has to be adapted before the entrance of about 5 CEE candidates (Poland, Czech Republic, Hungary, Estonia, and Slovenia) in the next few years (*The Economist*, 19 September, 1997: 27–28). Of course, the GATT-WTO policy and the new EU-CAP will work out differently for the agrarian firms dependent on the political geographical position of the rural area where these entities belong. In general, the global political and economic developments will differentiate the farming conditions at the regional and local level (Wilkin 1997). Because the variety in physical conditions and the related cultural dimensions of farming and rural life is great, the new global trends will not only change but also deepen the existing styles of farming.

> The styles of farming concept nearly always implies that we are talking about highly differentiated practices which are due to different and strategically chosen "positions" of farmers as family, cultural repertoires, markets, technological developments, relations with agribusiness companies and extentionists are concerned. . . . Despite the growing "grip" of markets and technology on the organization of the production process, these provide room for maneuver for farmers, that is, they allow for deferential positions. (Hebrinck and van der Ploeg 1997: 207).

As Hougart et al. (1995) has learned concerning rural Europe, from a cultural point of view the farming styles in Britain, France, Germany, Italy, Denmark and the Netherlands differ enormously. Probably these differences will increase, particularly when the new EU-CAP will partly imply a renationalization of the agricultural polity. At the same time a (collective of) firm(s) in a specific rural region can only survive as an actor in the world wide agro-food system if it

> . . . succeeds in imposing itself as an obligatory point of passage between the global and the local network. This means that, if successful, the project (of a firm: HG) should first have the ability to shape and mobilize the local network and that, second, the project is able to exercise control over all exchanges between the local and the global network. (Verschoor 1997: 207)

In that case it is right to label the farmer as a "rural entrepreneur." However, this label is often used not only for the advanced agrarians who have the power resources to create a robust economic position in the global agro-food networks, but also for the modest farmers, particularly in the EU, who try to continue as a family firm by expanding their variety of economic activities. For example to become a manager of a small camping site or a distributor of a specific regional product (cheese or asparagus), which promotes the region as an interesting tourist area. From this perspective the political and economic changes in agriculture can alter the sight of the countryside dramatically. Perhaps farmers in the EU will be important professionals in forestry, woodland, nature protection and leisure (Gilg 1996). Of course, in the trends that will change the rural areas, at least in the EU, the role of the national government has to be adapted as well. Although the policy makers at the national level often accept the challenge to plan and to steer the renewal of rural areas, it is doubtful if their power position allows them to play a top-down role. As far as this questions the planning approach of the national policymakers, this problem has been addressed elsewhere (Goverde 1997). In fact the problem has a wider scope. The government was always involved to protect farmers' incomes, to guarantee food supplies and to regulate the food prices. Nowadays these objectives are added by other collective purposes of fanning like the sustainability, the desire of nature protection, the preservation of the scenic beauty of the landscape, the recreational attractiveness and the social acceptability. According to Frouws (1997: 84):

> This change brought about a repoliticization of the agrarian question as the use of the land is more severely contested than ever before. Now that the insulating political protection of agrarian corporatism has largely disappeared, the social contract of farmers with society is being reconsidered.

If the civil servants like to get a legitimized position again in the governance of agriculture they should participate in the networks which contribute to redefine both farming as a profession and rural space. Perhaps this strategy will be enhanced by the EU, when the EC "priests" will lead the agrarian communities, at least the Europeans, to a new contract that includes "cross compliance," linking environmental conditions with measures of economic support practiced already before in the United States (Boonstra 1996: 43).

DIFFUSION OF POWER IN AGRO-FOOD (SUB-)NETWORKS: SOME REFLECTIONS

In this concluding section first a summary is made of the approach used in this study. Then some reflections are presented about the diffusion of power in the agro-food (sub)networks, which were studied. A conclusion will round off these reflections.

Summary of the Research Approach

From a historical perspective three component parts were constructed for the analysis of power in the agro-food system today:

1. The basic human activities in the agro-food system: economizing, orientating, disciplining, polity constructing.
2. The three main categories of actors: priests, warriors and farmers (used as metaphors in the descriptive frame of reference).
3. The concept of "a shift in the balance of power": from a religious agrarian regime to a military agrarian regime.

The first two components ("basic human activities" and "categories of actors") were used to order the available data concerning events, trends and forecasts in the real agrarian world. A matrix (see tables 6.1 and 6.2) gives insight into the dependencies between the different types of actors. This insight was used to select the key, but mutually related, cases in the agro-food system today (table 6.3). The third element ("shifts in the balance of power") was investigated by perceiving the agro-food system as a "network," consisting of loosely coupled, mutually dependent subnetworks concerning the selected key issues. These key issues were approached with a specific research design: a qualitative multiple case study. In this case study "the power balance analysis" was the main research method.

The concept of "policy network" combines insights from policy science (focusing on public policy processes) and ideas from political science and organization theory about the distribution of power and dependencies, organizational features, and interorganizational relations (Kickert et al. 1997: 1; 14–34). The theory of policy networks is in accordance with the idea of the diffusion of power, because it has been developed as a reaction to the model of rational comprehensive decision making. In this model governmental institutions were supposed to be the central and most powerful policy makers in a society. However, the concept of the diffusion of power is based on the idea that nongovernmental actors can influence public issues and collective actions seriously. Of course, the governmental actors will continue their specific societal function (maintaining public values and the public interest). However, the position of the government can no longer be perceived as the top of a hierarchy from which it steers the society. The governmental representatives are participants (partners or competitors) between other parties in the political arena. None of the participants in the agrarian policy-(sub-)network are able to realize their goals all by themselves. Therefore governmental and nongovernmental actors in the same network are interdependent. This mutual dependency implies the diffusion of power.

Diffusion of Power in the Analyzed Cases

The cases shortly presented above (section 5) illustrate a diffusion of power, particularly between state- and nonstate actors. However, the multiple case study as a whole has generated mainly knowledge about shifts of power in the selected issues. It does not imply that the diffusion of power can always be made clear in a way that some (combination of) actors can be reputed as more powerful than other participants nor that such reputations can be explained completely. However, concerning the analyzed (sub-)networks the following claims about the diffusion of power can be made plausible:

- In "biogenetic engineering" a diffusion of power was discovered not only between American state actors and nonstate actors as MNCs, but also between the "priests" on both sides of the Atlantic (the civil servants of the United States and the EU). The only opposition, European "farmers" (a coalition of farmers, environmentalists and consumers) entered the political arena rather late and oriented their power resources (petition, media support) to the European Parliament, an almost powerless participant in the biogenetic policy network.
- The case concerning the GATT-TRIP and the Plant Breeders' Rights showed an almost classical competitive interdependence between the (state and nonstate) "warriors" of the North and the South. The North participants want to protect (under the GATT-"free world trade"-regime: sic!) the access to their technological knowledge which as a mean of orientation is, of course, a very important power resource. Because the TRIP introduces new rules, procedures and institutions, the North creates a new power resource by these means of organization. This new power tool has been implemented already with the use of means of vi-

olence, another power resource, in some regions of the South. The South fears a new labor division in the process of globalization.

- The GATT-TRIP, if implemented and maintained seriously, is a regulative power resource which gives the holders [mostly MNCs in combination with governments of nation states or regional authorities (NAFFA, EU, ASEAN)] the capacity to change parts of the geo-political agrarian world order, first in countries dependent from rather monocultural crops, later in countries with differentiated harvests as well (Taylor 1993: 50–102).
- The balance of power between the EU- and the CEE-countries is always supposed to be asymmetrical in favor of the EU. However, the EU-CEE integration requires adaptations on both sides.[13] Of course, the EU has outstanding regulative powers: it sets the rules, the procedures and the timing. Although the CEE-candidates have to pay for their own membership, the EU will not receive an economic market of 100 million people free of charge.
- In general, the EU and the CEE seem to be symbiotically interdependent. However in the details of the negotiations some competitive interdependence will become manifest as well. The diffusion of power in the EU is quite different in comparison to the CEE countries. While it is well coordinated in the EU countries, in the CEE countries there are many social-psychological and political obstacles for a functional cooperation between state and nonstate actors. Apart from their objective economic power this is the main reason why the EU countries have a dominant power position. If a real countervailing power will not be developed in the CEE countries, there is a danger that the entrance into the EU will work out as a new type of colonization (particularly in fields of banking, assurances and premium funds). In order to realize a more equal balance of power in Europe, which can guarantee political stability in the long term, hopefully the EU negotiations will enhance the disciplining and polity constructing process to an adequate diffusion of power in the leading CEE countries.
- The EU management of the BSE crisis demonstrates how social cohesion can explain the policy processes in policy networks. Particularly, the EU as an intergovernmental authority is severely dependent on cohesion between (a majority of) sovereign members to break through the vetoing and hinder power of one member state.
- The case concerning the renewal of rural areas gives some ground to the idea that the chains of interdependence between the actors in agro-food networks have become extremely long. Therefore, the power between the levels in these networks has become very diffused. On the one hand, the farmers in the individual agrarian firms are extraordinarily dependent on the whole agrarian polity around them. Still

they have some room for maneuver. On the other hand, all the "priests" and "warriors" (politicians, civil servants, bankers, scientists, etc.) at higher levels in these networks (regional, national, international, global) are mutually dependent on the millions of local farmers as well. As far as the farmers have lost a serious part of their goodwill in particular western societies, all other actors are in trouble as well. Therefore, the real challenge for national governments in particular is to contribute to a new social contract concerning farming and the rural space in open interaction with the other agrarian participants.

CONCLUSION

This study developed an explicit attention to power in networks, particularly in agrofood networks. By studying several subnetworks within the global agro-food network a wide diffusion of power has been discovered. Still dominant shifts in the balance of power within these networks could also be made plausible.

From a methodological point of view the study implied some biases, although the descriptive frame of reference was deducted from a long term historical and rather comprehensive perspective. In fact the selection of key issues was based on actual debates in the global agro-food network. The impacts on rural life and farming of "related fields" (Friend and Jessop 1969) like civil and interstate wars, (transnational and rural-urban) migration movements, and physical erosion of rural areas were underestimated. Of course, these limits of our study concealed the relevance of means of violence as an important resource of power. The "warriors" in our cases were really a metaphor for competing civilized people. In the global reality, however, farmers are often and on a wide scale confronted with destruction by political and military violence. According to Long (1997:19) "these processes raise critical issues concerning the viability of certain types of livelihoods and modes of organization, and address fundamental questions about changes in cultural identity and social relations in what looks like being an increasingly transnational and de-territorialized 'rural' world."

The network approach was primarily used for descriptive analysis and explanation, not for prescription or for management recommendations. Further research in agro-food complexes should provide the evidence necessary to accept or to reject this approach for these aspects of policymaking. The presentation of the subnetworks in the cases could not go into details, particularly not concerning the structure of agro-food business complexes and how it is interwoven in practice with governmental institutions and governmental representatives. Although the approach made clear that the diffusion of power has not ruled out the nation states as a key actor in these agro-food policy networks, the balance of power in general seems to be shifting to international organizations. The national governments are perhaps no longer the kings in their jungles. However, nation states fulfill a key intermediary role in the dispersion and constitution of power concerning a secure, sufficient and sustainable food supply.

NOTES

1. The second part of this prelude is based on Goudsblom (1997: 74–83 and 89–96).

2. The conceptual relation between complexity (included uncertainty), cooperation and control on the one side and ideas about markets, networks, institutions on the other side is clearly worked out in Lanbooy (1991: 15–24).

3. The information about genetic engineering is reproduced here from *The Economist* 28(4), 1997, "The Year of the Triffids," 92–94 in "The green gene giant. Monsanto's boss wants to revolutionize farming, save the environment and make money. All at the same time," 76.

4. The last poll under 16.246 Europeans (end of 1996) reflected in the "Eurobarometer on Biotechnology" shows a decline in the optimism about biotechnology and genetic modification (in comparison to 1991 and 1993), although the knowledge about these issues was growing. Public opinion demonstrates little trust in the national governments as effective regulators of modern biotechnology. The researchers (*Nature*, June 1997; quoted in *NRC* 27(6)1997) announce that the public is not convinced by the risk analyses of the governments. Moral doubts and visions are important as well. Governments don't pay attention to moral evaluation. People recommend the UN and the WHO to do this job. Some figures: 75 percent demand for a special label on dairies with manipulated genes; 53 percent said regulation does not give enough protection against risks now; 39 percent want religious organizations to be involved in the design of relevant new regulations.

5. The GATT emerged as a "temporary" substitute to the International Trade Organization, the third of the Bretton Woods institutions but which the U.S. Congress failed to ratify (Nicolaides 1994: 230).

6. The United States was supported by the CAIRNS group, which gathered countries from different backgrounds. Industrialized countries, countries from the Eastern bloc as well as some developing countries. The following countries joined the group: Australia, New Zealand, Canada, Hungary, Argentina, Uruguay, Brazil, Chile, Colombia, Indonesia, Malaysia, the Philippines, Thailand, the Fiji Islands. The CAIRNS wanted to break the U.S.-EU dominance of the agricultural portfolio and to reduce subsidies on volumes of agricultural products (mainly EU). The first goal was not realized, the second one partly. Countries such as Singapore, the Philippines and Thailand, which tried to diminish the Japanese dominance in the Asian Case were supported by the United States also in order to promote an enlarged Pacific Block (Vernon 1996: 626).

7. During the 7th World Congress of the International Food and Agribusiness Management Association (IAMA, Jakarta, June 1997), the President Mr. Herman Wijffels

(top manager of the second bank in the Netherlands) reminded everyone that the world's population will need more food in the next 50 years than ever before in history (NRC 27(6) 1997).

8. These figures are reproduced in Tansey and Worsley (1995: 95) from the course Hobbelink, Henk (London: Zed books, 1991), 44 and 46.

9. The political agenda (*Agenda 2000*) about the future of the CAP is related to:

- The start of the European Monetary Union (EMU); which countries will have a common *valuta* (the euro) in January 1999?
- Institutional reforms (recently delayed: summit European leaders, Amsterdam, June 1997).
- The preparation of an EU position for the negotiations of the WTO, starting 1999.
- The midterm review of the EU Structure Funds: the new terms starts in 2000.
- The risks of increasing disequilibrium in agricultural markets, although the world demand for food will rise continuously.
- The changing image of the agro-food business in the eyes of the consumers (demand for higher quality control, better management of diseases, and less external environmental impacts).
- The demand for a more integrated approach to the future of the rural areas (multifunctional farming, employment inside and outside the agribusiness, environmental policies).

10. The countries involved are:

- Poland, Czech Republic, Hungary, Slovakia ("Visegrad" countries).
- Estonia, Latvia, Lithuania (Baltic States).
- Romania, Bulgaria, Slovenia.

11. These figures are reproduced in Tansey and Worsley (1995: 95) from the source Henk Hobbelink (1991), *Biotechnology and the Future of World Agriculture* (London: Zed books), 44 and 46.

12. BSE is probably caused by "scrapie," a disease in sheep that has been known for about 200 years. Scrapie infected sheep-rests from slaughterhouses has been mixed with other cattle fodder ingredients. The crucial variable is that the procreator of BSE in scrapie can pass obviously the barrier of species. BSE is not the result of activities by bacteria or viruses. The dominant theory is that "prions," which are particular proteins characterized by their capacity to change healthy proteins into bad ones, start their destroying activities in the milt and go via the spinal marrow to the brains. The incubation time of BSE seems to be rather long. BSE has killed about 19 (young) people in Britain now. British researchers could not find yet a specific deviant in the genes construction, the character or the (physical and social) behavior of the BSE victims. This implies that millions of people might have been infected by BSE prions. Therefore, an epidemic catastrophe can not be excluded in the (near) future yet. A therapy is not available at the moment (Hoogstraten 1997).

13. As the Treaty of Amsterdam and Agenda 2000 demonstrate, a lot of things have to be done concerning the renewal of the EU institutions, the EU budget and (mostly in the CEE) the physical and financial infrastructure.

REFERENCES

Anderson, Svein S. and Kjell A. Eliassen. 1993. *Making Policy in Europe. The Europeification of National Policymaking*. London, Thousand Oaks, New Delhi: Sage.

Benson, J. K. 1982. "A Framework for Policy Analysis," in *Interorganizational Coordination*, D. Rogers, D. Whitten, et al., eds. Ames, Iowa: Iowa State University Press.

Berkhout, Petra. 1996. "Met MOE en WTO het nieuwe millenium in. Gemeenschappelijk Landbouwbeleid ter discussie," in *Spil*, 141–42, 1996–3, 11–18.

Boonstra, Froukje. 1996. "Waar blijft de visie op plaats en functie van de landbouw in de maatschappij?" in *Spil*, 141–42, 1996–3, 40–44.

Crozier, M. and E. Friedberg. 1977. *L'acteur et le système: les contraintes de l'action collective* (Actors and Systems: The Politics of Collective Action). Paris, 1997. (English: Chicago, 1980)

Daugbjerg, Carsten. 1997. "Policy Networks and Agricultural Policy Reforms: Explaining Deregulation in Sweden and Re-Regulation in the European Community," in *Governance: An International Journal of Policy and Administration* 10(2) April: 123–42

The Economist. 1997. "'The Green Gene Giant,' 76 and Genetic Engineering. The Year of the Triffids." 28(4): 92–94.

———. 1997. "Welcome to Europe," (pp. 13–14) and "Europe, Eastward, ho, They Said Warily," (pp. 27–28).

Elias, Norbert. 1969 [1939]. *Uber den Prozess der Zivilisation*. Suhrkamp.

Friend, J. K. and W. M. Jessop. 1969. *Local Government and Strategic Choice: an Operational Research Approach to the Process of Public Planning*. London: Tavistock Publications.

Frouws, Jaap. 1997. "The Changing Parameters of Social Regulation and Governance in Agriculture." *Images and Realities of Rural Life, Wageningen Perspectives on Rural Transformations*, Henk de Haan and Norman Long, eds. The Netherlands: van Gorcum, 77–88.

Gilg, Andrew W. 1996. *Countryside Planning*, in The First Half Century, 2nd edition. London and New York: Routledge.

Goudsblom, Johan. 1997. *Het regime van de tijd*, especially the second part "Mensenmacht en mannenmacht" (essay 2 "de opkomst van religieus-agrarische regimes," 67–83, and essay 3 "de opkomst van militair-agrarische regimes," 84–96. Amsterdam: Meulenhof.

Goverde, Henri. 1997. "Sturing van plattelandsvernieuwing," in *Tijdschrift voor Sociaal Wetenschappelijk Onderzoek van de Landbouw* 12(2): 141–60.

———. 1987. *Macht over de Markerruimte*. KNAG/KUN. Amsterdam: Nijmegen.

Goverde, Henri and Jules Hinssen. 1994. "Machtsbalansanalyse," In *Methoden van Invloedsanalyse, Boom*, L. Huberts and J. Kleinnijenhuis, eds. Amsterdam: Meppel.

Harris, Marvin. 1978. *Kannibalen en koningen* (translated from English in 1977). Amsterdam: Boek, Utrecht.

Hebinck, Paul and Jan Douwe van der Ploeg, "Dynamics of Agricultural Production. An Analysis of Micro-Macro Linkages," in Images and Realities of Rural Life, Wageningen Perspectives on Rural Transformations, Henk de Haan and Norman Long, eds. The Netherlands: van Gorcum, 202–25.

Hocking, Brian and Michael Smith. 1995. *World Politics. An introduction to International Relations.* 2nd ed. New York: Prentice Hall, Harvester Wheatsheaf.

Hoggart, Keith, Henry Buller and Richard Black. 1995. *Rural Europe: Identity and Change*. London and New York: Arnold.

Hoogstraten, S. van. 1997. "BSE en volksgezondheid," in Beleid en Universiteit 8: om de toekomst van de landbouw, Vakgroep Algemene Agrarische Economie. Studium General Wageningen Agricultural University and Ministry of Agriculture, 11–17.

Kennedy, P. Lynn, Harold von Witzke and Terry L. Roe. 1996. "Multilateral Agricultural Trade Negotiations: A Noncooperative and Cooperative Game Approach." *European Review of Agricultural Economics* 23: 381–99.

Kerremans, Bart. 1994. "De Uruguay-ronde van de GATT. Eindpunt van de traditionele handelsdiplomatie?" *Internationale Spectator* xlvii: 374–80.

Kickert, Walter J. M., Erik-Hans Klijn and Joop F. M. Koppenjan. *Managing Complex Networks*, in Strategies for the Public Sector. London, Thousand Oaks, New Delhi: Sage.

Kol, J. and B. Kuijpers. 1997. "Failliet landbouwbeleid Europa definitief bewezen," in *NRC* 30(5).

Kralt, P. J. 1997. *Opening van een Policy Window: BSE-crisis*. Masters thesis. Wageningen Agricultural University.

Kuyvenhoven, A. 1997. "Evaluation World Food Summit: Discussion," in Beleid en Universiteit 8: om de toekomst van de landbouw, Vakgroep Algemene Agrarische Economie, Studium General Wageningen Agricultural University and Ministry of Agriculture, 74–77.

Lambooy, J.G. 1991. "Complexity, Formations, and Networks," in *Complexes, Formations and Networks*, M. de Smidt, E. Wever, eds. The Netherlands Geographical Studies 132, Royal Dutch Geographical Society, Utrecht.

Lehmbruch, Gerhard. 1991. "The Organization of Society, Administrative Strategies, and Policy Networks," in *Political Choice: Institutions, Rules, and the Limits of Rationality*, Roland Czada and Adrienne Windhoff-Héritier, eds. Frankfurt am Main and Boulder, Colo.: Campus Verlag/Westview Press.

Long, Norman. 1997. "Agency and Constraint, Perceptions and Practice. A Theoretical Position," in *Images and Realities of Rural Life. Wageningen Perspectives on Rural Transformations*, Henk de Haan and Norman Long, eds. Assen: van Gorcum, 1–20.

Marsh, Davis and R. A. W. Rhodes. 1992. "Policy Communities and Issue Networks: Beyond Typology," in *Policy Networks in British Government*, David Marsh and R. A. W. Rhodes, eds. Oxford: Clarendon Press.

Meer, A. H. van der. 1997. "Landbouw en uitbreiding Europese Unie,' in Beleid en Universiteit 8 : om de toekomst van de landbouw, Vakgroep Algemene Agrarische Economie. Studium General Wageningen Agricultural University and Ministry of Agriculture, 23–29.

Nicolaides, Phedon. 1994. "The Changing GATT System and the Uruguay Round Negotiations," in *Political Economy and the Changing Global Order*, Richard Stubbs and Geoffrey R. D. Underhill, eds. London: MacMillan, 230–45.

Ockenden, Jonathan and Michael Franklin. 1995. *European Agriculture. Making the CAP Fit the Future.* Chatham House Papers, The Royal Institute of International Affairs. London: Pinter Publishers.

Rhodes, R. A. W. and David Marsh. 1992. "New Directions in the Study of Policy Networks," in *European Journal of Political Research* 21: 191–205. London and New York: Routledge.

Sbragia, Alberta M., ed. 1992. *Europolitics. Institutions and Policymaking in the "New" European Community*. Washington D.C.: The Brookings Institution.

Schendelen, M. P. C. M. van (red.) 1993. *Nederlandse Lobby's in Europa*, 's-Gravenhage.

———. 1984. *Het Europees Parlement*. Utrecht: Aula.

Skogstad, Grace 1994. "Agricultural Trade and the International Political Economy," in *Political Economy and the Changing Global Order*, Richard Stubbs and Geoffrey R. D. Underhill, eds. London: MacMillan, 246–58.

Smith, Martin J. 1990. *The Politics of Agricultural Support in Britain: The Development of the Agricultural Policy Community*. Aldershot: Dartmouth Publishing.

———. 1993. *Pressure, Power and Policy. State Autonomy and Policy Networks in Britain and the United States*. New York, Tokyo, Singapore: Harvester Wheatsleaf.

Tansey, Geoff and Tony Worsley. 1995. *The Food System. A Guide*. London: Earthscan Publications Ltd.

Taylor, Peter J. 1993. *Political Geography*. World-Economy, Nation-State and Locality, 3rd ed. Essex, London: Longman.

Vernon, Raymond. 1996. "Passing through Regionalism: The Transition to Global Markets," in *The World Economy* 19(6) November: 621–33.

Verschoor, Grard. 1997. "Entrepreneurship, Projects and Actor-Networks. Reconceptualizing Small Firms," in *Images and Realities of Rural Life, Wageningen Perspectives on Rural Transformations*. Henk de Haan and Norman Long, eds. The Netherlands: van Gorcum, 245–66.

Wichers, A. J. 1965. *De oude plattelandsbeschaving*. Een sociologische bewustwording van de "overherigheid," Assen: Van Gorcum.

Wilkin, Peter. 1996. "New Myths for the South: Globalisation and the Conflict between Private Power and Freedom." *Third World Quarterly* 17(2): 227–38.

Williams, R. H. 1996. *European Union Spatial Policy and Planning*. London: Paul Chapman Publishing Ltd.

Zee, Frans A. van der. 1997. *Political Economy Models and Agricultural Policy Formation: Empirical Applicability and Relevance for the CAP*. Wageningen: Mansholt Institute.

7

Globalization, Technology, and Emancipatory Politics: Toward a New Multilateralism?

Michael G. Schechter

This chapter will investigate the relationship between globalization, emphasizing information and communications technology as an agent, and social forces, with a focus on transnational, emancipatory political movements, what will be referred to herein as the new multilateralism.

The chapter begins by discussing what is now occurring, that is, identifying the multiple means by which information and communications technology is transforming the international relations of social change (i.e., the ways in which an emerging multilateralism involving nonstate actors are exploiting information access). I will then turn to an assessment of the claims for the future, for the possibilities of a new multilateralism, centered on democratic social forces, but also including much more sinister actors including drug dealers and money launderers. I will assess the works of those that see information technology as the potential for emancipatory politics, as the key to building nongendered, nonracist,[1] transnational, democratic communities[2] and anti-statist and counter-hegemonic social movements.[3] Ricci, for example, notes that there are those who see the Internet as allowing direct democracy, participation, an unmediated free flow of information bypassing constraints of the media and lobbyists, etc.[4] Loader speaks of the "transcending qualities" of information and communication technologies

> . . . as a means to facilitate the demise of modernist forms of governance based upon territory, hierarchical managerial control of populations, and policing. Thus nation-state boundaries are said to be weakening both from the development of global economies where 'cyberspace is where your money is' and also from the lack of control over national governments from the lack of control by national governments of communications in cyberspace. Furthermore, the

> changing politics of identity characterized by the breakdown of social class, patriarchal and racial modes of political organization and their replacement by a diverse range of movements championing social difference may also be finding expression in cyberspace. In this context, cyberspace is regarded as the medium through which to explore concepts of emancipation, empowerment and the transcendence of physical subjugation.[5]

Whitaker's "utopian exhortation" (the phrase is Loader's) is among the most hyperbolic of this group, perhaps justifying inclusion with what Loader calls the "cyber-libertarians."[6]

> Democracy will spring not from the barrel of a gun but from the personal computer and modem. States and corporations will lose control over the flow of information. The People will rule the Internet.[7]

Skolnikoff's more qualified (academic?) statement is more representative of the thinking of this group:

> It is therefore a reasonable, though qualitative, conclusion that the introduction of information technologies (and other technologies that pay a synergistic role) tends, on balance, to have consequences that are biased in the direction of increased limitations on the centralization of political power and toward greater openness within a society.[8]

I will also discuss those that foresee a darker, commercialized,[9] hierarchical future[10] in which the currently privileged and marginalized remain so,[11] where some of the essentials for building more participatory politics are deemed absent and where the Internet is sometimes portrayed as an agent of "cultural imperialism," contributing to the spread of the highly individualistic American variant of capitalism.[12] Loader, perhaps revealing his own biases, calls the most pessimistic of this group, those prophesying a dystopia, digital "Luddites." [13] In general, this group is comprised of those who see that new means for information and communications technology are *not* the keys to a new multilateralism; indeed they may reinforce the established and emerging multilateralisms.

In this chapter, I contend that these disagreements, and the positions held by those between these ends on a continuum,[14] are less a consequence of disagreements over the potentials of technology than over politics, tradeoffs among competing values, and strategies for achieving particular political ends. The most obvious of these tradeoffs relates to government regulation of the Internet (i.e. in terms of "free speech" or the freedom of the "the market").[15] McChesney elaborates:

> Although the Internet clearly has opened up important space for progressive and democratic communication, the notion that the Internet will permit humanity to leap frog over capitalism and corporate communication seems dubious unless public policy forcefully restricts the present capitalist colonization of cyberspace.[16]

Accordingly it is contended that those who are enthusiastic about the impacts of information and communications technology on global politics are more moderate in their goals for change, more meliorist in their approaches, and more worried about tradeoffs with other often deeply rooted, longstanding values. Those with revolutionary aspirations, those who will not simply be satisfied with increased access to information vital to coping with environmental threats or means for publicizing human rights violations, etc., but seek alternative power distributions in the international system, find the new information and communications technology at best inadequate to their counter-hegemonic aspiration and, in some instances, counterproductive to their goals and strategies. Moreover, they are also willing to entertain thoughts about some tradeoffs, especially as these tradeoffs are often designed by and to privilege those in power, now or in the past. Throughout the chapter, I portray information and communications technology as a key agent, globalization as not being "ideology-less," and conceive of it as both a project and a process.[17] Accordingly, I believe it is essential that we ask how this aspect of globalization functions, who or what controls it and for what purpose. Is it likely to transform social structures? Whose interests are the likely changes going to serve?[18]

In sum, I argue that it seems best to think of cyberspace as a contested space that offers some potential for personal emancipation and perhaps even collective emancipatory politics. Even though it is true that the globalizing qualities of the Internet allow for "enhanced democratic economic regeneration on the one hand and the re-emergence of local cultural identities on the other," it seems naïve to act as if politics and power differences stop when information and communications technology is concerned, to believe that it is anarchical, ideology-free or totally unreflective of the socioeconomic and cultural context which gave rise to it: those currently in power are not easily displaced, much as the "cyber-libertarians" may wish it. Such a perspective seems to accord with (at least some of what) Frissen has to say; specifically, that the evolution of information and communications technology

> . . . is not a sketch of Utopia. Cultural post-modernization, in the sense of fragmentation, does not imply the disappearance of power, control and inequality. International networks are intelligently used by transnational corporations. Virtuality does not transform the capitalist system—to some extent it supports it. [Information and communications technology] is full of ambiguities.[19]

The Notion of Multiple Multilateralisms

Central to the MUNS (Multilateralism and the United Nations Systems) project[20] has been a distinction between the old multilateralism (which I choose to call the established multilateralism) and the new multilateralism. By the established multilateralism, I mean the key institutions (such as the UN Security, NATO, the OAS, the Bretton Woods "sisters" and the GATT) and interstate, "multilateral" processes chiefly established in the aftermath of World War II to aid in solving the world's problems.[21] Although, over time, these institutions and processes have all evolved (and been augmented; the WTO, EU, and G-7 "nexus,"[22] and the end of fixed exchange rates are obvious examples), they have a number of essential and enduring characteristics in common. Most important of these is that they are "top-down" institutions; they are hierarchically organized, contain limited membership executive committees, weighted voting procedures, have limited and formalized interactions with NGOs and almost none with social movements, and generally reflect the power distribution of the world as it evolved in the early years of the Cold War.

The emerging multilateralism[23] includes some "bottom-up" institutions, global ad hoc conferences—intergovernmental and nongovernmental (most frequently exemplified by the Rio Conference)—along with more traditional, hierarchically organized nongovernmental organizations (NGOs)[24] and intergovernmental organizations with which they work.[25] The nongovernmental organizations which are agents of the emerging multilateralism are differentiated from the new multilateralism in terms of their funding sources (i.e. they often get funds from states and intergovernmental organizations), modes of operation (i.e. representative rather than participator, hierarchical rather than anti-hierarchical, and often work in concert with statist institutions) and goals (i.e., the emerging multilateralisms' goals are not primarily emancipatory). In Pasha's language, "Often tied to global capitalism and its disciplinary institutions (for example the IMF and World Bank), or its *humanized* experience in philanthropic organizations, nonstate actors (of emerging multilateralism) do not offer an alternative for transformation.[26] Even in the best of circumstances, they work towards rejoining without upsetting global structures.[27] In the environmental field, the distinction is often made between environmental movements and resistance or deep ecology movements, with some organizations—like Greenpeace—as somewhere between the two.[28] The emerging multilateralism has benefited considerably from the explosion in information and communications technology, for example, through publicizing their activities on the World Wide Web, by the exchange of information between Northern–based NGOs and their Southern counterparts and by providing an important additional means for expanding their human (and thus financial) resources bases.

The new in the new multilateralism is used in the sense of contrasting with conventional usage rather than novel or necessarily recent.[29] It is multilateralism that is consistent with the MUNS project's critical approach and emancipatory goals: multilateralism serving the interest for *and* from the bottom up on the foundations of a broadly participatory global society. Its normative intentions are often deemed counter-hegemonic. It includes what many refer to as grassroots movements and citizens groups, many of which are only beginning to gain influence (and scholarly attention), and many of which have heretofore had limited transnational ties, rarely reaching beyond the communities in which they operate.[30] Indeed, Ricci contends that

> when scholars talk about global grassroots social movements, they often refer to two areas in which these movements have global tendencies; the environment and human rights. It is in these areas that we face common, global risks and in these cases there are not 'others.'[31]

But given the state of globalization in general and information and communications technology in particular, almost all social movements are affected by events beyond their local environs,[32] especially in terms of ideas, tactics and strategies.[33] The hope of the proponents of the new multilateralism is that with a more broadly educated and better trained in skills global populous and significantly more sophisticated and accessible technology, especially cyberspace,[34] that the new multilateralism will be able to gain popular support and replace multilateralisms that are out of synchrony with the global structure, defined in material, institutional and ideational ways,[35] and thus seem more capable of seeking the resolution of key global problems, including poverty.[36] In some instances the advocates of the new multilateralism see themselves as transnational community builders and of global citizenship.[37] Richard Falk, for example, argues for a globalization from below, from which will develop

> . . . a democratizing globalism [that] encourages identification with national ethnic and biological communities, whatever their contours, but gives existential force to the experience of humanities, of the species as sharing a destiny for better or worse.[38]

Thus, for advocates of the new multilateralism, among the key challenges are whether the notion of a virtual community[39] is oxymoronic[40] and the degree to which modern-day communications technologies facilitate BGOs and social movements that seek to transcend their original sectoral bonds and nondemocratic structures, a step often portrayed as essential if such movements hope to provide an alternative to those currently in power.[41]

Information and Communications Technology and the Study of International Relations and Globalization

Deibert is right that the International Relations field has traditionally . . . given little or no attention to the wider implications of large-scale shifts in the means through which humans communicate." The dominant state-centric theories where particular levels of analysis were often privileged, and even nonmainstream theories of International Relations that sometimes adopted a more structurationalist approach,[42] had their attention otherwise directed.[43] That historical trend, however, has been altered somewhat with the proliferation of work on globalization, of which a discussion of information and communications technology is often a part, and the rapid development of the Internet and the World Wide Web. Most recent works on International Relations discuss, albeit quite generally and often uncritically, the transformational impact of the new information technologies. They frequently focus on: 1) the way in which information and communications technology assists in breaking down the inside/outside barrier,[44] 2) the role such technologies have played in particular events, be it CNN (and the so-called CNN war in Somalia); the role of the fax, e-mail and electronic bulletin boards in the collapse of the former Soviet Union;[45] the role of the global media in "recasting" Turkish national identity (on the one hand, in breaking up the unitary national culture by feeding the so-called small worlds of real Turkey and on the other of homogenizing difference and particularity by connecting the "small worlds" across frontiers and creating "imagined communities," such as linking Turkish workers in Germany with Turkish culture);[46] or the Internet and its alleged role in the Chiapas uprising in the immediate aftermath of the signing of the NAFTA accord;[47] or in the Ayatollah Ruhollah Khomeini's successful revolution in Iran;[48] or 3) the presumed association between asymmetric expansion of the information and communications technology[49] and the increasing intra and inter-state economic stratification.[50]

More systematic and comprehensive, or at least open-ended, are those studies emanating from cultural studies scholars and by those working in the field of communications. Here the discussions are rarely linear (but multidirectional and multidimensional), and not simply writings of an impending utopia or dystopia. Indeed such scholars recognize the potential and the dangers of information and communications technology for changing peoples' lives and the possibilities for statist roles in influencing at least the pace of that change. Mowlana's is illustrative of this sort of work:

> With the coming of the so-called information explosion and information society, one of the most crucial questions facing Islamic societies pertains to the ultimate control of information processing and technology. In the face of the contemporary electronic age, there has been a gradual disappearance of the oral or traditional culture that has been a major resistance force in the face of cultural dominance. The concept of civil society as a secular society was introduced into the complex life of Islamic lands at the time when the forces of resistance were a minimum. . .
>
> The crucial question for Islamic societies is whether the emerging global information communications community is a moral and ethnical community or just another stage in the unfolding picture of transformation, in which the West is the center and the Islamic world the periphery. Throughout Islamic history, especially in the early centuries, information was not a commodity but a moral

> and ethical imperative. Thus, from an Islamic perspective, it seems that linguistic and political vocabularies, now at the center of global politics, both celebrate the arrival of a new communication age and hold the key to ultimate information control.[51]

The tension between cultural homogenization and heterogenization to which Mowlana alludes has been referred as the central problem of today's global interactions. It has globalized factionalism, which has consequences for the global perspective on media infrastructure and television developments as well as the new interactive medium of the Internet and new journalism structures.[52]

Information and Communications Technology and the Emerging Multilateralism

The connections between the expansion and particularly the consequences of information and communications technology and multilateralism, however, remain spotty. Most references are simply to the fact that it should be a great "boon" to nongovernmental organizations, for example by offering the opportunities for those in the North to do research for those in the South,[53] allowing for possible global coordination of union demands[54] and successful transnational labor campaigns,[55] or the dissemination of information needed on agricultural productivity in the South, or dealing with emergency situations.[56] A few are a bit more elaborate, although the connections to forms of multilateralism are not central to their investigations. Ronal Deibert and Joshua Karliner probably exemplify these works as well as do most anyone. Deibert rightfully notes that

> Although hypermedia does not generate . . . new social movements, they do create a communications environment in which such activities flourish dramatically. As computer networks have grown, transnational social movements have exploded, forming complex non-territorial based links that defy the organization of political authority in the modern world order.

In particular, Deibert notes that ". . . transnational environmental groups were among the first to realize the potential of the early computer networks as facilitators of their organization. EcoNet, for example, was formed in 1982–long before the popularity of the Internet–and now spans over 70 countries. He goes on to note that EcoNet is now ". . . only one part of the vast web of networks operating through the Internet and linked together under the broad umbrella called the Association for Progressive Communications (APC)." The APC, the primary provider of telecommunications for NGOs and UN delegates to such UN sponsored conferences as those convened in Vienna, Cairo, and Beijing,[57] clearly exemplifies the connections between "hypermedia" and the emerging multilateralism. Deibert goes on to note that many transnational social movements, not part of the formal APC network, also exploited Internet bulletin boards, newsgroups, and mailing lists. Moreover, "thousands of niche political movements from across the political spectrum and from all points of the planet have built a presence of the web."[58] While also emphasizing the APC, Karliner expands on Deibert's last point. He emphatically asserts that the "Internet can also serve as a tool for those campaigning on specific issues." He exemplifies this by reference to the Rainforest Action Network's ability to use its page on the World Wide Web to encourage thousands of individuals to send computer-generated faxes to the Mitsubishi Corporation to urge that company to curb its deforestation.[59]

INFORMATION AND COMMUNICATIONS TECHNOLOGY AND THE NEW MULTILATERALISM

Esther Dyson is among the champions of the liberating, democratizing and community-building potentials of information and communications technology. She argues, for example, that

> Used right, the Internet can be a powerful enabling technology for the development of communities because it supports the very thing that creates a community-human interaction. One benefit of the Internet is that it allows the formation of communities independent of geography. People need only share interests or goals and find one another. Conversely, people are not stuck in the communities they are born in – not entirely, at least.[60]

Obviously Dyson recognizes differences between traditional and virtual communities (what she called "terrestrial" and "online" communities), but she believes those differences should not be overstated. Rules and processes can be established to make them similar (e.g., in terms of making it difficult to leave a virtual community and establishing procedures for expulsion and empowering someone to resolve disputes and set the tone) and functional analogues can be found. For example, she notes that in addition to sharing food as a mark of a "terrestrial" community, people often ". . . share their labor, building houses for one family or another. On the Net, they share their time, ideas, and experiences – food for thought or discussion, so to speak."[61] She goes on:

> The secret is that the Internet doesn't actually *do* much; it's a powerful lever for people to use to accomplish goals in collaboration with other people. It's more than a source of information, it is a way for people to organize themselves.[62]

While her example focuses on consumer complaints,[63] the implications for collective political action are evident. For example, Dyson discusses, under the rubric of not-for-profit communities, those that support Native American culture and are involved in the global fight against child labor. She actually expects such groups to proliferate.[64]

Elkins' analysis of virtual ethnic communities extends Dyson's study in a number of important ways. He does not see virtual ethnic communities as replacing existing ethnic communities, be they concentrated or dispersed. Rather he sees, in the post-modern era, that many people will increasingly become members in multiple communities, some of which will be virtual. To some extent, he portrays virtual communities as a means for coping with the breakdown of traditional communities about which so much has been written. This, of course, includes the literature on "social capital" including Putnam's popular work, in which he portrays the evolution of the computer as contributing to the breakdown of the traditional community, without seeing the opportunities for community building on which Elkins focuses his attention.[65] While Elkins does not specifically address the counter-hegemonic or collectively emancipatory possibilities of such communities, he does see them as potentially personally emancipatory or at least liberating. He sees these post-modern virtual communities as offering individuals a "post-modernist step beyond the dichotomy of individual and community." Indeed, he opines that the threat of globalization to individuality dissolves as each individual freely chooses among multiple communities of which s/he is an integral participant.[66] Breslow reaches a similar conclusion likening the Internet to Foucault's arguments about anonymity (and personal and social empowerment). That is, it offers an individual ". . . the opportunity to escape the sociopolitical and sociocultural bonds which attempt to fix his or her identity, and thus his or her subjective potential."[67]

> Increasing numbers of people, upon discovering the Internet, are enamored by the technology's ability to publicly legitimate their self-expression and by the freedom it provides from traditional space and time barriers. A central question is whether, as is often claimed, this empowerment and the ability to connect with increasing ease to ever-growing numbers of like-minded people encourage a sense of community.[68]

Linklater provides a potential response and segue from this focus on virtual communities and revised or expanded personal identity to emancipatory group politics. He suggests that the emancipatory project has hindered so long as the marginalized have been constrained to think of the sovereign state as *the* basis for political community.[69] Works in critical theory have provided a way out through problematizing the sovereignty discourse;[70] students of virtual communities offer another means to achieve the same goal.

Sardar is much less sanguine about the possibilities of other communities. He contends that

> Communities are shaped by a sense of belonging to a place, a geographical location, by shared values, by common struggles, by traditions and history of a location – not by joining a group of people with common interests.

Furthermore, he implies, community's membership requires responsibilities: What responsibilities come from membership where you can simply resign by turning off your machine? To reinforce his point, Sardar quotes John Gray:

> Real communities can bear these burdens because they are embedded in particular places and evoke enduring loyalties. In cyberspace, however, there is nowhere that a sense of place can grow, and no way in which the solidarities that sustain human beings through difficult times can be forged.

To conclude his argument Sardar returns to his own voice:

> Real community creates context. It generates issues that are relations to time and space, history and contemporary circumstances, and require responsible judgment—which is why so many issues are difficult; they require balancing of opposing pressures. A cyberspace community is self-selecting, exactly what a real community is not; it is contingent and transient, depending on a shared interest of those with the attention span of a thirty-five second sound bit. The essence of real community is its presumptive perpetuity—you have to worry about the people because they will always be there. In a cyberspace community you can shut people off at a click of a mouse and go elsewhere. One has therefore no responsibility of any kind.[71]

Sardar provides one of the strongest arguments about the degree to which cyberspace maintains or even reinforces existing power relations.

> The supposed democracy of cyberspace only hands control more effectively to a centralized elite, the ideology of the free citizen making everyone oblivious to the more enduring deep structure of control. Decentralized domination solves two problems simultaneously, it makes the newer territory [cyberspace] manageable and submissive to the structures of control while keeping the citizens happy by giving them a sense of their importance as they are being used.[72]

Sardar even takes issue with one of the oft-stated strengths of cyberspace, namely that communicators' race and gender can be protected. The consequence of that from Sardar's perspective is not the growth of a gender-free and non-racist community, but one in which pluralist debate can be avoided, in which the marginalized can stay marginalized.[73] Whitaker, Venturelli, and Ake tie the issue more explicitly to the notion of a new multilateralism.

Whitaker recognizes the capacity of the new communications technologies to be "liberating and empowering" within authoritarian regimes.

> The fax machine and E-mail have indeed become revolutionary weapons in the hands of dissidents, and, satellite television, for all that it symbolizes cultural imperialism and the penetration of traditional cultures by Western capitalist values, also destabilizes brutal regimes and police states.

On the other hand, Whitaker sees the democratizing potential of the new communications technologies as "far less substantial in advanced liberal democracies." Venturelli reminds that: "All communications technologies, from the pen and printing press on have possessed democratic potential." But he adds:

> The danger is that the romantic attraction of such possibilities directs our attention away from what is actually happening: the growing appropriation of the digital spectrum for commercial exploitation and a shrinking spectrum for non-commercial exploitation. Liberty of expression is not inevitable.[74]

Even more to the point, Whitaker contends that virtual communities are entirely lacking in the social and cultural context that could rise to actual revolutionary movements:

> They literally disembodied, disconnected from the social roots of their participants, floating in cyberspace without the identities that enable and drive people to carry out actual struggles against real enemies. People who communicate with one another only in cyberspace often mediate those communications through masks, false identities that they consciously adopt as playful/deceptive shields to protect their real identities.[75]

Claude Ake, an advocate of direct democracy throughout his life, argued in a similar vein.

> Globalization is desocializing society, obliterating the conditions that make political consciousness and the political 'public' possible. Phenomenal advances in communications technology driven by global marketing and the information revolution which it has spawned is reconstituting consciousness as information, informed delivered in ever-increasing profusion and speed. And yet having established itself as consciousness, this information bears hardly any social experience. And yet having established itself as consciousness, this information bears hardly any social experience. To begin with this, it is not only a product of technology, it is technology. Form and content, message and medium are intertwined in what is really a subsumption, the subsumption of information into technology. In its technological materiality, information is not communication, but non-communication. It does not allow for reciprocity, especially antagonistic reciprocities which are dynamic; it is what Jean Baudrillard calls ' speech without response.'

> . . . In this context there can be only a politics of disempowerment for here is a context in which the critical role of political mobilization is made abstract and concentrated in the mass media, a context in which political will and political choice achieve concreteness only as opinion polls . . . They deny politics by creating a realm of necessity that demands submission rather than creating a realm of freedom that facilitates and enjoins creativity.[76]

In many Whitaker, Venturelli and Ake's analyses are all focusing on the limited potential for new communications technologies to *directly* empower new multilateralisms. Breslow makes a related argument, but then goes beyond that. Similar to them, he notes that

> . . . the Net promotes a sense of sociability, but it remains to be seen whether this sociability translates into solidarity. Political and social change over the course of this century have occurred as a result of solidarity, both social and physical; people get together to protest.[77]

Breslow's reading of history is that protest and thus change comes about when friends collude, those with one whom has a "storehouse of memories." On the other hand, the Net is portrayed as allowing people to maintain distance and anonymity, a phenomenon that he considers counterproductive to the "solidarity" needed for change.[78]

But Breslow also offers insights that allow us the opportunity to think of the connections facilitated by the Net in *less direct* ways. For example, Breslow argues that the Internet has facilitated the evolution of horizontally organized and spatially dispersed corporations that have an ability to readily relocate and therefore circumvent civic obligations.[79] That is, the post-Fordist nature of multinational corporations has been facilitated by the evolution of modern-day communications.[80] Those self-same processes, of course, have been frequently tied to the so-called "race to the bottom" (i.e. the loss of income by workers who are less mobile than capital and corporations).[81] While there are some very powerful arguments as to why the "race to the bottom" thesis has been overstated,[82] there seems to be some evidence that the public airing of the argument itself was useful in garnering support for transnational labor coordination, some of which has been facilitated by the Internet. Thus in these two seemingly or at least perceptually interrelated ways, communications techniques in the post-Fordist era of globalization appear to have facilitated the expansion of counter-hegemonic, although not necessarily "bottom-up" or democratic movements.

Among the key investigators writing about the new multilateralism are those working on the ground. Dave Carter is illustrative of such a scholar-participant. Not simply does he provide a "bottom-up" perspective on the new multilateralism but, as one would expect from one policy participant, he also provides some concrete suggests of how to get from where we now are to where he wishes us to be. Carter's valuable insights grow out of his own experience in developing the Manchester, England Host and "Electronic Village Halls."

> The main scenario being debated is essentially an optimistic one where the information superhighway will be able to support a wide range of new services that will empower citizens and provide for their full participation in an emerging "digital democracy." There is a serious danger, however, that this ignores the realities of power which support an "information aristocracy" rather than a "digital democracy." If citizens are not able to have access to the new telematics infrastructures and services, the outcome will simply reinforce existing patterns of inequalities with "information 'haves' and 'have-nots'" in our communities.
>
> At the same time, the development of new services and applications which take advantage of upgraded and enhanced infrastructures is currently dominated by the multinational corporate sector—either as suppliers or users—leading to a pattern of "development from above." If the new infrastructures are to benefit a much wider spectrum of people than is currently the case, there is a need for public support at the local level to support "development from below" in applications and services.
>
> One of the main constraints on the current development of advanced communications services is the lack of new applications that can generate enough demand to reach a critical mass of users. To extend the "electronic highways" metaphor, while the "superhighways" are being constructed, there are not enough "slip-roads" being built, there are virtually no "cars," let along public transport, in mass production and insufficient "driving lessons" available in order to support people in exploiting the opportunities which the "superhighway" offers in terms of speed and capacity.[83]

Carter suggests that if the goal is universal access to telematics services, then there is a need for a strategy for "social innovation in the community" (i.e., "development from below" in the form of experimentation, field trials and demonstration projects, including the so-called teledemocracy projects). Of course, Carter recognizes that his suggestions will have to confront those fearing that the call is for a kind of virtual communitarian democracy (i.e., ideological opponents) and the need for significant funding. While he does not expect funding to immediately gush forth from multinational corporations, he sees the market as providing space for experimentation and looks to local community organizations and higher education institutions as potential resource bases. In this context, he sees the "inherent conservatism and elitism with higher education institutions" as a key obstacle that must be overcome.[84] McChesney is one of the few others with similar goals and politics who has begun to develop a concrete strategy:

> Progressives. . . need to put communication on the political agenda and then work for nonprofit and non-commercial alternatives to the status quo. Potential support will come from those who do not benefit from the existing system. The

> heart of the movement must come from those portions of the population already organized for political activism. Regardless of what a progressive group's first issue of importance its second issue should be media and communication. This applies to all social movements . . . Alliances should be struck with progressive teachers unions and librarians who are battling the privatization and commercialization of their fields, often by the same forces. And any political party that claims to act on behalf of the bulk of the population, and against capital, must incorporate progressive media and communications into the core of its platform.[85]

Others, of course, have argued that major beneficiaries of information and communications technology may be drug traffickers and money launderers,[86] often involving those wishing to change the extant distribution of power and wealth, but can hardly qualify to be counted as part of the new multilateralism as that term has come to be used. Lenk provides one of the most extensive discussions of the "globalization of crime." As he notes:

> Until now (a) plans for (criminal, terrorist, etc.) action, (b) the marshalling of resources for such an action, (c) its execution and (d) the (destructive) effects of it used to be concentrated on a territory delimited by boundaries. From now on, these four phases of adverse action will become more and more dissociated in space. Information technology increasingly allows for the production of remote effects. If remote surgery is now possible, remote criminal attacks are as well. Destabilization of a village or a city may originate anywhere.
>
> Moreover, the same technology also multiples opportunities for monitoring nature, society and individual behaviors. Remote sensing and surveillance of all types are no longer the privilege of powerful military or civil state authorities. Governments are losing their Orwellian privileges of information detection. Remote sensing and other means of spying are available at increasingly low cost . . . It is easy to imagine which means will soon be at the disposition of organized crime.
>
> . . . information technology also augments the planning capacity of individuals and organizations. For designing complex criminal and terrorist projects, large organizations are no longer required. Major effects can now be produced by small groups. Hence organized crime may become less 'organized' than presently assumed.[87]

In sum, there appear to be considerable linkages between new information and communications technology and the new multilateralism as well as social movements with less normatively appealing goals. The linkages include what is both direct and indirect, realized and potential. The degree to which the new multilateralism is the major beneficiary of such communications technology is largely a consequence of power and strategy in the contested space that the information and communications technologies afford.

CONCLUSIONS

The new information and communications technology has affected all forms of multilateralism. Enthusiasm over its potential for achieving a new multilateralism is related to the political goals and strategies of those discussing it. Those whose goals include revolutionary change and direct democracy stress the differences between online communities and traditional communities. Those whose goals include replacing the dominance of the neo-American model of capitalism[88] are less optimistic about the political potentials of the Internet than those whose goals focus on increasing the numbers of participants in representative democratic processes. Those who are concerned about value tradeoffs, such as constraining free speech and free market capitalism are less sanguine about the possibilities of the Internet for arresting the spread of capitalism and American culture around the globe, much less the transnational criminal forces that have been among the major beneficiaries of the new information and communications technology. Although they can be portrayed as anti-statist and perhaps even counter-hegemonic they were certainly not what was meant by MUNS when it spoke of the new multilateralism.

As in any contested space, where power is differentially dispersed, only time will tell the degree to which the new multilateralism is the major beneficiary of such information and communications technology. In the interim, more investigation of specific cases is called for, especially involving less direct linkages between communications technology and the expansion of counter-hegemonic social movements and those authored by those working on the ground, whose analyses and advocacy of specific strategies for effectuating the new multilateralism seem particularly promising.

NOTES

1. See, for example: Reg Whitaker, "The Tower of Infobabel: Cyberspace as Alternative Universe," in *Socialist Register 1996*, Leo Panitch, ed. (Atlantic Highlands, N.J.: Humanities Press International, Inc., 1996), 186–87.

2. Sobchack draws a comparison between the democratic elements of the Internet and the evolution of enfranchisement without property requirements in the United States, underscoring, however, that it is naïve to think of the Internet (and especially the World Wide Web) as providing "free information." Much of what it provides people are free access to advertisements. Vivian Sobchack, "Democratic Franchise and the Electronic Frontier," in *Cyberfutures: Culture and Politics on the Information Superhighway*, Ziauddin Sardar and Jerome R. Ravetz, eds. (London: Pluto Press, 1996), 78 and 86–88.

Kinney discusses the vision of an "electronic democracy" with people voting from their homes, taking as much time to deliberate as necessary, debating with fellow citizens, "chatting" with elected officials, signing electronic petitions, etc. He goes on to ask how much hardware would cost to effectuate such a vision and, logically following from that, how widespread would access (and participation) then be. He also notes that there are some U.S. Congressional staffers who fear that e-mail overload will lead to members of the Congress ignoring incoming messages, making members of Congress even less accountable than at present (i.e., decreasing democracy in another way). Jay Kinney, "Is There a New Political Paradigm Lurking in Cyberspace?" in *Cyberfutures: Culture and Politics on the Information Superhighway*, Ziauddin Sardar and Jerome R. Ravetz. eds. (London: Pluto Press, 1996) 138 and 144.

3. As Kinney notes, those currently ". . . attracted to the Internet are largely from the fringes of society – folks, who for one reason or another, feel their message is not represented by the mainstream media." They use the Net to broadcast their "extreme views." To date, of course, American voices and sites have dominated the Net. Kinney opines that this might simply be the latest example of a "pioneer/settler philosophy of self-reliance". . . people with a tradition of staking their claims. "Is There a New Political Paradigm?" 143. Whitaker contends that ". . . it is already a notorious fact that it is the Right, not the Left, that has made the most of the political opportunities of cyberspace, in many cases the ugliest elements of the Right, offering racism as political pornography on the Internet." He also notes that major users of the "information highway" are "disproportionately" male, white, and the other familiar categories of privilege. "Of course, over time these things may change." "Tower of Infobabel" 177 and 186. See also: Michael Whine, "The Far Right on the Internet," in *The Governance of Cyberspace: Politics, Technology and Global Restructuring*, Brian D. Loader, ed. (New York: Routledge, 1997).

Ravetz contends that the "economics of electronic transmission will enable the more privileged sectors of the less privileged societies to participate with fewer disadvantages in global intellectual culture. Whether the new technologies will enable the less privileged among the more privileged to assert themselves is another questions. If nothing else, entry to the multimedia world now costs about as much as a used car." Jerome R. Ravetz, "The Microcybernetic Revolution and the Dialectics of Ignorance," in *Cyberfutures: Culture and Politics on the Information Superhighway*, Ziauddin Sardar and Jerome R. Ravetz, eds. (London: Pluto Press, 1996), 49. See also Nicholas Baron, "Computers and Capitalism: A Tragic Misuse of Technology," *Monthly Review* 47(4) 1995: 43–44.

4. Andrea Ricci, "Towards a Systematic Study of Internet Political and Social Communication in Europe," in *Media and Politics in Transition: Cultural Identity in the Age of Globalization*, Jan Servaes and Ricco Lie, eds. (Leuven: Acco, 1997), 161–62.

5. Brian D. Loader, "The Governance of Cyberspace: Politics, Technology and Global Restructuring," in *The Governance of Cyberspace: Politics, technology and Global Restructuring*, Brian D. Loader, ed. (New York: Routledge, 1997), 1–2.

6. Brian D. Loader, "Preface," in *The Governance of Cyberspace: Politics, Technology and Global Restructuring*, Brian D. Loader, ed. (New York: Routledge, 1997), xii.

7. "Tower of Infobabel," xii. Obviously there is significant variations in terms of access to information and communications technology. For example, electronic mail-based distribution lists, Usenet groups and World Wide Web (WWW) pages are public in orientation, whereas electronic mail, invited Internet relay chat or video conferencing and password protected file transfer protocol (ftp) or WWW sites may be

relatively private. For an elaboration, see: Loader, *Governance of Cyberspace*, 5.

8. Eugene B. Skolnikoff, *The Elusive Transformation: Science, technology and the Evolution of International Politics* (Princeton: Princeton University Press, 1993), 101. See also: Ithiel de Sola Pool, *Technologies of Freedom* (Cambridge: Harvard University Press, 1983), 5 and Ithiel de Sola Pool, *Technologies without Boundaries: On Telecommunications in a Global Age* (Cambridge: Harvard University Press, 1990) k, *passim*.

9. Hamelink summarizes: "In brief, the field of international communication and its major players can best be described in terms of a commercial market-place driven by the belief that a free market under capitalist conditions guarantees an optimal delivery of information and culture to everyone." Cees J. Hamelink, "International Communication: Global Market and Morality," in *International Communication and Globalization*, Ali Mohammadi. ed. (Thousand Oaks: Sage Publications, 1997), 97. Tehranian and Tehranian distinguish the World Wide Web from the Internet in this regard, noting that some of the users of the latter are quite resistant to commercialization. Majid Tehranian and Katharine Kie Tehranian, "Taming Modernity: Towards a New Paradigm," in *International Communication and Globalization*, Ali Mohammadi. eds. (Thousand Oaks: Sage Publications, 1997), 160.

Recognizing the anti-statist elements of the Internet as well as the socially progressive forces and commercial uses of it (and especially the World Wide Web) and the potential for state regulation (most recently exemplified by China's regulations against the use of the Internet to leak state secrets, political subversion and spreading pornography and violence), and censorship, Breslow believes it is best to portray the Web as a contested site. Harris Breslow, "Civil Society, Political Economy, and the Internet," in *Virtual Culture: Identity and Communication in Cybersociety*, Steven G. Jones, ed. (Thousand Oaks: Sage Publications, 1997), 236–37 and 240. For a discussion of the state's capacity in this regard, see Joel R. Reidenberg, "Governing Networks and Rule-Making in Cyberspace," in *Borders in Cyberspace: Information Policy and the Global Information Infrastructure*, Brian Kahin and Charles Nesson, eds. (Cambridge: The MIT Press, 1997), 99.

Loader finds it "somewhat ironic" that many of those who champion the libertarian credentials of the new international and communication technology ". . . now find themselves engaged in a kind of Habermasian contest to defend the earlier text-based interaction, which they believe promulgates democratic participation against the commercial interests which are hell-bent upon commodifying political discourse in cyberspace." "Governance of Cyberspace," 11–12.

10. As Sardar notes, the systems operators of the new technology (e.g., of electronic newsgroups and bulleting boards) can deny entry, cut, delete, censor, reroute communications and observe all that is going on. Ziauddin Sardar, "alt.civilizations.faq: Cyberspace as the Darker Side of the West," in *Cyberfutures: Culture and Politics on the Information Superhighway*, Ziauddin Sardar and Jerome R. Ravetz, eds. (London: Pluto Press, 1996): 32. Mowlana speaks of the distribution network in a similar manner, seeing it as centralized, tending toward "oligarchy." Homia Mowlana, *Global Communication in Transition: The End of Diversity?* (Thousand Oaks: Sage, 1996), 199.

11. "Age Matters, Sex Matters, Level of Education Matters in Internet Consumption in Europe." Ricci, "Towards a Systematic Study," 168.

12. Mike Holderness, "A Promising Solution Fraught with Peril," *CERES: The FAO Journal* 158, March–April 1996: 22.

13. "Preface," xiii.

14. Lipschutz exemplifies this "middle ground" position. He rejects the "popular notion of the Internet as anarchical and the great "equalizer of individuals; indeed, his research underscores that some environmental groups see themselves as in the vanguard and controlling a great deal in terms of resources and access to power. On the other hand, he expects local knowledge to gain greater "cachet and credibility" and, in doing so, for the environmental groups in the vanguard to fall back into the pack. That is, he believes that the hierarchical nature of the transnational environmental movement – which I would describe as emblematic of the emerging multilateralism – has not been significantly altered as it came to exploit new communications technologies. But, having said that, he implies that the sharing of knowledge from those currently lower down on the hierarchy – something that the Internet permits– may actually make the process more inclusive, even democratic as called for by advocates of the new multilateralism. Ronnie D. Lipschutz with Judith Mayer, *Global Civil Society and Global Environmental Governance: The Politics of Nature from Place to Planet*, Sheldon Kamieniecki, ed., *SUNY Series in International Environmental Policy and Theory* (Albany: State University of New York Press, 1996), 74. Kinney is one of those who describes the Internet, although originally funded by the U.S. government as the "closest thing to a functioning large-scale anarchist society that human culture has yet seen." "Is There a New Political Paradigm?" 143.

15. The question of whether "cyberspace" can promote democracy as well as protect privacy is examined in: Charles D. Raab, "Privacy, democracy, information," in *The Governance of Cyberspace: Politics, Technology and Global Restructuring*, Brian D. Loader, ed. (New York: Routledge, 1997).

Loader offers an interesting observation regarding the tensions related to access: "I am reminded here of the ubiquitous Microsoft toolbars and icons which are instantly recognizable around the world and which with the launch of Windows 95 will doubtless attempt to colonize the Internet." "Governance of Cyberspace," 11.

16. Robert W. McChesney, "The Global Struggle for Democratic Communication," *Monthly Review* 48, July–August 1996: 6.

17. These notions are elaborated in Michael G. Schechter, "Globalization and Civil Society," Paper prepared for Presentation Annual Meeting of the Academic Council on the United Nations System (ACUNS), Hotel Herradura Resort and Conference Center, San Jose, Costa Rica, June 27, 1997.

18. For a similar line of questioning, see: Mowlana, *Global Communication*, 195–96.

19. Paul Frissen, "The Virtual State: Post-Modernization, Informization, and Public Administration," in *The Governance of Cyberspace: Politics, Technology, and Global Restructuring,* Brian D. Loader, ed. (New York: Routledge, 1997), 124.

20. For a description of the MUNS program, see: Robert W. Cox, *Program on Multilateralism and the United Nations System (MUNS); Final Report* (Tokyo: The United Nations University, March 1996).

21. Cox provides a succinct explanation of the various ways in which the term "multilateralism" has been used in recent works in International Relations. Robert W.

Cox, "Introduction," in *The New Realism: Perspectives on Multilateralism and World Order,* Robert W. Cox, ed. (New York: St. Martin's Press, Inc., 1997), xvi–xviii.

22. The term developed is Gill's. Stephen Gill, "Global Structural Change and Multilateralism," in *Globalization, Democratization, and Multilateralism,* Stephen Gill, ed. (New York: St. Martin's Press, 1997), 8–9.

23. It overlaps with, but is different from global civil society. Civil society, as usually constructed, is seen in opposition to the state, in the case of global civil society this would seem to include statist institutions, such as intergovernmental organizations. While NGOs are part of both global civil society and the emerging multilateralism, those funded by states and IGOs are only a part of the former. Moreover, among the key actors in global civil society are transnational criminal gangs, not a part of the emerging multilateralism, given their goals and activities. For a more expanded discussion of the contested term "global civil society," see: Schechter, "Globalization and Civil Society."

24. Hirsch contends that ". . . many NGOs are hardly structured by the principle of autonomous self-organization, but rather can be defined as a quasi-state apparatuses, as well as financially dependent upon them. More often than not, NGOs even function as instruments for neo-liberal privatization strategies and of inter-state power struggles. In many respects, a significant form of "NGO business" appears to be developing with its own professional and commercial logic." Hoachim Hirsch, "Globalization of Capital, Nation-State and Democracy." *Studies in Political Economy* 54, Fall 1997: 54. See also: Noeleen Heyzer, "Toward a New Government-NGO Relations for Sustained and People-Centered Development," in *Government –NGO Relations in Asia: Prospects and Challenges for People-Centered Development*, Noeleen Heyzer, James V. Riker, and Antonio B. Quizon, eds. (London: Macmillan Press, Ltd., 1995), 6.

25. The relationship between intergovernmental organizations, especially the UN System, and NGOs that characterize the emerging multilateralism is dynamic. It also serves to differentiate IGO-NGO relations that existed as part of the traditional multilateralism, which Groom has described this way: "The UN system is above all a system of governments in which peoples are allowed in through the tradesman's entrance to ECOSCO, and then only in a highly circumscribed manner, under the aegis of Article 71 of the charter. The tripartite status of the ILO (International Labour Organization) is an outstanding exception to the notion that the peoples of the world are enfranchised, if at all, only through governments insofar as the UN system is concerned." A. J. R. Groom, "Reflections on a Changing Political System," in *Global Issues in the United Nations' Framework*, Paul Taylor and A. J. R. Groom, eds. (New York: St. Martin's Press, 1989), 287.

26. Hirsch makes a similar argument, concluding that ". . . the hope of an extensive pattern of NGOs serving as the building blocks in the construction of an international democratic civil society, could prove to be a dangerous misconception." "Globalization,' 54–55.

27. Mustapha Kamal Pasha, "Globalization and Poverty in South Asia." *Millennium: Journal of International Studies* 25, Winter 1998: 64.

28. See, for example, Bron Raymond Taylor, ed., *Ecological Resistance Movements: The Global Emergence of Radical and Popular Environmentalism* (Albany: State University of New York Press, 1995).

29. For an elaboration on origins and meaning of the term, see: Cox, "Introduction," xix.

30. See, for example, the discussion of the Chipko movement in the Himalayas of Uttar Pradesh in: Vikram K. Akula, "Grassroots Environmental Resistance in India," in *Ecological Resistance Movements: The Global Emergence of Radical and Popular Environmentalism*, Bron Raymond Taylor, ed. (Albany: State University of New York Press, 1995).

31. Ricci adds that even in these instances and even without taking into account ethnic and religious diversity and cultural variety, it is hard to anticipate speaking in terms of the "global we" when talking about things like the potential impact of global warming for many Pacific Islanders. "Towards a Systematic Study," 154.

32. Simon Dalby, "Crossing Disciplinary Boundaries: Political Geography and International relations after the Cold War," in *Globalization: Theory and Practice*, Eleonore Kofman and Gillian Youngs, ed. (New York: Pinter, 1997), 29.

33. Good discussions, albeit a bit overstated in the sense of over generalizing from the developed state perspective on the impact of globalization on breaking down the local/global dichotomy include: Kevin R. Cox, "Introduction; Globalization and its Politics in Questions," in *Spaces of Globalization: Reasserting the Power of the Local*, Kevin R. Cox, ed. (New York: The Guilford Press, 1997), and Erik Swyngedouw, "Neither Global nor Local: 'Globalization' and the Politics of Scale," in *Spaces of Globalization: Reasserting the Power of the Local*, Kevin T. Cox, ed. (New York: The Guilford Press, 1997).

34. This theme has been developed in James N. Rosenau, *Along the Domestic-Foreign Frontier: Exploring Governance in a Turbulent World* (Cambridge: Cambridge University Press, 1997) 58–61.

35. For a related hope, see: James N. Rosenau, "Citizenship in a Changing Global Order," in *Governance without Government, Order and Change in World Politics*, James N. Rosenau and Ernst-Otto Czempiel, eds. (Cambridge: Cambridge University Press, 1992).

36. While, as Rosenau notes, there is no reason to believe that ". . . a more analytically skilled person is more likely to be more radical, more liberal, or more conservative, or that someone more cathectically capable is likely to rank more conservation over consumption, slow growth over development, human rights over community order, or otherwise attach priorities in specific ways," there is some reason to hope and believe that those with new (including) technological skills, better connected to the world, will be less driven by habit and more by a readiness to act on the basis of adaptive learning. James N. Rosenau, *Turbulence in World Politics: A Theory of Change and Continuity* (Princeton: Princeton University Press, 1990), 336 and 338.

37. Jeremy Brecher, "The Hierarchs' New World Order—and Ours," in *Global Visions: Beyond the New World Order*, Jeremy Brecher, John Brown Childes, and Jill Cutler, eds. (Boston: South End Press, 1993).

38. Richard Falk, *On Humane Governance: Toward a New Global Politics* (University Park: The Pennsylvania State University, 1995), 88–89.

39. There are those who argue strongly against the phrase virtual community. "Such communities may well be formed in novel ways but they are not somehow 'unreal' because of that. What makes a community vital to its members is their treatment of the communications as meaningful and important." Lyon continues: "The real/virtual distinction turns out. . . to be a further – regrettable – instance of the binary oppositions typical of modernity, and which show up in first media age logic as sender/receiver,

ruler/ruled, and so on." David Lyon, "Cyberspace Sociality: Controversies over Computer-mediated Relationships," in *The Governance of Cyberspace: Politics, Technology and Global Restructuring*, Brian D. Loader, ed. (New York: Routledge, 1997), 31. See also Shawn P. Wilbur, "An Archaeology of Cyberspaces: Virtuality, Community, Identity," in *Internet Culture*, David Porter, ed. (New York: Routledge, 1997).

40. Porter is probably right when he says that for many accessing the Internet "there is an expectation. . . of exchange, of sociability, even of empathy in conversations that may involve personal concerns, playful banter or philosophical debate. Whether what comes out of all this virtual talk can be properly termed "community" is a complicated question. . . and one that will continue to provoke reassessments of the fundamental nature of "community" itself. David Porter, "Introduction," in *Internet Culture*, David Porter, ed.

41. Shepherd writes of the need to focus on when an NGO gains the coalitional form necessary in order to effect change, specifically in his mind to . . . provide an alternative to the current corrupt business and opportunistic traditional leaders [he is referring particularly to contemporary Africa] who sell themselves to the military for the spoils of power. . . George W. Shepherd, "NGOs and Human Rights in Africa." *Africa Today* 43(4) 1996: 423–25.

42. Adam's account of the tradeoffs that communities make when investing in information technology demonstrates the utility of working simultaneously at multiple levels of analysis and being sensitive to interactions amongst those levels. Lischen Adam, "Maintaining Connection," *CERES: The FAO Journal*, 158, March–April 1996: 32–33.

43. Ronald J. Deibert, *Parchment, Printing, and Hypermedia: Communication in World Order Transformation* (New York: Columbia University Press, 1997), 2. Pool was among the earliest to recognize the global political implications of information technology. See, especially the book developed out of a massive manuscript that he left at the time of his death. Pool, *Technologies without Boundaries*.

44. See, for example, Jan Aart Scholte, *International Relations of Social Change* (Buckingham: Open University Press, 1993), 47–49.

45. UseNet is portrayed as having been particularly influential as a way for information to be exchanged. Gladys D. Ganley, *Unglued Empire: The Soviet Experience with Communications Technologies*. Ablex Communication, Culture, and Information Series (Norwood, N.J.: Ablex Publishing Corporation, 1996), 186–89. See also: Scott Shane, *Dismantling Utopia: How Information Ended the Soviet Union* (Chicago: Ivan R. Dee, 1994).

46. Haluk Sahin and Asu Akosoy, "Global Media and Cultural Identity in Turkey." *Journal of Communication* 42, Spring 1993: 37.

47. See, for example, Holderness, "Promising Solution," 18–19. Jeremy Brecher and Tim Costello, *Global Village: Economic Reconstruction from the Bottom Up or Global Pillage* (Boston: South End Press, 1994), 6.

48. Hamid Mowlana, "The Communications Paradox: Globalization May Be Just Another Word for Western Cultural Dominance." *The Bulletin of the Atomic Scientists* 51, July–August 1995: 41.

49. In Mowlana's useful phrase: what is global is not universal. *Global Communication in Transition*, 199.

50. After noting that 80 percent of the world's population still lacks the basics of telecommunication, Holderness alludes to rural-urban differences, not likely to be

entirely overcome by use of cellular mechanisms rather than more traditional. "Promising Solution," 21.

51. Mowlana, *Global Communication*, 125.

52. Ingrid Volkmer, "Universalism and Particularism: The Problem of Cultural Sovereignty and Global Information Flow," in *Borders in Cyberspace: Information Policy and the Global Information Infrastructure*, Brian Kahin and Charles Nesson, eds. (Cambridge: The MIT Press, 1997), 29.

53. Holderness, "Promising Solution," 20 and 22.

54. Holderness writes of Guatemalan workers using the Net to gain recognition and wage increases from Pepsi Cola, "Promising Solution," 22.

55. Andrew Herod, "Labor as an Agent of Globalization and as a Global Agent," in *Spaces of Globalization: Reasserting the Power of the Local*, Kevin R. Cox, ed. (New York: The Guilford Press, 1997), 185. Herod specifically credits the use of electronic mail systems to inform workers and supporters around the globe directly about solidarity campaigns and to solicit information about those whom they choose to vilify. Andrew Herod, "The Practice of International Labor Solidarity and the Geography of the Global Economy." *Economic Geography* 71(4) 1995: 356.

56. Lishan Adam, "Maintaining Connection." *CERES; The FAO Review* 158, March–April, 1996: 32.

57. Deibert, *Parchment*, 159–60.

58. Deibert, *Parchment*, 161.

59. Joshua Karliner, *The Corporate Planet: Ecology and Politics in the Age of Globalization* (San Francisco: Sierra Club Books, 1997), 202.

60. Esther Dyson, *Release 2.0: A Design for Living in the Digital Age* (New York: Broadway Books, 1997), 33.

61. Dyson, *Release 2.0*, 37, 38 and 46.

62. Dyson, *Release 2.0*, 35.

63. Dyson, *Release 2.0*, 36.

64. Dyson, *Release 2.0*, 47.

65. Robert D. Putnam, "Bowling Alone: America's Declining Social Capital." *Journal of Democracy* 6(1) 1995: 65. Baron writes of computers as a source of "social alienation," the consequences of which will only be seen in generations to come. "Computers and Capitalism," 45. See also Breslow, who underscores that while the Internet does not cause the "heightened sense of privacy and social detachment" that he connects with movement to the suburbs, it enables it. Significantly, he also connects the movement to cheap suburbs with the evolution of post–Fordist corporatism, a phenomenon also enabled by the development of the Internet. Breslow, "Civil Society," 254.

66. Elkins' analysis is notable in two additional ways. He explicitly notes that not all people can be expected to participate in virtual communities, using the Amish as an obvious example. Secondly, he does not limit his attention to existing communications technologies. The key, according to Elkins, is the replacement of mass media with targeted or addressable media with specialized and more homogenous audiences. These include "deathstar" satellites with several hundred broadcast channels as well as the much more familiar e-mail, Internet and World Wide Web. David Elkins, "Globalization, Telecommunication, and Virtual Ethnic Communities." *International Political Science Review* 18, April 1997: 139–52. For more details on DBS, see: Skip Pizzi, "DBS Radio: Deathstar or Dud?" Error! Book mark nor Defined. See also Ed-

ward A. Comor, Communication Technology and International Capitalism: The Case of DBS and U.S. Foreign Policy," in *The Global Political Economy of Communication*, edited by Edward A. Comor (New York: St. Martin's Press, 1994).

67. Breslow, "Civil Society," 236.

68. Derek Foster, "Community and Identity in the Electronic Village," in *Internet Culture*, David Porter, ed. (New York: Routledge, 1997), 23.

69. Andrew Linklater, "Citizenship and Sovereignty in the Post-Westphalian State." *European Journal of International Relations* 2, March 1996: 129–30.

70. See, for example Joseph A. Camilleri and Jim Falk, *the End of Sovereignty? The Politics of a Shrinking and Fragmenting World* (Brookfield, VT: Edward Elgar Publishing Ltd., 1992) and R.B.J. Walker, *Inside/Outside: International Relations as Political Theory* (Cambridge: Cambridge University Press, 1993).

71. Sardar, "alt.civilizations.faq," 29

72. Sardar, "alt.civilizations.faq," 36

73. Sardar, "alt.civilizations.faq," 29–30.

74. Shalini Venturelli, "Prospects for Human Rights in the Political and Regulatory Design of the Information Society," in *Media and Politics in Transition: Cultural Identity in the Age of Globalization* Jan Servaes and Ricco Lie, ed. (Leuven: Acco, 1997), 74.

75. Whitaker, "Tower of Infobabel," 186.

76. Claude Ake, "Globalization, Multilateralism and the Shrinking Democratic Space," in *Future Multilateralism: The Political and Social Framework*, Michael G. Schechter, ed. (New York: St. Martin's Press, forthcoming in 1998).

77. Breslow, "Civil Society," 254.

78. Breslow, "Civil Society," 255

79. Breslow, "Civil Society," 251

80. Pellerin makes a related argument. Helene Pellerin, "Global Restructuring and International Migration: Consequences for the Globalization of Politics," in *Globalization: Theory and Practice*, Eleonore Kofman and Gillian Youngs, eds. (New York: Pinter, 1996), 87.

81. See, for example, Brecher and Costello, *Economic Reconstruction*, chapter 1. Baran writes of "telecommuting" as another instance in which the personal computer contributes to possible worker exploitation. "With the possibility of having people work form home on their PCs, employers are salivating over the prospect of paying people piecemeal. . . no medical benefits, no paid vacations, no requirements for office space. . . " Of course such a phenomenon also physically separates workers so the possibilities of collective action lessen, unless they occur virtually. Baron, "Computers and Capitalism," 47.

82. See, for example, Herod, "Labor," and Meric S. Gertler, "Between the Global and the Local: The Spatial Limits to Productive Capital," in *Spaces of Globalization: Reasserting the Power of the Local*, Kevin R. Cox, ed. (New York: The Guilford Press, 1997), and Dani Rodrik *Has Globalization Gone Too Far?* (Washington: Institute for International Economics, March 1997).

83. Dave Carter, "'Digital Democracy or 'information aristocracy'? Economic Regeneration and the Information Economy," in *The Governance of Cyberspace: Politics, Technology and Global Restructuring*, Brian D. Loader, ed. (New York: Routledge, 1997), 137–38.

84. Carter, "'Digital Democracy,'" 139–51.

85. McChesney, "Global Struggle," 16–17.

86. Williams sees the communication revolution as contributing to a global market place, including for illicit drugs. While not emphasizing the communication revolution as a key agent, Strange offers a good introduction to the relationship between globalization and such activities. Phil Williams, "Problems and Dangers Posted by Organized Transnational Crime in the Various Regions of the World, " in *The United Nations and Transnational Organized Crime*, edited by Phil Williams and Ernesto V. Savona (Portland, Oregon: Frank Cass, 1996), 9. Susan Strange, *The Retreat of the State: The Diffusion of Power in the World Economy* (Cambridge: Cambridge University Press, 1996), chapter 6.

87. Klaus Lenk, "The Challenge of Cyberspatial Forms of Human Interaction to Territorial Governance and Policing," in *The Governance of Cyberspace: Politics, Technology and Global Restructuring* (New York: Routledge, 1997), 130. Lenk ominously adds that coping with these developments is made more problematic because most policing activities remain territorially defined.

88. For a classic discussion of the varieties of capitalism and one in which the American variant is not put in a particularly favorable light, see: Michel Albert, *Capitalism vs. Capitalism: How America's Obsession with Individual Achievement and Short-term Profit has Led it to the Brink of Collapse*. (New York: Four Walls Eight Windows, 1993).

8

The CAP in the Global Agricultural Economy: Prospects for the Twenty-First Century

Wyn Grant

INTRODUCTION

The Common Agricultural Policy remains in place as an example of the effectiveness of political resistance to forces of economic, social, and technological change. Although a number of significant changes have been made to the policy, it still delivers substantial levels of protection and subsidy to European farmers. The percentage Producer Subsidy Equivalent (PSE) remains at around 50 percent and it has been estimated that even relatively large farmers in Britain and France receive 30 to 40 percent of their income from subsidies (*Agra Europe*, 21 February 1997: E4).

Nevertheless, considerable forces for change are pressing on the CAP both from within and from outside the European Union. Conceptually, there is a need to disentangle these forces, although it is important to remember that they have a complex interrelationship with each other. Three models of change and one of resistance to change are presented for review here, although it should be stressed that they are not mutually exclusive, nor do they exhaust the range of possibilities. Indeed, they are unified by the fact that the forum in which the conflicts they give rise to are played out is largely that of international trade negotiations. The first model is a delayed globalization model. The argument here is that globalization processes have been delayed in agriculture, which has been a laggard in this respect. However, a catching up process is now taking place, with pressures for change being channeled through the effective incorporation of agriculture for the first time in international trade negotiations.

The second model is one that focuses on tensions between the United States and the EU (while acknowledging the presence of the Cairns Group as a new complicating factor). There is a long history of difficulties between the United States and the EU over agricultural trade. The argument here, however, is that the latest U.S. Farm Bill will have consequences for U.S. production that will lead to a new set of tensions. Once again the forum in which these tensions will surface is that of the new round of WTO negotiations on agriculture scheduled to begin at the end of 1999, but already surfacing in international discussions.

The third model is one that emphasizes the importance of technological change in agriculture and in particular the role of biotechnology as the enabling technology of the twenty-first century. This could be presented as another dimension of the EU-U.S. tensions with American multinational drug companies seeking to overcome barriers to the sale of their products in the European market. There is a need, however, to think more generally about the transformative possibilities of biotechnology in agriculture.

The fourth model is one of resistance to change. It portrays the CAP as essentially a social policy that seeks to preserve a distinctive space in rural Europe for marginal farmers in remoter regions. Part of the argument here is that the Uruguay Round has actually increased resistance in Europe to globalizing tendencies (Rieger 1996). This welfare state model of the CAP is increasingly likely to become entangled with arguments about the need to develop forms of agriculture which are environmentally friendly in terms of their impact on landscape, wildlife and levels of water pollution. There is an inherent tension between an updated productionist vision of agriculture based on utilizing the latest technology, and funded by credit provided by financial institutions, and a different vision of agriculture. This second vision sees it as forming part of a particular kind of rural society, existing in harmony with and producing food which is valued for its "natural" qualities. Particularly in Northern Europe, this clash between alternative visions is likely to become politically more significant with the BSE episode focusing attention on some of the underlying issues.

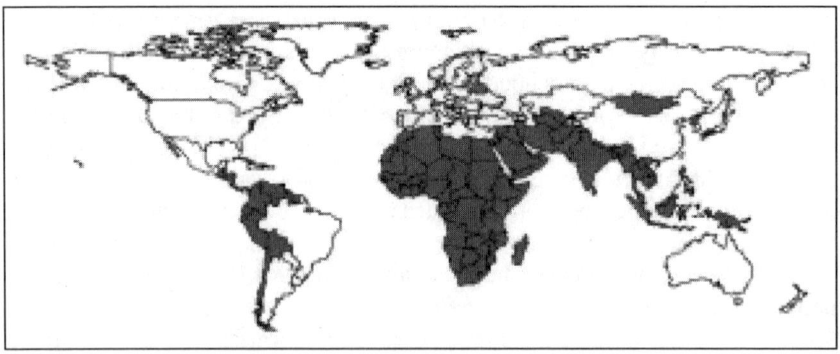

Map 8.1. The World of the Non-Aligned Movement

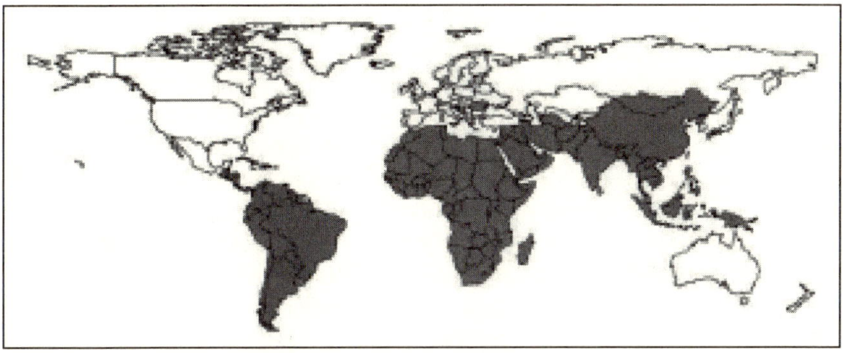

Map 8.2. The World of the Group of 77 plus China

A DELAYED GLOBALIZATION MODEL

There is something of an inherent contradiction between globalization and agriculture. As Higgott notes (1997: 5) "Globalization de-emphasizes the importance of land and territory, localization enhances it." Land is the key factor of production in agriculture and ownership of land in most countries has remained in the hands of family farmers operating on a relatively small scale compared with most businesses. It might be argued that agriculture is in many respects an inherently local activity.

Treated as a stylized fact, globalization may be seen to have three principal driving forces: international trade, foreign direct investment and the operations of international financial markets. A fourth catalytic factor is the international communications revolution, both in terms of telecommunications and various kinds and reductions in the time and monetary cost of international travel. Underlying all these forces are the activities of multinational companies which want to reduce barriers to international trade, are responsible for foreign direct investment, and are the driving force on the demand side for changes in the structure and functions of international financial markets.

Before proceeding any further, it is important to note the relative unimportance of mutinational companies in agriculture. There are, of course, important international agricultural trading companies such as Cargill and Dalgety and companies of this kind are key players in the politics of agribusiness. However, there is not the level of displacement that one finds in the food processing industry with companies such as Cadbury, Schweppes, Nestle and Unilever. Once again, this reflects the fact that farms are generally owned by individual entrepreneurs. In Britain, which has the most commercialized agriculture in Europe, there is an increasing tendency for farms to be managed by listed companies on behalf of their owners so as to maximize the return from the available assets. These companies, however, still operate on a national basis. Some British farmers have invested in farms in Eastern Europe, but the scale of such investment is still relatively low.

Foreign direct investment is thus largely absent in farming, and is still at a relatively early stage of development in first stage food processing sectors such as dairy products. In the financial sector, research undertaken by the author with William Coleman of McMaster University shows that distinctive national arrangements for the provision of agricultural credit have been eroded, although not at an even pace, and there has been some policy convergence alongside persisting national differences. (Coleman and Grant 1998).

In terms of financial instruments, there is an active market in agricultural futures. In many respects this represents just another speculative financial instrument, although contracts for wheat, maize and soybean "for decades. . . have provided the basis for physical market trading in these products throughout [the United States]." (*Agra Europe*, 25 October 1996: N4). The futures market is much more developed in the United States than in Europe: "The U.S. has twice the number of contracts, on twice the number of commodities, and does 17 times the trading volume." (*Financial Times*, 30 October 1996). Following the passage of the 1996 Farm Bill, which is likely to lead to greater price instability, it is likely that "Future markets . . . will become more important survival tools for farm managers." (Knutson, Smith, Outlaw, and Woods 1996, unpaginated). The leading futures exchange, the Chicago Board of Trade, is actively seeking to expand its activities in various parts of the world, but agriculture is lagging behind other sectors in terms of its involvement in sophisticated financial instruments.

Globalization processes in agriculture are most evident in trade, but it could be argued that trade forms a more conventional aspect of international exchange compared with the more dynamic forces driving globalization. Moreover, trade in agriculture has been highly distorted by various forms of import protection, domestic assistance and, above all, export subsidies. The United States and the European Union in particular have dumped surplus product on the world market, disadvantaging countries that might otherwise be in a competitive position in agricultural trade.

The author who has set out most systematically to examine globalization forces in agriculture is Le Heron who argues that globalized agriculture is an outgrowth of globalization forces inherent in capitalism. (Le Heron 1993: 16). His approach is refreshingly distinctive, but taking the underlying dynamics of capitalist transformation as a starting point does not adequately allow for the distinctive characteristics of agriculture as a sector. Le Heron does offer us (1993: 190) one vision of a possible future for agriculture in the twenty-first century:

> The term globalized agriculture encapsulates three interwoven ideas: increasingly, the historical forces organizing agriculture are global forces; increasingly,

> the main organizations bringing about significant changes in agriculture are organized globally; and increasingly the historical form of agriculture in this era involves the organization of integrated, often global, agro-production systems.

This paper is not taking the position that there are no global forces at work in agriculture. However, they are more limited in their extent than in many other sectors, their impact is more constrained, and they encounter more embedded forms of political resistance. This may seem like a restatement of the "agricultural exceptionalism" thesis at the international level, and in some respects it is. It is combined, however, with a recognition that exceptionalism, as embodied in the CAP, is under increasing and more effective attack.

It could be argued that the increasing importance of the World Trade Organization (WTO) in agricultural matters is supporting evidence for Le Heron's second point, that the organizations bringing about significant changes in agriculture are organized globally. An alternative way of viewing the WTO would be to see it as a mechanism for two trade super powers (the United States and the EU) to legitimize agreements they have arrived at elsewhere (in the case of the agriculture through the Blair House process). Cairns Group advocates would no doubt object to such a characterization as an oversimplification, but it contains a large enough kernel of brutal truth to be worth making.

The Uruguay Round was significant in relation to agriculture because it brought the sector effectively within the ambit of international trade negotiations after decades of exclusion (for the history of agricultural trade negotiations, see Swinbank and Tanner 1996). The substantive results in relation to agriculture were more limited than had been hoped for. As Hathaway and Ingco note (1995: 31), the agricultural agreement "does not represent a significant reduction in border protection or a major increase in access to protected markets. It appears that the level of protection afforded the most protected commodities, such as sugar and dairy products, was reduced the least." Discussions have to resume in 1999, but "It remains to be seen whether the major stakeholders in world agricultural trade want to pursue real trade liberalization." (Hathaway and Ingco 1995: 33) Or, to put it another way, will the United States be sufficiently driven by the consequences of its domestic policies to prize real concessions out of the EU?

Bilateral Tensions: the United States and the EU

The long postwar history of bilateral tensions between the United States and the EU over farm trade entered a new phase with the passage of the 1996 U.S. Farm Bill, the Federal Agriculture Improvement and Reform Act (FAIR). Variously described as a "milestone" and a "watershed" in U.S. agricultural policy which moves beyond the normal pattern of incremental change, FAIR expands on the market oriented policies of the two previous farm acts. It accelerates the reduction of the federal government's influence in the agricultural sector through traditional commodity programs.

FAIR introduces major changes in the methods used for making income support payments to farmers. The system of target prices and price-sensitive deficiency payments is abolished and instead there is provision for seven years of predetermined annual payments that are unrelated to production or to market price conditions. FAIR repeals most acreage controls that restricted cropping patterns, including the acreage reduction programs. The long established practice of "buying air," paying farmers not to grow crops, is effectively ended. Most planting constraints are eliminated so that farmers may now choose to expand their plantings of existing crops or switch more acreage to other crops in line with their expectations of market returns. It is anticipated that U.S. agriculture will become more price competitive in world markets as a consequence of the FAIR reforms. "Without the government (CCC) as an attractive market for commodity forfeitures, there will be increased dependence on export markets." (Knuston, Smith, Outlaw, and Wilson 1996: unpaginated) Although export subsidy payments will be reduced, relatively high levels of export subsidization will remain in place. Indeed, the U.S. agriculture secretary announced that more use would be made of the Dairy Export Incentive Program in 1997. Butterfat subsidies were resumed in an effort to boost flagging milk prices, a plan criticized from New Zealand as being contrary to the spirit of trade liberalization even if it was legal. (*Agra Europe*, 10 January 1997: M7)

It is important to place these developments within the context of the changing agricultural strategies pursued by the United States. "Until the 1970s, U.S. farm policy focused on stabilizing farming within a nationally regulated system of accumulation, with exports/food aid as a by-product of the domestic management of surpluses." (McMichael 1994a: 169) More recently, however, the United States has followed a strategy of re-orienting "farm support policies towards the (world) market sphere, and away from preserving a coherent national (family) farm sector." (McMichael 1994a: 164) Viewed in this context, it is no surprise that the FAIR Act puts particular pressure on dairy farmers, a bastion of family farming, with milk price support being reduced and then eliminated. The U.S. Department of Agriculture's Economic Research Service freely admits that dairy farmers will face lower net incomes and greater adjustments to their operations. Further pressure will be placed on medium sized farmers. These outcomes represent another victory for agribusiness interests, reinforcing Moyer and Josling's observation (1990: 34) that "Agri-business would seem to have an advantage in the farm bill lobbying process."

In this paper, however, the balance of domestic interests in American agriculture is a matter for concern only in so far as it has international implications. McMichael notes (1994b:291) that the U.S. negotiating stance in the Uruguay Round was "evidently based on a 'breadbasket of the world' conception." In some respects, this breadbasket strategy is "somewhat anachronistic in a world food economy where the center of gravity is shifting away from bulk, low-value products towards a brisk trade in high-value products." (McMichael 1994b: 291) The underlying logic is, as McMichael notes, based on rising middle class demand for animal protein products in less developed countries with supply constraints meaning that a concomitant rising demand for animal feedstuffs cannot be met locally.

In the American heartland, triumphalist accounts of FAIR see it as fulfilling the country's manifest destiny to be the world's leading supplier of agricultural products. It is worth quoting from a report emanating from Missouri at some length to give the flavor of the thinking:

> To make the case that the U.S. is probably the best positioned to supply these meat and feed grain needs to this growing world middle class is not difficult. The natural resources are here, the infrastructure is here, and just as important, the policies are now here. . . The FAIR Act will allow producers to move in response to market signals without being concerned about base protection. Add all these factors into the equation and you are hard pressed to determine who else can step up to the plate in a similar manner. (Young 1997: unpaginated)

The EU may wish to step up to the plate. In doing so, it may be at something of a competitive disadvantage. The French agricultural research institute, INRA, has suggested, "International comparisons of cost of production and productivity show clearly that, in the maize and oilseeds sectors, the U.S. benefits from significant comparative advantage." Removing price supports in the United States and reducing export subsidies should "improve both efficiency and competitiveness and make it possible to express the comparative advantage of the United States in the maize and oilseeds sectors as well as in the livestock industry which relies on these feedstuffs." (*Agra Europe*, 29 November 1996: P2)

Certainly, if as many forecast, the FAIR Act leads to an increase in U.S. production of wheat, maize and soy, and most of that extra produce is sold on the world market, new agricultural trade tensions are likely to appear between the United States and the EU. Some U.S. estimates suggest that soy production could increase by 20 percent in the period to 2004 compared with the 1993 to 1995 average. This in turn would reduce the world price for oilseeds. (*Agra Europe*, 3 January 1997: P2–P3) The EU oilseeds regime is particularly vulnerable to increased competition from U.S. producers, given that it offers producers a return equal to 2.1 times the cereal intervention price (adjusted by a world price reference). Professor Harry Ayer of the University of Arizona has argued, "The organization of the oilseeds regime in the EU is such that a decrease in the world price leads automatically to very large expenditure for supporting oilseeds producers. Already the oilseeds sector is one of the most costly, relative to the volume of production, and the number of farmers that are supported." (*Agra Europe,* 6 December 1996: P2)

It has to be said, however, that there is not unanimity about the effects of the FAIR Act on world agricultural trade. A number of distinguished agricultural economists have questioned whether its effects will be as far-reaching as has sometimes been suggested. Professor David Harvey conceded that FAIR would stimulate U.S. production and exports because it largely maintains traditional levels of support while removing production controls and preserving export subsidies. However, he argued that the new legislation was temporary. If high world prices for grains and other commodities were not maintained, agricultural lobbies could force the reintroduction of deficiency payments. (*Agra Europe*, 29 November 1996: P1) American experts such as Professor Ayer counter that the FAIR Act is part of a trend which started in 1971 and represents a shift in the political attitude towards agricultural support in the United States which in particular supports the decoupling of subsidies from production decisions. (*Agra Europe*, 6 December 1996: P1) One might add that concern about the reappearance of the budget deficit in the United States is likely to create formidable political resistance to any upward trend in agricultural subsidies in the United States of the kind that happened in the 1980s.

Leading German agricultural economist Stefan Tangermann stated that he was "not convinced that the end of supply controls for U.S. arable crops would inevitably lead to a surge in production and lower grain prices. Most estimates of the FAIR Act's effects on production were 'overstated' . . . because farmers no longer had an incentive to plant crops merely to maintain their base areas." (*Agra Europe*, 21 February 1997: E3) Indeed, by the spring of 1997, many analysts appeared to be emerging that the impact of FAIR would be much less than had originally been suggested. It was argued "that the scaling down of direct support of production and its replacement with decoupled direct subsidies will act as a disincentive to increased production." (*Agra Europe*, 14 March 1997: P2) The principal area of disagreement between analysts was "on the extent to which the world market will remain buoyant, sustain attractive price levels and thus stimulate increased output." (*Agra Europe*, 14 March 1997: P2) World prices remained generally favorable in 1997 and analysis by the U.S. Department of Agriculture showed "a significant increase in the area planted to the major crops and a substantial rise in production of the main grains, following the removal of planting controls and the elimination of production-linked subsidization." (*Agra Europe*, 12 December 1997: A2)

Nevertheless, there were signs of increased tension between the EU and the United States on agricultural trade matters. In part, these stemmed from the impact of FAIR on the likely negotiating stance of the United States. Following a difficult meeting with EU agricultural commissioner Franz Fischler at the World Food Summit in Rome in November 1996, the U.S. Secretary of Agriculture, Dan Glickman, suggested that the United States might become more aggressive in negotiating agricultural trade disputes with the EU. Glickman complained that there was a structural problem about the effective distribution of authority in the EU that made negotiation difficult:

> It's very difficult to get a clear position on who has legitimacy. I am concerned at how difficult it is to deal with the EU on a lot of issues, given its confederation. Anything that profoundly affects any (single) country makes it more frustrating and difficult to negotiate matters of serious trade concern. It's not always clear who has the authority. (*Agra Europe*, 22 November 1996: P5)

At the WTO ministerial meeting in Singapore in December 1996, the United States and the Cairns Group countries sought unsuccessfully to begin preparatory work on farm trade negotiations in 1997. This move was strongly resisted by the EU with the French agricultural minister bluntly stating, "France will not tolerate farm issues being discussed in Singapore." (*Agra Europe,* 13 December 1996: P4) The U.S. deputy agriculture secretary made it clear that "We don't want countries going away from here thinking they can relax and do nothing until 1999." (*Agra Europe,* 13 December 1996: P4) The United States has made it clear that it is going to push for the elimination of all agricultural subsidies in the next round of talks. This position is as unrealistic as the "zero option" was in the Uruguay Round. The U.S.'s attempt to put pressure on state trading bodies such as the Canadian Wheat Board and the New Zealand Dairy Board will bring it into conflict with its potential allies in the Cairns Group. In any case, the United States will not be able to take an effective negotiating position if the Congress does not grant "fast track" authority to the President.

The principal area of conflict between the United States and the EU will be over the future of the "blue box." (The Cairns Group has also signaled that it does not consider these concessions necessary). This was a device created to bring about an agreement over agriculture in the Uruguay Round. The EU's partially decoupled arable aid payments to farmers and the U.S.'s deficiency payments were placed in the "blue box" and hence outside the scope of the agreement. The FAIR measures end deficiency payments and hence the U.S. commitment to the "blue box." It is argued on Washington's behalf that its new subsidies are production neutral and hence may be placed in the "green box" and outside the scope of any future negotiations. The EU's compensatory subsidies to arable farmers are portrayed as not being production neutral because they are directly linked to production. In fact, both forms of subsidy tend to encourage production because they allow the grower to sell at a lower price than would be possible if the subsidies did not exist. "The problem for the EU is . . . that the breaking of the link between actual production and eligibility for payment in the American system is what makes the latter 'GATT-able' and the European system unacceptable." (*Agra Europe*, 20 September 1996: P5)

Even before the negotiations begin, there are a number of trade tensions between the EU and the United States ranging from bananas to veterinary equivalence which are leading to frictions. Perhaps the most politically contentious because they raise fundamental issues about the future direction of agriculture are those arising from developments in biotechnology and it is these questions that are analyzed in the next section.

BIOTECHNOLOGY: ANOTHER SOURCE OF EU-U.S. TENSION

The genetic engineering techniques opened up by the discovery of recombinant DNA justify biotechnology being regarded as the enabling technology of the twenty-first century, just as microelectronics has been the enabling technology of the last quarter of the twentieth century. Biotechnology opens up a new range of possibilities for farming and the food industries. It has also introduced a new set of trade tensions between the EU and the United States. The broad picture underlying these tensions is as follows: the research necessary to apply biotechnology to agriculture has been most extensively undertaken in the United States by American multinational companies. These new technologies have been widely adopted by American farmers, potentially increasing the competitiveness of their products in world markets. American multinationals also want to sell their new biotechnologically engineered products in the European market. However, there is significant consumer resistance to these innovations, and this translates into political resistance from the European Union.

This discussion will focus for reasons of parsimony on a soybean engineered by Monsanto of the United States. It should be emphasized that it is not the only product causing controversy. There has been a long history of tension between the United States and the EU over another Monsanto product, bovine Somatotropin (bST) which boosts milk yields in cows and has been widely adopted by larger U.S. dairy farmers. Often portrayed as the "gateway" biotechnology product, its commercial use is currently banned in the EU. (Grant 1991 and 1997) There is also a controversy in progress over a maize plant designed by Ciba of Switzerland which offers protection against the European corn borer pest: there is concern that its antibiotic resistance qualities may be transferred to animals and humans. Interestingly, there has been virtually no consumer resistance to a genetically engineered tomato puree based on tomatoes grown in California.

Soybeans are a very significant product in trade and consumer terms. "Soybeans, and the meal and oil made from them, account for 25 percent of U.S. agricultural exports to the EU, and were worth more than $2 billion (œ1.2bn) last year." (*Financial Times,* 15 October 1996) They are used in 60 percent of processed foods, including bread, biscuits, sweets and vegetarian products, as well as in baby and special diet foods.

Monsanto has engineered a soybean (by changing or supplementing the soy plant's genetic constituents) which is resistant to the company's own herbicide (Roundup) which would previously have damaged the crop as well as killing the weeds. As a result, weed control can now be achieved using a single spray that breaks down quickly in the soil. Roundup Ready soybeans also give the farmer more flexibility about planting dates, as they can plant and worry about weed control later. First reports indicated that "the transgenic seed yielded 20 percent more than its conventional neighbors and required fewer applications of chemicals" (*Financial Times*, 11 November 1996). Not surprisingly, American farmers are rapidly adopting the new seed. Over 1.5 million hectares of various transgenic crops were planted in 1996. (*Farmers Weekly*, 28 February 1997) It is anticipated that about 15 percent of the total U.S. soy area will be sown with genetically modified seed in the summer of 1997. (*Agra Europe*, 7 March 1997: N5)

These developments did not receive a welcome in Europe in the wake of the BSE episode. Greenpeace mobilized opposition to the genetically modified soybeans. When the first consignment arrived by ship in Hamburg in November 1996, it was greeted by a Greenpeace barge and two dinghies that projected anti-biotechnology slogans on to the ship's side. (*Agra Europe*, 8 November 1996: E2) A leading frozen food retailer in Iceland threw its weight behind the Greenpeace campaign, its chief executive declaring in a statement typical of the level of the debate, "It's like Frankenstein's soy beans." (*Financial Times*, 11 November 1996) Iceland has subsequently claimed that it has established a supply chain which means that its customers can buy products free of genetically modified material. The then UK environment secretary, John Gummer, portrayed the issue as a power struggle between the United States and EU, recalling visions of the EU as a bulwark against American hegemony:

> It is true that the Americans are trying to force this on to Europe without us making our own minds up about it. One of the important reasons for the EU is that we are strong enough to say to the Americans that we decide what we want in our food chain and not you. (*Financial Times*, 5 December 1996)

The EU's reaction to all this was characterized by considerable uncertainty with much of the initiative being ceded to member states. Genetically modified maize was given scientific clearance, but then France banned its farmers from planting it for the 1998 harvest, while Austria and Luxembourg announced that they would unilaterally ban both its sale and cultivation. (*Agra Europe*, 14 February 1997: E4) Labeling rules for genetically modified products have caused controversy within the Commission with the trade and industrial affairs commissioners wanting maximum flexibility and the environment and agriculture commissioners calling for a more stringent regime.

The biotechnology issue has much wider implications than introducing a new source of tension into U.S.-EU trade relations. Biotechnology is seen as offering an environmentally friendly way of feeding a growing world population. The argument advanced by advocates of biotechnology is that productivity improvements without the use of biotechnology are likely to be modest. There is relatively little scope for further improvements in plant productivity through conventional methods, and biotechnology opens up a new range of plant protection products that would reduce dependence on chemical sprays. Biotechnology is thus seen as offering the prospect of increased yields with less damage to the environment.

Bye and Fonte suggest that biotechnology offers the opportunity to move agriculture away from a Fordist model of standardized high quantity production towards a diversified model that is more responsive to consumer demand for high quality niche products. However, they recognize:

> This process will not lead in the foreseeable future to a biorevolution in agriculture, but rather to more acute contradictions and conflicts between the persistence of a technical model of production still oriented towards quantitative norms and the emergence of new demands and new functions for agriculture and the rural space. (Bye and Fonte 1994: 244)

The two earlier agricultural revolutions in the postwar period . . . the replacement of human and animal power by mechanization, and the widespread use of fertilizers and agrochemicals . . . were achieved in a very different political context. The emphasis was on maximizing production, an objective shared by consumers and unopposed by an environmental movement yet to emerge as an effective political force. In the wake of the BSE episode, the introduction of genetically modified products in Europe can easily be portrayed as a threat to consumer health and the environment. It is also possible to portray the situation in terms of well-worn political images such as the "arrogance" of hegemonic Americans. In this context, the positive transformative aspects of biotechnology tend to be submerged. In the European context, biotechnology becomes another arena in which resistance to change manifests itself.

RESISTANCE TO CHANGE

Rieger (1996) bravely sets out to defend the CAP from its critics. He portrays the CAP "as an integral part of the west European welfare state and its particularly moral economy." (Rieger 1996: 101) The CAP reform and the Uruguay Round "pushed west European agriculture in an even more nationalistic direction, which implies policies which try to block or even avert the potentially disturbing influences of international trade and of a highly interdependent, global economy on the economic and social situation at home." (Rieger 1996: 118) All the forces for change detailed above, as well as others that have not been discussed in this paper (such as enlargement and budgetary problems) may find themselves absorbed by a vision of the CAP as a defensive mechanism for a distinctive and important European social space. In practice, of course, most of the CAP assistance goes to large farmers, but this unpleasant aspect of reality need not prevent the use of the CAP as a barrier against globalizing forces. The current EU agriculture commissioner, Franz Fischler, a former Austrian agriculture minister with his own small farm, certainly has a distinctive vision of European farming. He has sought to recast the role of farmers as guardians of a rural landscape and society. Justifying payments to them, he has stated:

> Direct payments are there to pay for a very important service that the agricultural community renders to society as a whole. Farmers occupy the land and should continue to do so if we want to keep the kind of countryside we have created over the centuries in Europe and not allow our rural landscape to revert to wilderness. Farmers exercise a social and environ-mental role for which it is right that they should be rewarded. (Fischler 1996: 4)

In particular, "Fischler appears to be determined to preserve the small-holding as the bedrock of the structure of rural communities." (*Agra Europe*, 31 January 1997: P1). Fischler has sought to nudge the EU in the direction of a rural rather than an agricultural policy, an effort symbolized by a conference held at Cork in the autumn of 1996. However, for all the talk of the "Cork philosophy," it has received scant encouragement from the member states that fear that their existing subsidies might be diverted elsewhere under such a regime. Indeed, the Commission seems to have backed away from its support for a rural policy. In March 1997, the director-general for agriculture, Guy Legras, stated that "There was no question . . . of a common rural policy supplanting the CAP." (*Agra Europe*, 21 February 1997: E1)

The Commission has published its Agenda 2000 reforms for further reform, in outline in the summer of 1997 and in detail in March 1998. The controversy about these reforms, and whether or not they represent a useful step towards fundamental reform, cannot be examined in detail here. In any event, at the time of writing, they remain proposals that have to overcome substantial opposition from a number of member states, including France and Germany. What is significant about the reform proposals is the increasing emphasis on what is called the European Model of Agriculture which could be seen as an official statement of the resistance to change model.

The notion of a distinctive European model of agriculture was first advocated by the European farmers' organization, COPA, in the fall of 1997. Their secretary general commented that "This model meant that farmers' incomes kept pace with incomes in the rest of society" and also emphasized the multi-functional nature of farming in terms of its landscape and employment contributions. After its November meeting the Council of Agriculture Ministers produced a communique which referred to the "existing model of European agriculture" four times in six pages. The Council declared that it was "firmly resolved to continue developing the existing model of European agriculture and act to assert its identity both inside and outside the European Union." By March 1998 when the final Agenda 2000 proposals were published, the European Model of Agriculture (now referred to in capital letters) had "become a totem and a policy concept in its own right, to be respected whenever the policy is under internal and external attack." (*Agra Europe*, 20 March 1998: A1) In other words, although there is a more explicit acknowledgement of the social aspects of the CAP, the inefficiencies and market distortions it engenders are to be vigorously defended, particularly against international criticism.

CONCLUSIONS

The resistance to change model looks more robust than each of the three change models presented here. Globalization forces encounter the bedrock of national resistance in a more determined way than elsewhere. As a senior German official has stated, "European agriculture still requires tariff protection and domestic support for the major products. These demands should be made at the world trade talks with the utmost vigor." (*Agra Europe,* 21 February 1997: E3) As far as the second model is concerned, FAIR looks less like a forcing agent for change than was first anticipated. Nevertheless, EU-U.S. tensions over agricultural trade will persist and the United States (and the Cairns Group) will be determined to get more out of the next round of agricultural trade talks than they did last time. Biotechnology enhances EU-U.S. tensions, and may contribute to a growing competitiveness gap between the two producers that will make the EU even more resistant to change. However, its impact as a new technology is likely to be slower and more uneven than the two earlier waves of technological change in agriculture.

As Swinbank and Tanner comment (1996: 156) in relation to agriculture, "the policy-making arena is complex and difficult to understand and the outcome of the policy-making process is uncertain." One of the greatest uncertainties relates to the process of European integration, and in particular whether an EMU for core countries is achieved on schedule and without undue associated turbulence on the financial markets. The convergence criteria have created an additional pressure on agricultural budgets. If an EMU of core countries does occur, there will be some difficult questions to resolve about the subsequent operation of the green currencies that remain an important part of the CAP.

The most likely scenario for the opening years of the twenty-first century is as follows: U.S. agriculture will continue to become more competitive, agribusiness forces in the United States will remain politically strong, and better access to world markets will remain an important agenda item for the United States. However, the more globalization becomes a reality, the more it will be perceived as a threat by European agriculture. Hence, there will be more determined efforts to defend a distinctive European rural space under the banner of the European Model of Agriculture.

The shrewder people in the Commission and elsewhere see that the political way through these shoals is to change the CAP enough to keep its budgetary costs under control and to be able to offer enough concessions to prevent a complete breakdown of international trade negotiations. Presentationally at least, the CAP will have to appear more environmentally friendly and more closely related to specific social objectives. Elements of such an approach are to be found in the Agenda 2000 proposals, but they still fall far short of a fundamental change of emphasis away from the encouragement of intensive forms of agricultural production.

Not surprisingly, the millennium will not usher in any great changes in the conduct of agricultural policy domestically or internationally. It will remain a highly politicized arena, but one that is not very transparent or accessible to outsiders. As Rieger notes (1996: 100), "The CAP is very much a self-contained world, following its own logic." The global (or American) logic will slowly impose itself, but the EU has shown itself skilled at defensive politics in an international arena. One can thus predict more tensions, more conflict and changes which will often appear to offer more than they actually deliver.

REFERENCES

Bye, P. and M. Fonte. 1994. "Is the Technical Model of Agriculture Changing Radically?" in P. McMichael, ed. *The Global Restructuring of Agro-Food Systems*. Ithaca, N.Y.: Cornell University Press.

Coleman, W. and W. Grant. 1998. "Agricultural Finance Policies in a Globalizing Era: An Examination of Policy Convergence." *European Journal of Political Research*, Autumn.

Fischler, F. 1996. "Keynote Address." Agra Europe Outlook Conference, London.

Grant, W. 1991. *The Dairy Industry: an International Comparison*. Aldershot: Dartmouth.

———. 1997. *The Common Agricultural Policy*. London: Macmillan.

Hathaway, D. E. and Ingco, M. E. 1995. "Agricultural Liberalization and the Uruguay Round." Paper presented at World Bank conference.

Higgott, R. N.d. "Globalisation and Governance: Accommodating to Regionalization and Localization." Unpublished paper, University of Warwick.

Knutson, R. D., E. G. Smith, J. L. Outlaw and W. F. Woods. 1996. "1996 Farn Bill Review." Texas A and M University Agriculture and Food Policy Center, Working Paper 96-6.

Le Heron, R. 1993. *Globalized Agriculture*. Oxford: Pergamon.

McMichael, P. 1994a. "GATT, Global Regulation and the Construction of a New Hegemonic Order," in *Regulating Agriculture*, P. Lowe, T. Marsden, and S. Whatmore, eds. London: David Fulton.

———. 1994b. "Global Restructuring: Some Lines of Inquiry," in *The Global Restructuring of Agro-Food Systems,* P. McMichael, ed. Ithaca, N.Y.: Cornell University Press.

Moyer, H. W. and T. E. Josling. 1990. *Agricultural Policy Reform: Politics and Process in the EC and USA*. Hemel Hempstead: Harvester Wheatsheaf.

Rieger, E. 1996. "The Common Agricultural Policy," in *Policy-Making in the European Union,* H. Wallace and W. Wallace, eds. Oxford: Oxford University Press.

Swinbank, A. and C. Tanner. 1996. *Farm Policy and Trade Conflict*. Ann Arbor: University of Michigan Press.

Young, R. E., III. 1997. *The Long-Term Outlook for United States Agriculture*. University of Missouri Food and Agricultural Policy Research Institute Report.

Appendix 8.1 The Non-Aligned Movement

- Afghanistan
- Algeria
- Angola
- Bahamas
- Bahrain
- Bangladesh
- Barbados
- Belarus
- Belize
- Benin
- Bhutan
- Bolivia
- Botswana
- Brunei Darussalam
- Burkina Faso
- Burundi
- Cambodia
- Cameroon
- Cape Verde
- Central African Rep.
- Chad
- Chile
- Colombia
- Comoros
- Congo
- Congo (DPR; Zaire)
- Côte d'Ivoire
- Cuba
- Cyprus
- Djibouti
- Dominican Rep.
- Ecuador
- Egypt
- Equatorial Guinea
- Ethiopia
- Eritrea
- Gabon
- Gambia
- Ghana
- Grenada
- Guatemala
- Guinea
- Guinea-Bissau
- Guyana
- Honduras
- India
- Indonesia
- Iran
- Iraq
- Jamaica
- Jordan
- Kenya
- Korea (North)
- Kuwait
- Lao
- Lebanon
- Lesotho
- Liberia
- Libya
- Madagascar
- Malawi
- Malaysia
- Maldives
- Mali
- Malta
- Mauritania
- Mauritius
- Mongolia
- Morocco
- Mozambique
- Myanmar
- Namibia
- Nepal
- Nicaragua
- Niger
- Nigeria
- Oman
- Pakistan
- Palestine
- Panama
- Papua New Guinea
- Peru
- Philippines
- Qatar
- Rwanda
- St. Lucia
- Sao Tome & Principe
- Saudi Arabia
- Senegal
- Seychelles
- Sierra Leone
- Singapore
- Somalia
- South Africa
- Sri Lanka
- Sudan
- Suriname
- Swaziland
- Syria
- Tanzania
- Thailand
- Togo
- Trinidad & Tobago
- Tunisia
- Turkmenistan
- Uganda
- United Arab Emirates
- Uzbekistan
- Vanuatu
- Venezuela
- Viet Nam
- Yemen
- Yugoslavia (suspended)
- Zambia
- Zimbabwe

Appendix 8.2. The Group of 77 plus China

• Afghanistan • Algeria • Angola •
• Antigua & Barbuda • Argentina • Bahamas •
• Bahrain • Bangladesh • Barbados •
• Belize • Benin • Bhutan •
• Bolivia • Bosnia-Herzegovina • Botswana •
• Brazil • Brunei Darussalam • Burkina Faso •
• Burundi • Cambodia • Cameroon •
• Cape Verde • Central African Rep. • Chad •
• Chile • China (associate member) • Colombia •
• Comoros • Congo • Congo (DPR; Zaire)
• Costa Rica • Côte d'Ivoire • Cuba •
• Cyprus • Djibouti • Dominica •
• Dominican Rep. • Ecuador • Egypt •
• El Salvador • Equatorial Guinea • Eritrea •
• Ethiopia • Fiji • Gabon •
• Gambia • Ghana • Grenada •
• Guatemala • Guinea • Guinea-Bissau •
• Guyana • Haiti • Honduras •
• India • Indonesia • Iran •
• Iraq • Jamaica • Jordan •
• Kenya • Korea (North) • Kuwait •
• Lao • Lebanon • Lesotho •
• Liberia • Libya • Madagascar •
• Malawi • Malaysia • Maldives •
• Mali • Malta • Marshall Islands
• Mauritania • Mauritius • Micronesia •
• Mongolia • Morocco • Mozambique •
• Myanmar • Namibia • Nepal •
• Nicaragua • Niger • Nigeria •
• Oman • Pakistan • Palestine •
• Panama • Papua New Guinea • Paraguay •
• Peru • Philippines • Qatar •
• Romania • Rwanda • Samoa •
• Sao Tome & Principe • Saudi Arabia • Senegal •
• Seychelles • Sierra Leone • Singapore •
• Solomon Islands • Somalia • South Africa •
• Sri Lanka • St. Kitts and Nevis • St. Lucia •
• St. Vincent & Grenad. • Sudan • Suriname •
• Swaziland • Syria • Tanzania •
• Thailand • Togo • Tonga •
• Trinidad & Tobago • Tunisia • Turkmenistan •
• Uganda • United Arab Emirates • Uruguay •
• Vanuatu • Venezuela • Viet Nam •
• Yemen • Yugoslavia (suspended) • Zambia •
• Zimbabwe •

9

The Collective South in Multinational Environmental Politics

Adil Najam

Over the last decade, the term South has once again become the descriptor of choice for the set of nations that are variously referred to as the developing, less developed, underdeveloped countries, or simply the Third World. Especially in the context of global negotiations—and even more so in multi-national environmental negotiations—these countries are choosing, and sometimes demanding, that they be referred to as the South. It is the contention of this chapter that this is more than just a matter of semantics. Indeed, the term reflects a certain aspect of their collective identity and their desire to negotiate as a collective. It also reflects the type of collective that they are and wish to be. Equally, it is a reflection of the evolving global development agenda that these countries, and the multi-national policy system, are grappling with; particularly on issues related to sustainable development.

This chapter will focus, therefore, on the concept of the South. In particular, it sets itself the following goals. First, to establish the relevance of a South in post–Cold War multi-national policy and understand what the countries of the South mean when they choose to describe themselves as the South rather than as developing countries or as the Third World. Second, to establish whether there is, in fact, a recognizable South within the multi-national policy system and to determine the efficacy and relevance of the institutions of the collective South for this new phase of global policy negotiations. Third, to review the potential of the current phase of North-South dialogue in the context of what may be called the global politics of sustainable development. Finally, to review how this unlikely and unwieldy collective has held together despite the odds, and at what cost.

UNDERSTANDING THE SOUTH

The retreat of Cold War tensions has signaled a withering of old rivalries and a blossoming of new alliances; it has also allowed a new spate of issues—including trade, economic development, human rights, and environmental quality—to take center stage. The upheaval in the geo-strategic landscape has rendered alliances from another era defunct; all across Africa, Latin America, and Asia, regimes that never had real support at home find themselves deserted by the superpowers that had long sponsored their rule. In the former Yugoslavia, this led to the brutal dismemberment of a false state; in Somalia and Rwanda it triggered the disintegration of all notions of statehood. Alliances whose very rationale had been the ideological divide between East and West toil to adjust to a world whose fault-lines have shifted; some like the Warsaw Pact have crumbled, others like the North Atlantic Treaty Organization (NATO) struggle to seek a new mandate and new partners; yet others, like the Organization for Economic Cooperation and Development (OECD), turn their attention inwards as the battles move from being ideological to economic and the tensions are not as much with foes outside as between friends within. International institutions—no longer required to serve as Cold War sparring grounds—seek an expanded mandate, demand new powers; the World Bank with its gospel of structural adjustment and liberalization, the United Nations in its role as global conscience. It is within the context of this changing world order that the reemergence of the South as an "alliance of the powerless" needs to be understood (Williams 1993: 9).

What Is "the South"?

After more than a decade in hibernation, the phrase North-South again became the staple of scholarly as well as populist discourse on subjects related to multi-national politics and negotiation during the early 1990s. Despite their pervasive use, the terms North and South are seldom defined. This subsection focuses on the term South. More specifically, on what the countries of the South imply when they choose to self-define themselves as such despite, or because of, the historical baggage that the term carries. Implicit in this effort is the contention that understanding the term is not only integral to contextual zing North-South differences but is critical to understanding why the South behaves as it does in international politics. In 1980, the Independent Commission on International Development Issues acknowledged that neither North nor South is a "uniform or permanent grouping" and described them as generally synonymous with "developed" and "developing" countries (Brandt Commission 1980: 31). Emile Van Lennep (1983: 15)—then secretary general of the OECD—pointed out that the North-South concept, "like all powerful ideas . . . has the virtue of grand simplicity." He added that:

> It is true that over time the distinction between North and South has become less clear in an objective sense. But the fact remains that there are two sets of countries which are widely comprehended to consist of the developed and the developing, each set sharing certain broad characteristics and psychological affinities. We have the countries of the North, with advanced or relatively advanced income levels and social conditions and a more or less completed process of national integration. The South comprises countries where the development process is still very much in train, where dual economies and dual societies are characteristic, and where, in many cases, hunger and poverty remain the dominant way of life for millions of people.

This remains a still valid caricature of how the North-South divide is perceived by many. Indeed, the popular view that the North-South divide is a binary distinction between "haves" and "have nots" is a powerful, and not untrue, way of understanding the concept—as long as one remembers that what the South wishes to "have" is not simply economic development, but a say in the political decisions that affect its destiny (Krasner 1985; Thomas 1987). The danger, however, is that the distinction is too often distilled only to its economic dimensions, leading to the image of a South forever knocking at the North's door with a begging bowl in hand. Aware of this danger, the 1990 South Commission defined the term in a decidedly more political context. It talks not merely about economic poverty but about the "poverty of influence." For the Commission, the defining feature of the South is not merely its economic weakness, but also its political dependence. The self-definition of the South, therefore, is a definition of exclusion: these are countries that believe that they have been "bypassed" and view themselves as existing "on the periphery" (South Commission 1990: 1; *emphasis added*):[1]

> While most of the people of the North are affluent, most of the people of the South are poor; while the economies of the North are generally strong and resilient, those of the South are mostly weak and defenseless; while the countries in the North are, by and large, in control of their destinies, those of the South are very vulnerable to external factors and lacking in functional sovereignty.

To redress, what they consider to be an imbalance of influence, the developing countries have sought the vehicle of global negotiations, often referred to as North-South dialogue (see Gosovic 1972; Menon 1977; Murphy 1984). Although Jones (1983: 1) considers "North-South Dialogue" to be "very much a phrase of the 1970s," the terminology and the concept of the North-South divide is not new. Gordon (1978: 5–6) credits former British Ambassador to Washington, Sir Oliver Franks, with having coined the expression "North-South relations" in the late 1950s and having suggested that a worldwide cleavage along that axis might come to rival East-West relations as a central concern of world politics. By the early 1960s the term was already in use within the development community (Ward 1965: 3) and gained wider public recognition in the 1970s as part of the rallying cry for a New International Economic Order (NIEO). In NIEO debates, it gained legitimacy through its usage in UN documents and international forums. During the 1980s, as the NIEO movement faded from global attention, the term was also confined largely to specialized academic discourse. However, the publication of the South Commission Report in 1990 and the term's wide use by governments, nongovernmental organizations (NGOs), the media, and officials during the UN Conference on Environment and Development (UNCED) process revitalized it in popular environmental contexts.

At least till before the end of the Cold War, the East European countries of the Soviet bloc were seen as part of the North. Formally, then, North equaled East plus West. Practically, however, the North-South divide has been much more of a West-South divide (Weiss 1986a: 20). Historically, this would suggest a triangular schema with the North equaling West, and South and East being distinct actors. Along this line, Hansen (1979: 3–4), for example, used the term North as "a shorthand description for the world's rich, industrialized noncommunist states" and South for "the world's less developed or developing states" which "range from the suddenly rich but yet-to industrialize oil states of the Middle East to the so-called Fourth World states, the poorest countries of the world."[2] Although this triangular schema still best describes our popular division of the world, the end of the Cold War has disturbed the neat distinctions. The placement of East bloc countries within a North-South framework has become more difficult (Wallerstein 1993). Some East bloc countries now fit better within the North while others are distinctively Southern in character. Moreover, the end of the Cold War has created a set of new states—primarily in the Balkans and Central Asia—with a strong claim to being of the South, even though most of them are not (yet) represented in the institutions of the South (Najam 1993; Ayoob 1995). This has raised new concerns about the continuing validity of the concept in the post–Cold War world. While the nations that make up the collective continue to congregate under the Southern banner, at least some analysts seem to be saying: "it may work in reality, but does it make sense in theory?"

IS THERE STILL A SOUTH?

In proclaiming that "The 'Third World' Is Dead," the *New York Times* (Crossette 1994) has not been alone in prematurely pronouncing the demise of the South. Indeed, unwarranted obituaries have been, and remain, an enduring feature of the collective's decidedly rocky history. In its post–Cold War variant, the arguments go something like this: If the North was merely another name for the West, and now there is no East, then how can there still be a

South? Better still, if there is no longer a "Second" world, how can there be a "Third"? For those who remain fixated on notions that define the Third World or the South only in the narrow terms of Cold War polarizations, the conclusion is obvious: the emergence of Southern unity, they insist, was a result of Cold War politics; with the Cold War being dead, the alliance should also be buried. Oxley (1991: 102, 109), for example, opines that the North-South dichotomy has been "archaic" for quite some time, and has been rendered "ludicrous" by the end of the Cold War. With the Second World having surrendered to the economic ideology of the First, and with the South being as heterogeneous as it is, it is tempting to proclaim the Third World as a "mere historical curiosity," and the coalition of the South as "at best little more than an irrelevance and at worst an absurdity"; in the course of time it may turn out to be so; but that time is not yet (Williams 1993: 7–8; *also see* Grant 1996).

At the simplest and most pragmatic level, what Roger Hansen (1979: 2) had to say about why thinking in North-South terms was valid 20 years ago, seems equally valid today: "If over [130] developing countries time and again, in forum after forum, act as a diplomatic unit, they would seem to merit analysis as a potential actor of major importance in the international system."

Irrespective of what academic, or even popular, opinion may insist, if this group of states continues to act as a relatively cogent caucus in international forums, then it is simply irresponsible, not to say ridiculous, to label them deceased. At a deeper level of analysis, it is important to remember that for many of these countries, the desire for unity in the face of an international economic order that continues to place them at a systemic disadvantage still outweighs the internal diversity—which, in fact, has been a feature of the coalition's definition from its very outset. Most importantly, even if some Northern observers consider the South's agenda of 1970s "discredited" (Sebenius 1991: 87), it remains unfinished business for much of the South and a goal that is still seen as something that is very much worth pursuing (South Commission 1990; Mohammed 1992; Samper 1995; Grant 1996).

> The end of the Cold War has not resulted in making the Third World irrelevant as an explanatory category in international politics. . . . The relevance of the Third World, or the South, has been reinforced by the end of the Cold War because now the dichotomy between the developed, affluent, and powerful North and the underdeveloped, poor, and weak South is visible in even starker terms than earlier. . . . The end of the Cold War clearly has juxtaposed the vulnerabilities and insecurities of the South—an increasingly popular synonym for the Third World—with the power and affluence of the industrialized North. (Ayoob 1995: 61)

The validity of the South as an effective, or even a real negotiating collective had long been questioned on structural grounds. The collapse of Cold

War tensions only revived such criticism on historical grounds. Not surprisingly, then, the South's self-definition—or rather lack of any concreteness therein—has been vulnerable on at least two fronts: the structural criticism about the lack of homogeneity within the coalition, and the historical criticism about the irrelevance of the coalition after the demise of the Cold War. Let us review both streams of criticism.

The issue of heterogeneity has dogged the South from the start but many Southern scholars and leaders consider it to be a false issue because from the very beginning the South has accepted, even prided in, its internal diversity. According to Williams (1993: 10), a "crucial feature" of the collective is "the members' recognition of the essential heterogeneity of the group." While the South's defenders have not contested the inherent heterogeneity of the collective, they have consistently contested the assertion that this heterogeneity is a defining variable that might make the collective defunct (see Muni 1979; Brandt Commission 1980; Nyerere 1980; Sabri-Abdalla 1980; South Commission 1990). In essence, since the solidarity of the South "has never been based on some supposed general identity of economic interests by all developing countries" (Geldart and Lyon 1980: 101) therefore economic heterogeneity is insufficient—though not unimportant—for challenging the viability of the coalition. As Williams (1993: 10) argues, it may pose a "problem of management" but it is not "a sign of irrelevance or disintegration."

Additionally, available quantitative analyses suggest that the economic differentiation within the South has not grown as dramatically over the years as is popularly perceived, nor is it significantly greater than the economic differences within the North (Sabri-Abdalla 1980; Adams, 1993). Ultimately, the only litmus test of the South's alleged disintegration has to be whether its more fortunate members make efforts to distance themselves from their less well-off comrades in the common quest for international systemic change. Grant (1995: 569) reminds us that "there has been no stampede among the [Newly Industrialized Countries] to disassociate themselves from the Third World, especially as the portals of the industrialized countries of the North have not been flung open to them." In this respect, then, one can only agree with Thomas (1987: 3–4) that "the changes which have taken place in the last forty years have not sufficiently eroded the political, psychological or economic underpinnings of the grouping to warrant a reclassification. As a category in international relations, the Third World has not yet been rendered invalid." The question, of course, is whether the global changes over the last decade have somehow made the Southern collective defunct.

This is the thesis of the second stream of critique of the South as a viable collective; it argues that since the East-West rift has disappeared, therefore the South can also be declared deceased or, at the very least, it can be safely ignored (Van Evera 1990). Such a view seems to rest on the assumptions that a unipolar world implies an undivided world and/or that South unity came about only because of the Cold War. The first of these assumptions can only be credited to a flawed euphoria. For leaders of the South, the sense of subordination, alienation, and injustice that had initially brought them together, still persists. Not only has the end of the Cold War not triggered a buoyancy of hope in the South, it has raised new fears. As Malaysian Prime Minister Mahathir Mohammed (1992: 26) made passionately plain, "a unipolar world is every bit as threatening [to the South] as a bipolar world." As to arguments about the Southern collective being an artifact of the Cold War, it is true that Southern unity, especially within the nonaligned movement, emerged as retaliation to Cold War polarizations. However, the South sought for itself an identity separate from either bloc. Seen by the West as a "construct of the idle left" and often accused of being conceptually inconsistent by its critics, nonalignment has had a very precise meaning for its adherents. The essence of the South's political identity was not merely retaliation to *bi*-polarity, but to the very notion of *polarity*. Sabri-Abdalla (1980: 40) reminds us that "dependence, with all its corollaries has always been the root cause of Southern solidarity; as long as the perception of dependency remains intact, so will the South." Cedric Grant (1996: 569) explains:

> The transition from a bipolar world does not render [the South] anachronistic; nor does it justify the removal of the concept of the Third World from among the tools for analyzing international politics. On the contrary, the Third World, as an analytical concept, is likely to retain its usefulness so long as the world continues to be driven by serious economic and political disparities.

Having said the above, although the end of the Cold War does not render the South defunct, it does present it with a new set of dangers. The dangers entail not as much in the South disappearing as in being ignored in the wake of its own diminishing strategic utility. An articulation of the attendant fears of the South is captured by Chubin (1993: 88), who argues that "the South is under siege—from an international community impatient to meddle in its affairs. States of the South are losing their sovereignty, which in many cases was only recently or tentatively acquired." Not only is there the fear of a North more belligerent in using its hegemonic privileges, there is also the emergence of new claimants to the North's sympathy in the former Soviet bloc. The South is fearful of being marginalized further as attention and resources are diverted from development in the South to economic reconstruction in the East (Peng 1992; Adede 1994). While the dangers highlighted by the end of the Cold War have signaled to the South a need to revitalize its sagging coalition, new stirring around global environmental issues have offered them something on which to engage the North.

Neither the gravity of the threat nor the potential of the opportunity is lost on Southern leadership. If recent stirrings in the Group of 77 (G77) and the

Nonaligned Movement (NAM) are anything to go by, the South is not about to become a casualty of Cold War cessation. Two empirical studies of voting politics within the UN General Assembly demonstrate the tenacity and resilience of the South and the trend toward the reemerging prominence of the North-South divide in global affairs. Iida's (1988) quantitative analysis of developing countries' voting patterns in the General Assembly finds that the South's solidarity persisted—and was, in fact, higher than in the 1970s—during the 1980s when the fortunes of the South were at their lowest. Even more striking evidence is provided by Kim and Russett's (1996) study of alignments within the UN General Assembly since the end of the Cold War. Analyzing the voting roll-call data for General Assembly sessions from 1991 to 1993, they find (pg. 651):

> The North-South split now characterizes voting positions as much as the East-West split once did. The importance of North-South issues is not new, but during the Cold War years it tended to be conflated with and be overshadowed by East-West issues as a source of division. The resurgence of North-South voting renews and strengthens a long-standing alignment, one now likely to dominate the UN for a substantial period in its future.

A sense of new vulnerabilities, the persisting pangs of an unfinished agenda, and the opportunity of renewing a North-South dialogue under environmental auspices seems to have translated into a renewed assertiveness by the South, especially around the broad ambit of sustainable development. The evolution of what has been called ecopolitics (Pirages 1978; Alker and Haas 1993) seems to have given the South a new arena to rally in. With the global agenda no longer clouded by Cold War distractions, and with their own strategic utility to the superpowers evaporated, the countries of the South are reasserting their collective voice in international negotiations. The concurrent thrust of global environmental treaty making has provided them with an opportune arena in which to do so.

The reinvigoration that the South, especially the G77, seems to have enjoyed during and since the 1992 Rio Summit, and the prominence (re-)gained by the South as a relatively cohesive negotiating collective took many by surprise. Some thought the cohesion was unnatural while others predicted that it would be momentary. After all, the longstanding economic, political and geographic differences within the South could only be compounded by the environmental differences between them; the all-too-apparent differences between royalist, oil-rich Saudi Arabia and communist, economically struggling, Cuba can only be enlarged when one also factors that the first is a sparsely populated desert and the latter a populous small island state. In fact, at many turns during the 1992 Earth Summit, and in global negotiations since then, differences within the developing countries of the G77 have led to apparent fractures and frictions in the collective. For example, in the climate change negotiations, the influential oil-producing members of the G77 have had a significantly different agenda than the G77 members of the Alliance of Small Island States (AOSIS) and other coastal nations that are frontline states for possible sea-level rise (Moomaw, 1997; Elliot, 1998). In the negotiations on desertification, the dispute between African and non-African members nearly brought the G77 to a halt (Agarwal et al. 1999; Corell 1999). Negotiations on the biosafety protocol within the biodiversity convention also saw the developing countries differing significantly based on their trade priorities (Cosbey and Burgiel 2000).

However, the surprise is not that developing countries had different priorities on specific issues. It is that even when they chose to pursue their differentiated interests in global negotiations they nearly entirely did so within the framework of the G77. True to form, the collective has remained remarkably resilient in the face of conditions that should have predicated disintegration. Porter, Brown and Chasek (2000: 179) explain: "Despite growing disparities among the developing countries between rapidly industrializing countries such as China, India, Malaysia, and Brazil, and debt-ridden countries that have experienced little or no growth since the 1980s, such as most of sub-Saharan Africa, Vietnam, Myanmar, and Nicaragua, developing countries share a common view of the relationship between global environmental issues and North-South economic relations." It is this common view of the nature of the environmental problematique and its placement within a North-South framework that ensures that the collective South will continue to play an important role in future global environmental negotiations.

WHY "SOUTH"?

Before closing this section, something needs to be said about why the term South is being used here rather than the Third World. The two terms came into usage around the same time, were originally used to convey the same meaning, and still refer to roughly the same set of countries. However, in the context of popular, journalistic, and even academic usage their intent has substantially and substantively diverged. While South retains its intent of being a political entity, Third World has become a predominantly economic concept referring to poor countries, and more generally to the poor. The essence of the original Third World—which is all but lost in its current use—was that poverty was *a* symptom, rather than *the* cause of the commonality. What bound the countries of the Third World, despite all their differences, was not that they were economically impoverished but that they all felt politically disempowered. They had only recently become part of an international system that they had no hand in shaping, over which they had limited influence and no power, and which they considered unsympathetic to their interests. It was this system that they wished to change.

The important point is that the term Third World originally evolved as a *political* concept. As Merriam (1988: 20) reminds us, the term is "more than merely a sociological designation, it connotes a psychological condition, a state of mind encompassing the hopes and aspirations of three-fourths of humanity." It originally became popular amongst scholars and leaders of the emerging South as a political concept (Lyon 1984). Over the years its meaning has changed dramatically to an economic connotation (Muni 1979; Mountjoy 1980). As a political concept, the expression "neither [denoted] an inferior value structure, nor a descending numerical order" (Muni 1979: 128). As an economic concept, it has been corrupted to imply exactly that. This is not to suggest that Third World as a concept of simple economic gradation is without validity. Indeed, poverty is a major commonalty of these states; it is also the major banner used by them in articulating their demands. However, note that poverty is also evoked in a political context. As an economic term, Third World has become a useful concept. But it no longer does justice to its original political essence. That essence is better captured by the term South. It is this political essence that the scholars and leaders of the South attempt to capture by making South their descriptor of choice, and it is this political essence that is on display when these countries choose to negotiate collectively.

> Efforts to depict the Third World as an economic or cultural concept mistakenly attempt to reduce political behavior to a non-political explanation. . . . The unity of these countries arises, in the first place, from the inability of these states to exert significant influence on world events. . . . [M]aterial weakness and an inability to influence policy making provides a powerful stimulus of an alliance of the powerless. . . . [The] international division between the "haves" and "have-nots," did not by itself create the coalition although it established necessary conditions for bringing it into existence. (Williams 1993: 9)

It is critical, therefore, to remember that the Southern coalition is bonded together not just in a common desire for economic justice, but in a shared demand for a fundamental restructuring of international institutions and regimes. In *The Poverty Curtain*, Mahbub-ul-Haq (1976: 167) stresses that the struggle of the Southern collective is against "systemic discrimination"; as such "the basic struggle is for equality of opportunity, not equality of income." On a similar note, though in making a different argument, Stephen Krasner (1985: 27) argues that Southern solidarity is motivated by political control as much as by economic wealth and development; that "vulnerability, not simple poverty" is the motivating force for the Southern coalition. Viewing North-South issues with a political lens brings the enormity of the problem of global cooperation on anything—including the environment—into sharp relief. If bridging the enormous chasm of economic disparity between North and South seems like an insurmountable problem, then bridging the equally fundamental differences in the political aspirations of the two camps is even more so. Bringing about drastic changes in the international system that they consider antithetical to their interests is a fundamental goal of the South. The North is unprepared to accept any such change. It is here, as much as in the economic differences between the two, that we find the true essence of North-South conflict. Such a historical and political appreciation of what it means to "be of the South" needs to be cultivated if we are to make sense of the behavior of these countries in the global environmental politics and negotiation. This not only provides an explanation for the levels of emotion and frustration that North-South debates provoke, but also points to the conclusion that operationalizing global sustainable development is not merely about technical or market "fixes"; it is ultimately about reconciling deep-rooted normative differences about how the global multi-nation system—including the international environmental system—should be organized.

THE INSTITUTIONAL FACE OF THE SOUTH

The previous section argued that this essence is principally political, rather than economic; and that it builds on a set of shared vulnerabilities, grievances, and aspirations for the collective South to congregate around. One is justified in asking whether such a congregation exists only in the rhetoric of the South or whether it has institutionally manifest itself in international multilateral negotiations? This section sets out to answer this question.

Although the South is not—nor has it ever been—a simple concept to define, the wide acceptance and growing use of the term implies that even where the South defies precise definition, it enjoys general recognition. Nowhere is this recognition more manifest than in the institutional face of the South. Institutionally, the South consists of two distinct organizations, the Non-Aligned Movement (NAM) and the Group of 77 (G77). While distinct in their objectives, organizational structures and competencies, the two demonstrate a high degree of convergence in their membership and goals, and may be considered "separate parts of a single coalition" (Williams 1993: 11). While the memberships of the two organizations do not exactly mirror, the overlap between the 115 members of NAM and 132 members of G77 (plus China) translates into informal as well as formal coordination.

The roles played by the two in furthering the Southern agenda have been distinct, but complimentary. According to Sauvant (1981: 5), "while the Non-Aligned Countries [have] played a key role in making the development issue a priority item of the international agenda, the Group of 77 has become the principal organ of the Third World through which the concrete actions . . . are negotiated within the framework of the United Nations system."[3] Although the general distinction remains valid, the two mandates have been converging over the years. This section will provide an institutional history and description of both NAM and the G77, focusing more on the latter since that is the manifest negotiating arm of the modern South in contemporary multi-national policy negotiations.

THE NON-ALIGNED MOVEMENT (NAM)

Although its roots can be traced to earlier anti-colonial movements, the Afro-Asian Conference held at Bandung, Indonesia, in 1955 is generally recognized as the defining event for NAM, and the South as a negotiating collective. Twenty-nine countries from Africa and Asia and representatives from many liberation and nationalist movements participated. The heated debate on the concept of nonalignment remains the most enduring legacy of the event which was to convert what, till then, was a regional group into a cross-regional collective. (Jankowitsch and Sauvant 1978; Rajamoorthy 1992)

This was an era characterized by new states gaining political independence from colonial rule, a scramble amongst the superpowers for establishing "spheres of influence," and a growing concern amongst some of these new states that a world divided by the ideological animosities of the Cold War would only subvert their own hard-won independence. The debate on nonalignment was, therefore, both important and divisive. In the process, some who were present at Bandung (notably China and Japan) decided not to join the ranks of what later became NAM. However, the transformation from an Afro-Asian *conference* into a nonaligned *movement* did mean that new allies from Latin America and Europe could now be inducted. Prime Minister Nehru of India and President Soekarno of Indonesia, who had advocated nonalignment at Bandung, were joined in the following years by President Nasser of Egypt, Marshal Tito of Yugoslavia, and President Nkrumah of Ghana in championing the concept.

Since those heady days, twelve Summit meetings of Heads of State and Government have been held; most recently in South Africa in 1998 with the next one planned for Bangladesh in 2002.[4] NAM membership has now risen to 115 with the most recent entrant, the Dominican Republic gaining membership in 1999 (table 8.1 and map 8.1).[5] An important development since the end of the Cold War has been a greater openness to other groupings and states. Apart from a large number of future prospective members (or supporters) who attend the NAM Summits as observers, the number and range of "guest" representation at NAM Summits has increased to now include most Northern groupings and states. Also of note is the induction of some former Soviet states; something which G77 has been more hesitant in doing.[6]

The road for NAM has been far from smooth. Its relevance, never fully accepted by the Western powers, has come under serious internal question at least twice. The early 1980s saw the coalition fighting off internal threats to its continuity as member states repelled moves by the then Chair, Cuba, to promote the Soviet Union as the South's "natural ally." The early 1990s have seen it successfully fighting off a similar challenge to its continuing validity, this time from the replacement of superpower bipolarity with unipolarity. (See Jansen 1992; Chubin 1993; Grant 1995)

Indeed, NAM's achievements can seem dismal if we take its rhetoric literally—i.e. its stated goal of substantively redirecting the path of global politics either by ensuring its own functional independence or by contributing to world peace through influencing a weakening of the bipolar system. Having said that, while it is tempting to write off NAM as irrelevant, it is erroneous to do so (Jansen 1992; Williams 1993; Grant 1995). NAM's agenda has always been broader than its nomenclature. It has provided a forum to the nations of the South to stress their common concerns for independence and sovereign equality, de-colonization and anti-racism, economic and social development, sovereignty over natural resources, cultural equality, multilateralism, and the non-use of force or the threat of force. NAM's efficacy needs to be gauged not as much in the achievement of these goals, as in its ability to raise these issues at the international level. On that count NAM has been a reasonable success.

The durability of NAM through the turbulent 1980s, through internal differences, and through the demise of the Cold War highlights the continuing value the Southern leadership sees in it. This was demonstrated most strikingly at the 1992 Summit in Jakarta, Indonesia. What some had predicted to be a swan song for the organization turned into rejuvenation. At a preparatory meeting for the Summit, Egypt had proposed that with the Cold War having ended NAM should wind itself up and merge with G77. Instead, the leaders assembled at the conference came out with a vociferous vindication of the continuing utility of the movement in a unipolar world. Although the assembled heads of state and government acknowledged the need for "a realistic reordering of priorities" in light of the changed global setting, the Summit revitalized NAM and was one of the most comprehensive in its history—both in terms of attendance and the scope and depth of issues covered. It was especially important for articulating a rationale for the organization's continued existence in a unipolar world (Misra 1993). The South's view that "the desire to be independent is not dependent on the number of military blocs in existence at any given time," was most championed by the Malaysian Prime Minister Mahathir Mohammed (1992: 26):

> How can we remain non-aligned when the two ideological adversaries have disappeared? Where before we had the option to defect to the other side, now we have none. Our new option is to submit or resist. Both involve a loss of leverage, and weak nations with no leverage can only become weaker.

This process of revalidation was continued in Cartagena where the new Chair, President Samper of Columbia (1995: 10–11), proclaimed that "never before has it been so clear that we cannot face the challenges of the new international balance individually" and that "our integration into the world cannot be a solitary, suicidal adventure." More important than the rearticulating of goals, however, was the redefinition of strategies. In his concluding address, he stressed the need for NAM to take "the step from confrontation to cooperation, from conflict to consensus, from individualism to solidarity"; this was a more sober, more pragmatic NAM: "We cannot continue complaining. We have to move from idealism to reality" (quoted in Ferrer 1995: 25). The tone was echoed at the 1998 Summit in Durban, South Africa which declared that "unity of purpose and strategy among the nations of the Movement is of critical importance" but focused more on the challenges within the South than on differences with the North (NAM 1998).

Ultimately, NAM's greatest achievement is its resilience as a platform where its leadership can articulate their agenda. More than that, it has proved to be a forum where this agenda can evolve and respond to changing priorities. This resilience is, in large measure, a factor of its being an evolving institution; one that has had demonstrable impact in influencing and projecting the collective South's evolving agenda. Furthermore, NAM has provided weaker Southern states an opportunity to increase their participation in the multinational political economy beyond what the prevailing order might have permitted, while allowing the relatively stronger states the use of the collective's strength of numbers to enhance their own role in global politics.

If survival and redefinition have been the major successes, it may be because it has lacked any formal structure that could have imperiled its survival by resisting redefinition. This lack of structure, however, has imparted a certain sense of ad hoc-ism to NAM. This has translated into a lack of follow-through of decisions. A lack of resources, a profusion of unstable domestic political regimes in member states, unwieldy size, and the absence of any management structure has often led to the translation of genuine enthusiasm on the part of individual NAM leaders into inaction on the part of the collective. Without formal structure to ensure continuity, the onus of translating good ideas into real action is left entirely to individual member states who, despite all their good intentions, have too many other immediate worries distracting them from long-term NAM goals. An instrument of political summitry, NAM meets every three years to renew (or redefine) its vows. Operating through ministerial committees, NAM has no permanent institutional infrastructure to manage its activities between Summits. The Summits are held every three years, with meetings of foreign ministers held at eighteen-month intervals.

THE GROUP OF 77 (G77)

The Group of 77 has been described by Julius Nyerere (1980: 7), former President of Tanzania, as the "trade union of the poor" and by Roger Hansen (1979: 90) as "the most dynamic of the developing-country institutions." The G77 (1994b: 1) itself describes its goal as "provid[ing] the means for the developing world to articulate and promote its collective economic interests and enhance its joint negotiating capacity on all major North-South international economic issues in the United Nations system, and promote economic and technical cooperation among developing countries." Although it emerged around the same time as NAM, G77 has its own distinctive origins and, unlike NAM, was born within—and primarily as a result of—the changing composition of the United Nations in the 1960s.

> From January 1950 to November 1955 there was a deadlock within the United Nations system on the question of new members, and none secured admission. Then in December 1955 a tacit Soviet-American bargain enabled sixteen new members to join simultaneously and the doors of the United Nations were henceforth in principle open for further new members, so much so that in 1960 alone seventeen newly independent states were admitted—sixteen of them from Africa. Thus between 1955 and the early 1960s the basic political composition and character of plenary United Nations gatherings changed from being predominantly NATO-like to become more markedly Afro-Asian, even Third World, in character. (Geldart and Lyon 1980: 82)

The new UN composition meant that newly independent, developing, and nonaligned nations (the three terms identified almost the same countries) suddenly had a majority in the UN General Assembly. Although impeded by their unwieldy size and lack of experience in (or resources for) alliance politics, this unlikely group surprised—and annoyed—the major Western powers by incessantly demanding, and sometimes obtaining, more UN focus on issues of concern to them (see McDonald 1982; Adams 1993). The most important such issue was international trade; particularly, commodity trade. Under the intellectual leadership of Argentine economist Raúl Prebisch, the dynamic head of the UN's Economic Commission for Latin America and later the first secretary general of the United Nations Conference on Trade and Development (UNCTAD), the developing countries became increasingly convinced that existing economic institutions placed the South at a systemic trading disadvantage, that their poverty and "peripheral" status was historically defined, and that the only solution was to structurally change the international economic system. Based on the tenants of, what became known as, "dependency theory" they considered the existing international economic structures to be instruments of Northern interests and unsympathetic to their developmental concerns. They sought, therefore, an international trade organization controlled directly by the UN—where they were in majority and over which, they believed, they could exert greater influence. (See Gosovic 1972; Menon 1977; Jones 1983; Murphy 1984; Adams 1993)

In calling for an International Trade Organization in the early 1960s, the developing countries were, in fact, demanding a structural change that could accommodate their strength of numbers as well as their concerns; Western industrialized countries, however, preferred to rely on existing instruments.[7] The result of this tussle was the 1964 UN Conference on Trade and Development, which was convened as a "second-best compromise" for everyone, and has since become an institutionalized series of conferences. The conference is considered to be of "seminal importance" in the evolution of North-South dialogue (Adams 1993: 90) and it was there that the Group of 77 was officially born. Geldart and Lyon (1980: 85) recount:

> The first manifesto of the proto-G77 was released on October 18, 1963 in the UN General Assembly . . . when 75 member-states jointly sponsored a resolution entitled "Joint Declaration of the Developing Countries." The 75 endorsed with enthusiasm the opportunity offered by the forthcoming Geneva conference [UNCTAD-I] as, "conducive to the development of their economies and to the integrated growth of the world economy as a whole" . . . Twenty-one of these sponsoring states were from Latin America and the Caribbean, thirty-one from Africa, and twenty from Asia and the Middle East; the remaining three of the seventy-five were Cyprus, New Zealand and Yugoslavia . . . During the three-month-long proceedings of UNCTAD-I in Geneva, from March to June 1964, this informal group of 75 became the Group of 77 when Kenya, South Korea and South Vietnam added their signatures to the Group's Joint Declaration . . . and New Zealand withdrew . . .

UNCTAD-I came at a time of rising optimism and expectations in the South. A large number of countries had just gained independence, especially in Africa; developing countries were beginning to make their presence felt in international forums; and the industrialized world finally seemed to be responding. This enthusiasm, and the larger commonalty in aspirations, allowed the new nations to circumvent their internal differences. In a remarkable show of solidarity they arrived at Geneva as a single unit; a unified negotiating collective which, by its sheer numbers, could no longer be ignored. This collective of 77, otherwise disparate, nations was remarkable not only because it actually did speak with one voice, but also because it effectively changed (albeit temporarily) the direction of international polity (Gosovic 1972; Sauvant 1981). As Williams (1993: 13) records, UNCTAD-I "was the first conference at which the North-South divide took precedence over the East-West division." Through the late 1960s, UNCTAD allowed the G77 to become "the most comprehensively authentic voice of the Third

World" and the UNCTAD Secretariat in Geneva came to be seen as a principal voice and *de facto* secretariat of the G77. (See Gosovic 1972; Sauvant 1981; Weiss 1986a and 1986b)

The period 1971 to 1974 has been described as the "watershed years" for G77 (Geldart and Lyon 1980: 91). The raging monetary crisis, rising global inflation, expansions in G77 membership, the decision by the Organization of Petroleum Exporting Countries (OPEC) to quadruple oil price, the disastrous U.S. performance in Vietnam, and the onset of détente diplomacy set the stage for the G77's thrust for, what became known as, the New International Economic Order (NIEO). These were the heydays of Southern unity: NAM and G77 were in sync; OPEC seemed to demonstrate that unity could bestow power to the powerless; the "Charter of Economic Rights and Duties of States" was accepted at the UN General Assembly where the numerical strength of the G77 allowed it to win many victories over the industrialized countries; efforts to split the coalition over the oil issue were successfully repelled; and, finally, the North was forced—albeit reluctantly—into negotiations which it had so stridently resisted. The euphoria, however, was not to last long. The changed economic and political climate of the late 1970s and the 1980s left the NIEO movement, the hopes it had generated, and the solidarity it had fostered, much bruised. Twenty years after it was first formed "the impression that the Group of 77 had a kind of countervailing power has been exposed for its emptiness" and that the G77's "numerical superiority is insufficient to compensate for its lack of economic power" (Weiss 1986a: 2, 155). The G77 itself acknowledges that despite the great start, "the entire North-South dialogue was brought to a virtual standstill" by the 1980s (G77 1994a: 12).

Yet, despite the widely prevalent sense that the G77 has not been able to achieve its grandiose goals, the collective has refused to die. If anything, the 1990s has witnessed a mini-resurrection both of the South as a concept and the G77 as an institution. After the dormancy of the 1980s the new spate of global conference diplomacy has (once again) seen the G77 emerge as an influential and authentic voice of the global South. The shared views on international economic justice and the belief that unity might bestow power that had first crystallized the G77 as a negotiating collective have sustained it through the turbulent 1980s and beyond. Despite the failure to negotiate desired change, the ranks of G77 have swelled to a current membership of 132 plus China (table 8.2 and map 8.2).[8] In large part, this is because "the initial reasons for the formation of the coalition, i.e. individual weakness to pursue national goals, Western indifference or negativism to suggested reform, the existence of an institutional channel of communication which augmented the trend to mass aggregation and the persistence of economic weakness, have helped to maintain the coalition and increase its attractiveness." (Williams 1993: 13)

While the persistent inability of the G77 in achieving its goals has been a source of concern to its leadership, this has not been a reason to disband the group because not only have the underlying common interests that brought these countries together remained unmet—they have also remained unchanged. This reflects both a failure in having these goals met and a constancy of purpose in wanting to address them. In the absence of other alternatives, the relevance of the collective stems not from a track-record of success in negotiating collectively, but from the fear of inevitable failure in negotiating separately. This fear is articulated in an editorial in the South Letter (1994: 1): "Individual developing countries, even the most powerful and influential, count for very little in the grossly uneven match with powerful nations of the North; a North which seems to act in unison on all major North-South issues."

On the positive side, although the NIEO never achieved its goals, the fact that the initiative was able to gather steam is no mean achievement for the G77, which was its "chief negotiator." Indeed, as a collective the G77 has exerted substantial influence in the agenda setting stages of various UN deliberations—although it has not often succeeded in having its concerns redressed, it has had remarkable success in having them placed on the table. Similarly, it has had not inconsequential successes in shaping final compromises; most recently so during the 1992 Earth Summit and a whole series of subsequent global negotiations.[9]

The growth of the G77, even during its "down days" has been quite spectacular. Starting at 77, its membership now stands at 132 plus China. The most recent entrants are Eritrea and Turkmenistan who joined in 1997 and 1998, respectively.

The only two countries to have left its fold are Mexico and South Korea (in 1994 and 1997, respectively); both graduated to full OECD membership whose ground rules required them to give up their G77 membership. Structurally, G77 evolved simultaneously with (and possibly due to) the UN group system which, as institutionalized for UNCTAD-I, lumped Africa and Asia (plus Yugoslavia) in Group A, the Western alliance in Group B, Latin America and the Caribbean in Group C, and East Europe in Group D. Essentially, Groups A and C formed an alliance that grew up to become G77. In turn, the G77 has taken this system and built its own institutional template around it. G77 has historically functioned through three constituent regional caucuses—Africa, Asia, and Latin America and the Caribbean. This is a strategy for diversity management which allows each region within the collective the "voice" and the opportunity to have its views heard. Each group arrives at a regional consensus, which is then aggregated into a general G77 position by full consensus.

Indeed, the group structure imposes certain rigidity to G77 positions. It makes internal negotiations within the G77 burdensome and often means that the position the caucus adopts as a whole is not only watered down to the lowest common denominator but is so finely crafted that it is entirely inflexible. On the other hand, as Sauvant (1981) implies, the regional caucuses are the nearest thing that G77 has to an organizational structure; without them any form of decision making or management of over 130 national positions would become all but impossible. This points to the most enduring criticism of the G77 regarding its lack of any permanent organizational structure. Although G77 does have a skeletal staff at New York and Geneva, it is makeshift and inadequate. This, despite the fact that passionate calls for a more permanent servicing structure have been made for over twenty years, including most recently by the G77 South Summit held in Havana, Cuba in April 2000 (Gosovic 1972; Searwar and Lewis 1979; Hall 1980; Mahbub-ul-Haq 1980a, 1983; Ramphal 1980; Commonwealth 1982; Sewell and Zartman 1984; South Commission 1990; G77, 1994a, 1996, 2000b; Najam 1994a).

Annual Ministerial Meetings, convened at the beginning of the regular sessions of the UN General Assembly, serve as the major decision-making body (G77 1994b). Special Ministerial Meetings are periodically called to focus on particular issues or to prepare for important global negotiations. Technical expertise is provided by various committees whose composition, importance, and even nomenclature tends to vary from one year to the next. These provide neither continuity nor a repository of organizational memory. Various committees have been variously important at various points of time, the actual people involved change frequently and are forever distracted by other (non-G77) worries, and the approach to management tends to change with every new Chair.

Through the mid-1970s, as G77's size, visibility, and scope of issues covered increased, so did the arenas in which it operated. From being restricted only to the UNCTAD, it duplicated itself at all major international organizations and negotiations. Functioning as informal caucuses for diplomats from member countries, G77 "hubs" have sprung up at New York, Geneva, Rome, Vienna, Paris, Nairobi, and Washington where international bodies such as the UN General Assembly, the UNCTAD Secretariat, the Food and Agriculture Organization (FAO), UN Educational, Scientific, and Cultural Organization (UNESCO), United Nations Environmental Program (UNEP), etc. are based. In addition, G77 caucuses are active in most international negotiations where they adopt joint bargaining positions and strategies, and the group's chair serves as the spokesperson for the entire caucus. Although the various chapters have recently increased coordination, it is important to remember that, in general (Williams 1993: 13):

On its thirtieth anniversary, a report written for the G77 (1994a: 15–16) acknowledged:

> The intellectual challenge facing the G77 is greater than ever before. But it comes at a time when the supporting role of the international secretariats is weaker than in the past. The ability of the G77 to recapture its credibility as an effective negotiating partner is, therefore, critically dependent on its success in

> mobilizing the research and analytical resources needed for its work. In the present situation, the need for some kind of a secretariat of its own is compelling.

Despite its persistent structural limitations and its modest accomplishments, the G77 has been a legitimate and not an influential player in international multilateral negotiations. Born as a temporary caucus, it has become the dominant negotiating voice of the collective South in the UN system. While the G77 may not have achieved the radical systemic change that it envisioned, it has won valuable concessions and small victories on a number of issues at these and such forums. Not least of these victories is its own survival and acceptance as an enduring, even if not always effective, negotiating collective in the international negotiations.

THE SOUTH IN GLOBAL ENVIRONMENTAL NEGOTIATIONS

The timing of the 1992 Rio Summit was extremely opportune for the South. The UNCED preparatory process coincided with the fall of the Berlin Wall. While the latter instilled a sense of new vulnerabilities in the developing world and provided the motivation for revitalizing the collective South, the former offered an opportunity to engage the North in a new dialogue. The relevance of Rio was not lost on an influential group of Southern intellectuals, brought together by the South Centre (1991: 1–2) to propose a common negotiation strategy for the South:

> UNCED offers . . . an opportunity for engaging in more balanced negotiations between the North and the South, and it could yield results that the developing countries have been seeking for some time. Global action on the environment cannot succeed without the full participation and collaboration of the South. Indeed, UNCED is an international conference where the North is seeking environmental concessions from the South, and where the South can make such concessions in return for firm commitments by the North to restructure global economic relations. This potential give-and-take relationship makes it possible for the South to bargain for a comprehensive compact with the North.

The achievements of Rio did not match the South's exaggerated hopes (Agarwal 1992; Banuri, 1992; Najam, 1995a). The North was no more interested in bargaining for a "comprehensive compact" in 1992 than it had been in 1977. However, UNCED did place the spotlight firmly on the North-South conflict and moved the need for North-South dialogue back into prominence. A sampling of headlines from the Rio process testify to this regained prominence.

"North-South Divide Is Marring Environment Talks"
—*New York Times* (17 March 1992)
"Planning Talks Split on North-South Lines"
—*The Boston Globe* (5 April 1992)
"North-South Battles Dominate Run-up to Earth Summit"
—*Third World Resurgence* (May 1992)
"One Summit, Differing Goals"
—*International Herald Tribune* (2 June 1992)
"Poor vs. Rich in Rio" —*New York Times* (3 June 1992)

UNCED gave the South a forum, an issue, and an audience that it had been denied since the 1970s. The South—represented by an energetic G77—not only succeeded in reopening the North-South dialogue, they effectively made it *the* focus of the Summit. For a South that had gone to Rio fearful that the 1980s had left the North-South dialogue "in tatters," that the clock on international economic cooperation had been "turned backwards," and that the prospects for North-South cooperation were "bleak," the very fact that the dialogue was resuscitated was one of Rio's biggest achievement (quotes from Peng 1992; 27–29). North-South fault lines have similarly framed the spate of international environmental treaty negotiations that have followed UNCED. As we approach the tenth anniversary of the Rio conference, the South might justifiably feel frustrated at the lost promise of what then seemed like the "next generation" of North-South dialogue (Najam 1994a; Sandbrook 1997). However, it is also true that these negotiations have provided the South, as represented by G77, with opportunities to reshape the emerging global environmental agenda in terms of their enduring interests—they have attempted to do this by molding global environmental politics into the global politics of sustainable development. This has sometimes introduced new tensions for the Southern collective, both in terms of frictions with the North and fissures within.

This section seeks to understand the concerns and interests of the South within the evolving politics of sustainable development. This new phase of North-South dialogue, however, cannot be understood without understanding the legacy of an earlier era of North-South dialogue. This is important not simply for establishing historical context but because the North-South skirmishes now seen as a recurring feature of global environmental negotiation lie on the exact same continuum as earlier North-South conflicts.

FROM NIEO TO NIEO

It is a contention of this section that the South's current desire for, what could be described as, a New International *Environmental* Order (NIE[nv]O) is a reflection of the same fears and hopes that had prompted its earlier call for a New International *Economic* Order (NIE[co]O) in the 1970s (Najam 1995a). Moreover, to not appreciate this continuum is to misunderstand why the South behaves in global environmental negotiations as it does. The bulk of North-based environmental scholarship has steadfastly refused to acknowledge the importance of this continuum. A notable exception is Alker and Haas (1993: 166) who point out that "although it is not adequately describable as a return to the imperial/colonial world, contemporary global ecopolitics reflects somewhat analogous North-South geopolitical differences." However, even the scholars who do not invest much faith in seeking historical parallels to the South's current concerns would agree with Alker and Haas's (1993: 164) forecast of "a new era in which global ecopolitics will define many of the terms, if not the practices, of world politics" and that "North-South tensions are likely to be a salient conservative feature of this new era" (see Young 1989; Gardner 1992; Thomas 1992; Susskind 1994; Miller 1995; Elliott 1998; Agarwal et al. 1999; French 2000).

Hansen (1979: vii) defines the original NIE[co]O debate as a conflict about "conceptions about the management of society." On a similar note, Krasner (1985: 27) sees it as the South's fundamental challenge to the existing order of what he calls global liberalism; he points out that "vulnerability, not simple poverty" was the motivating force for these newly independent developing countries. In popular understanding, it is generally agreed that for the South NIE[co]O was a movement to restructure what it saw as an international system of iniquitous global economic relations; and for the North it became an effort to bring into the folds of the "global free market" the two-thirds of humanity that lived in the so-called Third World. Rallying its newfound unity and negotiating as a tight bloc, the G77 gained a major victory when a special session of the United Nations General Assembly was called in June 1974. The session legitimized the South's demand for the creation of a New International Economic Order by passing a resolution to that effect and drawing out a Plan of Action. This was followed, in December 1974, of a Charter of Economic Rights and Duties of States. The proponents of the new order demanded "full and complete economic emancipation" for the South and the way to achieve it was "to recover and control their natural resources and wealth, and the means of economic development." The developing countries decided to "change their traditional approach to negotiations with developed countries, hitherto consisting in presentation of a list of requests to developed countries and an appeal to their political goodwill." The new approach, they decided, would involve common action to strengthen their bargaining position, more economic activity among themselves and a strategy based on "the principle of relying first and foremost on themselves." (Menon 1977: 3–4)

The optimism reflected in UN resolutions proved misplaced and the differences persisted—North accusing South of being confrontational and

South blaming North for perpetuating an unjust order. However, the G77 did get one key demand met. Out of necessity rather than conviction, the North agreed to begin a process of wide-ranging North-South negotiations on international economic issues (see Gordon 1978; McDonald 1982). However, all attempts at genuine dialogue failed. By the 1980s, it was obvious that the momentum had been lost and North-South dialogue "appeared to be taking place largely between the conveniently deaf" (Mistry 1993: 170). As Mahbub-ul-Haq (1980b: 270) put it, "North-South negotiations [had] deteriorated to a ritual and a skillful exercise in *non*-dialogue." In subsequent years, as geopolitical and geo-economic events shaped new alliances, the South's unity as a bloc weakened. As the North's perception of the economic importance of natural resources in the South (particularly mineral and agricultural products) diminished, so did the perceived leverage enjoyed by the G77. As an increasingly indebted South struggled more than ever to resist the ravages of an unkind international economy, the control of the Bretton Woods twins—the World Bank and the IMF—became ever stronger. The NIE[co]O agenda rapidly receded from world attention, and so did discussions about North-South dialogue. It wasn't until the Earth Summit in 1992, that the relevance and need of North-South negotiations once again became the subject of broad academic, policy and even public discussion.

However, the environmental issue as an exemplar of the North-South divide predates Rio by at least twenty years. It is, in fact, striking that the vast literature on the history of the North-South conflict and the equally vast scholarship on international environmental politics treat the role of developing countries in the United Nations Conference on the Human Environment (UNCHE), held in Stockholm in 1972, as a mere footnote. In fact, UNCHE was one of the first global forums outside UNCTAD where the South consciously negotiated as a unified collective and adopted many of the very same substantive arguments and negotiation strategies which were soon to become the hallmark of NIE[co]O (Rowland 1973).

Indeed, from the very beginning, the developing countries recognized environmental concerns in the North as a distinctively North-South issue and, in some cases, as an effort to sabotage the South's developmental aspirations (see Mahbub-ul-Haq 1976). The intellectual leadership of the South very poignantly set out to redefine the environmental problematique in a decidedly North-South context. The most telling example was the so-called Founex Report (Founex 1972) produced by a distinguished group of Southern intellectuals as part of the UNCHE preparatory process. It is relevant to the argument here for two very important reasons. First, the tone and substance of the report mirrored, nearly to an exactitude, what was soon to become the rhetoric of the NIEO. Second, the tone and substance of the report mirrored, nearly to an exactitude, the rhetoric of the South at UNCED and at major environmental forums before and since. The point to be underscored is not simply that the Founex Report remains one of the most authentic and articulate enunciations of the South's collective interests on issues of environment and development, but that a) these interests have remained unchanged over time, b) they are the same interests which informed the NIEO ideology, and c) these same interests lie at the heart of today's global politics of sustainable development.

The constancy in the position of the South at Stockholm (which came at the very beginning of the first generation of North-South dialogue) and at Rio (which came at the very beginning of the second generation) supports the view that the two sets of dialogues lie on the very same continuum. The point is further supported in the accounts of UNCED negotiations by G77 negotiators. Chris K. Mensah (1994: 38), for example, points out that the Southern leadership had explicitly formulated its negotiation strategy around two key goals. First to "ensure that the South has adequate environmental space for its future development" and second, to:

> . . . modify global economic relations in such a way that the South obtains the required resources, technology, and access to markets which would enable it to pursue a development process that is both environmentally sound and rapid enough to meet [its] needs and aspirations . . .

In short, developing countries have constantly and consistently contextualized environmental issues as being part of the larger complex of North-South concerns. They consider the interests and priorities of their own collective to be shared enough to maintain a common position and the North's interests and priorities to be distinctively different from their own. It was, therefore, no accident that UNCED ended up being polarized along North-South lines.

The importance of the North-South dimension in international environmental affairs is widely accepted in the literature (see Young 1989; Mathews 1991; Porter and Brown 1996; Gardner 1992; Thomas 1992; Susskind 1994; Elliott 1998; French 2000). However, even in accepting the importance of the North-South split, there is hesitancy amongst many scholars to accept the "new" North-South environmental tensions as an extension of earlier North-South conflicts from the 1970s. In large part, this is because of the *fear*—as articulated by Sebenius (1991)—that entertaining the South's development agenda within the environmental dialogue might rekindle old conflicts and protract ugly polarizations. The hesitancy has also been propped up by the *hope* that the growing public perception of a collective threat to the global environment may translate into political momentum for collective international action (Porter and Brown 1996), or that a new ideological commonalty may grow around the concept of sustainable development (Sebenius 1991), or that the demise of East-West tensions might themselves ease North-South misapprehensions (MacDonald 1991: 42).

The experience from UNCED and subsequent environmental negotiations seems to suggest that polarizations across North-South lines are unlikely to disappear either by ignoring them or by wishing them away (Banuri 1992; Thomas 1992; Williams 1993; Dasgupta 1994; Hyder 1994; Agarwal et al. 1999; Najam 200b; Najam and Robins 2001). The resilience that the South has shown in pursuing, what it considers, its legitimate agenda of economic justice and international systemic change suggests that foreseeable global negotiations, including international environmental dialogue, will be dogged by this agenda. That this agenda of the South is beginning to look very much like a call for a New International *Environmental* Order should not come as a surprise to scholars of the subject. As Hansen (1980: 1120) had foretold, "in an era of linkage politics and strong Southern bloc institutionalization, the [South] will often attempt to accomplish in one setting what it is unable to accomplish in another."

This is exactly how the G77 has responded to the recent flurry of global environmental negotiations. Williams (1993: 19) points out that "the possibility of linking negotiations on global environmental change with demands for change in other areas of North-South relations is one crucial reason for the continued participation of developing countries in negotiations of environmental problems." Similarly, Porter and Brown (1991: 129) opine that "many developing countries, particularly the more radical members of the Group of 77, have viewed global environmental negotiations as the best, if not the only, opportunity to advance a broader agenda of change in the structure of North-South economic relationships." Williams (1993: 25) makes the point explicit: "it is not . . . a question of environment being co-opted into the North-South debate. It already exists in this debate and is conceived in North-South terms." This has to be seen as strategic behavior on the part of the South. It is not a mere coincidence that the times when the South has actually been able to force the North to the negotiating table have corresponded with periods when interest in global issues has been high. The confluence of important international conferences in the 1970s was not the principal cause of the peaking of NIE[co]O sentiments, but it certainly contributed significantly to the momentum that North-South dialogue was able to gain. By similar token, the spate of global conferences and negotiations in the 1990s has provided the South the opportunity and the platforms to re-ignite and reinvigorate their unfinished NIE[co]O agenda. One can only conclude that the leaders of the South will continue pushing this agenda through future negotiations and that the extent of their enthusiasm for the deliberations will be proportional to the extent to which this agenda is incorporated within the scope of the discussions and decisions.

NORTH-SOUTH DIALOGUE AND THE GLOBAL POLITICS OF SUSTAINABLE DEVELOPMENT

If it were the new vulnerabilities brought forth by the end of the Cold War that gave the developing countries the motivation to reinvigorate the collective South, and the concurrent onset of global environmental negotiations that provided them the forums in which to engage the North, it is the all-encompassing rubric of sustainable development that has enabled them to pursue the new North-South dialogue without having (yet) lost the North's attention while holding firm on their abiding developmental interests. The landscape of global negotiations in the 1990s is littered with myriad negotiations on myriad issues in myriad venues taking place with increasing frequency. These negotiations range from much trumpeted summitry on issues related to the environment, population, women, human rights, social development, food security, or human settlements to efforts aimed at building new global regimes on climate change, biodiversity, deforestation, desertification, or persistent organic pollutants, to the minutiae of overseeing the implementation of Agenda 21 in the UN Commission on Sustainable Development (CSD), sorting out the operational modalities of the Global Environmental Facility (GEF), or working out trade and environment conflicts within the World Trade Organization (WTO). While these negotiations differ in many respects, three elements are strikingly pervasive: the first is the preeminence of the North-South fault line as a defining feature of the deliberations; the second is the central role that the G77 plays as the negotiating voice of the South; and the third is the emergence of sustainable development as a matrix within which the substance of the discourse is recurrently couched. These elements, in conjunction, are the key ingredients of the new global politics of sustainable development.

Even though the mega-summits seem to be subsiding, we are likely to see a continuation of, if not a growth in, the trend toward more frequent and more complex international environmental norm-setting (Young 1993; Susskind 1994; Miller 1995; Najam 2000a). As Porter and Brown (1996: 147) point out, "today governments are involved every month in new rounds of international negotiations preparing for regimes that are soon to go into effect, reviewing and strengthening existing regimes, or negotiating new regimes." It is equally likely that the global nature of the environmental problematique will continue to make it one of the principal, though not the only, arena for continued North-South sparring. Moreover, the South has a strategic interest in continuing to define this dialogue in terms of sustainable development because this allows it to establish the crucial link between environment and development—a link that they have fought hard to establish and hold dear to their heart:

> It is significant that [Rio was] a conference on Environment and Development. This twofold topic marks the recognition of the "link" and of the interdependence of issues and solutions concerning what has in the past been treated as two separate agendas of international negotiations, on account of the insistence of the North. Because of this "link," it is possible to mount an integrated approach to the global challenges of sustainable development. (South Centre 1991: 1)

For optimists, the global politics of sustainable development is the embodiment of the hope that in trying to synergize the North's concern for environmental sustainability and the South's desire for economic and social development, the concept of sustainable development, loosely defined as it is—and, in fact, because it is defined as loosely as it is—will provide a broad framework within which a global compact that would meet the interests of both North and South could be built. For pragmatists, however, it is better understood as:

> . . . a struggle between the developing and developed countries to define sustainable development in a way that fits their own agendas. The developed countries, most of which are relatively rich, put environment first. By contrast, the developing countries, most of which are poor and still struggling to meet basic human needs, put development first. (Hyder 1994: 205)

Although the optimistic sentiment is certainly well-meaning, many are hesitant to accept that the new generation of North-South dialogue could be any more fruitful nor any less acrimonious than the old. This is especially true for those who still remember the entrenched antagonisms of the previous attempt. Wallerstein (1993: 118), for example, believes that "the next 20 years of North-South negotiations are not going to be more significant or efficacious than the last 20." Others, such as Grant (1995: 582), are more sanguine, even upbeat: "in many respects conditions are more favorable than at any other time for common ground to be established." Around the time of the Rio Summit there was a certain misplaced buoyancy amongst those who argued, if only for effect, that sustainable development might be the "trump card" that the South had been looking for all along. The North's new concern for global environmental problems, it was argued, provided the South with considerable leverage and bargaining power because without the participation of the developing countries many such problems cannot be addressed effectively.[10] A Caribbean official was reported as suggesting that "for the first time in more than a decade, the developing countries have an issue [i.e. the environment] where they have some real leverage" while India's environment minister went even further to proclaim that "the begging bowl is [now] really in the hands of the Western world."[11]

In retrospect, the enthusiasm was decidedly exaggerated and with time, it has certainly mellowed. Although the South was not entirely powerless in Rio, it soon found that its "leverage" lay not as much in influencing what went *into* the treaties as in what was kept *out* of them (Mello 1993). Such "negative power" has been a recurrent feature of the South's behavior in the global politics of sustainable development (Agarwal 1992; Mello 1993; Najam 1995a). Studies of just how much real leverage the environment might provide the developing countries on particular issues have yielded more sober, although not entirely pessimistic, assessments. In looking at the ozone case, for example, Rajan (1992: 147) found that the evidence does "not justify the view that the environmental issue has delivered into the hands of the South a potent new bargaining weapon." However, he would most likely agree with Miller (1995: 141), who focused on global regimes relating to the ozone layer, hazardous waste and biodiversity and found that "when there is a shared perception of environmental vulnerability, the Third World is able to gain a *modest* bargaining advantage" (emphasis added). Sell (1996), in looking at North-South environmental bargaining on ozone depletion, climate change and biodiversity, and Mello (1993), in analyzing the forestry negotiations at UNCED, arrive at similar conclusions. In short, the evidence suggests that while the South may have some leverage in the global politics of sustainable development its extent is limited, its application is largely to avoid defeat, and its use is conditional on the existence of a high level of concern, even alarm, for the said issue in the North.

From the South's perspective, such assessments are sobering but not melancholy. Its desire for systemic international change is enduring but, over the last many decades, it has been tempered by more realistic assessments—the impatience that once characterized the South is no longer as evident. Moreover, the defining essence of the collective South is the desire to minimize risk, rather than to maximize gain. Given the South's perceptions about the post–Cold War (im-)balance of power (Chubin 1993), vulnerability in a hostile international order (Ayoob 1995), and fears of the environment being turned into a tool for ecocolonialism (Adams 1993) the South's achievements in the global politics of sustainable development, thus far, although not spectacular have also not been disastrous. In fact, from its standpoint, the Southern collective has been able to do exactly what it set out to do: minimizing the risk of being bulldozed by a Northern agenda, maintaining a North-South focus to the dialogue, and eking out little victories (in terms of global transfers) whenever possible (see Hyder 1994; Mensah 1994). While this should be read as an appeal to lower one's sights on the extent of the potential for a new North-South bargain being constructed around the global politics of sustainable development, it should not distract from the point that a potential—no matter how small—does, in fact, exist. This potential emanates from two important differences between the first generation of North-South dialogue and its current incarnation.

First, unlike its predecessor, the second generation of North-South interaction is characterized by both sides wanting to establish a global dialogue, albeit with differing interests and agendas. For the South, such dialogue is itself a long-standing goal (Jones 1983; South Commission 1990). For the North, it is necessitated by the realization that global action on the environment cannot be successful without the active participation of the developing countries (MacDonald 1991; Sebenius 1994). This is a major sea-change from the 1970s when the South was calling for dialogue and the North was actively resisting (Weintraub 1980; Hansen 1980). Furthermore, there is a certain sense of urgency on both sides, since the effects of both environmental devastation and abject poverty compound visibly over time (Ramphal 1992). Second, by its very nature, it is often difficult to conceive global environmental problems in terms of victory and defeat, especially in the long run (Rajan 1992; Mensah 1994; Porter and Brown 1996). Unlike the oil or debt crises of the 1970s, the environmental crisis is not easily defined in win-lose terms. Although the jury is still out on whether and how the global environment might become a win-win issue, all indications suggest that it can very easily be transformed into a lose-lose proposition. This, too, marks a difference from earlier North-South dialogue that failed partly because it was perceived, especially in the North, as a zero-sum game (Gordon 1978; Hansen 1980; Mahbub-ul-Haq 1980b; Weintraub 1980; Sewell and Zartman 1984). Delayed sea-level rise, averted ozone depletion, or better protected forests may help some nations more than others, but in general, they will help all nations.

What the above means in terms of actual North-South negotiations is that there is already significantly greater agreement between North and South on the need for a potential New International *Environmental* Order than there ever was on the subject of a New International *Economic* Order. Having said that, while a common desire does exist in both camps—at least at the level of general principles—to tackle environmental problems, the hurdles to actually doing so are many and are profound. At the heart of the North-South politics of sustainable development are debates about the costs to be borne (including foregone benefits), the ability to bear these costs, the responsibility for causing the problem, and the ability to influence future decisions. These boil down to contentions about past responsibility, present ability, and future priorities. Serious differences persist between North and South, on all three. While much is made in the literature of the first two (past responsibility and present ability), the issue of future priorities is often overlooked:

> Developing countries have generally regarded the negotiation of global regimes on ozone depletion, climate change, biodiversity loss, and conservation of endangered species as a Northern agenda. Their own environmental priorities have been urban air and water pollution, the erosion and salinization of agricultural land, and toxic chemical contamination; but for most developing

> countries, economic growth, employment, and overcoming poverty have been the dominant concerns. Although developing countries are now active participants in many of these "Northern" regimes, their main concern is usually to ensure that their economic interests are protected. (Porter, Brown, and Chasek 2000: 178–79)

Bridging the deep differences that exist on all three axes is not an easy task and would require, at a minimum, innovative strategies from both North and South.[12] Till now, such strategies have not been forthcoming and both sides remain fixated on outmoded (and hitherto unsuccessful) strategies of dealing with the other. Given the deeply felt interests that the South has resiliently pursued for so long it is unlikely that it will voluntarily forsake its demands or be argued out of them. By similar token, given a realistic assessment of the South's bargaining leverage over the North, it is equally unlikely that the former will be able to browbeat the latter into simply accepting its position. If meaningful headway is to be made it will have to come through some mechanism that allows the interests of both sides to be met. That mechanism is creative issue-linkage. In this regard, sustainable development can be a potentially fortuitous term in that it can (given the right conditions) allow efficient packaging of issues of concern to North and South—issues that they might otherwise be hesitant to deal with individually. However, issue-linkage can be fraught with both dangers and opportunities. Some like Stone (1993: 115) fear that "adding cards to the deck raises the risk that the environment will get lost in the shuffle." However, Susskind (1994: 82) reminds us that issue-linkage can be "crucial to the success of negotiation[s]" that involve complex, multi-party, multi-issue bargaining. While there is certainly the danger of issue-linkage turning into blackmail—either by the North arm-twisting the South to follow its environmental dictates, or by the South threatening environmental inaction in the absence of a restructured international system—there is a strong case for both to seek issue-linkages in their pursuit of meaningful dialogue. After all, the very term sustainable development is itself the embodiment of creative issue-linkage and the promise of the global politics of sustainable development is, in fact, the promise of issue-linkage.

While issue-linkage that might incorporate the various interests is a potential strategy for breaking the impasse in North-South dialogue, it is by no means an easy strategy to operationalize. It would require a "level of political will . . . that [does] not appear to exist" (Porter and Brown 1991: 152). From the North it would demand "a spirit of compromise" so that the South sees itself engaging in a "genuine dialogue" (Williams 1993: 25). From the South it calls for setting "its [own] house in order," because "unless [the South] is able to get greater honesty, efficiency, and self-reliance into its own economic systems, it will be consistently portrayed as a beggar" (Agarwal

1992: 36). More generally, issue-linkage will only succeed if it is seen as "legitimate," if not seen as such by all parties, it would amount to nothing more than "blackmail" (Susskind 1994: 98).

The challenge, then, is to ensure that this generation of North-South dialogue does not plunge into the quagmire of frustration and acrimony like its predecessor. In the waning moments of the first generation of such dialogue, Sidney Weintraub (1980: 456) was arguing that "in order to negotiate effectively, the weak must find some lever to give them strength." At about the same time, Mahbub-ul-Haq (1980b: 276) opined that "it is possible that only a real international economic or political crisis will convince all sides to rush to the negotiating table." Today, some in the South believe that the environment could be that leverage; many in the North insist that the environment is that crisis. The jury is still out on whether it is either. However, a window of opportunity does exist, albeit small, in the potential of sustainable development becoming a win-win issue that could begin to start bridging the North-South chasm. The challenge is compounded by the opportunity—if the opportunity is missed, the common environmental crisis that the North and South are equally locked into could well collapse into common catastrophe.

Achievement and Impediment

Has the South, particularly as represented institutionally by the G77 in global negotiations, been an effective negotiation collective? The answer, as always, depends on whom you ask. At the end of the first generation of North-South dialogue, Weintraub (1980: 459–63) put it most bluntly: "The fundamentals of the international economic order have not been changed as a result of the North-South dialogue . . . No principles or rules have been substantially altered to accommodate the demands of the South . . . Stated broadly, the North has not agreed that systemic change is needed." Writing at about the same time, Sauvant (1981: 27) proclaimed that the "concerns of the G77 now influence nearly all considerations of international economic issues in the United Nations." Both statements remain correct today. The systemic change the South sought has not been achieved; yet, G77 remains a resilient actor in international affairs and has influenced the agenda, if not the results, of global negotiations. Calling the South a failure as a collective would be erroneous; if only because of its tenacity. Yet, its success (if it can be called that) is better measured by its survival than by tangible achievement.

Gauging Success

How should one gauge the achievements of the South? Firstly, any evaluation of the South and its institutions must begin with recognition of the nature of the collective. As a group that derives its strength—and its very identity—

from its shared weakness, *the South is designed to minimize the vulnerability of its members to the prevalent international regime, rather than maximize their domination over it.* It is with this yardstick that the achievements of the South need to be gauged. The motivation behind the creation and endurance of NAM and G77 is their members' acute realization of their own weakness. Although the rhetoric of the South is, understandably, laden with the hope of systemically changing the international order, the principal motivation is the fear that in not banding together, their individual vulnerability would be compounded. According to Williams (1993: 10), "[t]he Third World coalition is not necessarily a winning coalition but it minimizes the risk of defeat."

The importance of this realization of their own weakness is critical to understanding the tenacity of the South's institutions. Admitting their own weakness has meant that *even where the ideal aspirations are high, the realistic expectation of reaching them is low.* Moreover, starting from an admitted position of weakness allows for a redefinition of success—success becomes broader than achieving that which is better, and encompasses averting that which might be worse. After defining ideal goals and aspirations, Southern negotiators have most often focused on averting, or reducing, the damage that existing or proposed systems imply. *Success, therefore, is measured not in maximizing the gains but in minimizing the losses.* This flows directly from the South being, what Nyerere (1980: 4) called, "a unity of opposition." For example, in analyzing the South's performance at the 1992 Earth Summit, Agarwal (1992: 35) notes that the fear of giving up their development aspirations to Northern environmentalism compelled the South to search for negative gains (i.e., not losing too much). At Rio, as well as at the 1972 Stockholm conference, the South (as represented by G77) succeeded in ensuring that the issues and options that it liked least were kept *out* of the final texts but failed to bring the concerns and solutions that it did support *into* the texts of the agreements; as such, it exercised a negative power; the power to stop, rather than the power to shape (Najam 1995a).

Secondly, *the South is a creature of the United Nations system.* It is there that it has tried to exert its influence. Even NAM, which operates outside the UN system, is laden with references to the UN charter and has sought its influence via the world body. Krasner (1985: 8) has argued that "if the United Nations had not existed, it would have been impossible for the Third World to articulate a general program for altering international regimes." Literally born and raised within the UN, G77 realizes that it is there and not in the economic realm of Bretton Woods, that it enjoys a comparative advantage. This is important, in that *the South has sought, and continues to seek, change in economic regimes via a body that is principally political.* While that change has not transpired, the UN is much more of an economic animal today than it was thirty years ago; this is a testimony to the G77's influence.

Finally, *it is important to gauge G77's achievements not only by its continuing relevance today but by its cumulative impact over the span of its existence.* As Grant (1995: 576) points out, in view of the weakened state of the South in international relations by the end of the 1980s it is easy to forget that the South had earlier exerted considerable influence in international affairs:

> Many advances achieved by the UN in the 1960s and 1970s were due to collective action and moral pressure by the developing countries, through the NAM and its twin institution, the Group of 77. These countries increasingly determined the issues for the UN agenda and influenced their outcome. They were at the forefront of promoting international cooperation to deal with issues of global concern including apartheid, decolonization, development, disarmament and the Law of the Sea.

Indeed, there have indeed been occasional triumphs. Successful struggles against colonization and apartheid, the passage in the UN of the declaration for a New International Economic Order, the Charter of the Economic Rights and Duties of States, the emphasis on development within international discourse, the acceptance of "special needs" for developing countries, and occasional spurts of North-South dialogue are such achievements. In comparison to the original aspirations of the South, this is not much. However, it has been enough to keep the collective intact; the South realizes that "whilst coalition politics does not guarantee victory on any issues, it does produce the possibility of increased influence" (Williams 1993: 9–10). The politics of the South is the diplomacy of influence, not the politics of power. However, the South is aware that it has very few tangible achievements in its past, disillusionment in its present, and uncertainty in its future (South Commission 1990; G77, 1994a). The South of the 1990s is *not* the South of the 1970s—it is more diverse, less idealistic; more disillusioned, less impatient. But it remains—or rather, has reemerged—as a not inconsequential player in international policy, especially in international environmental affairs. The South's new pragmatism is reflected in the still firm, but much mellowed, approach to North-South relations taken by the South Commission (1990) and articulated in the 1992, 1995 and 1998 NAM Summits. The "street-politics" tactics of confrontation that the South adopted in the 1960s were warranted to ensure that the South's concerns were heard and placed on the agenda; however, to borrow once again from Weiss (1986a: 13) "it is difficult to remain *avant-garde* for [thirty-five] years."

The Lowest Common Denominator Trap

The story of this chapter has been the story of the remarkable resilience of the South as a collective. This resilience is remarkable not only because of the large differences that so obviously exist within this rather oversized and unwieldy group of countries, but even more so because it seems not to have brought them much in terms of concrete achievement. Indeed, it is the resilience itself—as manifest in the institutional survival and tenacity of the G77—that seems to be the collective's most important achievement. Preceding sections have tried to highlight why these otherwise disparate countries have held on to each other over such a long period. Here we focus on the cost they have had to pay in doing so. For the G77, this cost has been imposed most importantly in terms of the lowest common denominator positions that the collective has so often been reduced to. By this, we refer to the tendency of large groups to reduce their platforms to only those minimal positions on which all members are in full agreement. In practical terms, this means that the members with the most stringent position and those seeking the smallest movement define the collective's agenda.

There are a number of factors that facilitate this predicament of the Southern collective. To begin with, there is the self-perception of vulnerability and the attendant impulse for risk-minimization rather than gain-maximization. Having been (re-)mobilized principally because of the shared fear of the North imposing new environmental agendas on the developing countries, the South has been driven to group together much more by the desire to minimize individual losses than to create joint gains. This, combined with the memory of their 1970s NIEO adventures, militates against risk-prone grand strategy; for risk-averse members of the collective—fearful of the designs of the more powerful North and unsure of the limits of their own strengths—the lowest common denominator can seem like a cozy haven. It may promise much less in terms of rewards but it does promise to insulate against massive costs.

Yet, it is not a matter of self-perception alone. The reality of a large and unwieldy collective, lacking in formal management structures and facing chronic resource constraints goes a long way in explaining the predicament. In facing the dilemma inherent in the tension between creating and claiming value the South has found itself without the space, the time, or the resources to invest in the creation of joint gains because it has been so heavily burdened by the sheer size of the collective, the lack of any formal management structures, and severe resource constraints. The conundrum is that while the G77 has resisted formal management in the fear that it might make it a more rigid collective prone to control by leading states and secretariat staff, the absence of meaningful management routines has led to ad hoc rather than dynamic decision making, prey to a rigidity of its own. All of this has contributed to the lowest common denominator trap: a predicament where the South often finds itself getting, and sometimes even seeking, no more than the minimum that is acceptable to its most stringent members; in the process, value is left on the table in the shape of joint gains that might have been had if trades across differently valued issues had been facilitated (see Susskind 1994; Najam 1995a).

Finally, one should recall that global negotiation is an ongoing enterprise where the cumulated gains over a set of negotiations are more important than the specific goals for any particular negotiation episode. For the South, the limited goals of particular international environmental negotiations are removed from, and often secondary, to the larger goal of seeking systemic change in international structures. It is easy, therefore, to begin believing that unity over the long term is more important than (at least) specific interests in particular negotiation episodes. Although this is clearly a recipe for frustration in terms of the unmet or ignored interests that are bound to accumulate over time, the primacy of maintaining the façade of unity is key to the ethos of the Southern collective. For a group whose acquired unity has been deemed unnatural and transitory by so many (from within and without its ranks) for so long, maintenance of the expression of unity—even if it is merely cosmetic unity on the lowest of common denominators—becomes an important goal in itself.

Although the South has emerged as a remarkably stable and resilient collective in global environmental negotiations, the price of stability has often had to adopt lowest common denominator positions. This has constrained the G77's ability to negotiate effectively for the shared goals of the collective or the differentiated interests of its members. The unity of the G77, while not insignificant, is forever tentative; it is a unity that the G77 stumbled into; a unity that it has *learned* to stumble into. The impulse for risk reduction, low expectations, assumed habits of collaboration wrought out of a long history, and the need to herd a large and differentiated collective in the face of chronic resource constraints and no management effort has forced the South into the lowest common denominator trap. Getting beyond the lowest common denominator is deserving of concern because it serves as an important impediment to the larger interests of global environmental care, the collective interests of the Southern collective, as well as the differentiated interests of individual developing countries.

CONCLUSIONS

The goal of this chapter was to explore the motivations of the Southern collective in multinational negotiations related to the new politics of sustainable development. The purpose was to identify the defining features, the motivations, the *modus operandi*, and the agenda of the complex entity called the South which has become an increasingly important, even pivotal, actor in international environmental affairs. In doing so, we have focused on the collective behavior of developing states since there is a tendency in the literature to gloss over it or even ignore its import.

To recap, this chapter makes three sets of claims. First, the South is alive and well. The end of the Cold War has not spelled the demise of the South.

In fact, it has given the countries of the South a new motivation to coalesce their unity. Moreover, its supposedly growing economic heterogeneity has also not made the collective defunct. For the countries that describe themselves as the South, the term has never been a simple statement about shared economic impoverishment. It has been, instead, an articulation of their shared perceptions of political marginalization. It is the shared sense of being on the periphery of global decision making that is the defining feature of the Southern collective. For as long as this persists, so will the South.

Second, there is—and there has been for some time—a recognizable institutional face of the South and this face is becoming an increasingly familiar feature of international environmental affairs. The Non-Aligned Movement and the Group of 77 constitute the broad political and economic arms of the Southern collective. The latter of these, the G77, has consistently acted as the representative negotiating voice of the South in environmental negotiations. Although both groups suffer from the common malady of not having formal management structures to provide continuity and focus to their work, they each have fairly prescribed operating procedures, especially in relation to decision making. The continuing tenacity of these institutions, despite unfavorable environments, is their greatest achievement.

Third, the so-called global politics of sustainable development has allowed the South the opportunity to reinvigorate its sustaining agenda of global systemic change. The North-South differences now arising on issues related to the creation of, what may be called, a New International Environmental Order are best understood as lying on the exact same continuum as earlier North-South conflicts that had surrounded the ill-famed New International Economic Order. Although the concept of sustainable development does allow a small window of opportunity for a win-win compact to be crafted by incorporating the interests of both North and South, the evidence till now does not suggest that such a compact is imminent. Most importantly, the South (and the G77 as its negotiating arm) has to find a way out of the lowest common denominator trap that it has increasingly found itself in.

NOTES

1. Some Southern environmentalists build on such definitions to stress that the North-South distinction is not just a "developed-developing" difference, but primarily a "domination-dependence" divide; a divide created and perpetuated by centuries of colonialism which, they say, turned into neo-colonialism and is now in the danger of becoming ecocolonialism (Agarwal and Narain 1991; Peng 1992). During the UNCED process even government officials from the South began echoing this sentiment. Consider, for example, this statement by a Pakistani diplomat, Tariq Hyder, speaking for the Group of 77 (quoted in *SUNS*, 4 April 1992): "We [the South] do not want our freedom after independence, which has been so short, and in many ways so illusory . . .

to be constrained by new environmental conditionalities which could be equated with environmental colonialism."

2. Academic debate on whether there is a Fourth World, whether dividing the world into such spheres has any utility and where the socialist bloc countries fit in the schema were in rage in the 1970s. For a fascinating exposition of this debate see Wolf-Phillips (1979), Worsley (1979), Muni (1979), and Mountjoy (1980). In the shadow of the falling Berlin Wall, such discussion was revitalized in the 1990s (see David 1991 and 1992; Adams 1993; Najam 1993; Berger 1994; Ayoob 1995; Grant 1995).

3. The most recent manifestation of the relationship was in the declaration of the recent "South Summit" held in Havana, Cuba in April 2000 (G77 2000a). The meeting of heads of state and government of the G77 reaffirmed both the "imperative need to act in close unity" and the importance of collaborating with NAM though the Joint Coordinating Committee (JCC).

4. NAM Summits have been held at Belgrade, Yugoslavia (1961); Cairo, Egypt (1964); Lusaka, Zambia (1970); Algiers, Algeria (1973); Colombo, Sri Lanka (1976); Havana, Cuba (1979); New Delhi, India (1983); Harare, Zimbabwe (1986); Belgrade, Yugoslavia (1989); Jakarta, Indonesia (1992); Cartagena, Colombia (1995); and Durban, South Africa (1998).

5. Turkmenistan, Belarus and Dominican Republic are the most recent entrants. The applications of Bosnia-Herzegovina and Costa Rica were rejected in 1995 and 1998. Yugoslavia has been suspended since 1992.

6. Belarus, Uzbekistan and Turkmenistan are now full members.

7. Ironically, in 1995 a World Trade Organization (WTO) was created at the behest of the same industrialized countries that had strongly opposed an International Trade Organization in the 1940s and again in the 1960s.

8. Although China is not a full member of the G77 it holds a place of prominence as the only associate member; all resolutions and statements of the group are introduced on behalf of the Group of 77 and China. The membership of Yugoslavia has been suspended since 1992.

9. The G77's role at UNCED is discussed in Najam (1995a). The argument is that while the G77 was quite influential in shaping the agenda, its gains were "negative" in that it was far more successful in blocking the options it did not prefer (e.g. a global treaty on tropical forests) than it was in crafting its preferences into concrete decisions (e.g. large scale global transfers of resources). The South has had a similar impact on shaping the global population discourse (Najam 1994b and 1996) and in other episodes of global negotiation (see Banuri 1992; Rajan 1997; Agarwal et al. 1999).

10. MacDonald (1992: 41), for example, predicted that "the views of the developing nations will determine the direction, and probably the ultimate significance, of UNCED." The *New York Times* (17 March 1992) noted that "for the first time . . . the developing countries have an issue where they have some real leverage." Oran Young (1993: 447), argued that the South has "substantial bargaining leverage" and that "Northerners will ignore the demands of the South regarding climate change at their peril."

11. Both statements are quoted in Rajan (1992: 135–36).

12. Najam (1995a) proposes one such strategy for the South, which builds upon the lessons of negotiation theory and the experiences of the South. The 8-point strategy can

be paraphrased as: "Stop feeling angry at the North and sorry for yourself." It recommends that the South should focus on interests, not positions; cultivate its own power; be hard on issues, not on people; redefine the international environmental agenda; organize itself; develop its constituency; clean up its own act; and remember that good agreements are more important than "winning." The paper also argues that such a strategy would also lead to a more productive international negotiation process.

REFERENCES

Adams, N. A. 1993. *Worlds Apart: The North-South Divide and the International System*. London: Zed Books.

Adede, A. O. 1994. "The Road to Rio: The Development of Negotiations," in *The Environment After Rio: International Law and Economics,* Luigi Campigio, Laura Pineschi, Domenico Siniscalco, and Tullio Treves, eds. London: Graham and Trotman, 3–13.

Agarwal, A. 1992. "The North-South Environment Debate: Off to the Next Round." *Down to Earth* 15 July: 33–36.

Agarwal, A. and S. Narain. 1991. *Global Warming in an Unequal World: A Case of Environmental Colonialism*. New Delhi: Center for Science and Environment.

Agarwal, A., S. Narain and A. Sharma, ed. 1999. *Green Politics: Global Environmental Negotiations 1*. New Delhi: Centre for Science and Environment.

Alker Jr., H.R. and P. M. Haas. 1993. "The Rise of Global Ecopolitics," in *Global Accord: Environmental Challenges and International Responses,* N. Choucri, eds. Cambridge, Mass.: MIT Press, 133–71.

Ayoob, M. 1995. "The New-Old Disorder in the Third World." *Global Governance* 1(1): 59–77.

Banuri, Tariq. 1992. *Noah's Ark or Jesus's Cross?* Working Paper WP/UNCED/1992/1. Islamabad, Pakistan: Sustainable Development Policy Institute.

Berger, M.T. 1994. "The End of the 'Third World'?" *Third World Quarterly* 15(2): 257–75.

Brandt Commission (Independent Commission on International Development Issues). 1980. *North-South: A Program for Survival*. Cambridge, Mass: MIT Press.

Chubin, S. 1993. "The South and the New World Order." *The Washington Quarterly* 16(4): 87–107.

Commonwealth. 1982. *The North-South Dialogue: Making It Work*. Report of a Commonwealth Group of Experts. London: Commonwealth Secretariat.

Corell, E. 1999. *The Negotiable Desert: Expert Knowledge in the Negotiations of the Convention to Combat Desertification*. Linkoping Studies in Arts and Sciences No. 191 (Ph.D. Dissertation). Linkoping, Sweden: Linkoping University.

Cosbey, A. and S. Burgiel. 2000. *The Cartagena Protocol on Biosafety: An Analysis of Results*. IISD Briefing Note. Winnipeg, Canada: International Institute for Sustainable Development.

Crossette, B. 1994. "The 'Third World' Is Dead, but Spirits Linger." *New York Times*, 13 November sect. 4, 1.

Dasgupta, C. 1994. "The Climate Change Negotiations," in *Negotiating Climate Change: The Inside Story of the Rio Convention,* I. M. Mintzer and J.A. Leonard, eds. Cambridge: Cambridge University Press, 129–48.

David, S.R. 1991. "Explaining Third World Alignment." *World Politics* 43(2): 233–56.

———. 1992. "Why the Third World Still Matters." *International Security* 17(3): 127–59.

Elliott, L. 1998. *The Global Politics of the Environment*. New York: New York University Press.

Ferrer, Y. 1995. "Non-Aligned Movement: For Solidarity and Co-Operation." *Third World Resurgence* 64, December: 24.

Founex. 1972. *Development and Environment*. Report and Working Papers of Experts Convened by the Secretary General of the United Nations Conference on the Human Environment (Founex, Switzerland, June 4–12, 1971. Paris: Mouton.

French, H.F. 2000. *Vanishing Borders: Protecting the Planet in the Age of Globalization*. New York: W.W. Norton.

G77 (Group of 77). 1994a. *Thirty Years of the Group of 77: 1964–1994—United for a Global Partnership for Development and Peace*. Geneva: The Group of 77 and South Center.

———. 1994b. *Principles and Objectives of the Group of 77 for the Year 2000 and Beyond*. New York: Office of the Chairman of the Group of 77.

———. 1996. Report of the Eighth Annual Meeting of Senior Officials of the Group of 77, 26 September 1996 (Annex II: Summary of the Round Table on the Future of the Group of 77). G-77/AM(VIII)/96/RPT. New York: Office of the Chairman of the Group of 77.

———. 2000a. Havana Declaration of the G77 South Summit. Joint declaration released at the conclusion of the Group of 77 South Summit held in Havana, Cuba, 10–14 April 2000, at www.g77.org/summit/Declaration_G77Summit.htm.

———. 2000b. Havana Programme of Action. Group of 77 South Summit held in Havana, Cuba, 10–14 April 2000. Available online at www.g77.org/summit/ProgrammeofAction_G77Summit.htm.

Gardner, R.N. 1992. *Negotiating Survival: Four Priorities After Rio*. New York: Council on Foreign Relations Press.

Geldart, C. and P. Lyon. 1980. "The Group of 77: A Perspective View." *International Affairs* 57(1): 79–101.

Gordon, L. 1978. *International Stability and North-South Relations*. Occasional Paper 17. Muscatine, Iowa: The Stanley Foundation.

Gosovic, B. 1972. *UNCTAD Conflict and Compromise: The Third World's Quest for an Equitable World Economic Order through the United Nations*. Leiden, The Netherlands: A.W. Sijthoff.

Grant, C. 1995. "Equity in International Relations: A Third World Perspective." *International Affairs*, 71(3): 567–87.

Hall, K.O. 1980. "Strengthening Third World Negotiating Capacity," in *Dialogue for a New Order,* K. Haq, ed. New York: Pergamon Press, 45–59..

Hansen, R.D. 1979. *Beyond the North-South Stalemate*. New York: McGraw-Hill.

———. 1980. "North-South Policy–What's the Problem." *Foreign Affairs* 58, Summer: 1104–28.

Hyder, T.O. 1994. "Looking Back to See Forward," in *Negotiating Climate Change: The Inside Story of the Rio Convention,* I.M. Mintzer and J.A. Leonard, eds. Cambridge: Cambridge University Press, 201–26..

Iida, K. 1988. "Third World Solidarity: The Group of 77 in the UN General Assembly," in *International Organization* 42(2): 375–95.

Jankowitsch, O. and K.P. Sauvant. 1978. *The Third World without Superpowers: The Collected Documents of the Non-Aligned Movement* (4 volumes). Dobbs Ferry, N.Y.: Oceana Publications.

Jansen, G.H. 1992. "The Non-Aligned Movement Still Has a Role." *Third World Resurgence* (26): 25.

Jones, C.A. 1983. *The North-South Dialogue: A Brief History*. New York: St. Martin's Press.

Kim, S.Y. and B. Russett. 1996. "The New Politics of Voting Alignments in the United Nations General Assembly." *International Organization* 50(4): 629–52.

Krasner, S.D. 1985. *Structural Conflict: The Third World against Global Liberalism*. Berkeley: University of California Press.

Lyon, P. 1984. "The Emergence of the Third World," in *Expansion of International Society*, H. Bull and A. Watson, eds. Oxford: Clarendon Press.

MacDonald, G. J. 1991. "Brazil 1992: Who Needs This Meeting?" *Issues in Science and Technology* 7(4): 41–44.

Mahbub-ul-Haq. 1976. *The Poverty Curtain*. New York: Columbia University Press.

———. 1980a. "Beyond the Slogan of South-South Cooperation," in *Dialogue for a New Order*, K. Haq, ed. New York: Pergamon Press, 139–52..

———. 1980b. "North-South Dialogue: Is there a Future?" in *Dialogue for a New Order*, K. Haq, ed. New York: Pergamon Press, 270–87..

———. 1983. "A Plea for Human Sanity," in *Global Development: Issues and Choices*, K. Haq, ed. Washington D.C.: North South Roundtable, 3–8..

Mathews, J.T., ed. 1991. *Preserving the Global Environment: The Challenge of Shared Leadership*. New York: W.W. Norton and Co.

McDonald, J.W. 1982. *The North-South Dialogue and the United Nations*. Occasional Paper. Washington D.C.: Institute for the Study of Diplomacy, Georgetown University.

Mello, V.C.M. 1993. *North-South Conflicts and Power Distribution in UNCED Negotiations: The Case of Forestry*. IIASA Working Paper WP-93-26. Laxenburg, Austria: International Institute for Applied Systems Analysis.

Menon, B.P. 1977. *Global Dialogue: The New International Order*. London: Pergamon Press.

Mensah, C.K. 1994. "The Role of Developing Countries," in *The Environment After Rio: International Law and Economics*, L. Campigio, L. Pineschi, D. Siniscalco, and T. Treves, eds. London: Graham and Trotman, 33–53..

Merriam, A.H. 1988. "What Does the 'Third World' Mean?" in *The Third World: States of Mind and Being*, J. Norwine and A. Gonzalez, eds. London: Unwin Hyman.

Miller, M.A.L. 1995. *The Third World in Global Environmental Politics*. Boulder, Colo.: Lynne Rienner.

Misra, K.P. 1993. "Nonaligned Movement Back on the Rails: A Study of the Jakarta Summit." *International Studies* 30(1): 1–14.

Mistry, P. 1993. "Economic Relations between North and South in a New World Order," in *Facing the Challenge: Responses to the Report of the South Commission* edited by the South Center. London: Zed Books, 168–97.

Mohammed, M. 1992. "Why NAM Must Unite." Address by the Prime Minister of Malaysia (Dr. Mahathir Mohammed) to 10th NAM Summit. Reproduced in *Third World Resurgence* 26: 26.

Moomaw, W.R. 1997. "International Environmental Policy and the Softening of Sovereignty." *Fletcher Forum of World Affairs* 21, Summer/Fall: 7–15.

Mountjoy, A.B. 1980. "Worlds without End." *Third World Quarterly* 2(4): 753–57.

Muni, S.D. 1979. "The Third World: Concept and Controversy." *Third World Quarterly* 1(3): 119–28.

Murphy, C. 1984. *The Emergence of the NIEO Ideology*. Boulder, Colo.: Westview Press.

Najam, A. 1993. "An Identity Crisis for the South." *Down to Earth* 2(6): 47–48.

———. 1994a. *The Case for a South Secretariat in International Environmental Negotiation*. Program on Negotiation Working Paper. Cambridge, Mass.: Program on Negotiation at Harvard Law School, 94–98.

———. 1994b. "Prediction for Cairo: A Reaffirmation, A Reversal, Realignment, and a Refusal." *Environmental Conservation* 21(2): 105–10.

———. 1995a. "An Environmental Negotiation Strategy for the South." *International Environmental Affairs* 7(3): 249–87.

———. 1996. "A Developing Countries' Perspective on Population, Environment and Development." *Population Research and Policy Review* 15(1): 1–19.

———. 2000a. "The Case for a Law of the Atmosphere." *Atmospheric Environment* 34(23): 4047–4049.

———. 2000b. "Trade and Environment after Seattle: A Negotiation Agenda for the South," in *Journal of Environment and Development* 9(4): 405–25.

Najam A. and T. Page. 1998. "The Climate Convention: Deciphering the Kyoto Convention." *Environmental Conservation* 25(3): 187–94.

Najam, A. and N. Robins 2001. "Seizing the Future: The South, Sustainable Development and International Trade." *International Affairs* 77(1): 93–111.

NAM (Non-Aligned Movement). 1998. Durban Declaration for the New Millennium. Declaration of the 12th Summit of the Non-Aligned Movement held at Durban, South Africa, 2–3 September 1998. Accessed online at www.nam.gov.za/xiisummit/finaldocument/decl.htm.

Nyerere, J.K. 1980. "Unity for a New Order," in *Dialogue for a New Order,* K. Haq, ed. New York: Pergamon Press, 3–10..

Oxley, A. 1991. "North/South Dimensions of A New World Order," in *Whose New World Order?* Mara Bustelo and Philip Alston, ed. Annandale: The Federation Press.

Peng, M.K.K. 1992. *The Future of North-South Relations: Conflict or Cooperation?* Penang: Third World Network.

Pirages, D. 1978. *Global Ecopolitics: The New Context for International Relations*. North Scituate: Duxbury Press.

Porter, G. and J.W. Brown. 1991. *Global Environmental Politics*. Boulder, Colo.: Westview Press.

———. 1996. *Global Environmental Politics*. 2nd ed. Boulder, Colo.: Westview Press.

Porter, G., J. W. Brown and P. S. Chasek, ed. 2000. *Global Environmental Politics*. 3rd ed. Boulder: Westview Press.

Rajamoorthy, T. 1992. "The Origins of the Non-Aligned Movement." *Third World Resurgence* (26): 20–22.

Rajan, M.G. 1992. "Bargaining with the Environment: A New Weapon for the South?" *South Asia Research* 12(2): 135–47.

Ramphal, S.S. 1980. "Unity Alone is Not Strength," in *Dialogue for a New Order,* K. Haq, ed. New York: Pergamon Press, 11–21..

———. 1992. *Our Country, The Planet.* Washington D.C.: Island Press.

Rowland, W. 1973. *The Plot to Save the World.* Toronto: Clarke, Irwin and Co.

Sabri-Abdalla, I. 1980. "Heterogeneity and Differentiation–The End for the Third World?" in *Dialogue for a New Order,* K. Haq, ed. New York: Pergamon Press, 22–44.

Samper, E. 1995. Excerpts from the opening address of the new Chair of the Non-Aligned Movement, President Samper of Colombia. *South Letter* 24, Autumn/Winter: 10–11.

Sandbrook, R. 1997. "UNGASS Has Run Out of Steam." *International Affairs* 73(4): 641–54.

Sauvant, K.P. 1981. *The Group of 77: Evolution, Structure, Organization.* New York: Oceana Publications.

Searwar, L. and V.A. Lewis. 1979. "Proposal for Central Technical Support Unit for the Group of 77." Report prepared for the G77. *Mimeo.*

Sebenius, J.K. 1991. "Negotiating a Regime to Control Global Warming," in *Greenhouse Warming: Negotiating a Global Regime,* Jessica T. Mathews, ed. Washington D.C.: World Resources Institute.

———. 1994. "Towards a Winning Climate Coalition," in *Negotiating Climate Change: The Inside Story of the Rio Convention,* Irving M. Mintzer and J. Amber Leonard, eds. Cambridge: Cambridge University Press, 277–320..

Sell, S. 1996. "North-South Environmental Bargaining: Ozone, Climate Change, and Biodiversity." *Global Governance* 2(1): 97–118.

Sewell, J.W. and I.W. Zartman. 1984. "Global Negotiations: Path to the Future or Dead-End Street?" *Third World Quarterly* 6(2): 374–410.

South Centre. 1991. *Environment and Development: Towards a Common Strategy of the South in UNCED Negotiations and Beyond.* Geneva: South Centre.

South Commission. 1990. *The Challenge to the South: The Report of the South Commission.* Oxford: Oxford University Press.

South Letter. 1994. "Group of 77: Anniversary Resolution." *South Letter* 20, Summer: 1.

Stone, C.D. 1993. *The Gnat Is Older than Man: Global Environment and Human Agenda.* Princeton, N.J.: Princeton University Press.

Susskind, L.E. 1994. *Environmental Diplomacy: Negotiating More Effective Global Agreements.* New York: Oxford University Press.

Thomas, C. 1987. *In Search of Security: The Third World in International Relations.* Boulder, Colo.: Rienner.

———. 1992. *The Environment in International Relations.* London: The Royal Institute of International Affairs.

Van Evera, S. 1990. "Why Europe Matters, Why the Third World Doesn't: America's Grand Strategy After the Cold War." *Journal of Strategic Studies* 13(2): 1–51.

Van Lennep, E. 1983. "North-South Relations in the 80s: A Constructive Approach to New Realties," in *Global Development: Issues and Choices,* K. Haq, ed.. Washington D.C.: North South Roundtable, 14–22.

Wallerstein, I. 1993. "Wise, But Not Tough, or Is It Correct, But Not Wise?" in *Facing the Challenge: Responses to the Report of the South Commission,* edited by the South Center. London: Zed Books, 117–21..

Ward, B. 1965. *The Decade of Development: A Study in Frustration?* London: Overseas Development Institute.

Weintraub, S. 1980. "What Life Is Left in the North-South Dialogue?" *World Economy* 2(4): 453–65.

Weiss, T.G. 1986a. *Multilateral Development Diplomacy in UNCTAD: The Lessons of Group Negotiations, 1964–84*. New York: St. Martin's Press.

———. 1986b. "International Secretariat or Servant of the G77," in *The Nature of United Nations Bureaucracies*, David Pitt and Thomas G. Weiss, eds. Boulder, Colo.: Westview, 84–108..

Williams, M. 1993. "Re-articulating the Third World Coalition: The Role of the Environmental Agenda." *Third World Quarterly* 14(1): 7–29.

Wolf-Phillips, L. 1979. "Why Third World?" *Third World Quarterly* 1(1): 105–13.

Worsley, P. 1979. "How Many Worlds?" *Third World Quarterly* 1(2): 100–08.

Young, O.R. 1989. *International Cooperation: Building Regimes for Natural Resources and the Environment*. Ithaca, N.Y.: Cornell University Press.

———. 1993. "Negotiating an International Climate Regime: The Institutional Bargaining for Environmental Governance," in *Global Accord: Environmental Challenges and International Responses,* N. Choucri, ed. Cambridge, Mass.: MIT Press, 431–52.

10

Decision Making for Sustainable Development: Toward a New Paradigm

Joseph S. Szyliowicz

INTRODUCTION

Sustainable development can be (and has been) defined in many ways but there is a general consensus that development should be structured in such a way as to ensure that no further damage be done to the environment. If this is to occur, particular attention must be paid to the ways in which all societies make decisions concerning the projects that are designed to promote growth.

Traditionally, the primary focus of persons concerned with sustainability has been upon the macro level, with national and international economic policies and issues such as the maximum size of economies and their impacts upon the environment and resources. As one noted expert, David Brooks, has argued: "Sustainable development is not fundamentally about micro-economics or individual project analysis. It instead must focus on the big picture. . . . The key issues do not involve questions of how to allocate resources but how much the size of the economy." (Brooks 1990: 25)

The micro level issues, however, require at least as much attention because development is essentially achieved through projects. They embody the technologies that a state uses to achieve growth and if the projects are not well conceived, they will not only fail to contribute to a nation's development but will yield major negative outcomes and impacts. The world is already littered with projects that are failures. More are not needed and if sustainable development is to take place, well-planned and implemented projects are essential. Even David Brooks, despite his emphasis upon the strategic policy issues, concedes this point, for he rather surprisingly chooses to end his article with the following comment "Whether or not a project is 'sustainable' will become the standard of success in international development" (Brooks 1990). Such a standard will not become an international norm, however, unless the ways in which projects are planned and implemented undergo significant changes.

MEGA PROJECTS AND SUSTAINABLE DEVELOPMENT

Projects come in many shapes and sizes. They can be large or small, agricultural or industrial, experimental and demonstrational, capital intensive or labor intensive, designed to increase output or develop their new capabilities. Despite their variety, all projects possess certain commonalities, "purposefulness, some minimum size, a specific location, the introduction of something qualitatively new, and the expectation that a sequence of further development moves will be set in motion." (Hirschman 1967:1)

Although all projects have implications for sustainable development, it is the large projects, the "mega-projects" that deserve the most careful attention since, because of their scale, scope, and long life, they are the ones that have the greatest environmental and developmental consequences.

Megaprojects—large dams, steel mills, highways, tunnels, and airports—have become commonplace because they have a powerful appeal for practical reasons. When well conceived, they can serve as major stimulants to development in regions and nations. But one should not underestimate the universal appeal of mega projects as symbols of power and capability. In the developing countries they are regarded as evidence that a regime can harness modern technologies and gain international respect. Even in developed countries, citizens take pride in the great projects their communities implement.

Such projects have proliferated rapidly in recent years. In the 1970s their number increased thirty fold; over 1600, costing more than $100 million each, were planned during that decade (Murphy 1983). Since then their numbers and size have continued to grow as infrastructural demands expand throughout the world. Recent examples include the Three Gorges Dam in China and the new Kansai Airport in Japan.

Yet, as such projects proliferate, so do their problems. They often fail to achieve their planned goals, wreak unexpected environmental impacts, cost more than anticipated and are completed well beyond schedule, thus imposing heavy burdens which can be absorbed only with great pain and difficulty (Hirschman 1967; Szyliowicz 1991; Hall 1982). Numerous examples exist ranging from the Sydney Opera House to the Aswan Dam, to the new Denver International Airport. The latter, for example, grossly exceeded its original budget (the final cost was 300 percent more than the original projection of $1.5 billion), opened more than a year late, and began operations at passenger and flight frequency levels far lower than had been projected (Dempsey, Goetz, and Szyliowicz 1997).

Although most mega projects yield unanticipated and undesirable outcomes, it is essential to distinguish between those that turn out to be totally unfeasible or produce truly catastrophic consequences and those whose shortcomings can be more or less remedied. Specific examples of the former include the atomic airplane, the Chernobyl nuclear plant disaster, and the space shuttle Challenger. The latter, which includes the Aswan Dam, DIA, the Sydney opera house and, perhaps one day the Chunnel, are projects that encounter significant difficulties and whose costs (financial, environmental, and other) are much higher than necessary. But these can sometimes be overcome or minimized so that the project can function and sometimes even become a valued success. The Sydney opera house is a fine example.

Neither category, however, promotes sustainable development. Outright disasters are to be avoided if at all possible but even those that are salvaged, the "white elephant," though less tragic in terms of human suffering, impose heavy and unnecessary costs upon peoples and communities. The noted economist Albert Hirschman has argued that these might be unavoidable and even desirable: "If the project planners...had known in advance all the difficulties and troubles that were lying in store for the project, they probably would never have touched it." But, that would have been unfortunate "for the difficulties and the ensuing search for solutions set into motion a train of events that not only rescued the project, but often made it particularly valuable." (Hirschman 1967:14)

Whether such an optimistic, even panglossian view, is justified, whether the "hiding hand" does work to transform bad projects into "particularly valuable" ones is not at all obvious. Certainly the experience with mega projects that has accumulated in recent years suggests that such optimism cannot serve as the basis for planning and decision making.

Many scholars have attempted to identify the reasons why mega projects so seldom yield satisfactory outcomes. At first the focus was upon the development of better methodologies but, despite the progress that has been made in refining such techniques as cost benefit and cost effectiveness analysis, environmental and social impact analysis and the like, the failure rate has remained high. Accordingly the focus shifted to such factors as size, technological complexity, the lack of appreciation of differences in cultures and the impact of local and global environments (Schulman 1980; Murphy 1983; Morris and Hough 1987). The role of the environment has received increased attention because it affects projects by creating uncertainties and unexpected difficulties of all kinds (Hall 1980).

What remains unclear, however, is why planners and decision makers are unable to anticipate the risks and uncertainties inherent in any project and to design, manage, and implement them successfully. Dealing with risks and uncertainties is a fundamental issue dealt with in management schools and sophisticated managerial tools and techniques have been developed to deal with this problem. Obviously the answer must be sought elsewhere. What has been missing in the mega project literature is an explicit focus upon the political context in which decisions are made.

Some important work does exist on this topic which suggests that the fate of mega projects is determined not only by poor forecasts (a point to which we shall return below) but by such inherently political factors as the nature of bureaucracies, the role of citizens, and the financing and administration (Feldman 1987). However, this analysis does not go far enough for political variables influence all aspects of a mega project.

One of the most important is the degree to which the project can maintain flexibility. Scholars have demonstrated that large projects are inherently inflexible because of technical economic and social considerations such as high capital costs, long lead times, centralization, and technical demands. Hence, such projects frequently can not adapt to changing conditions and turn into white elephants (Collingridge and James 1991; Collingridge 1992; Morris and Hough 1987). What is overlooked in these analyses, however, is the role of political variables. Precisely because of their economic, technical, and social complexities, transportation and other major projects involve many actors and agencies, each with its own agenda and priorities. Once such a coalition has been formed, it becomes extremely difficult to make any changes for considerable bargaining and negotiations between organizations and groups is required. Power plays a critical role for the key turning points in any project can only be explained by the nature of the political process. In each case the outcome will be influenced by power distributions and the perceptions and belief systems of key actors. Such considerations also drive planners and decision makers to "frontload" projects. Regardless of its quality, a project that has been launched and in which substantial investments have been made is much less likely to be stopped than one that is still largely in the planning stage.

Second, even the appraisals and analyses are influenced by the nature of the political system. Forecasts, a critical element in any planning effort, are notoriously inaccurate even though in this area too, sophisticated tools and techniques have been developed. The errors are almost always the same. Costs are underestimated, demand greatly overestimated. Why should this be the case, given the great technical advances and refinements in methodology that have taken place? The most persuasive answer lies in the fact that forecasts are not made in a vacuum, they are made in a political environment. One scholar who has analyzed various transportation projects in the U.S. has concluded the following:

> Having interviewed public officials, consultants and planners who have been involved in these cases, I am absolutely convinced that the cost overruns and

> patronage overestimates were not the result of technical errors, honest mistakes, or inadequate methodology. In case after case, planners, engineers, and economists have told me that they have had to "revise" their forecasts many times because they had failed to satisfy their superiors. The forecasts had to be calculated to produce numbers that were dramatic enough to gain federal support for the projects whether or not they could be fully justified on technical grounds. (Wachs 1995: 274)

Under these conditions suggestions to promote sustainable development by improving project selection through the incorporation of environmental considerations into appraisal techniques (Pearce and Warford 1993) stand little chance of success unless the process permits such calculations to become genuine elements of the decision process. Any attempt to understand and improve the process of mega project planning must take into account such variables as the structure of power in which the project is planned and implemented and the nature of the decision process involved.

Transportation projects are perhaps even more influenced by their political environments than other mega projects because of their particular characteristics. These include transportation's saliency in every day life and its role in national economies which give any project great political visibility and arouse controversy. Furthermore transportation projects are always extremely large and involve not only huge investments but usually consume large quantities of land and affect the lives of many people. And, since many powerful actors are inexorably involved, ranging from environmental to business groups, heated debates that quickly become politicized are the norm (Wachs 1995).

TRANSPORTATION AND SUSTAINABLE DEVELOPMENT

The transportation sector is of particular importance for two significant reasons. First, transportation accounts for a large percentage of all mega-projects. One recent estimate of needed infrastructural projects, for example, is as follows (Levy 1996:16):

Type of projects	*Number*	*Cost (in millions)*
Power	201	$160
Transportation	493	$352
Water	94	$22.5

The large number of transportation projects should not be surprising since every country in the world recognizes the central role that transportation plays in economic growth and feels compelled to meet the demands that growth places upon the transportation sector. Hence, it is not surprising that airports, highway projects, container ports and subway systems are all proliferating around the world or that governments everywhere are struggling to develop innovative means of financing their infrastructural requirements in transportation. Furthermore, whatever the sector involved, any mega project is more or less dependent upon transportation for the shipment of inputs and outputs.

Second, this sector's characteristics and negative externalities place it at the center of any strategy designed to achieve sustainable development. The reason is simple. Existing transportation systems yield widespread and pernicious impacts. The degree to which they violate principles of sustainability can readily be understood if one considers the following criteria that have been advanced to measure the environmental limits of particular activities. These are (Daly 1990):

1. Renewable resources should not be used faster than their regeneration rates.
2. Nonrenewable resources should not be used faster than substitutes become available.
3. Pollution emissions should not exceed the assimilative capacity of the environment.

The transportation, sector, however, universally violates all of these criteria.

To begin with, transportation systems consume enormous amounts of materials of all kinds like millions of tons of concrete and steel to build highways, airports, and other facilities. Nor can one overlook the millions of tons of plastic and ferrous and nonferrous metals that are required to build the vehicles that use the infrastructure. Even more important is the degree to which the transportation sector consumes nonrenewable resources in the form of fossil fuels, notably oil. Globally, this sector consumes more than 60 percent of the world's total oil products. Oil now accounts for 98 percent of all energy utilized by transportation, an increase from 92 percent in 1960. Many governments have attempted to design policies to promote the use of other sources of energy for transportation but these efforts have obviously had little impact. Within the sector, motorized transport accounts for over 80 percent of all the oil used, aviation accounts for about 15 percent, rail and shipping for the remainder (OECD 1996).

With the continuing dominance of automobiles in the OECD countries and the growing automobility of the non-Western world, it should not be surprising that the use of oil continues to rise inexorably while few new fields are being discovered. As a result, experts agree that the world is rapidly running out of oil. The best current estimates are that world oil reserves will last for another 35 to 50 years. In actuality, however, the world will probably never run out of oil since diminishing supplies will lead to higher prices, the exploitation of hitherto noneconomic fields and sources (such as oil shale and tar sands) and increasing reliance upon alternative energy sources. Still, the seriousness of this issue should not be underestimated for one can readily imagine high price volatility with unsettling effects upon national economies. Furthermore, oil tends to come from politically unstable regions (notably the Persian Gulf with two-thirds of the world's known reserves) thus raising important questions about national security.

This heavy reliance upon oil leads to a tremendous amount of pollution. There are three major areas of concern. First, is air pollution caused by carbon monoxide, hydrocarbon and lead (in those areas where leaded gasoline continue to be used) from motorized vehicles? Studies have demonstrated that transportation is responsible for almost 90 percent of carbon dioxide emissions and a large percentage of other pollutants. This is particularly evident in large cities throughout the world. Second is noise pollution that inflicts psychological and physiological damage upon people. Third, is water pollution that is caused not only by the seepage of fuels and other contaminants at airports, garages, filling stations and the like, but directly through the use of waterways (Dron and de Lara 1996).

Further aggravating the situation is that transportation impacts are felt not only locally and regionally but their cumulative impacts contribute in major ways to ozone depletion and global warming. And, additional pollution is created by the manufacture and disposal of vehicles and infrastructure.

The impacts of pollution are most evident in urban areas where they often pose significant health risks. But pollution's effects are being felt regionally and even globally and range from aesthetics to impacts on forests, water resources, and crops. At the global level, emissions from vehicles are a major factor in global warming.

Nor can one ignore other ways in which existing transportation systems are not consonant with sustainability. They consume vast amounts of land for roads, airports, and railroads and more for parking facilities, manufacturing and maintenance plants. Over 65 percent of Los Angeles is paved. Furthermore, automobiles have created urban sprawl that in turn generates additional demands for transportation that can be met only by more automobiles. The increasing reliance upon this mode of transport also has negative consequences for social life. Although automobiles provide people with freedom and mobility, they do so only for those who can utilize them. Such groups as the poor, the elderly, the handicapped can easily be marginalized and isolated from community life if alternative transportation modes are not available. In short, transportation can isolate groups and regions from the mainstream and poorly devised highway and other infrastructural projects can carve up communities as happened frequently during the interstate construction phase in the United States in the 1970s. Nor can one overlook the heavy costs imposed by accidents and congestion (OECD 1996).

What is even more troublesome in terms of sustainable development is that the negative trends in transportation are accelerating. Globally the number of people and the amount of freight moving by road continues to increase. Although the proportion of trips by automobile has remained constant in the OECD countries, the increased mobility translates into a substantial growth in personal automobile travel. In the United States, for example, intercity passenger traffic by automobile increased by 57 percent between 1980 and 1996 whereas rail passenger traffic rose by only 26 percent (Eno Foundation 1997). In the rest of the world, private automobile usage is growing exponentially—in China, for example, by 100 percent a year. Similarly, freight is moving increasingly by road. In Europe, for example, 51 percent of freight movements were by road in 1970 as compared to 70 percent in 1990 (OECD 1996).

Clearly existing transportation systems in the developed world are not only unsustainable, they are on a course that promises to exacerbate what is already a dangerous situation. And, the developing countries appear to be replicating the patterns of the West. Many of their urban centers are among the most polluted and congested in the world. Sao Paulo, for example, has 4.5 million cars as compared to 2.1 million in New York City (NYT 1997). One expert has vividly described the situation as follows:

> Major changes are needed in the priorities for transportation policy in the Third World if development is to meet human needs rather than benefit only the world's current elite groups. The costs of failing to redirect transport policies today will be paid in the decades to come through a sharply reduced quality of life in the world's cities, increased conflict between the mobile elite and the mobility-restricted poor, and reduced capacity to solve the problems of capital shortages, unpayable debt burdens, toxic air pollution, and global climate change. (Replogle 1995)

What is required is a new vision of transportation and the development of theoretical and empirical approaches that make possible the creation of sustainable transportation systems. Such a system must be intermodal—it cannot be based on roads and motor vehicles alone, for all the reasons cited above.

Yet, almost every project in the U.S. and in most other countries is designed on a modal basis with few or no connections to other modes of transportation. The result has been the creation of several parallel systems that are not integrated into a coherent whole, a situation that has contributed to freight and passenger congestion, to accidents and fatalities, and to a tremendous waste of time and energy, and resources. Why a shift to such a systemic perspective is essential has been summarized as follows:

"Just as an ecological system is healthiest when it displays great diversity and differentiation, so too is a transportation system healthiest and most robust when diverse modal options are available to those moving people or goods. A transportation system dependent on only one or two modes of transportation is far more susceptive to inefficiency, disruption, and system failure than is one in which numerous different modes are allowed to operate." (Replogle 1995)

Intermodalism, however, is not synonymous with sustainability. It is a necessary but not a sufficient condition. A sustainable transportation system must possess certain other characteristics. It must be environmentally benign, efficient and flexible, and safe and secure. Each of these focus areas also incorporates three dimensions—technology, planning and policy, and ethics. Anyone concerned with safety and security issues, for example, must address the technologies involved, planning and policy processes, and numerous ethical issues. Such an approach permits the analysis of the strengths and weaknesses of each mode and of the ways in which the latter can be remedied so as to permit the emergence of a sustainable intermodal system. (Goetz, Szyliowicz, and Dempsey 1996)

Thus renewed attention must be paid to the ways in which decisions are made about the mega projects that form the backbone of the transportation sector. Two issues are paramount—the intermodal emphasis and a process that leads to better outcomes. Unfortunately, numerous recent examples illustrate the extent to which transportation mega projects, ranging from transit systems (San Francisco's BART, Miami's MetroRail) to highway projects (Embarcadero Freeway in San Francisco, London's motorways) to airports (Kansai, Mirabel) violate the basic principles enunciated above.

DECISION MAKING APPROACHES

Mega project planners and decision makers are not primarily concerned with such considerations as maintaining flexibility or ensuring that genuine public participation take place. Their thinking continues to be dominated by the rational actor model which views planning as a systematic, step-by-step process which involves such stages as problem definition, value clarification, goal selection, formulation of alternatives, evaluation of alternatives, selection of a course of action, and its implementation. Planners and decision makers must marshal all the relevant information. All possible alternative solutions are generated and analyzed. The optimal alternative is eventually selected for implementation (Levy 1994). A rational approach in planning should result in maximizing the benefits of the project and minimizing its costs but, as has been emphasized above, this has frequently not been the case.

This approach to planning and decision making has been severely criticized over recent decades. Theoretical analyses and empirical studies have demonstrated that planning and decision making is rarely, if ever, conducted according to the dictates of the rational model and that different approaches can yield greater insights into decision making processes and produce better results (Simon 1955; Lindblom 1959; Etzioni 1967; Hirschman, 1967; Allison 1971; Rondinelli 1977; Rycroft and Szyliowicz 1980; Feldman and Milch 1982, 1985; Hall 1982; Linstone 1984; Wachs 1985; Szyliowicz 1991; Greenaway, Smith, and Street 1992; Szyliowicz and Goetz 1996; Goetz and Szyliowicz 1997).

Despite this extensive body of scholarship, however, the rational actor model retains its primacy as a guide for planning large technological projects (Wachs 1985; Baker, Michaels, and Preston 1975). It remains the dominant approach because of its strengths — its logical, problem-solving orientation. Complex projects can be disaggregated into various subsystems, each of which can be analyzed through rigorous methodological approaches. Hence many planners continue to regard the rational model as the optimal approach which should be adhered to as closely as possible.

They continue to cling to it even though numerous other approaches have been developed including incrementalism (Lindblom 1959, 1979; Weiss and Woodhouse 1992), satisfying and organizational behavior perspectives (Simon 1955; March and Simon 1958), mixed scanning (Etzioni 1967), bureaucratic politics models (Allison 1971), cognitive and cybernetic paradigms (Steinbruner 1974; Axelrod 1976; Jervis 1976), and multiple perspectives (Linstone 1984), among others. Despite significant differences, these share a fundamental belief that it is necessary to be flexible, monitor feedback, and make adjustments through a process of trial-and-error learning. Accordingly, they have been conveniently grouped into a second general approach to planning and decision making and labeled the "strategic" or "adaptive" approach. They differ fundamentally from the "analytic" approach, characterized by the rational model, with its rigidity and impractical demands for complete and unambiguous information, large amounts of time and monetary resources, control over the external environment, accurate causal models, and a complete and consistent way to order preferences (Szyliowicz and Goetz 1996; Morone and Woodhouse 1986).

Clearly, the "adaptive" models hold considerable promise in terms of making plans and decisions that promote sustainability. The rational actor model which supposedly guides decision making mostly serves as a facade to legitimize decisions that political coalitions or powerful leaders wish to implement. This pattern does not lead to projects that promote sustainability. Doing so requires the development of a new approach to decision making.

A recent French government study that recognized the need for a new approach, suggested that it be based on the following principles (Dron and de Lara 1995; 39 ff):

1. Introduce rationality, transparency and evaluation methods in decision making.

2. Take into more realistic consideration the irreversible effects of infrastructural decisions.
3. Enact policies that ensure that prices reflect the actual costs
4. Inform the public and the decision makers about the nature of transportation and organize a public debate that will lead to a national policy.
5. Formulate specific environmental objectives.
6. Develop an effective political will to promote intermodalism.

That an appeal for rationality takes priority reflects an eternal longing of the French; that the appeal is necessary highlights the degree to which the rational actor model remains a mirage—even a culture that prides itself on its adherence to logic and clarity has failed to make its decisions on the basis of the rational model. This fact underlies the need to shift towards the "adaptive" models described above.

Not only do the "adaptive" models not make impossible demands upon planners and decision makers, they enhance the possibility of maintaining flexibility, an essential element if better outcomes are to be achieved. As emphasized above, changes are inevitable because any project encounters "uncertainties." Planning for sustainability aggravates the situation because numerous additional unknowns must be dealt with. These include the difficulties of anticipating and assessing environmental and other impacts and of forecasting technological and scientific change (Meadowcraft 1997: 184).

Working within the framework of an "adaptive model" does not mean that decision making should be "irrational." The rational model retains its importance as an ideal towards which it is necessary to strive. Its strength lies in its ability to provide a formal framework within which analyses (based on its premises) can be carried out. But it should not be regarded as a rigid template to be imposed upon a process that involves other rationalities.

The notion that there are different forms of rationality has been explored by scholars (Diesing 1962). Perhaps the most useful typology of rationality for our purposes, however, derives from Jurgen Habermas's communicative theory from which three separate rationalities can be derived. These are: 1) instrumental rationality which lies at the heart of the rational actor model, 2) communicative rationality which views people as the ultimate sources of knowledge and reality, and 3) emancipatory rationality which emphasizes freedom, participation, and self reflection (Khisty 1996).

Accordingly, any new approach to decision making should be based on "communicative discourse," that is, one that accepts instrumental rationality but incorporates the other rationalities as well. Such an approach places certain requirements upon the decision process—that it be transparent and sensitive to such considerations as irreversibility. It also accords the public (as well as the other major stakeholders) a central role because only in this way can people free themselves from exploitation. New structures and processes must be accompanied by changes in existing elite and mass values.

Achieving genuine, informed, public participation, however, is a complicated matter that entails various costs. In democratic societies some form of public participation is often mandated by law but public participation may take many forms and occur at different stages. The goal of the exercise is usually to legitimate a project; seldom is the public provided with meaningful opportunities to participate in making the fundamental decisions. As one transportation scholar noted recently (Khisty 1996: 171): "Although public involvement in the transportation planning process is vital, it is not uncommon to observe citizen groups involved . . . as mere passive onlookers and, at best, commenting on draft reports and the recommendations ready to be implemented."

Although real costs of time, money, and other resources are incurred if the public is involved in a meaningful way, for a range of educational and other activities are involved, these are more than offset by the benefits that can accrue. Genuine and effective public participation legitimizes decisions, allows issues to be aired, facilitates the generation and analysis of various options, and permits for more effective oversight. And, if the public recognizes the need for flexibility in the face of changing conditions, political leaders can modify projects much more easily than otherwise. The focus on participation does not fit the rational actor model for it incorporates a different view of rationality, one that at least implicitly guides the alternative planning and decision models that were labeled "adaptive" and which, as noted above, facilitate flexibility in making and implementing project decisions.

Public participation in transportation (as in many other technological sectors) is complicated by the technical nature of many of the issues involved. One scholar has identified this "problem of democracy" as follows (Meadowcraft 1997;185): "Any planning process involves specialist inputs and expert decision making. But if sustainability planning is to have any chance of success, it must also be based on popular inputs. How are the two to be reconciled?" This dilemma cannot be resolved easily but various mechanisms have been developed that hold promise of resolving this dilemma. Perhaps the best known is the "consensus conference," pioneered in Denmark, which has generated widespread attention in Europe and been applied in the U.S. (Durant 1995; Sclove 1996)

Other mechanisms that can be used to enhance the quality of public participation also deserve consideration. One problem area that plagues public participation is that people are often discussing projects based on questionable assumptions. Such assumptions and forecasts are usually formulated by planners but seldom are they subject to critical analysis. At least two possible approaches to resolving this problem have been suggested in various contexts. One involves working within the group by appointing a "devil's advocate." One or more decision makers are explicitly charged with questioning every aspect of a proposed policy or project. Although promising, this approach is no panacea for the assigned opponent can merely add legitimacy to a process or become marginalized (Jervis 1976). Even if this mechanism does not lead to better proposals, publication of the proceedings can serve an important educational function for the public. The concept of "transparency" is obviously critical in this regard.

The second approach moves beyond the group. It requires that the community and others scrutinize the assumptions within a risk analysis framework that assigns probabilities to various options. This approach will not necessarily lead to a community consensus over highly politicized and controversial projects because many factors can prevent such an outcome (Lewis 1995). Still, such a procedure which has at its core opportunities for all viewpoints to be considered and analyzed minimizes the danger of polarization and enhances the possibility of achieving an outcome that is acceptable.

Yet, for most planners and decision makers, a search for the holy grail of optimal efficiency remains the goal. A more effective approach would focus on keeping options open, creating robust and resilient organizations, other key dimensions of flexibility — the ability to hedge and to make adjustments as conditions change. Moreover, it is essential to accept the reality that the attempt to optimize efficiency often yields illusory savings. In many cases it is advantageous to invest in back up systems that may be viewed as redundant and unnecessary, creating reserves to deal with unexpected contingencies and developing organizational cultures that values learning and adaptation to new conditions and takes public involvement in the decision process seriously (Goetz and Szyliowicz 1997).

CONCLUSION

Development of any sort is highly dependent upon and influenced by the structure and functioning of the transportation system. There is now a widespread feeling that transportation must be viewed through a new paradigm because the narrow approach that has prevailed until now has created a system that is not consonant with current and future needs. Its infrastructure has been largely designed to meet economic needs, narrowly defined. The problem, however, goes beyond mega projects, important though these may be. It is also necessary to consider new policies such as pricing reforms that will facilitate the development of sustainable intermodal systems.

At the project level, it is clear that the ways in which planning and decision making takes place need to change. Continued reliance by planners and decision makers of the rational actor model is not only futile but will do little to resolve the serious problems that confront transportation or transform this sector into one that is consonant with sustainable development. New models that incorporate flexibility and which are more appropriate to the political and other realities of transportation planning in the modern world are required.

Clearly, transportation has entered into a new era. The serious problems of infrastructure which plague the United States and many other countries cannot be resolved effectively or efficiently without new approaches that incorporate the principles outlined herein. The first step in addressing these challenges is to ensure that elites and the public recognize the shortcomings of existing practices. Whether dealing with projects or policies a new public consensus is required. A new vision will not be realized until elite and public values change. There are, fortunately, many signs that such change is underway, but much remains to be done in all countries and at the international level.

Of equal importance is the development of more powerful theoretical tools that will enable us to better understand and predict decision processes and be of greater utility for practitioners and decision makers. In this area, political scientists have much to contribute though to date, the discipline has paid relatively little attention to such topics. Success or failure in mega projects will always be determined by the ways in which the political system operates, the attitudes and skills of its elites, and the patterns of public participation. Only if the conditions for success are created, will projects—and policies—in transportation and other sectors that promote sustainable development be designed and implemented. The costs of failing to do so are becoming higher all the time.

REFERENCES

Allison, Graham T. 1971. *Essence of Decision: Explaining the Cuban Missile Crisis.* Boston: Little, Brown, and Company.

Axelrod, Robert. 1976. *Structure of Decision.* Princeton, N.J.: Princeton University Press.

Baker, Robert F., Richard M. Michaels and Everett S. Preston. 1975. *Public Policy Development: Linking the Technical and Political Processes.* New York: Wiley.

Brooks, David. 1990. "Beyond Catch Phrases: What Does Sustainable Development Really Mean." *IDRC Reports* 25, October.

Collingridge, David. 1992. *The Management of Scale: Big Organizations, Big Decisions, Big Mistakes.* London: Routledge.

Collingridge, David and Peter James. 1991. "Inflexible Energy Policies in a Rapidly Changing Market." *Long Range Planning* 24: 101–08.

Daly, H. 1990. "Towards Some Operational Principles of Sustainable Development, Ecological Economics." Cited in *Pollution Prevention and Control: Environmental Criteria for Sustainable Transport.*" Working Paper of the PPGC Task Force on Transport, OECD, Paris, 1996.

Dempsey, P., A. Goetz and J. Szyliowicz. 1997. *Denver International Airport, Lessons Learnt*. New York: McGraw Hill.

Diesing, Paul. 1962. *Reason in Society*. Urbana, Ill: University of Illinois Press.

Dron, D. and M. C. de Lara. 1995. *Pour une politique soutenable des transports* Paris: La Documentation Francaise.

Etzioni, Amitai. 1967. "Mixed-Scanning: A Third Approach to Decision-Making." *Public Administration Review* 27: 385–92.

———. 1986. "Mixed-Scanning Revisited." *Public Administration Review* 46: 8–14.

Evans, J.S. 1991. "Strategic Flexibility for High Technology Manoeuvres: A Conceptual Framework" *Journal of Management Studies* 28: 69–89.

Feldman, Elliot J. 1985. "Patterns of Failure in Government Megaprojects," in *Global Dilemmas*, S.P. Huntington and J.S. Nye, Jr., eds. Cambridge: The Center for International Affairs, Harvard University and University Press of America.

Goetz, A. and J. Szyliowicz. 1997. *Revisiting Transportation Planning and Decision Making Theory. Transportation Research, Part A.*

Goetz, A., J. Szyliowicz and P. Dempsey. 1996. "Transportation and International Sustainable Development: A Preliminary Conceptualization and Application." Paper presented to OECD International Conference on Transportation and Sustainable Development, Vancouver.

Greenaway, John, Steve Smith and John Street. 1992. *Deciding Factors in British Politics: A Case-Studies Approach*. London: Routledge.

Hall, Peter. 1982. *Great Planning Disasters*. Berkeley: University of California Press.

Hirschman, Albert O. 1967. *Development Projects Observed*. Washington, D.C.: Brookings Institution.

Jervis, Robert. 1976. *Perception and Misperception in International Politics*. Princeton, N.J.: Princeton University Press.

Joss, S. and J. Durant, eds. 1995. *Public Participation in Science: The Role of Consensus Conferences in Europe*. London: Science Museum.

Khisty, C. J. 1996. "Education and Training of Transportation Engineers and Planners Vis-a-Vis Public Involvement." *Transportation Research Record* 1552.

Levy, John M. 1994. *Contemporary Urban Planning*. 3rd ed. Englewood Cliffs, N.J.: Prentice-Hall.

Levy, S.M. 1996. *Build, Operate, Transfer*. N.Y.: J. Wiley and Sons.

Lindblom, Charles E. 1959. "The Science of Muddling Through." *Public Administration Review* 19: 79–88.

Linstone, Harold A. 1984. *Multiple Perspectives for Decision-Making: Bridging the Gap between Analysis and Action*. New York: North-Holland.

March, James G., and Herbert A. Simon. 1958. *Organizations*. New York: Wiley.

Meyerson, Martin and Edward C. Banfield. 1955. *Politics, Planning, and the Public Interest*. Glencoe, Ill.: The Free Press.

Morone, J.G. and E.J. Woodhouse. 1986. *Averting Catastrophe: Strategies for Regulating Risky Technologies*. Berkeley: University of California Press.

Morris, Peter, and George Hough. 1987. *The Anatomy of Major Projects*. New York: John Wiley.

Murphy, K.J. 1983. *Macroproject Development in the Third World*. Boulder, Colo: Westview Press. *New York Times*, May 11, 1997,

OECD. 1996. *Pollution Prevention and Control: Environmental Criteria for Sustainable Transport*. Paris.

Replogle, M. 1995. "Sustainable Transportation Strategies for Third-World Development." *Transportation Research Record* 1294.

Rycroft, Robert W. and Joseph S. Szyliowicz. 1980. "The Technological Dimension of Decision-Making: The Case of the Aswan High Dam." *World Politics* 32: 36–61.

Schulman, P. R. 1980 *Large Scale Policy Making*. New York: Elsevier.

Sclove, R. 1996. "Town Meetings on Technology." *Technology Review*.

Simon, Herbert. 1955. *Administrative Behavior*. New York: MacMillan and Co.

Steinbruner, John D. 1974. *Cybernetic Theory of Decision*. Princeton, N.J.: Princeton University Press.

Szyliowicz, Joseph S. 1991. *Politics, Technology, and Development*. St. Antony's College Series. London: McMillan Press Ltd.

Szyliowicz, Joseph S. and Andrew Goetz. 1996. "Getting Realistic About Megaproject Planning." *Policy Sciences*.

Wachs, Martin. 1985. "Planning, Organizations and Decision-Making: A Research Agenda." *Transportation Research* 19A: 521–31.

———. 1995. "The Political Context of Transportation Policy," in *The Geography of Urban Transportation*, S. Hanson, S., ed. New York: Guilford Press, 269–86.

Webber, Melvin M. 1976. "The BART Experience—What Have We Learned?" *The Public Interest* 45: 76–108.

Weiss, Andrew and Edward Woodhouse. 1992. "Reframing Incrementalism: A Constructive Response to the Critics." *Policy Sciences* 25: 255–73.

11

The European Union and International Environmental Cooperation

Charlotte Bretherton and John Vogler

Students of international environmental politics have increasingly recognized the significance of various nonstate actors. Analyses of the positive contribution of epistemic communities (Haas 1990) and NGOs (Princen and Finger 1994) are prominent in the literature. Less attention has been paid to another "new actor"—the European Union, or to be more legally precise in many circumstances, "the European Community acting within its competencies."[1] Yet in terms of its presence in the world system, as measured by trade volumes or pollutants emitted, the EU with its single market must rank with the United States. Even a cursory reading of commentaries on recent international environmental politics will reveal that the Union is viewed as a significant player in its own right. Europe has interests and aspirations, takes up positions, is urged to act, negotiates and implements. Usually this is no more than a convenient shorthand, used with at least some awareness of the complex and often arcane relationships between fifteen Member States and the European Community—operating, since the Treaty of Maastricht, within the broad framework of the European Union. Yet it also reflects the legal reality that over the last twenty years the community has come to participate in no less than thirty-one major multilateral environmental agreements (MEAs).

These developments have a number of implications for international environmental cooperation. Arguments about the expanding role for the European Union might be seen as a contemporary version of the universalism versus regionalism debate that characterized discussion of the evolution of international organization and the promotion of peace more than a generation ago. In 1945 E. H. Carr wrote about a dangerous fascination with the "lure of universality":

> A world organization may be a necessary convenience as well as a valuable symbol. But the intermediate unit is more likely to be the operative factor in the transition from nationalism to internationalism. (Carr 1945: 45)

This has echoes today in discussions of the political response to global environmental change. The fact that we may be able to identify the global scope of some processes of environmental degradation and to conceptualize them in terms of a single global system does not necessarily mean that effective remedial action can only be taken at a global level. On the contrary the regionalist position is in the words of Inis Claude's (1965: 96) influential treatment:

> . . . that the regional unit is capable of more effective organizational action than the global unit; the stress is placed here on the nature of the unit rather than the nature of the problem. This consideration points to one of the most basic dilemmas of international organization: the disparity between *needs* for organization and *capacity* for organization.

Claude also points out that there is another regionalist proposition, which may seem appropriate to present circumstances, that the ultimate world system would have not one but several cores and that world organization would be formed by the combination of regional building blocks. Whether the EU could or should play such a role in the development of the architecture of international environmental cooperation is a difficult and largely unexplored question. Nitze (1990) suggested that separate regional approaches could provide the pillars of an overarching world climate change regime.

On the other hand, it might be asserted that the sheer scale of the EU militates against the kind of effective local action that is required. Clearly, however the EU is not a highly centralized political system and both future enlargement and the broad application of the subsidiarity principle may reinforce a tendency towards decentralization, at least to the Member State level. Moreover, the Commission makes strenuous efforts to forge direct links with regional and local authorities and NGOs at the grassroots level (reflected, for example, in the concept of partnership, which is a condition governing allocation and administration of structural funding under the European Regional Development Fund). At the same time the EU is, first and foremost, a huge single market and trading bloc with an evident propensity to expand its borders. This highlights the need for such a globally significant unit to behave in an environmentally responsible manner. Considerable importance attaches to the extent to which the trade promotion strategies and many of the other external policies of the Union—such as its pursuit of fishing opportunities outside European waters—can be subject to the disciplines of sustainable development set out in the Maastricht and Amsterdam treaties.

These are matters of great significance but they are essentially beyond the scope of this paper that has a narrower focus on the mechanics of international environmental cooperation. The question posed here is whether the development of the EC/EU as an actor in its own right either supplanting or, more usually, operating alongside the Member States has been conducive to the effective negotiation and implementation of MEAs. The starting point is an investigation into the nature of this participation and the extent to which the EU can be regarded as an actor distinct from the aggregate of its fifteen Member States. This turns out to be a rather more complex subject than one might imagine from the press reporting of, say, EU-U.S. deliberations at the 1997 Kyoto Conference of the Parties to the Climate Change Convention. Here the EU is often treated as if it were a state alongside the other parties, which include its own Member States. While, despite the enthusiasm of European Federalists, the EU is not comparable to a state it can appear in various guises as an independent and potent actor in international negotiations. The determinants of the EU/EC's status as an actor and the ways in which it actually participates in international environmental diplomacy form the first part of this paper.

In the second part, we turn to a brief analysis of the possible advantages and disadvantages of EU as opposed to Member State involvement in international environmental cooperation. Here opinions have differed markedly. At one extreme Benedick's (1991) first hand account of dealing with the EC and its Member States during the Montreal Protocol negotiations portrays them as a real impediment to progress. On the other, the authors of the Community's *Agenda 2000* claim:

> The Union has, on various occasions, confirmed its leading role in this field where it is particularly well placed for taking the leadership in international negotiations in order to reconcile conflicting interests (European Commission 1997b: 29).

BASES OF EU PARTICIPATION IN ENVIRONMENTAL DIPLOMACY

The burgeoning of EC/EU involvement in international environmental diplomacy during the 1980s and 1990s is the external consequence of well-known internal policy developments. From a position in which the 1958 Rome Treaty (TEC) was entirely silent on environmental matters, there is now a very substantial body of EC legislation and environmental policy backed up by full Community competence in critical areas such as atmospheric pollution and the disposal of hazardous wastes. As their transboundary and indeed global aspects increasingly appeared on the international agenda the Community was necessarily drawn into international environmental politics alongside its

Member States. At the same time, in a process reinforced by progressive insertion of sustainability requirements into the Community treaties, an important environmental dimension opened up in the trade, agricultural and fisheries policies which had long been at the heart of the EC and where the Commission's powers to conduct external relations on behalf of the Community as a whole were at their strongest. However the EU is not really a single actor; rather it is, often simultaneously, several different actors. Thus, under certain circumstances it resembles an international organization; in others a state; in yet others it resembles neither. To complicate matters further, the boundaries are indistinct; competencies shift over time and the EC/EU can change its character during the course of a negotiation. Nowhere is this more evident than in the conduct of international environmental diplomacy.

As a starting point there are really two modal types involved in EU external policy. First, exclusive Member State competence where unanimity voting in the Council gives each of the fifteen Member State governments an effective national veto, the Commission has, at best, a subsidiary and implementing function and the role of spokesperson and leader is assumed by the Council Presidency acting with the support of the previous and the next Member State government to hold that position (the troika). The paradigmatic example is provided by Common Foreign and Security Policy conducted within Pillar II of Maastricht. There is here an attempt to establish a distinct EU policy but the degree of autonomy is sharply constrained and efforts will often be dogged by inconsistency between Member States. Once a policy has been decided, however, the EU has the authority to deploy a range of inducements and sanctions deriving from Common Policies and involving the Commission.

At the other end of the spectrum lies what is known in Brussels as external relations—areas where exclusive Community as opposed to Member State competence has been achieved. The classic manifestation from the Treaty of Rome onwards involves the conduct of trade relations, the Common Commercial Policy under Articles 113, 228 and 229 [133, 300 and 301].[2] Here the Commission initiates policy, conducts negotiations and maintains relations with the relevant international organizations and deploys a range of trade policy instruments—notably anti-dumping penalties.[3] When external relations are conducted in this way there is no question that the EC appears at its most potent as a single actor in the shape of the Commission. Even here, however, there is still an authority relationship between the Member States and the Commission. While the Commission proposes policy the General Affairs Council agrees negotiating mandates and concludes agreements, although it will act by qualified majority. During negotiations and in the day-to-day conduct of Commercial Policy the Member States will continue to keep a watching brief over the Commission via the Article 113 Committee, which is composed of national trade officials.

The difficulty that arises in the field of external environmental policy is that *neither* model generally applies. Instead there is usually a situation of mixed competence where Member States and the Commission have concurrent powers. This introduces a number of complications into environmental diplomacy where the actor characteristics of the EU can shift even within the course of a single day's negotiation. The exact form in which the EC/EU appears in various environmental policy settings will depend upon, and be disputed in relation to, two sets of considerations: 1) competence as agreed and adjudicated by Community institutions and 2) external recognition by the rest of the international system.

INTERNAL AND EXTERNAL COMPETENCE

Competence is the EU term for "powers" in relation to the institutions and the Member States.[4] The location of competence has continually shifted during the life of the European Community, subject as it is to complex political wrangling between Member States jealous of their sovereignty, a Commission and Parliament eager to extend their reach and regular adjudication by rulings of the European Court of Justice (ECJ). Needless to say, this has provided a fertile field for ingenious legal argument over the interpretation of the treaties and of such arcane concepts as teleology, pre-emption and exhaustion.[5]

Initially, exclusive competence for the Community was limited to one or two areas in which it was expressly provided in the Treaty of Rome. However, as the Community's policies developed, conflicts began to emerge between internal legislation and the external agreements made by Member States. In an important leading case the ERTA judgment of 1970, the ECJ went well beyond the provisions of the Treaty of Rome by establishing the doctrine of parallelism: that is to say when the Community acquires internal competence over a subject it also acquires external competence—*in interno in foro externo*.[6] This had major and continuing implications for the conduct of external environmental policy and provides the decisive link with the development of internal policy.[7] Competencies cannot be precisely listed, because the issues involved in each new negotiation will be different and the internal situation within the Union may alter. The determination of competence can often be a difficult and niggling politico-legal process that pits the institutional ambitions of the Commission against the determination of some Member States to resist "competence creep." The situation may be further complicated by tensions within the Commission between the various DGs responsible for aspects of external policy.[8]

As we have seen, where questions under consideration relate entirely to trade, agriculture or fisheries there is exclusive Community competence and Art 113 [133] type procedures apply. Thus, for example, at the UN Conference on Straddling Stocks and Highly Migratory Fish Stocks, concluded in August 1995, the EC had exclusive competence and the Commission negotiated for the Community on a Council mandate.[9] Even here there can be problems, for at the time of the Council Conclusion on this particular agreement the Spanish government objected to exclusive competence. An example of the lengths to which politico-legal disputes over competence can go is provided by EC accession to the 1981 Convention on Antarctic Marine Living Resources (CAMLR). Member States objected to exclusive competence on grounds of teleology. The CAMLR is a new type of fisheries agreement, in that its Article II involves a total ecosystem view of marine conservation. Clearly its purpose is not simply to preserve fish stocks (a Community competence) but also to protect other forms of life dependent upon them—notably penguins. Penguins are, of course, birds. However, Community competence for the preservation of birds under its Bird Directive only extends to Europe, not the Southern Ocean. Consequently objections were made to exclusive Community competence in those parts of the Convention relating to total allowable catches (Macrory and Hession 1996: 132).

Most environmental issues involve mixed agreements and concurrent competence[10], where representation is legally shared between the Presidency and the Commission. For example, trade and air pollution issues in the stratospheric ozone negotiations, leading to the 1987 Montreal Protocol, gave the Community competence, while other matters were reserved to Member States. The boundaries of competence were under active dispute within the Community delegation during the negotiation of the Montreal Protocol which overlapped the EC's own deliberations on the Single European Act. This was to reduce the number of areas in which Member States alone could make agreements. Since then competence disputes have moderated somewhat through the clarifications on environmental policy provided by the Single European Act and the Treaty of Maastricht 1992.

Nonetheless, for the majority of external environmental policy issues competence continues to be divided and negotiations mixed. A good, current example is provided by the 1989 Basel Convention for the Control of Transboundary Movements of Hazardous Waste and their Disposal. It has trade aspects where there is 100 percent Community competence, science and development assistance aspects where competence is reserved to Member States, and environmental aspects where competence is concurrent. Negotiations under the 1992 Biodiversity Convention are also marked by divided competencies, with a strong Community position on trade and intellectual property, but Member State competence in other areas.

In the long drawn out process of developing the Framework Convention on Climate Change (FCCC) the Member States have been dominant but the Commission and aspects of Community competence have been increasingly involved.[11]

EXTERNAL RECOGNITION

Sovereign states alone were the traditional parties to public international law, but since World War II international organizations have acquired objective legal personality—that is to say a status that exists even if denied by the governments of some sovereign states. The European Economic Community was provided with such a personality in the Treaty of Rome, along with the right, subsequently extended to cover environmental questions, to conclude international agreements in specific areas.[12] Thus, it will be noted that the European Economic Community (since 1993 The European Community) appears as a signatory of recent multilateral environmental agreements; the Montreal Protocol, the Framework Convention on Climate Change and the Convention on Biodiversity, alongside the Member States. The European Union, as established by the Maastricht Treaty of 1992, does not have personality in international law, although at the 1996 to 1997 Inter-Governmental Conference there were unsuccessful moves to endow it with such status.[13]

The development of the EC as a negotiating actor in the environmental field also depended upon what other participants were willing to accept that while the EC's own Member States have not always been willing to allow the separate representation of the Community. There have been continuing disagreements as the Commission has sought to extend its external competence and provide the Community with a distinct voice in environmental diplomacy. An important foundation was laid during the negotiations to establish the 1979 Long-Range Transboundary Air Pollution (LRTAP) Convention. In this first foray of the EC into a multilateral environmental negotiation, the Commission was involved alongside Member States because it had competence in matters of atmospheric pollution. Initially the Soviet Union was opposed to any EC participation but was subsequently prepared to agree to a new formulation designed to cope with this new actor which was not a state but which was to be recognized as a Regional Economic Integration Organization (REIO). This was apparently in the expectation that similar status would be accorded to COMECON—a long-standing Soviet ambition (Interview Commission). In such a way the concept that has covered EC recognition in all subsequent major multilateral environmental conventions was born. Soviet aims were never realized and, to date, the EC is the only extant example of the REIO that is provided for in the operation of the various conventions.

Having REIO status has come to mean that the EC can be party to a convention without any of its Member States being a party. However, when one or more of the latter are also parties "the organization and its Member States shall decide on their respective responsibilities for the performance of their obligations under the convention or protocol" (Vienna Convention 1985: article13(2)). Voting rights are accorded equivalent to the number of states that are parties, subject to the proviso that the organization shall not exercise its right at the same time as any member state and vice versa (Vienna Convention 1985: article 15). As one U.S. diplomat rather wearily put it, "We don't mind what they do as long as they all don't want to vote at the same time" (Interview). Development of the REIO concept was not easy, particularly during the stratospheric ozone negotiations 1985 to 1997. Since that time, however, the REIO provisions have been repeated, practically verbatim, in the FCCC and Biodiversity Conventions.[14]

Aside from the REIO pattern, established for multilateral negotiations under the various conventions, the EC has no automatic right of participation. Such rights have been negotiated on a case-by-case basis—and have frequently been contested by Member States. In practice the EC currently has full member status in only three international organisations (as opposed to treaty-based organizations such as UNCTAD or various conferences of the Parties in which the EC operates as an REIO). They are the Food and Agriculture Organization (FAO), the European Bank for Reconstruction and Development (EBRD) and the World Trade Organization (WTO).

Much high profile environmental diplomacy is conducted under the auspices of the UN General Assembly. Here the EC has had very incomplete and ambivalent status. The relevant 1974 General Assembly Resolution merely grants it observer rights, and nonvoting status is the rule in most organizations in the UN family.[15] This is true of UNEP. However observer status, in this case, has been modified to allow regular consultation and exchanges of documents between the Commission and UNEP (Macleod, Hendry, and Hyett 1996: 337). Just before the Rio Earth Summit (UNCED) in April 1992 the EC was finally granted full participant status in an amendment to the draft rules of procedure, on the express understanding that this applied only to the forthcoming conference and not beyond (Brinkhorst 1994: 612; Mensah 1996: 32). This meant that the EC briefly acquired rights equivalent to those of participating states, except for voting and the submission of procedural motions. The outcome was the result of what a DGXI official describes as a huge battle" with Member States arising from the possible implication for the EC's status at the UN (Interview). A permanent memorial is to be found on the first page of *Agenda 21,* which contains the footnote:

> when the term Governments is used, it will be deemed to include the European Economic Community within its areas of competence. In relation to *Agenda 21* these areas of competence are, indeed, very extensive—ranging across substantial areas of the document (European Commission 1997a).

Although the same formula was used for EC participation in subsequent UN conferences on Habitat, Health and Environment and the Food Summit of 1996, it took three weeks of preparatory discussion to insert it into the documentation for the General Assembly Special Session, which reviewed UNCED in June 1997. Not only were some Member States unhappy, but there was also opposition from regional groups such as the Latin American Mercosur, which regarded the special treatment afforded the Community as discriminatory. Commission officials also had to ensure that President Jacques Santer was afforded equivalent status to national leaders attending (Interview Commission). Similar difficulties occurred in relation to participation in the Commission for Sustainable Development (CSD), established as a follow-up to UNCED.[16]

The situation in terms of participation rights as with competence is, thus, not static and the Commission has to argue its way towards establishing and maintaining the participation of the Community. For example, at the UNEP/FAO sponsored negotiations to establish legally binding prior informed consent (PIC) procedures for trade in hazardous chemicals and pesticides, the Community initially attended as an observer but was able to upgrade its participation to include voting rights on the grounds that it had been, since 1991, a full member of the FAO and that the legal instruments under consideration would fall within the exclusive competence of the Community (Interview Commission).

ENVIRONMENTAL DIPLOMACY AND THE CONDUCT OF NEGOTIATIONS

Where there is Community competence, the process of negotiating an international agreement commences with the Commission exercising its right of initiative and seeking a mandate from the Council of Ministers; "which shall authorize the Commission to open the necessary negotiations," voting by qualified majority.[17] The politics of formulating and agreeing on a mandate may be both lengthy and significant and represents the first of a number of points in the process at which Member States can assert their interests and determine the development of Community policy. In environmental policy the preliminary phase of formulating the Commission's approach will normally involve interservice consultations between the various interested DGs, analogous, in many ways, to the interdepartmental policy coordination (or bureaucratic politics) that is the stuff of national foreign policy making. The Commission's DGXI, responsible for many but not all aspects of environmental policy, is surprisingly small in size compared with national ministries and other Commission DGs. This, coupled with the intersectoral character of many issues, will make the internal deliberations quite extensive and often difficult involving complex lobbying between private sector groups, governments and Community institutions (Sbragia 1996; Wurzel 1996).

In some areas the Commission will not have competence and be relatively inactive (in most negotiations there is some existing legislative base to sustain a Commission mandate) and there will be a reliance upon a lead country approach involving inputs from key Member States which have particular interests and expertise.[18] In fact less than half the Member States are usually active and three or four positions are likely to emerge rather than 15. Where there can be no Commission proposal for a mandate the formal responsibility falls upon the Member State holding the Presidency of the Council of Ministers (assisted by an informal version of the troika involving the past and future presidencies). Thus, for example, the March 1997 Council decision on a common 15 percent reduction target for the FCCC Kyoto Conference of the Parties was engineered by the Dutch Presidency. If a small Member State, such as Luxembourg, holds the Presidency it will only be able to employ two or three of its own officials to specialize on environmental issues and there will necessarily be greater reliance on other Member States and upon DGI of the General Secretariat of the Council.[19] Depending upon the issues under discussion the Commission will also be consulted and cooperation here is markedly better than under the analogous Pillar II CFSP procedures. It is also worth remembering that negotiations are not isolated events. They occur within the context of existing international organizations and their secretariats with which the Commission has a continuous and active relationship involving technical and budgetary matters. This "special relationship" exists even with the Climate Change Secretariat in Bonn (Interview Commission).

Third party governments, especially those which, like the U.S. government, are in continual policy dialogue with the EC and have missions equipped to cope with its internal complexities, will also attempt to obtain intelligence and influence this phase of EC decision making. This effort is paralleled by NGOs and by corporate interests notably in the form of the EU Committee of the American Chamber of Commerce in Belgium, which takes a very active interest in environment and trade questions. Smaller countries will obviously not have such facilities and will relate to the Brussels system in a piecemeal fashion depending upon their particular national interests.

Dealing with the EU in its various institutional manifestations is quite unlike dealing with other governments:

> There is no other organisation like the EU—it operates differently—the dynamics of policy are different. The Commission itself is a very politically sensitive body. Which nationality gets which post in a DG is crucial. The United States, in dealing with the Commission, is typically drawn to the UK and Irish (officials) with a similar cultural outlook, and to Germans and Scandinavians. The French and the Southern Europeans are more reticent. Unofficial "finding out on the Brussels circuit" is very important. Sometimes people at the Commission will tell you which Member State to square. You have to be very vigilant in Brussels—so much is going on that it is difficult to keep your finger on the pulse of every issue (Interview, Brussels Mission).

When a Commission proposal emerges it is initially considered by the Council Working Group on the Environment involving officials from the Permanent Representation of Member States and from the Commission. This is one level below the Committee of Permanent Representatives (COREPER) and does the detailed work on the mandate. Having been agreed by COREPER the mandate will then be considered by the Environment formation of the Council of Ministers, although because its meetings are relatively infrequent it may also be approved by another formation of the Council. The negotiating mandate that is finally agreed is a confidential document and under the revised terms of Art 228 [300] it will be adopted by different decision-making procedures depending upon the issues under consideration. The mandate will establish competencies in what is usually a mixed negotiation; provide a set of binding directives and give greater or lesser freedom of maneuvre to the Commission, and of course to itself, in the conduct of negotiations (Macrory and Hession 1996: 135–36). Preparation for a conference involves the same basic procedures, although there will be no mandate but instead a common platform.

In a mixed negotiation there are likely to be difficulties at the margins of competence. For, with the best will in the world, the actual course that the talks will take and the issues that will be raised cannot always be predicted. On occasion it may be possible for a direct link to be established between the EC delegation and the Council. For example, during the Basel Convention negotiations in Geneva there was a parallel Council meeting in Luxembourg, which allowed constant reference back, updating and amendment of positions. Generally this will not be possible and for a week-long negotiation there will be no opportunity to activate COREPER and consequently decisions will be left to coordination meetings held at the negotiations. With a longer negotiation there can be reference back to Brussels as was the case in the 1995 Jakarta meeting on a biosafety protocol to the Biodiversity Convention. Here Member States felt that the Commission was going too far and matters were put on hold while other delegations were left in ignorance of the Community's position.[20]

The particular manifestation of the EU presented to other parties to an international environmental negotiation will also be determined by the Council acting with reference to Art 228 [300]. If competence is exclusive the Commission will negotiate, but the delegation will include at least one Member State representative and there may be a full Art 113 type committee.[21] In a mixed negotiation, there will be separate Commission and Member State delegations that will divide up responsibilities, including speaking responsibilities, according to competence. Normally when there is a common position which is not an exclusive Community competence the Member State which is President in Office of the Council will speak for all using the formula "On behalf of the Community and its Member States (Macrory and Hession 1996: 136).

After some early problems, members of EC delegations and outsiders have come to live with this "bicephalous" arrangement in mixed negotiations. Once a coordination meeting has taken up a position all are bound by it. Both Member State and Commission sources have attested to the improvement in Community solidarity at negotiations. One Member State negotiator observed that over the last three years, in which he had been an active participant, there had been a notable "tightening up" allowing less space for Member States to go their own way (Interview). Most problems seem to occur within UN General Assembly fora, where as we have seen, the status of the EC/EU is uncertain and there continues to be a certain "lack of Community discipline." In this context diplomats, accustomed to intergovernmental negotiations, have been faced with novel interventions from "little environmental women" who say "Sorry, I will talk on this matter because it falls within Community competence" (Interview Commission). The precise division of competence in any negotiation is a confidential matter. From the perspective of Member State officials the question of whether competence issues will be "pushed" rather than merely "raised" as a matter of routine can often depend upon the presence or absence of particular personalities with parochial agendas to pursue. Of importance too is the extent to which there is an atmosphere of trust between the officials dealing with a specific negotiation. On occasion more time can be spent arguing about who will speak, than about the substance of what is to be said (Interview Member State Official). These internal discussions will frequently interact with the negotiations proper. As one member of a Commission delegation put it:

> Negotiation is a three card game. We don't tell third parties which articles are covered by Community competence and which by Member States' (competence). They would never let you say this and it allows us to wash our dirty linen in private (Interview Commission).

The "washing of dirty linen" and the day-to-day planning of negotiating strategy is conducted in EC coordination meetings. These are held every morning during a negotiation, and sometimes at midday and in the evening too. This can be onerous for Member State representatives who may find themselves rising at 6 a.m. and being forced to hold national delegation meetings late at night.[22] Much depends upon the leadership role of whichever Member State holds the Presidency. If the Presidency is not strong the Commission sees its role as "doing the work for them" and also acting as a "sheepdog" to round up straying Member State representatives (Interview Commission). On the other hand even a "strong" Presidency will, on occasion, delegate responsibility for making first drafts of EC positions to Member State representatives, who either volunteer or are requested to take the lead. This may also suit the Commission, which can lack the resources itself to undertake the task. In circumstances where competence is shared, Commission officials assist the Presidency but do not supplant it as formal negotiator.

The final stage of a negotiation involves signature and ratification. Article 228 [300] does not specifically mention the signature of agreements, but the practice is to seek Council approval for this. There is then the ratification procedure that is described, in EC terminology, as the Council Conclusion. An important aspect of this Conclusion is that the Council will make a formal statement of the legal bases upon which the agreement is concluded, involving citation of the relevant Treaty articles. Normally the decision-making procedure involves qualified majority voting and consultation of the European Parliament within a strict timetable (McGoldrick 1997: 91–92; Macrory and Hession 1996: 138–39). Implementing legislation, if this is required, must be on the table at the same time. The process can extend over two years or more.

THE EU AND INTERNATIONAL ENVIRONMENTAL COOPERATION: AN EVALUATION

As we noted at the outset the sheer scale of the EU will make it (however configured) the main protagonist of the United States in the business of international environmental cooperation. Yet what has the involvement of this variable and idiosyncratic entity meant for the efficient creation and implementation of MEAs? What follows attempts to sketch in some of the arguments and evidence that might be used in determining this question.

Interest Aggregation

One apparent benefit of EU "actorness" is that by coordinating the activities of fifteen states in one unit, the geometry of international negotiations will be greatly simplified. Some of the international cooperation literature goes further than this in asserting that agreements amongst a restricted set of powerful players are most conducive to effective agreements (Krasner 1985: 262–64; Feldman 1992: 44–46). This is not just an abstraction from game theoretical experiments but also a commonly held oligopolistic rather than a hegemonic view of regime formation, which would fit well with the bargaining structure to be found in the GATT/WTO or in the Montreal Protocol negotiations, dominated, as they were at the outset, by two blocs—the Toronto Group and the EC—representing most of the then producers and users of CFCs (yet by the 1990 London meeting the interests of other potential consumers and producers had to be considered). Most other environmental negotiations, including those for climate change, have had a more multilateral character, but it remains true that if the United States and European Union can coordinate their positions, their influence is, in the diplomatic words of one participant, "not insignificant" (Interview Brussels Mission).

The existence of blocs and rather different from a bloc, powerful regional actors like the Union, will not in itself lead to desirable outcomes, but is simply a fact of international life that will have varying consequences. For example during the Vienna Convention and Montreal Protocol negotiations the EC managed with difficulty to act as an entity but hardly a very positive one. As a British participant explains the Member States ". . . marched in step for a reason that owed little to their individual views on the ecological consequences of CFCs: their mutual obligations under the Treaty of Rome" (Szell 1993: 36). Arguably, the CFC ban would have arrived rather sooner if the majority of Member States had been allowed to make natural alliances with outsiders who also sought progress rather than being bound by Community discipline. The EU because of its internal architecture is, of course, more than a bloc. It thus has a stability, joint policy making capability and longevity not experienced with single issue coalitions of states such as the Toronto Group in the stratospheric ozone negotiations or the JUSCANZ (Japan, United States, Canada, Australia, and New Zealand) group in the climate talks.

There is also a positive case to be made out for the Union if it can, by acting as a unit, reconcile differences between economies at varying levels of development, in very different situations and with opposing administrative traditions, all or any of which might otherwise have precluded agreement or at least led to a less desirable outcome (this effect may apply with greater force after the eastern enlargement of the EU). Commission staff often refer to the "added value" derived from a common approach to environmental problems. An important example is provided by the way the EC has developed its "bubble" concept, whereby regional partners negotiate differential contributions to a common target for emission reductions. The mechanism for this was first devised within the EC as a means of successfully concluding the Large Combustion Plant Directive (Nitze 1990: 24–25).[23] Subsequently, it has provided a framework within which very different national requirements for greenhouse gas emission reductions (or in the case of the Southern members of the Union, increases) can be accommodated within a common negotiating position.[24] The common EU position of a 15 percent reduction for a basket of three greenhouse gases was outwardly impressive in comparison to the United States and Japanese approaches to the Kyoto Conference of the Parties to the FCCC.

There were, however, two problems directly related to the EU's lack of actor capability. The United States and other negotiating partners raised the objection that, unlike a single state, the EU could not be held collectively liable for its common commitment to a 15 percent reduction. Other parties in the preparatory AGBM (Ad hoc Group on the Berlin Mandate) were able to "use it as a stick" to beat the EU, demanding that the Union deal with its own internal legal problems before they would be prepared to negotiate (Interview Member State Official). The target, as we have seen, did not have a legal basis in Community competence and there is no Commission mandate. Neither was the target entirely credible given the absence of internal policy to achieve it. The furore occasioned by the Commission's previously unsuccessful attempts to bring forward a carbon tax will be recalled, along with the rooted objections of Member States to the extension of Community competence in the fields of energy and taxation. Common carbon/energy taxation and energy saving measures have been fraught with problems and have been the subject of extensive industrial lobbying since before the Rio Conference (Skjaereseth 1994). The failure of the first attempt to legislate a carbon tax was the occasion of the well publicized refusal to attend the conference by the then-Environment Commissioner Carlo Ripa de Meana.[25]

Enhanced Effectiveness

When an international agreement has been concluded it is obviously more desirable that undertakings be enacted for a whole region simultaneously than for fifteen states to go their own way at their own pace. Thus, for the Montreal Protocol, the Commission initiated and the Council agreed a regulation binding on all Member States, which precisely followed the requirements of the Protocol. Not the least of the reasons why this type of common implementing action was necessary was the need to avoid the trade-distorting effects that would have followed more piecemeal, nationally based compliance. Similarly EC directives have bound members to take concrete implementing measures to give reality to the intentions of the LRTAP across the Union.

One should not, however, be too sanguine about the implementation and effectiveness of international agreements, even if they lie within Community competence. This will depend upon a range of institutional and other factors (Greene 1996). There are several models of regime effectiveness (Vogler 1995: 152–82). Effectiveness may simply be defined in terms of legal effect and technical compliance; and here the EC would appear to rate quite highly due to its well-developed system of incorporating Community into national law, whereby the EC's external agreements are binding upon the Member States.[26] Despite this, there were some worrying compliance failures regarding the Montreal Protocol in the early 1990s, when various Member States did not submit required data on CFC production and consumption and the Commission refused to disaggregate EU-wide data, on grounds of commercial confidentiality (Greene 1992: 14–15; Victor 1998: 142). The climate change regime is only at the beginning of its development but compliance with FCCC obligations to submit national greenhouse gas inventories has also been patchy across the EU with only 9 of the 15 having reported by mid 1997.[27] This could, of course, be used as a compelling argument for the establishment of Community competence in this area such that the Commission could supervise a uniform approach.

A more significant model of effectiveness focuses upon the ways in which international regimes actually do modify the behavior of firms and individuals in intended directions. Here the EU is engaged in a two level, or often three level, process whereby Directives and Regulations agreed at Union level have to be made effective in concrete ways through the enforcement and monitoring of rules at national and local levels. There have been some successes, and recent experience with the implementation of the Montreal Protocol has been encouraging, with EC institutions playing a "key coordination and standard setting role" (Greene 1998: 109). This remains an under-researched area subject to charge and countercharge, where an awareness of the importance of implementation is often recognized by theorists of European integration—but only as an afterthought to the main analysis (Jordan 1995: 1). Doubtless there are numerous failings in terms of actual behavior modification in relation to the international commitments of the EU. Nevertheless procedures for monitoring Member States' behavior and obtaining legal redress for non observance of rules are considerably more highly developed than is the case for intergovernmental organizations.

A SOURCE OF CONFUSION?

An argument against the increasing involvement of the EU in global environmental negotiations is that, despite various theoretical advantages, experience has shown that it is simply incapable of coordinating itself in ways that will not hamper and confuse the negotiating process. Here we must return to the politico-legal minefield of competence and the external projection of the EU's internal difficulties. The most authoritative exponent of a critical view has been the principal U.S. negotiator of the Montreal Protocol—Richard E. Benedick. The thesis, in his personal account, *Ozone Diplomacy: New Directions in Safeguarding the Planet,* is that uncertainty about Community competence and the laborious, not to say contentious, procedures of the EC delegation proved a tiresome obstruction in the path of the enlightened agreement sought by the U.S. negotiators.

> In its approach to CFC regulation throughout the negotiations leading up to Montreal, the EC Commission seemed to many observers generally more concerned about European political and economic union than about the urgency of protecting the ozone layer. . . In accord with its expanding federal role, the EC Commission insisted on being sole speaker for all 12 countries at the negotiating table. It could not enforce this discipline, however, when the frustrations of individual delegations became too intense. . . .Bitter behind-the-scenes struggles occurred at internal EC caucuses that preceded, and often accompanied, the negotiating sessions (Benedick 1991: 35).

The author goes on to provide rich detail on the problems of the EC Presidency during the negotiations, the difficulty of obtaining a mandate for the Commission from the Council and the general inflexibility that resulted. It is also charged that the delays in the entry into force of the Protocol stemmed from EC demands that its members ratify simultaneously.[28]

The view from the other side of the table has been put by UK delegation leader Fiona McConnell. Criticizing the inevitable one-sidedness of Benedick's account, she paints a rather different picture, where "The Commission's relations with Member States in general and the UK in particular were smooth and harmonious throughout the Montreal meeting" (McConnell 1991: 319). This seems very much a matter of perspective. However, McConnell makes two further points that are worthy of note. First, the problems of reaching consensus are hardly unique to the EC. Second, the real problem for the Community may be that its procedures are simply misunderstood by others. Referring to a number of "misapprehensions as to Community procedure" on Benedick's part, she writes that ". . . if someone of his distinction, working cheek by jowl with us for so long, can make such fundamental errors of interpretation, then the Community should ask itself why it is still misunderstood" (ibid.). Without doubt there continues to be a problem here. In the diplomatic community there are, it appears, a small minority of "cognoscenti" in EU matters (mostly trade specialists). Beyond the Missions in Brussels there is a great deal of ignorance of the niceties of EU procedure and much time is spent by those posted to Brussels explaining to home departments the complications of the system and the way it might be influenced (Interview Brussels Mission).

On occasion misunderstanding can still cause friction with third party governments. They may feel misled when what they are told by the Commission or a Member State is contradicted by the outcome of the coordination meeting. Then there are the delays and uncertainty prompted by Community procedures and reference back to COREPER. Looked at in another light these complicating factors provide avenues for diplomacy that the various players have not been slow to utilize. On occasion, too, the Commission and the Presidency appear to third countries to be much more confrontational and unfriendly than individual Member State delegates would be. When this is felt to be the case some form of internal struggle or negotiating ploy is suspected (Interview Brussels Mission). The leghold traps issue from 1991 provides a paradigm example of the way in which internal trade versus environment disagreements, and Community institutions at loggerheads, can either leave third parties (in this case Canada) in a state of frustration where what was thought to have been agreed is suddenly not agreed or, by the same token, can hand negotiating advantages to those wishing to obstruct common action (in this case the United States)[29].

LEADERSHIP OR LOWEST COMMON DENOMINATOR?

A related criticism is that the internal workings of the Union render it incapable of exercising decisive leadership. This elusive quality, the ability to seize moments of opportunity and to take others with you, receives some emphasis in the international cooperation literature (Young 1989: 234–35). A negative view of the Community, in this respect, would highlight the divergences between Member State positions in a whole range of environmental policy areas and conclude with a well worn phrase about "convoys moving at the speed of the slowest vessel." This is Haas's conclusion on the Baltic and North Sea negotiations where the "EC has exercised a major restraint on agenda setting and international decision-making" and "EC competence has yielded non-decisions" (1993: 140–41). Such a view had validity before 1987, when the Council routinely voted by unanimity but the effect of the Single European Act and 1992 TEU was to greatly expand the areas covered by qualified majority voting. Thus the "convoy" analogy might have been appropriate to the beginning of the Montreal Protocol negotiations. Here Denmark and Germany pressed for immediate and extensive action while Britain and France, in line with the interests of their chemical industries, took a more negative initial attitude. Consequently the EC played a rather passive role; "condemned to immobility without being able to react to compromise proposals" (Jachtenfuchs 1991: 265).

Certainly Benedick and others can contrast this with the impetus provided by the initial U.S. demands for CFC production cuts. However, it should be recalled that this was only after substantial internal conflicts and changes of direction in U.S. policy, that he himself documents. Proponents of the EC's side can reply with some justification that the final comprehensive package involving production and consumption cuts, and then a phase out, owed much to the Europeans and produced a more extensive and effective agreement than had initially been on offer. As Haigh (1992: 246) notes, ultimately it was the Community that was able to come to a rapid decision, by the Council in December 1990, to exceed the requirements of the Protocol and opt for a complete phase out of CFCs by 1997. On the tenth anniversary of the Montreal Protocol it was the Community which pressed, for the moment unsuccessfully, for further action in respect of an accelerated phase out of the consumption of HCFCs and the introduction of production controls.[30] By way of comparison the U.S. has in a number of recent negotiations, according to a Commission negotiator, "raised sitting on its hands to an art form" (Interview Commission).

Levy (1993: 108–109), a more impartial observer, makes a favorable comparison between the LRTAP structure run by the ECG and the Community:

> Unlike LRTAP, European Community negotiations frequently get beyond least-common-denominator politics. This can be attributed to the fact that the EC member states are negotiating numerous issues, and have grown accustomed to practising give and take in order to facilitate agreements. Governments are used to losing on some issues and winning on others. Another contributing factor is

the European Commission (which is considerably larger than the ECG and much more independent) and the European Parliament.

Elsewhere, too, it is possible to point to examples of EC leadership where internal legislation already exists and provides both a basis for competence and an incentive to negotiate proactively. In this and other areas (notably trade liberalization) the need to concert the policies and standards of a group of often divergent states within the single market has provided models of good practice which are often incorporated sometimes verbatim into wider international agreements.[31] Thus the EC took the initiative on the transboundary movement of hazardous waste, based on its internal Directive 84/61 (Kempel 1993: 48–49). The Commission also highlights its role in moving the Basel Convention forward on the matter of a total ban on exports of hazardous waste from OECD to non OECD countries. This would represent the extension of existing practice in the EC-ACP relationship (Commission 1997: 102). In 1992 the Community was the first to adopt legislation on the export and import of certain dangerous chemicals and the Commission has been in the forefront of negotiations to establish a binding Prior Informed Consent (PIC) procedure which would involve mandatory notification in relation to chemicals such as asbestos and potentially dangerous pesticides. Arising from its competencies in relation to land-based sources of marine pollution the Community has also been an active participant in the 1995 Washington Conference and has promoted, within UNEP, the opening of negotiations on persistent organic pollutants. The negotiations leading up to the signature of the FCCC at Rio in 1992, and subsequent meetings designed to flesh out the Framework Convention with control measures, are now the subject of a substantial literature (Vellinga and Grubb 1992; Mintzer and Leonard 1994; Nilsson and Pitt 1994; O'Riordan and Jager 1996; Paterson 1996). This is not the place to examine them, or indeed the difficult internal disputes involved. What is clear from all the accounts, however, is that the EU as an entity has been at the heart of these deliberations from the beginning, despite its competence problems and the wide range of Member State energy interests. EU leadership amongst the developed parties is not really subject to question. It extends from an initial policy of binding commitments to emission reductions in the INC before Rio to the subsequent Conferences of the Parties. According to one observer at Berlin in 1995, the EU countries remained the "most proactive" in seeking specific "targets and timetables" and the most sympathetic to the demands of developing countries for equitable treatment (Grubb 1995: 3). This leadership role was, by all accounts, maintained through to the 1997 Kyoto Conference. The resulting Protocol to the FCCC was inevitably a compromise, but one which reflected the influence of the EU as a major protagonist (there was an average developed country commitment to greenhouse gas reductions of 5.2 percent (8 percent for the EU) by 2008 to 2012 but the agreement also reflected U.S. objectives in terms of "flexibility" and emissions trading).

There is, thus, a fair degree of evidence that whatever the situation may have been before the Single European Act, the EU can claim a leadership role in recent environmental diplomacy. This trend has been reinforced by the accession of Sweden, Finland and Austria all of whom regard themselves as leaders in environmental policy and who have in the past been severe external critics of the EC's failings (Andersen and Liefferink 1997).

CONCLUSION

A proper conclusion as to the EU's "actor capability" in international environmental politics would require a much fuller survey of the whole range of its activities than has been possible here. There is, nonetheless evidence, that even when competence is absent or disputed, it has managed to be relatively coherent and proactive. In what has been described by a DGXI official as a "good second phase" after the establishment of the single market, there has been an acceptance by insiders and outsiders that Community competence must come into play across a wide range of environmental negotiations; and that it does, in fact, provide "added value" as well as complications. This has been a consequence both of external opportunity provided by the proliferation of environmental diplomacy in the late 1980s and 1990s and of developments internal to the Union. Naturally the creation of a mass of EC environmental legislation and establishment of Community competencies in this area provided the basis but the actual conduct of external policy on behalf of Member States with widely differing national approaches and interests was significantly facilitated by the extension of QMV by the Single European Act and the 1992 Maastricht Treaty.

Comparisons with other actors will be inevitable (particularly the United States and Japan which are the EU's main negotiating partners). Such observations should take into account not only the common features—U.S. external environmental policy is just as subject to bureaucratic infighting as are the "interservice groups" of the Commission—but also the differences. It may not make a great deal of sense to compare the EU with some idealized form of state, for the EC/EU in its various manifestations is an entity *sui generis*. This has consequences for the conduct of negotiations and for the broader role played by the EU in international environmental politics. Its "leadership" has a different character. Because of the need to integrate different national views and legal traditions the Union will usually tend to take more time to arrive at a position than its main interlocutors and radical change is difficult. By contrast the United States can alter its position sometimes on a daily basis. The sheer economic scale of the EU and its unique reach in terms of its network of relations with the South makes the EU, in the words of one official, "a slow moving but weighty ship" which once it has set its course will often exercise more influence on the outcome of negotiations than the United States, which for the moment at least has renounced the kind of leadership role it played during the Montreal Protocol negotiations (Interview Commission).

The European Union and, more particularly, the Community "acting within its competences" is undoubtedly a formidable player in international environmental diplomacy, and is recognized as such by third parties. This in itself represents a substantial achievement in less than two decades, and constitutes the externalization of momentous shifts within the Union. Nevertheless its capability as an actor is still problematic and its "variable geometry" in negotiations a source of perplexity to outsiders. Yet the overall trend has been towards increasing Community competence (although this may not continue) and the "bedding in" of procedures for the conduct of mixed negotiations and the creation of mixed agreements in areas which often exhibit a high level of technical and political complexity. The sheer scale of the European Union means that, whatever its internal arrangements as regards competence, it remains an indispensable partner in negotiations on global environmental questions. There are grounds for believing that operating as the EC or EU as opposed to fifteen separate states can make a positive contribution to international environmental cooperation. Yet there are also problems, and it is important for both practitioners and analysts to understand the unique and often frustrating characteristics of the European entity with which they have to deal. In the interests of the development of environmental cooperation there is much to be said for the Commission's view that they would be best served by the extension of Community competence. This is unacceptable to some key Member State governments. For them, any efficiency gains that might be achieved, for example, in constructing the Climate Change regime would be heavily outweighed by losses of national sovereignty in critical areas such as energy policy and taxation. Whether this position is sustainable in the long run, as the Union is enlarged and the single currency introduced, remains to be seen.

NOTES

1. The title European Union has formal application only since the entry into force of the Treaty on European Union in November 1993 and is used as an umbrella term for the three pillars of the post-Maastricht construction (Pillar I—the European Communities; Pillar II—Common Foreign and Security Policy; Pillar III—Justice and Home Affairs). The title European Union is used below both in general discussion and in those specific circumstances where it is appropriate. While anxious to avoid

an excessively pedantic (and confusing) approach, it is on occasion necessary to the argument, or to historical accuracy, to employ alternative titles—European Community, European Economic Community, etc.—enjoyed by the various manifestations of the "actor." The present article is derived from a larger project on the European Union as a global actor. This has generated extensive evidence from interviews held with officials in Brussels and elsewhere during 1996–1997. Such sources cannot be attributed but are indicated in the text as (Interview).

2. Under Article 12 of the Treaty of Amsterdam all the existing treaty articles are to be consolidated and renumbered. The new numbers for articles mentioned are given in square brackets following the existing numbers.

3. The Council acting by qualified majority vote (QMV) agrees the negotiating mandate of the Commission and "concludes" any agreement reached—a process that also involves consultation with the European Parliament. The Commission is "assisted" in its negotiations with outsiders by a special 113 Committee composed of Member State representatives.

4. "Competence can be defined as the authority to undertake negotiations, conclude binding agreements, and adopt implementation measures. Where competence is exclusive, it belongs solely to the Community to the exclusion of the member states. Where it is concurrent either the Community or the Member States may act but not simultaneously" (Macrory and Hession 1996: 183).

5. A sense of this is provided by the arguments given in Macrory and Hession (1996) as to the determination of competence in the climate change negotiations. A major recent source is Macleod, Hendry, and Hyett (1996), while McGoldrick (1997) provides a clear guide through the legal thickets.

6. The circumstances of the 1970 ERTA Case 22/70 Commission v. Council were as follows. Since 1962 there had been negotiations for a European Road Transport Agreement involving EEC and non-EEC member states which were renewed in 1967. In 1969 the EC adopted Regulation 543/69 concerning the harmonization of social provisions for drivers, which provided the basis for the Commission's assertion of its right, rather than the member states, to pursue external negotiations on the ERTA. The ECJ found in favor of the Commission in what, at the time, was seen as a very extensive interpretation of community competence—that "as and when such common rules come into being, the Community alone is in a position to assume and carry out contractual obligations towards third countries affecting the whole sphere of application of the Community legal system."

7. Subsequent judgments and practice have augmented the legal basis upon which the Commission has asserted its right to be involved in the conduct of international environmental negotiations. The most important of these subsequent rulings involved "potential competence." This extended ERTA principles to areas where, although there were no common rules in existence, participation of the Community in an international agreement "is necessary for the attainment of one of the objectives of the Community."

8. The Commission is no more a monolith than member state governments and there can be acute tensions between individual Commissioners and DGs over specific areas of competence leading to what are known in EC parlance as problems of "coherence"—exemplified by the long-running difficulties between DGI (trade) and DGXI (environment) over the issue of a ban on trade in furs from animals caught by

leghold traps. Commencing in 1991 there were arguments within the Commission over whether trade policy should override animal welfare obligations and competence disputes both within and between Community institutions. Inevitably the dispute interacted with trade negotiations with the main fur exporters, Canada, Russia and the United States causing delay and frustration for animal rights campaigners and indeed the EC Environment Council of Ministers and the Commissioner.

9. This pattern is also evident in FAO sponsored negotiations on the 1995 Code of Conduct for Responsible Fisheries (where the Commission described itself as "major actor") and the 1993 Agreement to Promote Compliance with International Fishing and Management Measures by Fishing Vessels on the High Seas (Commission 1996: 67–68).

10. Unlike the sphere of external trade, the Community enjoys merely "concurrent competence" in environmental policy. "That is to say that in the absence of Community measures, Member States retain authority to regulate this sphere" (Scott 1998: 89).

11. At the beginning of the process of negotiating the Climate Change Convention there was little Community competence and the Commission was not a formal participant in the Intergovernmental Negotiating Committee. Nonetheless, the EC was a signatory in 1992 and at the FCCC's Ad Hoc Group on the Berlin Mandate (AGBM) meetings the Union negotiated "as 16" using the format of fifteen states and the Commission, but competence remained problematic and there was no formal negotiating mandate for the community, in part because of the controversial nature of the taxation instruments that the EC might employ in order to give substance to Art.4 commitments of "developed" parties to the Convention. Member state governments continued to be wary that any ground given to the Commission here might prove to be the "thin end of the wedge" of extended Community competence.

12. Article 210 of the Treaty of Rome reads simply: "The Community shall have legal personality." Article 228 provides for the "conclusion of agreements between the Community and one or more States or an international organisation." Article 130r(5) of the Single European Act extended the operation of Article 228 to international environmental agreements.

13. See CONF 2500/96, Brussels, 5 December 1996, chapter 13, 94–95, in which it was proposed to endow the Union with legal personality. This would be distinct from the Community's personality and representation would be by the Presidency or Secretary-General of the Council rather than the Commission. In the event the UK resisted this and all that appeared in the draft Treaty of Amsterdam was an article (J.14) allowing the Council to conclude agreements acting unanimously on a recommendation of the presidency, CONF 4002/97, Brussels, 8 July 1997.

14. The relevant provisions are Arts. 6, 4(2b), 18 and 22 of the United Nations Framework Convention on Climate Change, UN Doc.A/AC.237/18 (Part II) Add.1, 15 May 1992.

Also, Arts. 2,31,and 35 of the Convention on Biodiversity, UNEP, Na.92-7807, 5 June 1992. An exception is the 1973 Convention on International Trade in Endangered Species (CITES), where the absence of an REIO clause means that the Community, as such, has no speaking or participation rights even though it has internal competence over the issues covered by the Convention. Under these circumstances it is understood that Article 5 [10] of the Treaty of Rome imposes a "duty of solidarity" on Member States to pursue a common Community position.

15. Resolution 3208 (XXIX), 11 October 1974.

16. There was a two year long argument within the United Nations Economic and Social Council (ECOSOC), the parent body of the new CSD. To the usual disputes about competence and voting strength was added a new consideration arising from the fact that membership of the CSD was to be limited to fifty-three. This meant that the Commission was demanding membership of a body to which only some of the EU's constituent Member States would be elected. The issue was only resolved in 1995 after the CSD had already held two sessions. "Full participation" by the EC was defined as speaking rights, the right to put propositions but not to vote; and all this on the understanding that there would be no increase in the representation to which members of the Community would otherwise be entitled (Mensah 1996: 32).

17. See Article 228 of the Treaty of Rome, as substantially extended and amended by the SEA and the TEU.

18. Interview evidence, DGXI. The lead states mentioned in terms of climate change were the UK, Netherlands, Germany, and Denmark. With the very notable exception of the UK, these are the "troika" of advanced environmental modernizers often mentioned in the literature on EC environmental policy. See Sbragia (1996: 241).

19. DG I of the Council General Secretariat covers environmental protection, foodstuffs, and health and is staffed by ten administrators. It has a logistical and drafting function and assists the presidency in the preparation of negotiations.

20. This was seen by EC officials as providing a negotiating advantage leading to a "favorable outcome." (Interview).

21. Continuing member state representation when the Commission has competence is provided by "special committees." The best known of these is the 113 Committee for trade negotiations. Its role is explicitly mentioned in the revised Article 228 where (TEU) "The Commission shall conduct these negotiations in consultation with special committees appointed by the Council to assist it in this task and within the framework of such directives as the Council may issue to it."

22. Interview evidence from a national official relating to the AGBM meetings of the FCCC.

23. The Directive was negotiated between 1983 and 1988 and provides one of the EC's responses (alongside the 1987 Vehicle Emissions Directive) to the LRTAP. The original intention was to set uniform nitrogen and sulfur emissions targets for power stations in excess of 50 megawatts. In the end the intra EC negotiations could only be included by setting differentiated national targets (Boehmer Christiansen and Skea 1991: 234–46).

24. In advance of the Kyoto Third Conference of the FCCC Parties, the Council agreed (3 March 1997) to a common position that will seek emission reductions in a three gas "basket" (Carbon dioxide, methane, and nitrous oxide) of 15 percent by 2010. This was based on highly differentiated national "contributions" from the fifteen Member States. Heavily industrialized countries with the most polluting industries—Luxembourg, Germany, Austria and Denmark—have agreed 25 percent reductions, while Belgium, the Netherlands and the UK will make cuts of 10 percent. France and Finland, deemed to be low polluters, will stabilize at 1990 levels while the "cohesion" states of the EU—Greece, Portugal, Spain and Ireland—are allowed small increases (*Times*, 4 March 1997).

25. He described the UNCED as this "parade of vanity and hypocrisy. . . . We are not only not saving the earth we are not even saving our own consciences" *Guardian* 30 May 1992. Commission President, Jacques Delors, did attend but was not allowed to address the Conference and, in what may or may not be a significant indicator of actor capability, was forced to hitch a ride home on Mitterand's presidential Concorde.

26. For a discussion see Macleod, Hendry and Hyett (1996: 122–41).

27. J. Lanchbery, verbal evidence, 5 September 1997.

28. Similar comments, particularly about the interest of the Commission in "expanding its turf" and the lack of a constructive and flexible mandate from the Council, are to be found in an article by a European commentator and are quoted with approval by Benedick. See Jachtenfuchs 1990.

29. The problem dates back to a 1991 Regulation banning the import of furs from countries that had not outlawed the use of inhumane traps. The issue involves the competencies of DGI for trade and DGXI for animal welfare. Arguing the adverse trade implications and possible reference to the WTO: DGI was able to win an internal struggle with DGXI to prevent the Commission from implementing the ban that had been agreed by the Environment Council. This aroused the anger of the European Parliament, which threatened legal action against the Commission. Meanwhile, in order to resolve the problem, a draft agreement on humane standards was negotiated with Russia and Canada (but not the United States) which was generally regarded as inadequate by the animal welfare lobby. At the June 1997 Environment Council no decision was taken on the framework agreement, leaving Canadian representatives in "dismay" and the United States able to continue with a policy of inactivity in the face of what it perceived as the internal chaos within the EC. Interview evidence and *European Voice* 23–27 June 1997.

30. A proposal made with Switzerland at the Ninth Meeting of the Parties, Montreal, September 1997. The agreement reached on a developed country phase out date for methyl bromide of 2005, with a 50 percent reduction by 2001 was in line with the June Environment Council's negotiating mandate for the Commission. UNEP Information Unit for Conventions: http://www.unep.ch/iuc/, online press release 17 September 1997.

31. A small example is provided by Art.9 of the OSPAR Convention relating to freedom of environmental information which is a replica of the relevant EC internal Directive (Skjaeserth 1998: 340).

REFERENCES

Andersen, M. S. and D. Liefferink, eds. 1997. *European Environmental Policy : The Pioneers*. Manchester: Manchester University Press.

Benedick, R. E. 1991. *Ozone Diplomacy: New Directions in Safeguarding the Planet*. Cambridge, Mass.: Harvard University Press.

Boehmer-Christiansen, S. and J. Skea. 1991. *Acid Politics: Environmental and Energy Policies in Britain and Germany*. London: Belhaven Press.

Brinkhorst, L. J. 1994. "The European Community at UNCED: Lessons to be Drawn for the Future," in *Essays in Honour of H.G. Schermers* Vol.II, D. Curtin and T. Heukels, eds. Dordrecht: Nijhoff, 609–17.

Cameron, J., J. Werksman and P. Roderick, eds. 1996. *Improving Compliance with International Environmental Law*, London: Earthscan.

Collier, U. 1996. "The European Union's Climate Change Policy: Limiting Emissions or Limiting Power?" *Journal of European Public Policy* 3(1): 122–38.

Conference of the Representatives of the Governments of the Member States. 1996. *The European Union Today and Tomorrow: Adapting the European Union for the Benefit of its Peoples and Preparing it for the Future*. Dublin II, Conf 2500/96: Brussels, 5 December.

European Commission. 1995. *Intergovernmental Conference 1996: Commission Report for the Reflection Group*. Brussels: May.

———. 1996. *Report from the European Commission to the UN Commission on Sustainable Development on the European Community's Progress Towards Sustainability*. Prepared for the Fourth Session, Brussels: April.

———. 1997a. *Agenda 21 the first five years: European Community progress on the implementation of Agenda 21 1992–97*. Luxembourg: Office for Official Publications of the European Communities.

———. *Agenda 2000: For a stronger and Wider Union,* vol.1, Doc/97/6 Strasbourg.

Feldman, D.L. 1992. "Institutions for managing global environmental change," *Global Environmental Change* 1, March: 42–58.

Greene, O. 1992. "Implementation Review: the Framework Convention on Climate Change and the Montreal Protocol." Paper to British International Studies Association Annual Conference: December.

———. 1998. "The System of Implementation Review in the Ozone Regime," in Victor et. al., 89–136.

Grubb, M. 1995. *The Berlin Climate Conference: Outcome and Implications*. Briefing Paper No. 21. London: RIIA.

Grubb, M. and D. Anderson, eds. 1995. *The Emerging International Regime for Climate Change: Structures and Options after Berlin*. London: RIIA

Haas, P. 1990. *Saving the Mediterranean: The Politics of International Environmental Cooperation*. New York: Columbia University Press.

———. 1993. "Protecting the Baltic and North Seas," in *Institutions for the Earth*, P. Haas, R. L. Keohane and M.A. Levy, eds. Cambridge, Mass.: MIT Press, 133–82.

Haigh, N. 1996. "Climate change policies and politics in the European Community," in *Politics of Climate Change: A European Perspective*, T. O'Riordan and J. Jager, eds. London, Routledge, 155–84.

Hession, M. 1996. "The Role of the EC in Implementing International Environmental Law," in *Improving Compliance with International Environmental Law*, J. Cameron, J. Werksman, and P. Roderick, eds. London: Earthscan, 177–84.

Jachtenfuchs, M. 1990. "The European Community and the Protection of the Ozone Layer." *Journal of Common Market Studies* XXVII(3): 261–77.

Jordan, A. 1995. *Implementation Failure or Policy Making? How do we Theorise the Implementation of European Union (EU) Environmental Legislation*. CSERGE Working Paper GEC 95-18.

Kempel, W. 1993. "Transboundary Movements of Hazardous Wastes," in *International Environmental Negotiation*, G. Sjostedt, ed. Newbury Park: Sage, 48–62.

Levy, M. A. 1993. "European Acid Rain: The Power of Tote-Board Diplomacy," in *Institutions for the Earth: Sources of Effective International Environmental Legislation*, P.M. Haas, R. O. Keohane, and M. A. Levy, eds. Cambridge Mass.: MIT Press, 75–132.

Macleod, I., T. Hendry and S. Hyett. 1996. *The External Relations of the European Communities: A Manual of Law and Practice*. Oxford: Oxford University Press.

Macrory, R. and M. Hession. 1996. "The European Community and Climate Change: the Role of Law and Legal Competence," in *Politics of Climate Change: A European Perspective*, T. O'Riordan and J. Jager, eds. London: Routledge, 106–54.

Marks, G., L. Hooghe and K. Blank. 1996. "European Integration from the 1980s: State-Centric v. Multi-level Governance." Journal of Common Market Studies 34(3): 341–78.

McConnell, F. 1991. Review of "Ozone Diplomacy." *International Environmental Affairs* 3(4): 318–20.

McGoldrick, D. 1997. *International Relations Law of the European Union*. London: Longman.

Mensah, C. 1996. "The United Nations Commission on Sustainable Development," in *Greening International Institutions*, J. Werksman, ed. London: Earthscan, 21–37.

Mintzer, I. M. and J. A. Leonard, eds. 1994. *Negotiating Climate Change: the Inside Story of the Rio Convention*, Cambridge: Cambridge University Press.

Nilsson, S. and Pitt, D. 1994. *Protecting the Atmosphere: the Climate Change Convention and its Context*. London: Earthscan.

Nitze, W. 1990. *The Greenhouse Effect: Formulating a Convention*. London: RIIA.

O'Riordan, T. and J. Jager, eds. 1996. *Politics of Climate Change: A European Perspective*. London: Routledge.

Paterson, M. 1996. *Global Warming and Global Politics*. London: Routledge.

Peterson, J. 1995. "Policy Networks and European Policy Making." *West European Politics* 18(2): 389–407.

Princen, T. and M. Finger. 1994. *Environmental NGOs in World Politics: Linking the Local and Global*. London: Routledge.

Sbragia, A. 1996. "Environmental Policy: the 'push-pull of Policy Making" in H. Wallace and W. Wallace, eds. 3rd ed. *Policy Making in the European Union*. Oxford: Oxford University Press, 235–55.

Scott, J. 1998. *EC Environmental Law*. London: Longman.

Skjaerseth, J. B. 1994. "The Climate Policy of the EC: Too Hot to Handle?" *Journal of Common Market Studies* 32(1): 25–45.

———. 1998. "The Making and Implementation of North Sea Commitments: The Politics of Environmental Participation," in Victor et. al., 327–80.

Somsen, H. 1996. "The European Union and the Organization for Economic Cooperation and Development," in *Greening International Institutions*, J. Werksman, ed. London: Earthscan, 181–204.

Szell, P. 1993. "Negotiations on the Ozone Layer," in *International Environmental Negotiation*, G. Sjostedt, ed. Newbury Park: Sage, 31–47.

Vellinga, P. and M. Grubb, eds. 1993. *Climate Change Policy in the European Community*, London: RIIA.

Victor, D.G. 1998. "The Operation and Effectiveness of the Montreal Protocol's Non-Compliance Procedure," in Victor et. al., 137–76.

Victor, D. G., K. Raustilia and E. B. Skolnikoff, eds. 1998. *The Implementation and Effectiveness of International Environmental Commitments: Theory and Practice*. Cambridge, Mass.: MIT Press.

von Moltke, K. and A. Rahman. 1996. "External Perspectives on Climate Change: A View from the United States and the Third World," in *Politics of Climate Change: A European Perspective*, T. O'Riordan and J. Jager, eds. London: Routledge, 330–45.

Wallace, H. and W. Wallace, eds. 1996. *Policy-Making in the European Union*. Oxford: Oxford University Press.

Werksman, J., ed. 1996. *Greening International Institutions*. London: Earthscan.

Wurzel, R. K. W. 1996. "The Role of the EU Presidency in the Environmental Field: Does It Make a Difference Which State Runs the Presidency?" *Journal of European Public Policy* 3(2): 272–91.

Young, O. 1989. *International Cooperation: Building Regimes for Natural Resources and Environment*. Ithaca and London: Cornell University Press.

12

Bioregionalism and Political Boundaries: Concepts and Constraints

Peter Woolstencroft

INTRODUCTION

Since the 1950s the rapidly expanding environmental movement has spawned a wide range of analyses of the intersections between the natural world, society, and the state. Moving from its early low-drawer and issue-specific formulations (especially conservationalist) to broader, more general responses, environmentally centered thought began to challenge dominant social-economic interests. From about the mid-1970s drive by the urgent messages of the Club of Rome's *The Limits of Growth* and similar publications, analysts of environmental issues took on a more global perspective and thought in terms of "ecology." For some the world itself—Gaea—was a living organism. More politicized and less technocratic, ecological thinking focused on basic socioeconomic-political values of society, especially industrialized ones and, indeed, in the case of many Green parties and various writers, the state itself.[1] Many far reaching and radical formulations were produced as ecologists grappled with the continuing and deepening crises of environmental degradation and their connection with the organization of political systems.

One approach, the deep ecology movement, primarily associated with Arne Naess, equates humans with all other forms of life and denies human primacy over the world.[2] Rejecting large-scale political units, deep ecologists search for appropriate human communities grounded in regional ecology, their lifestyles developing in light of their region's characteristics. Instead of the standardization produced by modern science, technology, and economic processes the norm would be one of diversity.[3] A related, but more influential approach, social ecology, for which the driving force over three decades has been Murray Bookchin, advocates "municipal libertarianism." The municipality, rather than the large, bureaucratic, and cumbersome nation-state, is the central arena of political life; and, as with deep ecology, local control will lead to diversity.[4]

Within this wide tradition, one body of thought, represented by the term "bioregionalism,"—has moved "beyond the disciplinary interests of the pioneering geographers and naturalists who first gave it form and become the conceptual basis for a full-fledged social-ecological transformation."[5] In its simplest expression, it calls for congruence between political and natural boundaries. The premise is that boundaries—the building-blocks of the state's structure, including those that differentiate one state from another—are generally drawn in a way that is unconscious of nature. Existing political boundaries not only stand in the way of effective environmental policies, but more importantly, preclude the development of environmentally sensitive life attitudes. Restructuring of political units so that their boundaries follow natural lines will provide the necessary condition for the emergence of ecological consciousness necessary to arrest and correct the pervasive environmental deterioration of the modern world.[6]

Over the past decade, the bioregional idea has enjoyed rapid diffusion (though it still is very much North American-centric, with some European antecedents and interest),[7] accompanied by a large body of popular and academic commentaries; the formation of community groups; the holding of local and regional conferences; five continental congresses; the establishment of institutes and publishing series, including academic journals; theses and dissertations; the development of interest in rehabilitation; and proliferation of lively internet sites.

The movement from environmentalism to ecologism has attracted the attention of practitioners in a wide range of disciplines, especially economics, political philosophy, and political science. Bioregionalism, as with other radical perspectives, has received a wide range of judgments, positive and negative. For Robin Eckersley, it is eccentric and politically naïve;[8] for David Pepper, it is romanticized ruralism;[9] for Andrew McLaughlin, it is an incomplete vision, but one that is useful because it guides visionary gradualism in a world carved into political sovereigns that have little bioregional logic and which will not be easily or immediately dissolved.[10] And McLaughlin credits the bioregional movement for generating interest in addressing cities as an ecological problem because they "as currently organized are imperial centers reaching out great distances, drawing in food, water, and energy, and dispersing their wastes outward."[11] Dimitrious Roussopoulos, finds bioregionalism's focus on boundaries "refreshing"; and asserts that "making the primary place of political decision making the ecological context in which we live leads our future towards a 'natural' internationalism."[12] Judith Plant points to "the bioregional project" as being especially congenial with ecofeminism's striving for life-giving and for providing family-nurturing ring having a primary role in societal arrangements.[13] And, last, Jeremy Rifkin claims that the redrawing "of political boundaries to match ecosystem boundaries is among the most formidable and pressing political issues facing every country in the world as humanity makes the transition from geospheric to biospheric consciousness."[14]

Recently, geopolitical thinking emerging from globalization of economic processes has focused on the emergence of trans-system regional entities that serve as the "ports of entry" in the world economy. Certain regions, having mobilized their locational strengths, human resources, and investment climates, are the high-growth leaders in the world's economy. This new form of regionalism, while having very different perspectives on the development of post-industrial capitalism and transnational corporations, has a number of commonalities with bioregionalism. For each, the primacy and importance of "place" is a postulate that structures the analyses and argumentation. And each presupposes that existing political boundaries are not only malleable but that they should be eliminated or bypassed.

This paper, working within the perspectives of political geography relating to frontiers and boundaries, analyzes the development of bioregional concepts; the utilization of bioregional concepts in discussions of political reorganization; and constraints in the implementation of bioregionally centered changes in the reform of political institutions such as the contemporary state. Its argument is that much of the earlier forms of bioregionalism contain fantasy elements that work against their incorporation into mainstream thinking about politics and the environment. There are, nonetheless, important issues contained in the view that political boundaries should have a natural footing rather than following the haphazard patterning characteristic of almost all political boundaries. However, the identification of core political issues in the call for bioregionally centered political systems leads to a number of conceptual and empirical problems that, in sum, render the approach questionable, despite the validity of its contention that existing political systems are systemically dysfunctional from the perspective of environmental problem solving.

The newer versions of regionalism, which see the effects of existing political boundaries as being attenuated if not eliminated, raise questions about the function of boundaries in a world where economic processes erode the capacity of governments to provide for "national" economies. This, in turn, leads to questions about the character of representative democracy in the modern world economy.

THE CONCEPT OF BIOREGIONALISM

Every discussion of bioregionalism acknowledges the influence of a small set of writers and advocates, most notably Peter Berg, Freeman House, and

Kirkpatrick Sale, especially his *Dwellers in the Land—The Bioregional Vision*.[15] Many have been activated by their powerful yet poetic evocation of a peaceful, environmentally sensitive, economically self-sufficient society very much different from the dominant and ever-expanding industrialized model. Bioregional thinking has been expressed in many ways: architecture and planning;[16] design;[17] literature;[18] agriculture (giving rise to "permaculture" or permanent agriculture or permanent culture); and movements dedicated to land reinhabitation and ecological restoration.[19]

Although the term bioregionalism originated, obscurely, in the 1970s, correlated ideas have a much longer lineage.[20] The term region has a long history in geography; but its association with Social Darwinism and extreme connections between land and people (exemplified in the work of Haeckel) plus the difficulty of identifying and sustaining natural regions, led to the demise of this approach.[21] The concept of ecoregion, an important part of the bioregional argument, also has a long history, with first publications appearing in 1899.[22]

The biologist J. B. S. Haldane, in his paper, "On Being the Right Size," claims that "just as there is a best size for every animal, so the same is true for every human institution."[23] Alexander explains the link between size and manageability in terms of communications. With population growth "the channels of communication needed for democracy and justice and information are simply too clogged, and too complex: bureaucracy overwhelms human processes.[24] Sale, for his part, cites, amongst others, Turner's emphasis on regionalism and Mumford's focus on regional planning as important intellectual antecedents.[25] Mumford, for instance, is tied by McLaughlin to bioregionalism with the argument that regional autonomy allows for diverse cultural evolution.[26] Pepper connects Leopold Kohr's *The Breakdown of Nations* to E. F. Schumacher's *Small is Beautiful* (to whose society Sale first presented his bioregional vision).[27] In the United States, regionalist movements from the 1920s to the 1940s, stressed place, local control, self-sufficiency in ways similar to the bioregionalists of the last quarter of the century.[28]

Following in the tradition of ecologically driven schemata for the transformation of society,[29] bioregionalism requires an enormous paradigm shift:

> . . . before our industrial society begins first to abandon the notion of controlling and remaking the world in the name of a global monoculture and then to realize that maybe what it calls *provincial* [italics in original] is merely the kind of minding your own business attention to local reform that might just save the world.[30]

Moving from globalism to localism entails changes in thinking in terms of the scale of human settlement, the organization of economies, the nature of political organizations, social relationships, and the evolution of societies. Table 12.1 outlines the nature of these changes conceived by Sale and, indeed, other bioregionalists.

Table 12.1. Paradigm Shift: From Industrio-Scientific to Bioregionalism

	Bioregionalism Paradigm	*Industrio-Scientific Paradigm*
Scale	Region	State
	Community	Nation/World
Economy	Conservation	Exploitation
	Stability	Change/Progress
	Self-sufficiency	World Economy
	Cooperation	Competition
Polity	Decentralization	Centralization
	Complementarity	Hierarchy
	Diversity	Uniformity
Society	Symbiosis	Polarization
	Evolution	Growth/violence
	Division	Monoculture

Source: Kirkpatrick Sale, *Dwellers in the Land,* p. 50.

The concept of bioregionalism is based on three core ideas, each of which is of interest to political geographers. First, place is a primary condition in human action: connectedness to the land is seen as essential for healthy people, communities, and society. One particular claim: If people live in a close association with the land, indeed in accord with the land, they develop environmentally sensitive and economically sustainable attitudes. Second, the appropriate boundaries for political organization are found in nature. For Rifkin, only

> when political and ecosystem boundaries are made compatible with one another will it be possible to regulate properly economic activity so as to make it sustainable and congenial with the temporal and spatial limitations of the environment human communities dwell in.[31]

Third, decentralization should be the organizing principle of economic, social, and political life. Sale, for example, calls for self-governing bioregional communities linked with each other by a "loose" confederation.[32] The explication of these ideas will lead to a fuller understanding of the concept of bioregionalism.

THE CENTRALITY OF PLACE

Andrew McLaughlin writes that attachment to place is central to bioregionalism.[33] Pepper connects bioregionalists' love of place with that of Wordsworth's as well as utopianists such as Morris.[34] The centrality of place is seen in the writings of Sale, who assumes that not only must people become "dwellers in the land, to come to know the earth fully and honestly, the crucial and perhaps only and all-encompassing task is to understand place, the immediate, specific place where we live."[35] Aldo Leopold, whose works, especially *A Sand County Almanac,* are often cited by bioregionalists, is imbued with this spatial naturalism. In his essay, "The Land Ethic," Leopold proposes that: "A thing is right when it tends to preserve the integrity, stability, and beauty of the biotic community. It is wrong when it tends otherwise."[36] Bioregional theorists view human institutions as having evolved in such a way and having become so large as to pull people from what used to be the case, a sustained nexus between humans and their spatial contexts. Retrieval of this relationship calls for radical change in how humans are organized. For Brian Toker, a "healed relationship with the earth must transcend the artificial boundaries that mark these different spheres (personal, social, political), for the attitudes and cultural patterns that sustain our civilization's present ways have been around far longer than most of our present political or social institutions."[37] State organization is the primary culprit, because its size, bureaucratization, and standardization overwhelm people. Such a view is expressed by Yi-Fu Tuan: "the modern state is too large to be known personally, its shape too evidently artificial to be perceived as a natural unit."[38]

In the spirit of "thinking globally and acting locally," Rifkin sees that a "new green politics will need to reopen the global commons." Reestablishing a sense of "ground" in the biosphere means re-participating with

> the earth at every level of human existence. Breaking out of the arbitrary enclosures that have separated the ecosystems of the earth into exploitable domains and commercial corridors is the single most pressing task on the biospheric political agenda.[39]

The centrality of place, since it is predicated on the belief that lifestyles will reflect natural surroundings, will lead to social diversity, with the local community, rather than higher-order political aggregations, determining the limits of anti-social behavior; spatial contexts will override the universalization of human values.[40]

NATURAL BOUNDARIES[41]

Sale's call for bioregionalism argues that instead of a nation-state the basic political unit will be the bioregion, which will be self-sustaining and characterized by the fact that "its people and features would be part of a close organic unity."[42] The claim for natural boundaries is found in Sale's definition of a bioregion:

> any part of the earth's surface whose rough boundaries are determined by natural characteristics rather than human dictates, distinguishable from other areas by particular attributes of flora, fauna, water, climate, soils, and land forms and by the human settlement and cultures those attributes have given rise to.[43]

Berg and Dasmann write that a bioregion refers to both "a geographical terrain and a terrain of consciousness—to a place and the ideas that have developed about how to live in that place."[44] Other writers more or less follow in the footsteps of Sale, Berg and Dasmann. Bioregions for the Todds are "a cluster of ecosystems arranged topographically and climatically" which require incorporation of a human element.[45] Jim Dodge, much more expansively, proposes a wide range of criteria including watersheds; biotic shifts (percentage changes in plant/species composition by region); topography; human cultures, perceptions, and behaviors; land elevation; and, finally, "the force of the place itself."[46]

Although setting of boundaries is a central part of the bioregional project, the issue has not attracted much systematic attention. Sale has been the most explicit in addressing a number of issues associated with the delineation of regions.[47] More recently, Doug Aberley has given a lengthy account of bioregional mapping that moves beyond Sale's contribution to address some theoretical and technical cartographic issues.[48] The development of Geographic Information Systems has made it much easier to produce overlay maps that allow for the identification of commonalities and to determine regional borders. Bioregionalists recognize two possible approaches to the boundary problematic: one involves "a system that will allow bioregions to be drawn in universal order"[49]; the other, much preferred by bioregionalists, combines natural and human features.

The second approach is evident in Sale's definition of a bioregion that incorporates many variables, human and nonhuman. Boundaries will probably not be rigid but fluid—"but the general contours of the regions themselves are not hard to identify by using a little ecological knowledge" and, indeed, may be intuited. Natural regions are nested within higher order aggregations; in the North American context, the largest—the "ecoregion"—Sale estimates to be of "several hundred thousand square miles" and would number about fifty. Validity for the identification of ecoregions is that the "culture areas of the major native groups in North America overlapped ... almost exactly with broadly defined major bioregions."[50] Below ecoregions are a series of "georegions" and "morphoregions," corresponding with various aggregations of naturally bounded regions. The obvious indeterminacy contained in overlapping boundaries for Sale is resolved locally: "the task of determining the appropriate bioregional boundaries—and how seriously to take them—will always be left up to the inhabitants of the area." In a similar vein, Berg argues that the "final boundaries of a bioregion are best described by the people who have lived within in it, through human recognition of the realities of living in places."[51] Bioregional boundaries and "the various scales at which to create human institutions" can be left to people provided they have honed "their bioregional sensibilities and making acute their bioregional consciousness." Once regions have been set "informed discussion will eventually merge borders into a biocultural logic."[52]

> A "soft" or "fuzzy" boundary is not problematic because it tends to encourage a blend, a cross-fertilization of cultures at the bioregional edges, to blunt the possessiveness and defensiveness that rigid borders so often cause, and to keep in check the human propensity to stamp our lines and purposes on nature's.[53]

Addressing the issue of fuzzy boundaries (and even "seasonal elasticity"), David McCloskey, in arguing that ecoregions, regions are natural holistic "emergents" stipulates the following guidelines. First, "an authentic ecoregional boundary" must come from the land and reflections of people. Second, while there are edges, they "serve as clear and powerful articulations of diversity." Third, "ecoregional boundaries are multiple, not singular, in nature" with their regions being "bounded wholes in space and time" where the most significant features "converge in a distinct and sustained way." Fourth, "the place, species, and peoples have evolved together."[54]

Aberley addresses the boundary problematic in more explicit terms. External boundaries of bioregions can first be delineated by "physiographic determinism," by which is meant the development of maps showing such things as "watershed information with I animal communities, with vegetation types, with physiographic (landform) regions, etc." Aberley recognizes that what is missing from the use of natural I elements in the definition of bioregions is "that there is no easy way to give human scale to the territories defined." The solution is "to make human occupation of any land area a part of the bioregion definition equation." For Aberley, "the essence of the bioregional ideal . . . is to irrevocably marry human activity into processes of sustainable land, animal, plant, and atmospheric interaction."[55] The finding of bioregions involves:

- Watersheds.
- Watersheds are usually related to "biogeoclimatic or ecoregion areas where a particular grouping of vegetation, climate, and landform predominate."
- "Bioregions often correspond to the territories of single or associated aboriginal peoples."
- "Your bioregion is likely the region that you know; places that are foreign to you or which are generally unfamiliar are probably "somewhere else."[56]

DECENTRALIZATION

Sale argues that "the ecological law with which bioregionalism should logically begin is decentralism, centrifugal force, the spreading of power to small and widely dispersed units. . . . So it is in the natural world, where nothing is more striking than the absence of any centralized control."[57] This regional approach has two important manifestations—politics and economics.

Arguments for political decentralization, of course, have many sources, but the bioregionalist version is predicated on the assumption that one of the flaws in modern state organization is that the diversity of bioregions is not incorporated into higher order political decision making. Liberal democracy resolves disputes on a majoritarian basis, with conflicts between territorially-grounded interests not resolved on the basis of ecological criteria (or, often, the recognition of ecological considerations).[58] In bioregions the political process will be (largely) consensual because citizens confronted with the "reality" of a particular bioregion will develop a shared understanding of their interests and alternatives. Economically, large-scale decision making is impervious to bioregional needs and capacities. Sale's vision is that the "economy that comes into being within a bioregion also derives its character from the conditions, the laws, of nature." Bioregional economies would be oriented toward "balance" or "steady state" rather than "perpetual change" and "continual growth" in the name of "progress." In accord with nature, such economies would be self-sufficient because "just as nature does not depend on trade, does not create elaborate networks of continental dependency, so the bioregion would find all of its needed resources . . . within its own environment.[59] Bioregionally based political units would resist the material blandishments of the integrated world economy by "utilizing readily available resources in imaginative ways to provide food, clothing, shelter, transportation, and energy."[60]

THE CRITIQUE OF BIOREGIONALISM

The spread of the bioregional concept has engendered many criticisms, in considerable part arising from its utopianism and looseness.[61] In this paper the focus is on issues that have a grounding in political geography. One line of inquiry concerns the possibility of natural boundaries. Three issues, each of which lead to discussion about the functions of boundaries, are pursued. The first has to do with the possibility of change from the existing system of political boundaries; the second deals with the range of possibilities that nature presents; and the third examines the resolution of disputes. The second critical line pertains to place as a value in human affairs. The third area of analysis is decentralization, primarily considered from the point of view of inequalities.

At the outset, it must be stated that the boundary issue as presented by bioregionalists writing about land-based bioregions ignore the problem of oceanic ecoregions which, of course, constitute a large fraction of the earth's surface. Political geographers have discussed boundaries in terms of "artificial" and "natural," with the latter reflecting landscape characteristics or functional features, such as economic activity. Bioregionalists think in much grander terms. What are the possibilities of wholesale change in boundaries of the kind imagined by bioregionalist thinkers? The problem is exemplified by figure 12.1, a map of Cascadia, one of bioregionalist proponents' favorite examples, which incorporates land from the United States (six states) and Canada (two political units, the province of British Columbia and the Yukon Territory).

Political geographers have described political boundaries as being conservative in character; once established, they are rarely changed, even if the historical reasons have long lost their weight or their meaning.[62] Constitutional protection in federations and entrenched interests, along with societal inertia if not indifference, account for the conservatism of political boundaries. Transnational change would require an enormous shift that in the absence of war, extraordinarily severe economic difficulties, or massive social disruption is hard to contemplate.

Within a nation, of course, a feature of the physical landscape or some aspect of society may be a dominant factor in a boundary decision; but the important element is that the primacy of the feature reflects political purposes, preference for one from among many choices. Political geographer, Ladis Kristof, in a seminal article observed that a "boundary does not exist in nature or by itself. It always owes its existence to man."[63]

Of course, a people, perhaps even for the panoply of reasons offered by bioregionalists, may determine that wholesale redrawing of political boundaries to reflect ecological boundaries warrantable. The issue is the likelihood of being able to do so. Sale's belief that peaceful resolution of overlaps seems very naive, even if the pertinent populations have a high degree of biological consciousness.

A more serious problem arises from the nature of ecological boundaries.[64] At the macro-level, differentiation between one ecoregion and the next is a function of

> climatic regime, defined as the diurnal and seasonal fluxes of energy and moisture. As these fluxes change, the kinds and patterns of dominant life forms change, as do the kinds of soils. As a result, ecosystems of different climates differ significantly.[65]

Generally, for ecological regions to reflect climatic regimes they would have to be large entities. Consider the continental United States: It can be divided into six climatic regimes. Generally they are large (with three covering the easternmost two-thirds of the continent). Their smooth, almost flowing, lines of demarcation should not be regarded as hard. Climate buffers serve to mark one climate zone from another, but the central parts of each climate regime is clearly different from adjoining ones.

Other regimes (food webs, trophic levels) are secondary factors, though from the point of view of humans these are of immediate importance. The boundaries of biotic regions "are recognized by perceived changes in the ecological relationships of vegetation, landform, drainage, and soil,"[66] a view that is similar to that of Aberley's.

For Aberley, resolution of disputes will reflect perceptions of "what seems right." Political geographers would not argue against "what seems right" underlining boundary decisions. But for bioregionalists to welcome indeterminacy in boundaries is to miss the point made by political geographers that the boundary represents resolution of a conflict over where it ought to be. Once the need for boundaries is recognized it must be satisfied. The fact of the boundary reflects recognition that some form of separation was necessary and the chosen line, all things considered, made acceptable sense.

Although the potential use of other nonclimatic criteria to delineate ecological regions is welcomed by bioregionalists, two serious problems remain with the attempt to construct naturally-based political boundaries: the first deals with ecological spatial variability; the second with the possibility of developing integrated regional models. The issue of ecoregional variability can be seen from examining the relationship between climate, soil, and forests. Compared to climatic regimes, soil regions are much more diverse, with seven found in irregular distributions in the eastern half of the United States. And increasing complexity is evident when natural forest vegetation zones are mapped. The resulting picture is one of dispersed heterogeneity and linear irregularity. Yet, these ecoregions are interdependent, in that forest regions are tied to climate and soil conditions.[67]

Bailey in his various writings has illustrated how ecoregions can be spatially divergent. Figure 12.2 (appendix) gives one instance of the argument.

The point is that—contrary to Sale's assumption that there would be about 40 ecoregions easily identified and delineated, in North America—in fact; the determination of the number and shape of bioregions is highly problematic. The degree of the problem is evidenced when the history of integrated regional models is examined. Attempts to develop models for the interaction between social systems and their environments have a long and contested history. Integrated regional models—considered especially important by their proponents for societies to address pressing environmental issues—are in their infancy. Elizabeth Blood observes that at present, modelings of human and environmental change have been discipline specific (physical, ecological, social) and generally focused at the individual, ecosystem or global scale.[69] Scholars discussing integration efforts, while hampered by disciplinary differences in scale, processes, and language, agree that "interactions among human, ecological, and atmospheric systems largely occur at the regional scale (areas larger than ecosystems or landscapes but subcontinental) and that these interactions drive regional structure."[70] The difficulties in developing integrated regional models belie the ease that Sale assumes will characterize the identification of bioregions.

For a number of reasons, watersheds are thought to be attractive ways to construct bioregions. Generally, they have more or less stable boundaries which are easily determined and their relative discreteness make agreement between peoples in adjoining bioregions more likely than would be the case with other, "softer," determinations.

However, the watersheds criterion is problematic in a number of important ways. The first problem relates to the question of scale, which arises from the fact that watersheds are nested in higher-order aggregations, ranging from local streamsheds to large watersheds. The connections between levels are acute because

> ecosystems are spatial systems and are consistently inserted, or nested, into each other, each level subsumes the environment at the level below it. Therefore, it conditions or controls the behavior of the system below it.[71]

The logic of the above observation is that delineating bioregions on the basis of watersheds leads to larger, rather than smaller, entities. But Bailey identifies four problems with using watersheds for determining ecological regions:

- Large areas (perhaps as much as 20 percent of the United States) do not have clearly defined drainage networks.
- Watersheds may flow through very diverse climatic and topographic regions.
- Lack of coincidence between surface water and ground water systems.
- Watersheds do not necessarily have similar aquatic environments.[72]

In conclusion, while there are many possible ways of drawing "natural boundaries"—watersheds, plant species, even historical/cultural divisions of primal peoples—at base, there is reason to share the "suspicion that, as entities drawn on a map, bioregions may be less natural distinctions than conventional choices, as arbitrary as national boundaries."[73] Less rhetorically, the best perspective on the bioregional boundary problem is that the optimal criteria are climate and landforms; generally, the latter determines smaller regions and the former structures larger ones; but, as has been pointed out, climatic zones, generally, cover large landmasses; and landforms, generally, are more compact but are spatially heterogeneous and irregularly shaped.[74] And while ecologists view the landform criterion positively, they are acutely aware that "the relationship of landscapes to other ecological conceptions is far from simple."[75] They await progress—conceptual, methodological, and empirical—in the development of "unified ecological models."[76]

The establishment of naturally contoured boundaries will not just happen, of course, but requires the development of strong place-centered attitudes with attendant ecological sensitivities. Bioregionalism, falling within the anarchist tradition, advocates "independent development" and assumes that "spatial organization is a determinant of economics, society, and politics."[77] The argument that place is a motive force in human behavior is problematic for a number of reasons. First, it must be squared against other forces, such as ethnicity, language, and religion, which have shown great resiliency and holding power, despite the secularization and homogenization of modern societies. This point has been made in a variety of ways by a number of commentators. Anderson, in arguing that geography is not the only value in human organization, observes that linguistic, religious, and other cultural boundaries do not necessarily follow bioregional lines.[78] Milbrath argues that while we are in our "region" we also are part of "much broader cultural and religious traditions, and in worldwide communities of like-minded people." Furthermore, our economically interdependent world "would require the most draconian measures to force economic actors to think and act regionally." And (but perhaps less obviously), if people really found regions to be meaningful units for organizing their lives and to which they would like to give allegiance, they already would have done so.[79] Edward Wilson, in his discussion of human nature does not accord place any standing and, indeed, writes that "ultra-environmentalists start with the premise that man is a creation of his own culture." Disturbingly for the bioregionalists' cause, nature as a source of values is a highly contested proposition in philosophy, the debate having produced a large body of literature and a journal, *Environmental Ethics,* devoted to such matters. Rubin, a writer not at all friendly to bioregionalism and other biocentric philosophies, is on the right track when he judges that bioregionalists' attachment to place "takes on a religious and even mystical significance."[81] And it must be concluded that bioregionalists focus single-mindedly on one dimension of the relationship between humans and their environments, and, in so doing, reduce the complexity of the world—human and nonhuman — to just one factor. Paradoxically, however, while they pursue a world built monotheistically their model is built on diversity in political expression and activation.

One continuing theme running through bioregionalist literature is the call for decentralization, which is valued for its enhanced potential for political participation, diversity in political expression, and effective control and decision making. Within the more extreme parts of the ecology movement, nature and its claims are in some sense postulated to be equal to or superior to humans and their institutions, thereby contesting the democratic humanism that is seen as a centerpiece of western political thought.[82] This paper does not address the issue of anthropocentrism (the view that humans are superior and ought to be the center of political action). The question of the structure of government in a bioregional world is discussed in terms of how scale and political systems are handled. The focus is two aspects of this relationship. The first deals with the size of bioregions and how they are defined. The second is a matter of democratic theory.

Bioregional decentralization raises a number of issues. Bioregionalists speak about self-sustaining entities, but such conditions are hard to guarantee. In fact, it would appear intuitively obvious that bioregions would vary enormously in terms of their carrying and sustaining capacities. Compare, say, northern California with northern Canada; one with a moderate climate, the other not; one with a diverse and productive environment, the other not. In a world were equality is a strong force and where people are aware of spatial differences, people would move from one to the other, thereby threatening the sustainability of the "richer" region. The response in all probability would be the assertion of the boundary as a separating device.[83]

The scalar quality of bioregions is also problematic. Smaller units would have greater potential for participation; yet, from the standpoint of environmental problem solving, smaller units would be dysfunctional given that most significant threats to the environment are at the macro-level. And here we come to the conceptual incoherence of bioregionalism in the decentralized system, the local level—the bioregion—will operate in noncapitalist (if not anti-modern) ways but, globally, there will be no central control. As Penner notes, "it is difficult to conceive of Ecotopia without more or less, planning and a lesser or nonexistent role for markets.[84] In other words, while decentralization "gives each member of the community more control over that community's decisions. But the smaller the community, the less and less the community decisions will ordinarily matter to the ultimate outcome."[85] In a world devoid of universal acceptance of bioregional precepts, some societies will be less ecologically sensitive than others will. In a world that is at best a "loose confederation" they may even calculate that environmental costs and economic benefits justify externalities.

THINKING IN BIOREGIONAL TERMS

The critique of bioregionalism may be thought to invalidate the approach. To the contrary, despite its overstatements and utopianistic reach, there is value in thinking about humans and their world in bioregional terms. Ironically, while bioregionalism casts a wide net and thinks in terms of global transformation, its most fruitful manifestations are at the local level. In the 1960s, conflicts in California over the diversion of water from northern California to the south saw its opponents in their successful battle take on the premises and argumentation of bioregionalism.[86] Rifkin refers to the development of air quality control boards in California.[87] Daniel Press traces the development of bioregionally oriented groups in California and the movement to increase region-wide forest planning to the point of merging existing boundaries.[88] Pepper cites permaculture projects in England that, paradoxically, reflect the actions of county councils working within their jurisdictions.[89] A recent Canadian inquiry on the future of Toronto's waterfront, adopting "the ecosystem approach" and referring to "the Toronto bioregion," found that "institutional arrangements in the bioregion are often part of the problem; bureaucratic systems are often rigid and jurisdictions fragmented."[90] Foster's bioregionally oriented accounts of how governments traversing ecological regions developed common conservationalist policies make the point that effective policies and procedures can be developed without eliminating the political entities themselves.[91] The creation of overarching bodies to handle specific regional issues serves to develop sensitivities towards other bioregional issues. The critical factors are an institutional presence and successful legitimation for successful bioregional action and progress.[92] Press, noting that bioregional conflicts call up fears of the loss of political power and economic prospects, cogently concludes:

> bioregionalism will have to squarely face the conundrum of the urban-rural, collective versus individual interests, and competing ecological goals. More broadly, the success of any policy innovation demands on how well it addresses concerns over social justice, technocracy, and economic imperatives.[93]

Eckersley's discussion of Sale's bioregional argument notes that Sale assumes that there is a clear community of interest among the various communities within a bioregion; that they are relatively homogeneous; and that they are organically bound together by an ecological identity. But in the falsity of Sale's assumptions, the issue is: "What political forms will best promote bioregional goals?"[94]

THE NEW REGIONALISM AND POLITICAL BOUNDARIES

The irony however, is that developments in the global economy raise doubts about the possibility of developing institutional arrangements for handling environmental problems at the macro-level. Kenichi Ohmae, a prolific business strategy writer, in his recent book, *The End of the Nation State,* discusses changes in politics and economics within the context of nation states and the emergence of new economic regions.[95] Emergence of the global marketplace—driven by international capital and transnational corporations, the escalating development of information technologies, and the rise of materialistic individualism—has led to the decay of the traditional nation-state. Political boundaries now constitute a "cartographic illusion" inasmuch as the important determinants of economic activity and growth in the modern global economy have erased their role.[96] Regional states, described as "natural economic zones," now serve as "ports of entry" in the new economy. Unlike megacities they are not locked into central governments, but accept the logic of global competition.[97] That logic, however, is not built on standardization and homogenization and on the recognition of spatial differences in markets acquired not through "nation-based organizations, but through a region state-focused network of capability and competence."[98] This assertion of "place" as an important variable, along with the dismissal of the importance of boundaries, brings Ohmae's "region states" and "bioregional" entities into alignment. The difference is that the first is economistic and the latter is not. The overlap is even seen in Cascadia, once the ecotopia of bioregionalists, and now an idea that has been taken over by business-oriented groups to show how the Pacific Northwest will be an actor in the global economy.[99]

Students of political boundaries, like Jean Gottmann and Edward Soja, amongst others, have identified a number of their functions: security; barriers, filters, and screens; organization of cognition, affect, and energy; and reference points for individuals and groups. If Ohmae (and others) were right, then people in region states would live in a world in which boundaries increasingly become indistinct. The logic for region states in a global economy is to not interfere with the decision making of transnational corporations: their role is to provide a place that attracts investment. Ironically, then, economic forces of the modern world are creating entities that look very much like what bioregionalists have been calling for: regional, with "soft" borders, place-focused, with federal-like links between entities. Bioregionalists will not value the economistic character of the new regionalism. What about the environment? Only proverbial time will tell, of course, but Wendt argues that, as regions become richer, they are more willing and able to address environmental issues; and environmental consciousness is one of the "quality of life" factors in investment decisions.[100]

Political systems, their sovereignty marked by boundaries, provided the context in which liberal democracy developed roots and flourished. Politicians, by setting agendas and working toward their fulfillment, legitimated the system of elections, party competition, and voting. The nature of democratic politics in the new regional systems is very much uncertain.

What do politicians do in a limited system of government?

What is meant by elections, political competition, and voting in a world of borderless politics?

NOTES

1. Robert E. Goodin, *Green Political Theory* (Cambridge, UK: Polity Press, 1992), 157.

2 Naess, Arne, *Ecology, Community and Lifestyle* (Cambridge: Cambridge University Press, 1989).

3. I.G. Simmons, *Humanity and Environment: A Cultural Ecology* (Harlow: Longman, 1997), 289.

4. Murray Bookchin, *The Philosophy of Social Ecology* (Montreal: Black Rose Books, 1990).

5. Brian Tokar, *The Green Alternative: Creating an Ecological Future* (San Pedro: RandE Miles, 1987), 27.

6. For an early statement of this view, see Sam Love, "Redividing North America," *The Ecologist* 7(7) August/September 1977: 318–19.

7. See Love, "Redividing North America" and Christopher Alexander et al., *A Pattern Language* (New York: Oxford University Press, 1977), 12. Kirkpatrick Sale taught a bioregional course at Schumacher College in Devon; see his "Putting Dartia on the Map," in Doug Aberley, ed., *Boundaries of Home: Mapping for Local Empowerment* (Philadelphia: New Society Publishers, 1993), 27–31. Some European political developments and interpretation related to ecological issues have "regionalist" overtones; see Dieter Steiner and Markus Nauser, eds., *Human Ecology: Fragments of Anti-Fragmentary Views of the World* (London: Routledge, 1993), especially 288–95.

8. Eckersley, 168, 170.

9. David Pepper, *Modern Environmentalism* (London: Routledge, 1996), 188.

10. Andrew McLaughlin, *Regarding Nature: Industrialism and Deep Ecology* (Albany: State University of New York Press), 210.

11. McLaughlin, *Regarding Nature: Industrialism and Deep Ecology*, 206–207; for an example, see Peter Berg, "A Metamorphosis for Cities: From Gray to Green," *The Trumpeter* 8(1) Winter 1991: 9–12.

12. Dimitrious I. Roussopoulos, *Political Ecology* (Montreal: Black Rose Books, 1993), 79.

13. Judith Plant, ed, *Healing the Wounds: The Promise of Ecofeminism* (Philadelphia: New Society Publishers, 1989).

14. Jeremy Rifkin, *Biosphere Politics: A New Consciousness for a New Century* (New York: Crown Publishers, Inc., 1991), 289.

15. Peter Berg (and Raymond Dasmann), "Reinhabiting California" in Peter Berg, ed,, *Reinhabiting a Separate Country: A Bioregional Anthology of Northern California* (San Francisco; Planet Drum Foundation, 1978), 217–20. Kirkpatrick Sale, *Dwellers in the Land: The Bioregional Vision* (San Francisco: Sierra Club Books, 1985); an important antecedent work by Kirkpatrick Sale is *Human Scale* (New York: Coward, McCann, and Geoghegan, 1980). A recent statement by Sale is "Principles of Bioregionalism," in Jerry Mander and Edward Goldsmith, eds., *The Case Against the Global Economy* and *For a Turn to the Local* (San Francisco: Sierra Club Books, 1996), 471–84. See also Sale's "Mother of All: An Introduction to Bioregionalism," in Hildegarde Hannum, ed., *People, Land, and Community* (New Haven: Yale University Press, 1977), 216–36.

16. Christopher Alexander, et al., *A Pattern Language: Towns, Buildings, Construction* (New York: Oxford University Press, 1977).

17. Ian L. Mchaig, *Design with Nature* (New York John Wiley and Sons. Inc, 4th ed., 1997); Sim Van Der Ryn and Stuart Cowan, *Ecological Design* (Washington, D.C.: Island Press, 1996); Nancy Jack Todd and John Todd, *From Eco-Cities to Living Machines: Principles of Ecological Design* (San Francisco: Sierra Club Books, 1984).

18. Thomas Berry, *The Dream of the Earth* (San Francisco: Sierra Books, 1990).

19. Stephanie Mills, *In Service of the Wild: Restoring and Reinhabiting Damaged Land* (Boston: Beacon Press).

20. Donald Alexander says that the word *bioregionalism* was first used by a Canadian, Allan Van Newkirk, in 1974; Donald Alexander, "Bioregionalism: Science or Sensibility," *Environmental Ethics* 12(2) Summer 1990: 161.

21. David Pepper, *Modern Environmentalism,* 188.

22. Robert G. Bailey, et al., "Ecological Regionalization in Canada and the United States," *Geoforum* 16(3) 1985: 266.

23. Cited in Alexander, A Pattern Language, 11.

24. Alexander, *A Pattern Language,* 11.

25. Sale, "Mother of All: An Introduction to Bioregionalism," 229–30.

26. McLaughlin, *Regarding Nature: Industrialism and Deep Ecology,* 208.

27. Pepper, 1996: 307.

28. Robert L. Dorman, *Revolt of the Provinces: The Regionalist Movement in America, 1920–1945,* (Chapel Hill, N.C.: University of North Carolina Press, 1993; the connection is drawn in Patrick Mazza, "Uncovering the hidden history of regionalism: The American regionalist insurgency of the 1920s–1940s, see www.tnews.com/text/regionalist_insurgency.html.

29. See Pepper, *Modern Environmentalism,* for a comprehensive delineation of value differences between various environmentally and non-environmentally centered ideologies.

30. Sale, "Principles of Bioregionalism," 472.

31. Rifkin,, *Biosphere Politics,* 289.

32. Sale, *Dwellers in the Land,* 96; Eckersley, 69

33. McLaughlin, *Regarding Nature: Industrialism and Deep Ecology,* 207–208.

34. Pepper, *Modern Environmentalism,* 195, 213.

35. Sale, "Principles of Bioregionalism," 472.

36. Aldo Leopold, *A Sand County Almanac* (New York: Oxford University Press, 1949), 224–25.

37. Brian Tokar, *The Green Alternative: Creating an Ecological Future* (San Pedro: Rand E. Miles, 1987) 26.

38. YI-Fu Tuan, *Topophilia* (New York: Columbia University Press, 1974), 101. Tuan makes the interesting point that the earth is a natural unit; and, possibly, in some ideal future, "our loyalty will be given only to the home region of intimate memories and, at the other end of the scale, to the whole earth." (102)

39. Rifkin, *Biosphere Politics,* 312.

40. Charles T. Rubin, *The Green Crusade: Rethinking the Roots of Environmentalism* (New York: The Free Press, 1994), 194.

41. Bioregionalists are not alone in their call for "natural" boundaries; for one such exposition, see Joel Garreau, *The Nine Nations of North America* (Boston: Houghton and Mifflin, 1981).

42. Pepper, *Modern Environmentalism,* 188.

43. Pepper, *Modern Environmentalism,* 55.

44. Berg and Dasmann, "Reinhabiting California," 218..

45. Nancy Jack Todd and John Todd, *From Eco-Cities to Living Machines* (Berkeley: North Atlantic Books, 1994), 44.

46. Jim Dodge, "Living by Life: Some Bioregional Theory and Practice," in *Co-Evolution Quarterly* 32, Winter 1981: 6–12.

47. The 1992 North American Bioregional Congress showed a widening interest in mapping; Doug Aberley, "Mapping the Experience of Place," in Doug Aberley, ed., *Boundaries of Home: Mapping for Local Empowerment* (Philadelphia: New Society Publishers, 1993), 18; this volume contains a number of interesting articles on maps and bioregionalism.

48. Doug Aberley, "How to Map your Bioregion: A Primer for Community Activists," in Doug Aberley, ed., in *Boundaries of Home: Mapping for Local Empowerment,* 71–129.

49. Doug Aberley, "New Terrain: Current Mapping Thought," in Doug Aberley, ed., *Boundaries of Home: Mapping for Local Empowerment,* 47.

50. Gary Snyder, "Bioregional Perspectives," in Van Andres, et al., eds., *Home! A Bioregional Reader* 17; Love, "Redividing North America," 319.

51. Peter Berg, "What Is Bioregionalism?," *The Trumpeter* 8(1) Winter 1991: 6.

52. Kirkpatrick Sale, "Principles of Bioregionalism," 475–78.

53. Sale, *Dwellers in the Land,* 59.

54. David McCloskey, "On Ecoregional Boundaries" in Doug Aberley, *Boundaries of Home: Mapping for Local Empowerment* (Garbriola Island, B.C.: New Society Publishers, 1993), 60–63.

55. Aberley, "How to Map Your Bioregion: A Primer for Community Activists," 74–75.

56. Ibid., 77.

57. Sale, 1985: 91. See also Kirkpatrick Sale, "Free and Equal Intercourse: The Decentralist Design," in *Putting Power in its Place: Create Community Control,* Christopher Plant and Judith Plant, eds., (Gabriola Island, BC: New Society Publishers, 1991), 20–27.

58. Gerald B. Thomas, "The Politics of Hope: An Eclectic Vision of the Future," in *Environmental Politics and Policy,* James P. Lester, ed. (Durham: Duke University Press, 1995), 354–57.

59. Sale, 1997, 223.

60. Rifkin, *Biosphere Politics,* 310.

61. Major critiques are Don Alexander, "Bioregionalism: Science or Sensibility?" *Environmental Ethics* 12: 161–73; Robyn Eckersley, *Environmentalism and Political Theory: Toward an Ecocentric Approach* (London: University College Press, 1992), 167–70; Lester W. Milbrath, *Envisioning a Sustainable Society: Learning Our Way Out* (Albany, New York: State University of New York, 1989), 211–16; and David Pepper, *Modern Environmentalism,* 306–309.

62. Edward W. Soja, *The Political Organization of Space* (Washington, D.C.: Association of American Geographers, 1971), 16. It is interesting to note that Soja speculated that "a new technological revolution has created a vastly different global situation from that which stimulated the rise of the nation-state." (p. 16).

63. Ladis K. D. Kristof, "The Nature of Frontiers and Boundaries," *Annals of the Association of American Geographers* XLIX: 130.

64. Milbrath, *Envisioning Sustainable Society,* 214.

65. Robert G. Bailey, "Multi-scale Ecosystem Analysis," in *Global to Local: Ecological Land Classification,* R. A. Sims, I. G. W. Corns, and K. Klinka, eds. *Global to*

Local: Ecological Land Classification (Dordrecht: Kluwer Academic Publishers, 1996), 22.

66. J. Stan Rowe, "Land Classification and Ecosystem Classification," in *Global to Local: Ecological Land Classification,* Sims, Corns, and Klinka, eds. (Dordrecht: Kluwer Academic Publishers, 1996), 18.

67. David M. Smith, "The Forests of the United States," in *Regional Silviculture of the United States,* John W. Barrett, ed. (New York: John Wiley and Sons, Inc, 1995), 8–15.

68. Diana Liverman, "Modeling Social Systems and Their Interaction with the Environment: A View from Geography," in *Integrated Regional Models: Interactions Between Humans and Their Environment,* Peter M. Groffman and Gene E. Likens, eds. (New York: Chapman and Hall, 1994), 67–78.

69. Elizabeth Blood, "Prospects for the Development of Integrated Regional Models," in *Integrated Regional Models: Interactions Between Humans and Their Environment,* Peter M. Groffman and Gene E. Likens, eds. (New York: Chapman and Hall, 1994),145.

70. Blood, "Prospects for the Development of Integrated Regional Models," 145.

71. Robert G. Bailey, *Ecosystem Geography* (New York: Springer-Verlag, 1996), 11.

72. Bailey, *Ecosystem Geography,* 36.

73. Rubin, *The Green Crusade,* 194.

74. Rubin, *The Green Crusade,* 194.

75. T.F. H. Allen and Thomas W. Hoekstra, eds., *Toward a Unified Ecology* (New York: Columbia University Press, 1992), 86.

76. Allen and Hoekstra, *Toward a Unified Ecology*, 282–332.

77. David Pepper, *Modern Environmentalism* (London: Routledge, 1996), 33

78. Don Alexander, "Bioregionalism: Science or Sensibility?" 167.

79. Milbrath, 214.

80. Edward 0. Wilson, *On Human Nature* (Cambridge, Mass: Harvard University Press, 1978), 18.

81. Rubin, 195.

82. Eckersley, 56–57.

93. Pepper, 308.

84. Pepper, 308.

85. Goodin, 51.

86. Ted Simon, *The River Stops Here* (New York: Random House, 1994. Simon describes the conflict arising from the proposal of the U.S. Army Corps of Engineers and California water authorities to inundate Round Valley in Northern California in order to move water to the south and the development of bioregional thinking on the part of those who led the successful fight against the plan; see pages 134 and 324.

87. Rifkin, 290.

88. Daniel Press, *Democratic Dilemmas in the Age of Ecology* (Durham, NC: Duke University Press, 1994), 106.

89. Pepper, 309.

90. *Regeneration: Toronto's Waterfront and the Sustainable City: Final Report* (Toronto: Royal Commission on the Future of the Toronto Waterfront, 1992), 60.

91. See Charles H. W. Foster, *The Cape Cod National Seashore: A Landonark Alliance* (Hanover: University Press of New England, 1985) and *Experiments in Biore-*

gionalism: The New England River Basins Society (Hanover: University Press of New England, 1981.

92. Charles Foster, *The Cape Cod National Seashore,* 84.

93. Press, *Democratic Dilemmas in the Age of Technology*, 107.

94. Eckersley, 169.

95. Kenichi Ohmae, *The End of the Nation State: The Rise of Regional Economies* (New York: The Free Press, 1995).

96. Ohmae, *The End of the Nation State*, 7–16.

97. Ohmae, *The End of the Nation State*, 60–100; Ohmae identifies as exemplars northern Italy; upper Rhine; Wales; San Diego/Tijuana; Hong Kong/Southern mainland China; Silicon Valley/Bay area; Pusan in South Korea; and Fukuoka and Kitakyushu in Japan.

98. Ohmae, *The End of the Nation State*, 101.

99. *What Is the Future of Cascadia?* (Seattle, Discovery Institute, 1993); cited in Patrick Mazza, "Lifeplace or Marketplace?: Bioregions, Region States and the Contested Turf of Regionalism," see www.tnews.com/text/lifeplace-marketplace.html.

100. Henry Wendt, *Global Embrace: Corporate Challenges in a Transnational World* (New York: HarperBusiness, 1993), 245–56.

Index

About the Contributors

Charlotte Bretherton is Professor of International Relations at John Moores University, Liverpool, UK.

Stephen Clarkson is Professor of Political Science at the University of Toronto, Canada.

Jonathan Crystal is Assistant Professor of Political Science at Fordham University, Bronx, New York.

Henri J. M. Goverde is Associate Professor of Public Administration at the Nijmegen School of Management and Professor of Political Science at Wageningen University.

Wyn Grant is Professor of Politics at the University of Warwick, Coventry, UK.

Bart Kerremans is Associate Professor of International Relations at the Catholic University of Leuven, Leuven, Belgium.

Quan Li is Assistant Professor of Political Science at The Pennsylvania State University, University Park, Pennsylvania.

The late **Stuart S. Nagel** was Emeritus Professor of Political Science at the University of Illinois at Urbana-Champaign and Secretary-Treasurer of the Policy Studies Organization.

Adil Najam is Assistant Professor of International Relations and Environmental Policy at Boston University.

Zdzislaw W. Puslecki is Professor of Economic Science and Head of the Department of International Economy at Adam Mickiewicz University, Poznan, Poland.

Paul J. Rich is Titular Professor of International Relations and History, The University of the Americas-Puebla, Mexico. President of the Policy Studies Organization, Dr. Rich is a Fellow of the Hoover Institution, Stanford University, and President of Phi Beta Delta, the international honor society for achievement in international education.

Michael G. Schechter is Professor of International Relations at James Madison College, Michigan State University.

Dale L. Smith is an Associate Professor and Chair of the Political Science Department at Florida State University, Tallahassee, Florida.

Joseph S. Szyliowicz teaches at the Graduate School of International Studies and Center for Transportation Studies at University of Denver at Boulder, USA.

John Vogler is a Professor in the Department of Politics, International Relations, and the Environment at the University of Keele, Staffordshire, the United Kingdom.

Peter Woolstencroft is Associate Professor of Political Science at the University of Waterloo, Ontario, Canada.